A Citizen's Guide to

Public Accountability

*Changing the Relationship
Between Citizens and Authorities*

Henry E. McCandless

co-published by
Citizens' Circle for Accountability
www.accountabilitycircle.org
and
TRAFFORD

National Library of Canada Cataloguing in Publication Data

McCandless, Henry E. (Henry Emerson), 1935-
A citizen's guide to public accountability : changing the relationship between citizens and authorities
Includes index.
ISBN 1-55212-957-8
1. Political participation. 2. Democracy. 3. Power (Social sciences) I. Title.
HN110.Z9P6 2001   323'.042   C2001-903358-3

TRAFFORD

This book was published *on-demand* **in cooperation with Trafford Publishing.**
On-demand publishing is a unique process and service of making a book available for retail sale to the public taking advantage of on-demand manufacturing and Internet marketing.
On-demand publishing includes promotions, retail sales, manufacturing, order fulfilment, accounting and collecting royalties on behalf of the author.

Suite 6E, 2333 Government St., Victoria, B.C. V8T 4P4, CANADA

Phone	250-383-6864	Toll-free	1-888-232-4444 (Canada & US)
Fax	250-383-6804	E-mail	sales@trafford.com
Web site	www.trafford.com	TRAFFORD PUBLISHING IS A DIVISION OF TRAFFORD HOLDINGS LTD.	
Trafford Catalogue #01-0359		www.trafford.com/robots/01-0359.html	

10   9   8

To the memory of my daughter Lesley,
who fought for purity in all things
but lost to schizophrenia.

Foreword

To be asked to write a foreword to this important and timely work is, for me, both an honour and a source of sadness. An honour, because of the uniqueness of the book, and the integrity and knowledge of its author, my friend Henry McCandless; a source of profound sadness, because I realize again that, in Canada as elsewhere, Public Accountability is a severely endangered species. Attempts at its nurture and preservation appear to raise even less enthusiasm than, say, the protection of whooping cranes or snapping turtles.

Yet, as a civilized country Canada will not survive unless there is viable public accountability. It is an essential component of the civic habitat; without its practice, citizens are helpless. They are like fish in an increasingly poisoned ocean.

But Canadians need not feel helpless and compelled to acquiesce to the destructive impacts of power exercised without public accountability. There are ways to cope, and this book is a guide on how to cope and how to detoxify a civic habitat, polluted by the unchecked use of power — be it legal, commercial or regulatory power.

The book is an exquisite map, drawn by someone who has lived and worked in positions that required asking as well as answering questions of public accountability. What I like so much about Henry McCandless's map is its scale and perspective. Within our social terrain, he clearly lays out the reciprocal relationships between those who exercise power and governance, and those who are governed or administered.

On the micro-scale the map indicates the areas of accountability of elected officials and civil servants, those in governance roles and their CEOs, and lawyers, doctors and others. It provides citizens with navigational information so that they can move and act in specific areas. Here is the methodology of "taking to account."

The illumination of the macro-scale, achieved through the dissection of case histories and public policy issues, offers an additional and complementary perspective. On this scale the map shows how the lack of public accountability has affected the public good. Each case, in which transparency and public answering is not achieved — or not achieved in time — appears to alter the civic terrain. The navigational obstacles become larger, seem more deeply anchored and tied, and well-known landmarks seem to vanish. The author, as both navigator and observer, records these changes and their consequences.

Woven through the book, both explicitly and implicitly, is the notion of standards. In terms of the image of the map, standards are the coordinates, the landmarks, the navigational directions. The erosion of standards, the disregard of markers and signals are tickets to trouble. And surely there is trouble across the land; and who would want more trouble?

I have always felt that, as a society, we have misdirected many of our public policy discussions. Too much attention has been focused on the ends or outcomes of an endeavour and far too little on the means of getting from here to there. Yet, finally, it may matter more how we do things than precisely what we do.

As citizen, I see public accountability coupled with transparency of process as the essential link between means and ends. As a *Canadian* citizen I have the legitimate expectation that those in authority can and will be held to account so as to clarify both ends and means. (Public consent is required for both.)

How? By a large number of collective public steps, using the information and the spirit of this book.

The new technologies that have helped to complicate public accountability, technologies that can be used to hide or fudge lines of responsibility, can also assist citizens to forge coalitions for accountability and due public process. But in the end, public accountability is a citizen-to-citizen effort. Those who have to be taken to account may well evade the answering; they may not respond to invitations and may not appear at meetings.

In such cases, meetings and hearings have to include empty chairs, to identify those who chose to hide from public view. Questions posed, but not answered, need then to be made public as well as brought forward to those involved and their "superiors."

It is important to remember, that prevention of disaster and of miscarriage of justice, and the assurance of equity are not the only fruits of the systematic practice of holding to account. Answering publicly how trust and responsibility have been discharged will also reveal good practices, jobs well and carefully done, and models to follow — not only schemes and patterns to avoid.

Before us, then, is truly a GUIDE, a way for citizens to develop and enhance good civic practices and thereby not only prevent disasters, but also maintain and strengthen the fabric of the common good.

May this guide be used creatively and often.

Toronto November 2001   *Ursula M. Franklin C.C. FRSC*

TABLE OF CONTENTS

Preface

In a memorable CBC radio documentary on George Orwell in January 1984, narrator George Woodcock quoted Orwell: "When I sit down to write a book.... I write it because there is some lie I want to expose, some fact to which I want to draw attention, and my initial concern is to get a hearing.... My aim is to expose lies, hidden agendas, recklessness and inattention to duty." While concerned with the same things, this book is less courageous. It is simply to suggest a legitimate and public means of making authorities themselves expose what Orwell said should be exposed, and to propose a way for citizens to control those to whom they give or allow authority. In 2001, it is a pretense to suggest that citizens control anything.

A book explaining accountability and why citizens must hold to account needs to be rigorous if it is to be useful. This is because authorities, seeking to evade their public answering obligation, will look for weaknesses in the argument. For example, if authorities say, "We already answer for our responsibilities," we can ask them to publicly state the specific standard of public answering they think they are meeting, compare that with what we think is a reasonable public answering standard in their circumstances, and decide whether their answering is fair and complete. If the law doesn't require adequate answering from the authorities, we tell our legislators to install the requirement. As for the claim that public answering in society is too complex a matter for citizens to handle beyond visits to polling booths, readers of this book can tell for themselves.

Guidance in holding to account has to be more than descriptions of wrongs and evaded responsibilities, with no proposed action steps. Public interest organizations and citizens able to act on their own must be offered strategies that can make a difference to the fairness of the decisions made by a wide range of authorities.

This book is in no way a polemic against authorities such as executive governments and corporations. They do what they want when we don't hold them to account. The book explains where we stand today in public answering for important responsibilities and what can be done to produce adequate answering. But because of the stakes globally, and the current broad erosion of standards in society, citizens now have to play hardball to exact the level of public answering from authorities that should have been required years ago – when people in modern-day power were learning how to evade their responsibilities and answering obligations.

Being serious in holding to account means that we have to shift from giving deference to people in authority to stating fair expectations for them, making them tell us their intentions, their reasoning for their intentions, their performance standards and, later, making them tell us their results and how they applied the learning they gained from what they did.

This book argues that we can help prevent harm in society by exacting adequate public answering before the fact. It argues that accountability and holding to account are powerful yet simple concepts, that authorities in a democracy can't refuse to answer, and that we must put the force of law behind authorities' obligations to answer publicly and to a standard. But we have an obligation to do something fair and sensible with validated public answering that is given in good faith.

We start with four horror stories to illustrate how lack of public answering obligations for different types of authorities led to horrific outcomes for the people affected, with no convincing evidence to date of learning gained and applied by the authorities who caused or allowed the harm. Canadian examples are used for the most part, but these can be interpolated to other countries. The point of the book is that public answering can be exacted by citizens in any country, because holding to account doesn't tell authorities what to do. It only asks them to answer for their responsibilities – to explain – and this is an unassailable request. Citizens are not impotent. We *can* hold to account if we decide to and, if we do, we will help increase safety and fairness in society.

The Introduction sums up the state we have put ourselves into by failing to apply the precautionary principle to civics. It suggests broadly what we can do about it if we are to sensibly commend, alter or stop what authorities intend. It is in effect a summary of the argument. The rest of the chapters explain what is reasonable in public answering, the accountabilities of important groups of people, and how citizens can hold to account. The first two appendices illustrate ways of exacting answering by authorities.

As the reader will see, newspaper and radio news items handily identify important responsibilities of people that call for public answering, even if the articles and news clips don't deal with the answering obligations. Readers will also note that the articles cited are a very small sample of the range of authorities' responsibilities that citizens must oversee. The groundrules for public answering don't change when countries turn their attention to new public issues, such as terrorism. Governments seeking greater executive power and authority must comply with answering rules that are set by the citizens. We have to install basic legislated rules for public answering which, with audit of the answering, will produce a self-regulating effect on authorities.

Most of the points made in this book come from the insights other people, such as Dr. Michèle Brill-Edwards, MD, of the Alliance for Public Accountability, Nicole Morgan, George Windsor and activist writers in various journals. I have simply tried to see pattern and how holding to account would help.

But in proposing standards for public answering, the crux of the book, I am indebted most to Dr. Ursula Franklin, Professor Emeritus of the University of Toronto. In her 1989 Massey Lectures, *The Real World of Technology*, Dr. Franklin stressed the crucial issue I had missed as a professional auditor viewing public accountability – the issue of *who* would benefit and *who* would bear the costs of something proposed that affects the public in important ways. Being in the business of serving accountability relationships, auditors obviously know why public accountability reporting is needed. But they aren't used to reporting on the "who," let alone before decisions are taken by authorities. Dr. Franklin's encouragement was influential in my decision to write a book on the subject. The book's subtitle I owe to the late Ottawa activist Terry Cottam, who pioneered in applying the public answering obligation in his work in the late 1990s.

I thank all those who critically read drafts of chapters, and Joy Hamilton's edit helped immensely. Bruce Batchelor and the staff of Trafford Publishing gave me exemplary help. I am very grateful for both the encouragement and forbearance of my wife Kitty, who never complained about my "crusading" at all hours in the Alliance for Public Accountability, or my endless hours of writing. Also my mother, Stella Jenkins who, in reading a few early chapter drafts, told me, "Punch some holes in your text and let some air in." I'm not sure I succeeded, but four-wheel drive is necessary in thinking about holding fairly but relentlessly to account.

Henry E. McCandless
Victoria, BC
November 2001

Introduction

The State We're In[1]

We like to believe, regardless of the evidence, that people in authority will do the right thing. Or, if we don't think they will, we expect that someone will deal with it. ("Authorities" means elected and appointed officials and governing bodies having authority or power to make decisions that affect citizens in important ways.) Yet the horror stories of authorities not doing their duty and later denying their responsibility ought to have shaken us out of blind faith. The question is whether we really want to know the truth about authorities' intentions, and what we would do if we knew it.

In Canada we've seen tens of thousands of wrecked lives and deaths from contaminated blood, the result of authorities' abdication. Now we see the same abdication in our water supplies. We've seen coal miners killed in a demonstrably unsafe mine, people wrongly convicted, military top command operating by whim, huge sums of public money spent on political patronage, and successive federal governments handing over policy sovereignty through international trade agreements that are likely to be Canada's Culloden. We accept government ministers' assertions as valid, yet they are simply decrees: the ministers give no supporting evidence.

Health care is one example. Families across the country now struggle, having to become their own physicians, nurses and care-givers because government ministers in the 1990s slashed health care funding. We allowed our health ministers to duck their duty in performance control to make government delivery of health care work, and be efficient. The ill and their families try to deal with a vaunted Canadian health care system that is not a system. Public outcry for restoration of health services results in government spending for quick-fix appearances. Rather than deliver on their management contract with Canadians, provincial executive governments continue to allow or even engineer the transfer of control and delivery of health services to the private sector on a cost-plus basis. This means that the public purse is to supply the corporation owners' profits, with no evidence required for professed greater efficiency or fairness, and no performance answering obligation for the private operators. The federal government postures on protection of Medicare at the provincial level but seems only an onlooker, abdicating its Medicare stewardship and health protection obligation to Canadians.

Canada's blood disgrace showed all health ministers across the country what they were each responsible for, but we have yet to see individual or collective responsibility being taken by them to ensure other killings and harm don't happen. That is because they haven't accounted to us. Globally, enforced debt reduction, deregulation and privatization in Southern countries is destroying their capability to cope in health. In Canada we have no excuse for allowing the destruction of what most Canadians have clearly said they want to keep. But again, we haven't asked for the answering for responsibilities that tells us what our governments intend.

Citizens' beliefs and attitudes about Medicare are not the same thing as citizen intention and action. Only citizens can force adequate health care funding, coupled with adequate management control over its delivery to make government-run health care fair, effective, efficient and economical. Inattention to management duties in government helps those who wish to hand things over to corporations. Legislators know this. But to assess what's wrong in health care delivery and fix it, we must do certain things. We must state what we think are reasonable performance expectations for health ministers, health-related senior civil servants, district health board members, doctors and care facility managers and staff, test the standards with those who must meet them, compare our expectations with valid readings of their actual performance, and ask for their answering.

Abdication to privatization means that governments think they can walk away from their responsibilities and answering obligations – that they wouldn't have to ensure safety; they wouldn't have to make their own health care operations efficient and effective; they wouldn't have to protect the integrity of medical research; they wouldn't have to set and meet the service quality standards that citizens have repeatedly said they are willing to pay for; and they wouldn't have to answer for how well privatized operations served citizens. We have no assurance that the federal government isn't allowing health care for Canadians to become just another market commodity supplied by transnational corporations under free trade agreements that the government claims are beyond its control. In health, environment and other issues, it is as if some of our executive governments are at war with the citizens they are supposed to serve.[2]

Reliance on "market" is the repudiation of policy in the public interest. When business interests try to make politicians and their constituents think that Medicare won't work, which means overturning the legislated agreement between governments and citizens, we need full, fair and validated public answering for the reasons. Business must state how they would serve citizens more fairly, effectively and economically, and governments must state their intentions and reasoning. The same goes for overturning protection of public education, the environment and wildlife. It also applies to replacing the idea of natural food and plant processes with genetically-engineered foods and trees.

Why are we in the state we're in? One reason is that we have failed to apply the precautionary principle in the way we look at governments and corporations. This is the idea that reasonable doubt or an alert of possible harm is reason enough to take precautionary action. Instead, in most safety and social issues, we allow "reverse onus." This is the notion that if we citizens are worried about the intentions of governments, corporations or other authorities, we must conclusively prove that those intentions will cause great harm. In going along with this notion, we've been patsies.

To make the precautionary principle work, we must make our authorities answer to us for upholding it. We have always had the right and power to do this, but we haven't made them publicly explain their intentions before the fact and tell us why their intentions are *not* harmful. Thus we get no effective public answering before the fact that can help us prevent harm. Instead we have decay in standards and resolve.

Simply saying that authorities "must be made accountable" adds nothing. Authorities making decisions have always had the fairness obligation to publicly explain their intentions and reasoning before taking their decisions. The point is that we have never made them give adequate public explanation before the fact. We have confused responsibility, the obligation to act, with accountability, the obligation to answer for responsibilities – which means having authorities report their intentions and their reasoning, and later what resulted from their actions.

Or we confuse accountability with blame, punishment or forced answering in a court. We haven't achieved adequate public answering because we haven't said, relentlessly, "We think it reasonable that you report your intentions, reasoning and performance standards before the fact, and your evidence that your intentions are fair and won't lead to harm or injustice." When authorities do claim to answer, we don't audit the fairness and completeness of their answering, which means that we don't exact valid answering from them.

When we have to face up to obvious threats to safety or justice, we tend to supplicate or to lobby and fight, but usually too late. And if we manage to create a climate of opinion or use the courts to stop something, we simply delay authorities' intentions. Their agendas don't change, and the intentions are simply put on hold to be rolled out again later in a different guise. Notable examples of this are the Organization for Economic Cooperation and Development's late 1990s Multilateral Agreement on Investment, proposing the subordination of countries' core policies to the profit aims of corporate boards. The World Trade Organization's 1999 Seattle round and the 2001 Free Trade Area of the Americas' meeting in Quebec didn't show a different aim.

When risk turns into actual harm, we collectively react to it but don't learn from it. Witness the June 2000 contaminated water in Walkerton, Ontario, repeating in a different form in North Battleford a year later, with likely more to come elsewhere. But more than a decade earlier, the blood deaths and families wrecked from hepatitis C were obvious lessons in the precautionary principle for the provincial and federal governments responsible for safeguarding health. Once something happens we leave it to others and simply hope for the best. Or we look for someone to blame, contented to blame the operating manager rather than the directing minds responsible for the overall management control that included safety control.

When the regulating manager is the executive government, the strategy for government lawyers is to blame the on-site managers, as in Walkerton, or, when it's clear that the government regulators failed in their duty and the inquiry commissioner knows it, as in the blood disgrace, the government's lawyers go after the inquiry commissioner. In the case of the *Exxon Valdez*, the media went after an alcoholic ship captain, not the senior managers and the company board ultimately responsible for the company's safety control systems. The boards of directors of the Canadian Red Cross and the parent corporation of the Westray mine have never been called to account. The major churches ran the schools where Aboriginal boys were abused, and their hierarchy denied or failed to act on what was happening. But the entity with senior precautionary management control responsibility over the schools was the federal executive government. After the "blame games" and court processes, we then allow our politicians to say, "Let's move on" without telling us what they have done to assure prevention of harm in the future.

We don't try to understand or fix the underlying syndromes and hold the responsible people to account for fixing them. Despite investigative journalists' reporting and public interest organizations' efforts, people in power are not made to answer or to change their intentions. After the fact, we put blind trust in public inquiries and their government-decided mandates. Then we watch them bog down in predictable legal wrangling, back away from underlying causes, fail to recommend who in future should answer to whom for what, and even fall short in redress. Since the executive governments forced to commission these inquiries know all this, we ought to know that they can drive inquiry commission trucks into the ditch. When inquiry recommendations survive, governments can easily ignore those that go to the bone, and civil servants can be ordered to produce yet more regulations. Regulations at present are too often lowest-common-denominator compromises that don't include public answering for compliance or public answering by those with the enforcement duty.

Executive governments pretend that their protection responsibilities can be shifted to a "self-regulating" business sector, unaccompanied by public answering obligations, or to boards or other bodies that they hold out as expert decision-makers but which can only be advisors to the still-accountable ministers.

In the face of this, citizens' groups exhaust themselves trying to dig out information to fight with that should have been made public in the first place. Most people have to do this after a full day's work at their regular jobs, and they lack back-up groups to provide a second wind. At the major policy level, governments wanting to escape existing policy and to overturn established values and standards need only push through several upheaving changes all at once. They know that the combined effect will overwhelm the challenge capability of citizens' groups. With impunity, they reject their obligation to publicly explain their reasoning and the likely outcomes. The impunity comes from their legislative majority.

Whenever executive government negligence or deception does get exposed, arrogance carries the day. Rather than answer fairly, a government minister can successfully decree that fact is not fact, or that a damning inquiry report got it wrong – as in the Somalia inquiry. The issue blows over and we're back to business as usual. Journalists turn to other events and don't see the issue through. Citizens go back to their glazed state, incapable of dealing with ministerial, military and corporate arrogance. Nothing changes, even with changes of government.

We may complain about this or that arm of the civil service, but then we live with it. Politicians thus don't have to pay attention to management. Yet the integrity and management of our institutions determines the quality of our society. Today's senior civil servants, in serving the wants of ministers, vanquish citizens and junior civil servants who question. They then create the required "spin" for whatever happens, perhaps not even realizing whether their actions undermine fairness. Success in their organizations means pleasing their superiors or potential corporate employers. "Success" has nothing necessarily to do with serving the public interest. In the civil service we now have "situational ethics," adjusted to fit the aims of political agendas. No public interest performance standards have been set for senior civil servants, and ethics in the civil service are continually re-defined to fit with the agendas and "business ethics."

We can no longer say that we know the ability and motivation of our elected representatives who form our executive governments. But the same goes for our senior civil servants. This is because there is no public answering by either of these groups for whose needs they are honouring. For example, how do we know that our Members of Parliament haven't discovered that they can hand over their intervention duties in society to corporate boards and "the market," yet still keep – and increase – their salaries and pensions? If people think that senior civil servants may be serving corporations' interests rather than the public interest, the civil servants aren't setting the record straight because they are not accounting publicly for their intentions and conduct, let alone having their assertions validated. Collectively they have the power to choose between answering to the public and being held suspect by the public.

Today in government, deception, spin and appearances reign. Back-bench elected representatives, impotent in their legislatures, fail to ensure safety, fairness, effective spending and protection of the environment through the laws they create. Opposition parties make appropriate noises but fail to force adequate public answering from the government front benches because they don't know how to force it and may see no end value in it.

We haven't set the fundamental performance and public answering standards that our elected representatives should meet in their duty to regulate safety, justice and fairness in society. We haven't protected them from themselves, and we haven't given back-benchers their marching orders to control their leaders rather than be controlled by them, and to answer to us for doing so. Compliance with the law, probity and value for money are all part of elected representatives' fairness duties. Government ministers, including the first minister, should serve and answer to the caucus that employs them. But it works the other way around: back-benchers must please the prime minister and ministers if they want perks and want to "get ahead."

Nor have we required our universities and other research institutions to publicly account, to show whether they put the public interest ahead of pleasing corporations in their research and teaching. We need validated public answering from them to show whether they place the precautionary principle before cash from the corporations funding their research.

In the business sector, the large transnational corporations' aims are predictable, unabashed and evident to all. Their directing minds understandably seek to nullify sovereign countries' core policies to make control of their corporate environments easier. Why would we expect them to do anything else? Yet we let them do it by allowing our political leaders to escape their duty to protect our sovereignty, culture and social, health and environment policies. We let our leaders blame it on some combination of the United States, "uncontrollable globalization" and "international financial forces," as if nothing happening in our own country can be attributed to identifiable Canadians in authority, and nothing can be done. As one senior citizen put it, "We don't seem to have any real Canadians at the top." Without public answering to a standard, we don't have the evidence to allay the concern that instead of "real Canadians" at the top in parliaments and in the civil service making national decisions, we have modern-day Quislings. But if we have them, it is because we didn't ask them to state their intentions and validate their answers.

The problem with turning everything over to corporations – even if we ignore that their unabashed goals are competitiveness and the creation of wealth for owners and managers – is that those in stewardship positions who would turn things over haven't told us the outcomes they seek, for whom, whose wants would be honoured, whose needs would not be, and what the results would likely be. We haven't required our political leaders to propose means for collaborating and sharing responsibilities across countries to keep the planet going.

Supplication to authorities clearly doesn't work. Nor do "calls for" this or that, which may be newsworthy and build awareness but don't change authorities' agendas. Fighting and lobbying may stop some intentions some of the time, but temporarily halting an agenda won't change an underlying intention. And when groups with narrow interests form to claim an injustice and win something, they may simply collect their award and leave the scene, not staying to help make authorities publicly account in the future. The large public interest organizations are good at awareness-building and have broad fronts of concern. But thus far they haven't made holding to account one of their strategies, even though they have effective public podiums to force public answering from directing minds. They have the resources to lay out the public answering reasonably to be expected from authorities, and collectively they have the clout to force authorities to publicly state their intentions, reasoning and results. They could then use their knowledge to publicly validate authorities' answering.

Examples of harm and injustice easily come to mind because they make the news. Less obvious is the erosion of standards in society leading to erosion of leadership in the public interest, which in turn leads to further lowering of standards, in a spiral effect. People can start to think that if their government is jettisoning standards of decency and is operating by appearances, this should somehow be an acceptable guide for citizens.

Senior citizens, who know what standards are but who collectively allowed their erosion, may be more interested in protecting indexed pensions than making authorities answer publicly for their intentions and conduct. "It's out my control," the retired may say, even those who are able-bodied enough and have the time to work on holding to account. The major churches, coping with lawsuits from their own past wrongs and denials, will be advised by their lawyers and public relations people that now is not the best time to exert their moral leadership to bring about adequate public answering by authorities.

Also not obvious is citizens' undue deference to authority. Deference lets authorities off the answering hook. Citizens in countries such as Canada, new and geographically exempt from the historical savagery and slaughter of older cultures, can refuse to believe that people in authority could be ill-intentioned or callous. The blood deaths showed callousness, and in Canada a quiet tax audit or relentless pursuit by Justice Department lawyers would do the trick for someone challenging the federal executive government too close to the bone. It may be a challenge to overturn centuries of conditioning in citizen deference to authorities in a single decade, but answering standards *can* be installed, within a decade, by citizens who want them installed. Adequate public answering *can* be exacted.

People may say, "But citizens holding to account isn't the way things work." Exactly. We are talking here about "ought." Or, people will say, "But elections are how we hold to account." That is a myth we have all been taught to believe. Elections don't produce timely public answering that allows us to control something, pull back from it or redirect authorities' actions. The aim of today's election campaigns is simply to condition sufficient voters to think in a certain way as they enter the polling booth.

The political labels of Left, Right and Third Way distract attention from the answering obligation, which is politically neutral. "Right" seems to mean ignoring responsibility for social justice and lobbying to give self-interest primacy through the force of law – leaving citizens to their own devices. "Left" today seems to mean only fractious exhortation, missing the opportunity to be the natural champions of adequate answering from authorities. "Third way" seems to be a foggy middle ground with no proposed innovation in the use of power by citizens. None of these labels suggests how legitimate needs are to be identified and met, and illegitimate wants rejected. None of these camps sets out how their specific aims, to the extent they exist, translate into sensible citizen direction for authorities and public answering from the authorities. The obligation to answer isn't a partisan issue; it's a universal social imperative in fairness. But we achieve adequate public answering using political processes. Whichever political party becomes a genuine and enduring force producing adequate answering by authorities will never lose its support with the people.

Today our public questioning of authorities is ineffective or it's not done at all. Citizens are thus losing control, while everything wrong is attributed to the lack of "political will" – a statement that doesn't identify who has what responsibility. Any legal challenge of authorities' decisions relies on processes that are increasingly influenced by the executive governments who appoint and administer the judiciary. Back-bench legislators in the governing parties still pretend to be in control, but on key issues they would have difficulty refuting the argument that they might as well not be there. Question Period in the legislatures is only a partisan ritual dance.

We haven't required those who receive significant money from the public purse to tell us specifically how they are serving the public interest. This includes not just politicians and civil servants but also consultants who serve the executive governments that hire them. A terrible problem is civil servants increasingly thinking that what they do to serve a minister's wants and to get ahead is quite alright. They have no trouble looking in the mirror. We have set no performance and public answering standards for our senior civil servants. When their actions not in the public interest are about to be exposed, the responsible bureaucrats tend to be promoted, shifted or generously retired. When heads roll uphill, it's no wonder that citizens revert to sullenness or denial.

Increasingly, the key decisions affecting societies are being made those who have or control money or control business decisions. Key decisions are not being made by the citizens who constitute the society. At the global level we have no evidence of progress in fairness; only evidence of the widening gap between the rich and the poor. Whether in Canada, any other country or globally, the issue isn't the "what" of processes called "capitalism" and "globalization"; it is the "who" – whose wants are being honoured at the expense of whose needs, and who is directing how that happens. "Public participation" and "public consultation" only go so far. And when there is consultation, decision-makers don't tell us their reasoning for how they used the input from consulted groups, and who was not consulted and why, and their criteria for genuine consultation.

We have done it to ourselves. Because it has been easier, we have chosen to put blind faith in authorities and to avoid knowledge of their intentions. As the late Aimée Paxton, a former nurse, put it, "Today, no one can stand the truth." We have got ourselves into a mess, but no one has been standing over the planet putting up the rent and rendering us all helpless as citizens. The cartoon character Pogo said it all: "We have met the enemy and he is us."

What Does Holding to Account mean?

In 1976, federal Auditor General James Macdonell made a much-quoted statement to the House of Commons, which was that Parliament had lost, or was close to losing control of the public purse. Today, citizens have lost, or are close to losing, effective control of fairness in society. The precautionary principle says that those disagreeing with this proposition and the indicators for it have the obligation to produce the evidence to refute it. We haven't applied the precautionary principle to those in authority. We haven't required those with important responsibilities to adequately explain their intentions before they act, so we can be well enough informed to commend, alter or halt their intentions.

We have many good observers of syndromes in our society, but their writing seldom proposes who should take what steps next Monday morning to start fixing the syndromes and how we ensure that the steps are taken. We have yet to install the means to prevent officials ducking knowledge of what's going on when it is their responsibility to know. The accountability issue is about *citizens* having the will to know what is going on and why, the will to install the needed public answering obligations, and the will to exact and validate the answering and act responsibly on honest answering.

If we want reasonable standards of fairness and safety in society we had better do something to achieve it, not just sit around complaining and agreeing with observers' descriptions of the state we're in. "Defiance" has a nice ring, but, like sullenness stemming from distrust, it doesn't lead anywhere or fix anything. We have to skip defiance and move from undue deference to holding fairly to account. That means we must install reasonable performance and answering standards for all authorities. We must make them report on their responsibilities and performance and validate their answering. Otherwise, we won't know authorities' intentions and we won't overcome deception. Nor will we have the information we need to influence authorities' decisions before the fact.

Adequate answering means full and fair answering. Holding to account means exacting that answering. Public interest organizations may say, "It's naive to expect useful answering from people in authority. They will simply lie. Trying to hold to account is a waste of time." But requiring the answering and validating it should lead to a reasonable degree of self-regulation by authorities. They won't want to look silly by publicly stating intentions that are obviously unfair, or performance standards for themselves that take no effort to meet. And if authorities later lie about their actual results they can be found out by knowledgeable public interest organizations, or professional audit, or both. Requiring validated public answering causes ill-intentioned authorities to shoot themselves in the foot. The idea is to create a self-regulating influence on decision-makers who are responsible for safety, justice and equity. The key to this is making authorities answer *publicly*. And if we exact adequate public answering before the fact, it produces a useful basis for discovering and debating the fairness of authorities' real intentions and performance standards. This helps limit deception.

The general sequence in holding to account is straightforward. First, we identify and rank the legislated duties and commonsense responsibilities of executive governments, legislative assemblies, corporate and institutional boards and other authorities in serving the public interest. This is feasible, through citizens' working groups for different types of responsibilities such as health care and protection, workplace safety, education, justice issues, environmental protection, legislator effectiveness, and so on. These groups should involve the appropriate elected representatives.

Then we identify reasonable performance standards for the authorities in their circumstances, and reasonable standards for their public answering. Writing the standards can't be left to government bureaucrats or to academics funded by executive governments. We then ask the authorities to publicly state their intentions and reasoning, and their own standards, as they see them, for their performance and public answering. If authorities balk at making these public assertions, we ask our elected representatives to lean on them.

Then we tell the public whether we think the authorities' stated intentions for their performance and answering serve the public interest and, if we think they don't, we report why not.

The purpose of holding to account is to better predict what authorities will do that would affect us in important ways, and to have reasonable knowledge of their ability and motivation in carrying out their responsibilities. We need assurance about both ability and intent. For example, in wrongful convictions of people, at what point does the question of competence of police and officials shift to the question of their motivation? The same is true for legislators in an assembly, ministers in a cabinet, senior civil servants or board members of corporations. If we are uncertain we won't trust our authorities, and if we don't trust them, society doesn't work properly.

We must therefore include basic standards for public answering in our laws and constitutions. Otherwise, countries' sovereign powers will be handed over to corporations and within-country power arrangements in parliamentary systems will remain elected dictatorships. Authorities will simply do what they want. When we have the requirement for adequate answering installed in the law, holding to account and auditing the answering should take less time and effort than citizens on their own trying to pry out the intentions of stonewalling authorities to learn what to fight. If we have to fight we should do it in the best way we can, but if we don't make our legislators install the public answering requirement we will continue to allow diminishing fairness and the abuse of power. Validation of authorities' answering is feasible. For example, audit attestation of the fairness and completeness of corporations' and governments' financial reporting has been running for a hundred years.

But confining the public's attention to financial answering has meant that the few legislated reporting requirements already in place in the public and private sectors are largely limited to budgets and financial statements after the fact. We have allowed business custom and the law to keep public answering to the narrow range of financial disclosure.

We must break out of this norm and require authorities to publicly report their fairness intentions and the reasoning, performance standards, actual performance, compliance with the law and who got what as outcomes, and what the authorities learned and how they applied it.

When authorities explain their intentions and reasoning and we challenge them, power is shared, just as it is shared in genuine public consultation. Public answering after the fact makes authorities' mistakes visible, which of course they don't want. But authorities have a legitimate concern: will their answering be used unfairly by political opposition simply looking for "ink"? Those in power therefore don't volunteer to answer. But others seeking to take over political power also may resist working for better answering standards if there is a chance they will be in power themselves. This is evident from the reluctance of opposition political parties – even those who we would most expect to champion public answering – to propose adequate answering standards when the need for them is obvious.

It is time to stop supplicating, but to fight only when it's necessary. Each time we fight, the authorities get a better handle on how to counter it. What they are not used to, and have no strategy to deflect, is being told to publicly account, and to a standard. We must insist that our governments and the larger corporations tell us how their intentions would produce fairness, and what difference their actions have made thus far, to whom. As matters stand, the rich get richer and the poor poorer because our elected representatives allow it. But legislators in sovereign states are still in control of the laws that regulate corporations and other authorities in their countries and set their public answering obligations. Where this control is in doubt, legislators, collectively across the globe, are still in control of the collaboration needed to produce effective laws governing fairness and accountability.

Public interest organizations are key because they act for citizens. In their areas of interest their leaders can organize task groups to draft basic performance and answering standards for the directing minds of authorities and for senior civil servants. These organizations also have the knowledge to audit the answering.

As individuals, we can help public interest organizations bring about public answering by handing our elected representatives basic expectations rather than supplications. But there is a problem: many of us would feel uncomfortable marching in a placard parade, but even more uncomfortable making appointments with our elected representatives and asking them a series of questions that simply ask for explanation, such as:

- How have you informed yourself about Proposal X?
- What would you say are your responsibilities in the issue, as you see them?
- What will you do to have citizens reasonably understand who would benefit from Proposal X and why they should, and who would bear what costs and risks, and why they should?
- What do you see as your own performance standards in this issue?
- How do you plan to account to your constituents for your duty in Proposal X?

Even in a democracy, this may seem too daunting for many. But it isn't difficult to write a non-supplicating letter to an elected representative that politely sets out a few right questions and the writer's expectations for answers. If we get no response, we can politely write again – and yet again – until the elected representative tells us his or her intentions.

If authorities won't answer adequately for their responsibilities, and if elected representatives won't make them, and if public interest organizations can't create a climate of opinion strong enough to force them to answer, citizens and their organizations can use another approach. This is to audit the authorities direct. Once we free ourselves from blind faith we can take an audit view. An audit is simply a capable assessment of performance and answering against reasonable expectations, reported publicly. But it is to be done fairly, with some rigour.

In the citizen audit approach, citizens' groups or public interest organizations can identify who has what commonsense responsibilities and public answering obligations for responsibilities they think are important. Using the information available – most of it public – citizen audit groups can assess any authority's apparent performance and its actual public answering against reasonable expectations for it. Citizen audit would make use of journalists' and media coverage of people's responsibilities in an issue, keeping in mind that journalists won't set out the public answering that is missing. The citizen audit report invites the authority's governing body to account – to present its own view of its intentions, performance and quality of answering. Citizen audit reports simply ask authorities to do what they should have done: to account and to submit their answering to validation. The report would give the reasons why they should.

The horror stories of the past few decades tell us that we can no longer operate on blind trust, or claim to know the intentions and abilities of the directing minds of our institutions. We must in effect cancel public trust in authorities and have them earn it back through honest public answering before and after the fact. Validated answering will help us tell who is serving the public interest and who is not.

The days of elections giving power of attorney must end. As the servant of the people, executive government has become greater than the master, and the directing minds of the large transnational corporations answer to no one. Executive governments answer to the legislatures poorly, arrogantly, deceptively or not at all. Quasi-government organizations presumed to serve the public interest don't show by their answering who their real clients are. Thus citizens must stop deferring to authorities and start holding people in authority to account, fairly yet relentlessly.

When we think about it, installing the answering requirement and holding to account qualifies as innovation in the use of power in society. It is the job of citizens, as the ultimate governing body, not only to decide who will allocate power and who will see that it is used only in the public interest, but also to make authorities account for the use of the power given to them. Once citizens and their organizations become accustomed to exacting adequate answering, they will wonder why it took so long to do it.

Public answering won't stop deception and corruption, but it will help to limit it. Since valid trust in our institutions is needed to have society work properly, we must place in positions of leadership and authority only those willing to account fully and fairly for their responsibilities. Those who seek office but won't commit to answering to an agreed standard must be denied the office, and those in office who refuse to account must be placed in credibility receivership. Those who seek power can have all the status they want, but in return they must answer adequately to us. The more autonomy we give authorities the better their answering must be. But when we insist that authorities answer to us, we must not only validate their reporting but also do something fair and sensible with answering given in good faith.

At the global level, the public answering obligations of national executive governments are illustrated by a late 1990s comment of a Canadian senior citizen about the United States: "The United States sucks whatever it wants from wherever it wants, anywhere in the world, and we can't stop them." As to Americans' view of themselves, the editor of *Harper's Magazine* in August 2001 cites a writer in TIME magazine:

> America is no mere international citizen. It is the dominant power in the world, more dominant than any since Rome. Accordingly, America is in a position to re-shape norms, alter expectations and create new realities. How? By unapologetic demonstrations of will.[3]

We need to know the extent to which this view reflects the view of those who decide the intentions of the United States and its businesses. In the day-to-day civil affairs of people on the planet, what outcomes in justice does the United States seek, for whom? International coalitions needed to deal with terrorism are a separate matter: the "with us or against us" condition cannot be used to force world compliance with Americans' business aims.

If we pursue the two citizens' observations above to identify who has what answering obligation, it takes us beyond the words "United States" to identify the particular directing minds producing what Southern countries and activists argue is unjust in America's aims. While we obviously don't attribute everything that happens in the world to the United States, the U.S. affects the world in very important ways. In fairness, that makes its directing minds publicly accountable to the other countries. It is therefore reasonable that the world's six billion people ask the United States executive government and Congress, representing only five per cent of the world's population but directing the world's most powerful entity, to state the specific outcomes or end-states they intend, for whom, and why, and how the U.S. intends to produce those outcomes. A mission statement of the United States confined to isolationism or goals of "individual liberty, free enterprise and limited intervention by government" (or anyone else's government) won't produce a civil society, even within the US itself.

But the public answering obligation applies as well to the executive governments and legislatures of the other Northern countries – Canada included. They must make clear, through their answering, whether they put corporate business interests first. Do they in fact intend to allow corporate sales to come before safety, social justice and the environment? Do they authorize or encourage the sale of arms to those who they know are fomenting the growing regional conflicts around the world that kill untold numbers of citizens and destroy these countries' economies?

Just as the mission of the Salvation Army is to make citizens out of the rejected, holding to account can make competent citizens out of the deferential and apathetic, by making it possible for citizens to be in control. Holding to account is not a political movement. It is simply a discipline that can use citizens' energy more efficiently than fighting as the first recourse in working for a fairer society. Validated answering can expose practices that authorities deny exist or won't fix. Nor is achieving better public answering a partisan political policy: it is politically neutral because it doesn't honour some people's needs but not others. It helps to make clear people's legitimate needs and distinguishes them from authorities' wants. Because of its self-regulating potential, the public answering requirement is a fairness governor on authorities' self-serving aims.

Effective holding to account is a reasonable indicator of citizens' competence. It requires only courage to face up to what is going on, common sense based on fairness, and a shift to working smarter, not harder to control people in authority. The test is whether we can say as citizens, "We're not patsies and we're not just shrugging our shoulders. We're in control." Mahatma Gandhi and Dr. Martin Luther King showed that we don't have to use aggression to achieve justice – that there are other ways to achieve it if they are used. Holding fairly yet relentlessly to account surely fits with the way such leaders worked for justice.

One question for the next decade is whether citizens will cease to be outraged by anything. Will we stumble on in a bewildered and battered state, ultimately accepting whatever authorities decide for us, or will we choose to control our society? Unless we say, "enough is enough," the horror-story assembly lines will carry on, likely picking up the production pace until citizens say to authorities: "We give up; do whatever you want to us."

To get going on holding fairly to account, we must clarify the concept of public accountability and know what holding to account means for important responsibilities and why it's important. We must learn how to achieve the needed public answering from authorities. The work to be done includes drafting and installing standards for legislated public answering for major responsibilities. But we don't wait for the law to evolve; in the meantime we work to exact adequate public answering.

The four horror stories that introduce Part I are not journalism. They show what happens when we don't have public answering for important responsibilities. If citizens don't want public answering because they don't want to deal with it, that is the personal business of each. But in all honesty, we can't trust authorities if we have no evidence for it. It *is* feasible to install the public answering obligation for authorities. It *is* feasible to apply the precautionary principle to set fundamental rules for authorities' performance and answering. And it *is* feasible to validate authorities' answering to limit deception. Creating an answering society fundamentally changes the relationship between citizens and those in authority. It can be done because we already have the institutions and structures in society to do it. Adequate public answering will have a regulating and stabilizing influence in the way society works, and that will lead to greater fairness in society.

Endnotes

[1] The title of Will Hutton's book *The State We're In*, (Vintage, London, 1996) aptly applies to public accountability.

[2] For example, former Canadian federal minister Monique Bégin, quoted in a February 2000 *Ottawa Citizen* article, said that in strategy sessions around the cabinet table during her ministerial time from 1976 to 1984, everything was put in the context of war and of battle. When citizens spoke up it was interpreted as a challenge to the government, and Ms. Bégin felt that by the year 2000 the situation was likely worse. Many Ontario citizens felt that the new government of Premier Harris and his "60s brats" advisors was literally at war with citizens.

[3] Charles Krauthammer, quoted in Lewis H. Lapham's "The American Rome," *Harper's Magazine*, August 2001, p.31

Part I

Accountability

CHAPTER 1

Four Horror Stories

Introduction

These cases illustrate what can happen when people with important responsibilities don't account for their responsibilities, and are not made to answer. Each case summarizes what happened and what adequate public answering would have disclosed about the authorities' performance. The information for the first three cases is taken from public reports. For the court martial case, further supporting documents were supplied by the family of the officer court martialled.

Certain terms used mean the following in the context of the cases:

Responsibility means the obligation to act in a role or duty, to the limit of one's power or authority, and to cope reasonably with external constraints. This includes informing oneself adequately to carry out a duty diligently. But commonsense responsibility is as important as legally-prescribed responsibility, because existing laws are weak in setting performance standards and answering obligations. Thus responsibility is defined in this book as the obligation to act in the public interest in a role or duty. If someone given a directive perceives it not to be in the public interest, that person has to decide whether to serve the public interest or the wants of those assigning the action. There are obvious cases where command control legitimately takes over, such as in wartime operations, but a civil servant's responsibility in the operations of government, and that of a professional in the private sector, is to serve the public interest.

Accountability means the obligation to answer for the discharge of responsibilities, through explanation to those having a significant legitimate interest in what the decision-makers intend and do. People whose responsibilities and decisions significantly affect the public cannot confine their answering to reporting only to their superiors. The answering obligation, like the answering itself, is both before and after the fact and is explained in Chapter 2.

Holding to account means obtaining adequate answering for responsibilities. For important answering, this means having the answering validated. But it also means responding fairly to answering given in good faith. It is an active or ensuring role rather than passive, because in most cases the answering has to be exacted.

The precautionary principle says that a decision to proceed with an intention flows from diligently identifying and assessing the nature and extent of the risks involved, in terms of risk to safety, fairness, justice or risk to the environment. When the risk of proceeding cannot be ascertained with reasonable assurance, such as valid scientific evidence, and some measure of decision error is likely or certain, the decision-makers act on the side of being cautious rather than taking chances that are unnecessary. The purpose of the precautionary principle is to prevent action leading to harm. It requires proponents and authorizing decision-makers to demonstrate the safety of proceeding with an intention – or a decision not to act – as opposed to requiring concerned citizens to demonstrate that the intention is unsafe. For example, the term "risk management" in health is misleading, because the key protection responsibility is deciding the level of risk to be *accepted* by the public, not simply to act in a task. "Risk management" could be simply the management of risk appearances.

Directing mind means the person, group or official governing body who ultimately determines or authorizes intentions affecting citizens in important ways. The intentions may be carried out by a government department or agency, a corporation or some other entity. The term "directing mind" comes from Lord Denning's view of the management and board of directors of a company as the company's "directing mind and will," expressed in one of his court decisions as a judge in the mid-1950s. This is described in Case 3. Holding to account therefore can't be effective without identifying who must answer for the responsibilities in question, which is the true directing mind. For government, the directing mind is the ministers of the Crown in the executive government, or their counterparts in other forms of government. For local government it is municipal councillors. For corporations it is the members of the governing body – the board of directors or governors. For Crown corporations the ultimate directing mind is the responsible minister.

Management control means, in essence, causing to happen. Therefore, it also means causing not to happen that which shouldn't – especially important in safety and health risks. Management control means engaging effectively the abilities, motivations, processes and structures needed to achieve agreed achievement objectives and cope with external constraints beyond an entity's control. Motivation is the most important element because it determines the level and direction of effort. Management control includes obtaining the information needed to tell whether responsibilities are being properly discharged. Safety control, value for money, compliance with the law and financial control are all part of management control. Responsibility for the adequacy of management control in an organization lies with the organization's directing minds.

Fundamental rules are rules of conduct in an organization, as few in number as possible, that are not to be broken. Waiver of them requires the consent of those setting the rules.

Compliance means meeting reasonable expectations for conduct stemming from fundamental rules and authoritative direction. Examples are compliance with the intent of laws (not just the letter of the law), spending authorizations, contracts, and other direction considered authoritative.

Critical Success Factors are the necessary and sufficient sub-objectives which, if met, mean that a main objective is likely to be met. Governing bodies must know how the critical success factors are working in their organizations.

— — —

The harm in the following cases resulted from directing minds failing to discharge their responsibilities in the public interest, including their control duty (they may have controlled in their own interest), choosing not to know what was going on, or simply failing to learn and carry out their duties and control responsibilities in the public interest. Directing minds can successfully reject their accountability and exonerate themselves if they are not held publicly to account for their responsibilities.

CASE 1

The Blood Disgrace[1]

What Happened

In the 1980s, over 60,000 Canadians received blood or blood products that killed them fairly quickly, shortened their lives or gave them life sentences of reduced capacity. The suffering of their loved ones is an extension of the harm. The estimates of the commission of inquiry were at least 2,000 infected with HIV and 60,000 with hepatitis C.

Part of this Canadian disgrace is that we don't even know the total number killed or injured from HIV and hepatitis C contracted through blood transfusions. The victims' charge of callousness levelled at those responsible comes from the authorities' recklessness in the risk they made blood users take, especially in the early 1980s. In 1998, every Member of Parliament in attendance on the government side stood in the House of Commons to vote down compensation for victims receiving contaminated blood before 1986 – in effect saying to the public that there was no effective safeguard before then. That is false but the MPs got away with the pretense, and still today the media report that there was no test for hepatitis C before 1986.

As we start the next century with a revised blood system, the health ministers across Canada who put the system together have not told us who has what specific responsibility for preventing a recurrence of harm, the extent to which the health ministers are following the precautionary principle, or what they think the preventive control is for the replacement system. Blind faith reigns for legislators and citizens alike: we have no effective public answering in place for the Canadian Blood Services agency. With no answering by those with the ultimate responsibility, nothing changes fundamentally.

The 1980s blood and blood products contaminated with HIV and hepatitis C were distributed in Canada by the Blood Transfusion Service of the Canadian Red Cross Society, whose blood experts would have been expert in risk awareness. So long as the Red Cross could successfully claim its products to be safe, the income from donated blood turned into saleable blood products would continue. There was also a regulator. The federal Minister of Health, through the Health Protection Branch, had and still has the statutory duty to control the safety of manufacturing processes for blood components, blood products and their distribution. The Minister also has the duty to establish whether claims about a product's safety are true.

The job of ministers of health across Canada is safety and protection. Yet in the 1980s these ministers, who directed the Red Cross's blood transfusion services through the ministers' Canadian Blood Committee chose to concern themselves only with the Red Cross's spending, not the safety of its distributed blood. And the federal accountable ministers and senior civil servants hadn't staffed or resourced the Health Protection Branch to permit adequate regulation of blood. There were no blood experts and not even inspectors to check Red Cross transfusion centres. The health ministers knew, or ought to have known that the Red Cross was unique in being unregulated by the federal Health Minister. Two decades later, the federal government still lacks this competence for its regulatory duty under the *Food and Drugs Act*, despite probable future blood contamination from new contaminants.

The failures of the regulator and the Red Cross came to public attention as the horrors unfolded in the 1980s. Citizens in other countries were alerted, but Canadians were not. Their outrage was supported by the 1990s Commission of Inquiry on the Blood System in Canada, headed by Justice Horace Krever. Commissioner Krever reported to government ministers in November 1997, also publishing his report for the public.[2] One of his recommendations was that all the blood-injured be compensated. No one has been criminally charged – not even people who, because of looming liabilities, had authorized the destruction of years of Blood Committee minutes in 1989. This act was the subject of a 1977 report by the federal access to information commissioner.

The federal, provincial and territorial ministers of health responded to the disgrace by establishing a replacement national blood agency, but largely the same operations. Ministers have never stated to Canadians the safety control and public answering standards for future blood safety and accessibility that they think are necessary and sufficient. These collective and accountable ministers of the Crown have not made clear to Canadians, and especially the blood-injured, exactly what they intend as future safeguards in response to the recommendations of the Krever inquiry. Regardless what ministers want Canadians to believe, they remain the directing minds for the new agency and have the duty to ensure not only accessibility but also adequate safety and adequate public answering standards. The federal Minister of Health has full statutory power and duty to set adequate safety performance standards for the national blood system.

The federal Minister and the other ministers have yet to state what they perceive as their duty, so that Canadians can hold them to account. They have yet to state what public answering standards they intend for themselves, as the new Canadian Blood Services' overseers, and what performance accounting they require from the governing board of the agency. Given the death-count and the extent of lasting harm from the 1980s, it should be inconceivable that legislatures across Canada haven't examined what the ministers intend as their responsibilities, performance standards and public answering obligations. But our legislators haven't even asked for this answering. Governing-party legislators won't because they simply support their ministers, but opposition parties can, and would have the public behind them.

The following chronology is background for understanding the responsibilities and answering obligations in the blood disgrace. It does not include all significant events and decisions, nor does it attempt to summarize the Krever report. Even so, the outline clearly shows that people with key responsibilities did not do their duty from the time of the first blood alerts in 1982.

— — —

By the 1960s it was well known in scientific ranks that donor blood used for transfusions and blood products was contaminated with hepatitis. Reasonably successful testing, known as the surrogate ALT test, was available to detect the disease we now know as hepatitis C. Despite published studies supporting the efficacy of testing to prevent over half of post-transfusion hepatitis cases, the Red Cross did not test its blood donations, and the federal regulator took no visible interest.

By the end of 1982, the risk of AIDS from transfused blood was known and steps were being taken in the United States and other countries to deal with it. But not in Canada.

By 1983 it was found that heat-treating blood products made from blood plasma reduced the AIDS risk. Given the known successful hepatitis C testing, and the fact that AIDS was being transmitted through blood transfusions, 1983 was the critical year for Canadian federal regulatory officials to act under their statutory duty. The fact that they and their ministers didn't act is presumably the reason why all Members of Parliament present on the Liberal benches rose one day in April 1998 to vote down, 154 votes to the united Opposition's 140, Justice Krever's inquiry report recommendation that all the blood-injured be compensated, not just those harmed after 1986.

Once the significant risk of blood contamination became known in the medical world, those with significant responsibilities for blood safety had an immediate vigilance obligation to inform themselves for their duty and take precautionary steps. For the federal Minister of Health and the Health Protection Branch, this meant identifying the risk and deciding what level of risk to accept under the precautionary principle embedded in the federal *Food and Drugs Act*. In 1984, with other countries installing mandatory testing and providing public information, Canadian officials were still dragging their feet, issuing only "good health" pamphlets that ducked the issue. Even as late as the fall of 1984, after Canadian laboratory tests had found antibodies in donated blood and it was clear that the blood being distributed in Canada by the Red Cross was lethally contaminated and producing AIDS, the federal government, as supreme regulator, still failed to act. Failure to act was a decision.

Blood and blood products meet the definition of drugs as defined in the federal *Food and Drugs Act*. Blood and blood products are thus regulated under the Act and its regulations, administered by the Minister of Health and his department. For example, Section 12 of the Act, together with the regulations, reflects the Act's legislation of the precautionary principle. It prohibits sale of blood and blood products unless the Minister indicates that "the premises in which the drug was manufactured and the process and conditions of manufacture are suitable to ensure that the drug will not be unsafe for use." But the government took no steps to bring the Red Cross under regulation. As Commissioner Krever's report into the blood system put it 18 years later, "During most of the period of the contamination of the blood supply, the Red Cross was the only pharmaceutical corporation in Canada that was in effect unregulated." A 1982 Health Protection Branch draft regulations amendment to strengthen the regulation of biological drugs, which include blood and blood products, was shelved and not acted on until 1989.

The federal executive government at all times had full power to act to save lives. But the "environment of decision" in the early 1980s included two political influences. First, federal ministers' goals of de-regulation and attracting big foreign pharmaceutical corporations to Canada came before aims of strengthening regulations for safety. Government department resources were deployed accordingly. Secondly, a federal election loomed for September 1984. No incumbent senior minister would want exposure of what was happening if it would make ministers publicly answerable for thousands of needless deaths and wrecked lives. At stake was not just public blame and massive legal liability but also the unthinkable – possible criminal liability not only for Red Cross officials but also for identifiable provincial and federal ministers and senior civil servants who had failed to act.

Despite growing public concern and the fact that heat-treating and surrogate ALT hepatitis C testing were being done elsewhere, the Canadian Red Cross continued to ship untreated blood and blood products. The federal Minister and Health Protection Branch had the power to stop the shipments, but didn't do so. Thus the Red Cross was able to define the availability of replacement heat-treated blood as the estimated time when their own untreated stock would be used up.

Not until 1985 did Canadian authorities finally concede the obvious connection between blood transfusions and hepatitis C. Even then, Canadian recipients of contaminated blood were not traced and alerted as far as was possible with the Red Cross's and hospitals' abilities to trace. As late as 1986, when American blood agencies had already installed hepatitis C screening at virtually all blood centres, the Red Cross refused to screen.

Red Cross officials claimed that the testing was unproved and would cost $10 million a year. Testing for the antibody for the hepatitis C virus was finally implemented in Canada in 1990.

At no time did the federal or provincial health ministers or the board of the Canadian Red Cross report to Canadians what they saw as the emerging blood risk. They did not report their own statutory duty and their intentions and reasoning, nor did they report what they saw as their own performance standards under the precautionary principle. At no time did any of these authorities disclose the trade-offs they were making among saving lives, keeping costs down (including the cost of writing off contaminated blood!), achieving political policy aims, and reducing their own exposure.

In 1989, under the direction of the newly-appointed executive director of the Canadian Blood Committee, a committee of the overseeing Canadian health ministers, the audio tapes and transcripts of the Committee's meetings from its inception in 1982 to 1989 were unlawfully destroyed. These records documented ministers' decisions for the blood system, taken on the advice of senior civil servants. In 1989 federal health department officials knew that access to information requests had been filed for the minutes and that lawsuits against the Red Cross and federal government were already being launched. Who ordered, authorized or permitted the executive director, Dr. Jo Hauser, to destroy the minutes has never been made clear, and to date no one has been sanctioned or fired, let alone jailed.

In 1996 the federal Information Commissioner, John Grace, launched an investigation into the 1989 destruction of the Blood Committee minutes, based on the public revelations. His report, released the day after Dr. Hauser resigned from Health Canada, confirmed that the purpose of the destruction was to avoid exposure but found no punishment teeth in federal records-related legislation, and did not deal with criminal liability.

The blood-injured had called for criminal charges to be laid, asking why the RCMP had not acted at the outset of harm. They contended that the RCMP had not launched a criminal investigation because elected officials and senior bureaucrats would be involved. When the Krever final report was published, the RCMP responded that they were reviewing the report, together with other information they were now getting from individuals. This was to assess whether a criminal investigation should be launched. The RCMP said they would be "proactive" in seeing whether the report pointed to a criminal investigation, but also said that no one had lodged a complaint. They also warned that it would be a complex and lengthy case. Thousands would have to be interviewed before charges could be laid, because the RCMP would not be able to use the Commission's evidence as evidence in criminal proceedings. In 1997 Dr. Michèle Brill-Edwards, former senior physician for drugs regulatory matters in the federal Health Protection Branch and co-director of the Ottawa-based Alliance for Public Accountability, pointed out the Criminal Code provisions covering violation of federal statutes. The RCMP then announced that it was launching a criminal investigation.

When the Alliance for Public Accountability followed up in March 1999, the RCMP replied that its task force "continues to investigate all aspects of the Canadian Blood System between 1980 and 1990, as identified by complaints from the public." The RCMP was still at it through 2000, with the public still not knowing whether it would lay charges.

The Krever Commission

Commissioner Krever's 1993-1997 inquiry into the blood system in Canada stemmed from hearings on the blood contamination held in the early 1990s by a federal parliamentary committee. The majority on the committee were government members. The committee did not report to the House its view of the responsibilities and accountabilities involved (if in fact it had any view on this), thus abdicating a core function of parliamentary scrutiny. Instead, the committee left everything to Commissioner Krever, and left the executive government to decide what he would and would not examine. For example, Commissioner Krever would not be allowed to name those whom he concluded had failed to discharge key responsibilities, and he did not address authorities' answering obligations.

In February 1996, Commissioner Krever's progress was halted by the predictable legal wrangle over who could be named in his report and who would not. An inquiry citing a person for misconduct may be important for possible civil charges by victims and their families, and for criminal investigation and charges by the Crown. Many took court action to prevent being named. Counsel for the blood victims maintained that the victims' right to know why they were dying and who was responsible came before officials' perceived risk to their own reputations.

The federal court of appeal ruled that 17 could be named, comprising 14 Red Cross blood managers and three federal government officials. But 47 people receiving the Commissioner's notice of possible naming would not be named. These were people whom Krever had said were never intended to be named but only notified to give them the chance to rebut any tarnishment from association. Since the *Inquiries Act* is not new, this dispute should have been foreseen and prevented. The result is that those with the most senior responsibilities, up to and including the responsible health ministers, have never been named.

In the middle of the naming dispute, the Ottawa *Hill Times* broke the story that Bill C-95, a new *Department of Health Act*, would have the effect of removing statutory responsibilities from the federal Minister of Health. The Minister's duty to uphold the *Food and Drugs Act* was to be eliminated by simple removal of a key responsibility clause in the existing *Department of Health and Welfare Act*. The deletion had been pointed out to MPs by counsel for blood victims, Lori Stoltz, who had been alerted to its implications by Dr. Brill-Edwards. But the parliamentary committee, with its government majority, took no action until the *Hill Times* exposed the issue. The clause was then reinstated in Bill C-95. The big newspapers didn't carry this story.

In 1996 the Krever Commission requested early-1980s government documents on executive government decisions about federal draft regulations. These would have up-graded safety standards for biological drugs, which include blood and blood products. The requested documents would have shed light on ministers' views of their responsibilities and intentions concerning proposed regulations amendments circulated to the industry in 1984. The government rejected Krever's request, claiming cabinet secrecy.

The government counsel's disdainful parting shot at Justice Krever came in December 1996, at the close of the extended hearings. Said the Crown's lawyers in their summary, the "true object" of Krever's inquiry "is not a purposeful contribution to the safety of the Canadian blood supply, but a search for scapegoats." The statement achieved its media purpose. The immediate *Ottawa Citizen* headline read: "Government Slams Blood Inquiry Head." The government's lead counsel then predictably apologized to Justice Krever, saying that he did not mean to "impugn you or your office."

The Krever inquiry hearings ended on 18 December 1996. The Commissioner's lengthy report, made public in November 1997, laid out much information of use for the future, and included the recommendation that all blood victims, not just those harmed after 1986, should be compensated. But it did not explain to Canadians the statutory protection powers and duties of the federal ministers of health, whose departments' failure to halt the contaminated blood distribution act led to the deaths and injury. And it did not summarize for Canadians who had what statutory and commonsense responsibilities and accountabilities; whether those involved discharged their obligations and, if not, why not; and who in future should account publicly for what responsibilities.

The Replacement Blood System

The 1996 naming-names wrangling that delayed the Krever report allowed the federal government to shift to a political strategy of "let's pre-empt Krever's report," not waiting for Commissioner Krever's recommendations about what would be needed for a safe blood system. Starting in March 1996, the federal Department of Health gathered provincial officials to create a replacement national system which it would "reconcile" with whatever Krever recommended.

Since the federal government wished to say that views of blood user groups had been heard, federal health department officials convened a meeting of representatives of blood user and victim groups and other groups in January 1997 in Toronto. The Department's 1996 consumer group consultation rounds, which stemmed from complaints of departmental secrecy, had been criticized as putting consumers into roles that gave the appearance of participation but without real input or power.

The January 1997 Toronto meeting was no different. It was conducted by Health Department officials as a "tell and sell." Only lower-level departmental officials attended, not the decision-makers, and they ducked explaining the crucial elements of the replacement system. These elements were the letters patent powers, responsibilities and accountabilities of the proposed national blood corporation intended by the federal, provincial and territorial health ministers. Since the ministers were to meet in March 1997 to discuss the recommendations of their deputy ministers, the federal government obviously knew what was to be proposed to the ministers but did not share its intentions at the Toronto meeting.

Federal Health Minister Allan Rock held a second meeting in Toronto in early November 1997, adroitly timed between the October 1997 press release on the new blood system by the federal/provincial/territorial health ministers, and the release date for Commissioner Krever's final report. Although it was billed as a "stakeholder" meeting, one research doctor who attended the Toronto meeting called it "simply window dressing." Doctors, researchers and other stakeholders were invited to "meet the challenge" and to deliberate in discussion groups on operational aspects of the intended new system. Kept off the agenda yet again were the intended key responsibilities of the new blood authority and the intended performance answering standards, both for the new agency's board and for the overseeing health ministers.

Behind the scenes, the proposed letters patent and by-laws intended for the new corporation had been drafted in mid-1997. The legal provisions drafted for the corporation's safety mandate and performance standards differed significantly from what the nation's health ministers' later stated in their October 1997 press release on the new Canadian Blood Services. The press release version was used at the podium of the November 1997 Toronto meeting by the director of the Transition Bureau for the new agency. The draft legal documents limited the ministers' responsibilities for blood safety and accessibility, set out no public answering obligations for the agency's directing minds, and required no external assessment of the agency's performance other than the usual external audit of the corporation's financial statements.

Minister Rock then appointed an advisory board for the Blood Services agency, giving the impression that it was expert and would be responsible for safety – which tended to imply that the Minister himself would no longer be responsible. The Minister has yet to tell Canadians who will produce what public answering for the provincial, territorial and federal ministers' overseeing role, and for the agency's operating responsibilities for maintaining a national blood service providing feasible maximum safety. The responsibilities include effective trace-back when danger is detected.

Thus Canadians lack assurance that they now have greater safety in blood.

The Missing Public Answering

The main responsibilities and accountabilities lay with the federal, provincial and territorial health ministers and the Red Cross, but those of the federal government are the most important. As the statutory regulator of blood safety in Canada, the federal health minister has supreme power and authority over the safety of blood and blood products.

Timely and validated public answering by those having the protection responsibilities could have alerted citizens and their elected representatives to the blood risk early on. Public concern might then have forced the federal Ministers and the Health Protection Branch to act to prevent at least half the deaths and wrecked lives.

Had reasonable public reporting requirements been in place, audit of the fairness and completeness of the forced reporting could have produced answers to the following questions:

- For blood safety precautions, who had what responsibility to act, when, and to what standard of performance?
- Who had the obligation to tell blood users, legislators and Canadians at large:
  - how well the Health Protection Branch and Red Cross were informing themselves about blood risks
  - the level of risk they intended Canadian blood users to accept?
- Was timely accounting for the intended and actual performance of the responsible officials being given to the public?
- Was the management control reasonably to be expected for ensuring safety diligence in each cluster of responsibilities operating effectively?
- If people with key responsibilities were not doing their duty, why? What were the underlying reasons and possible syndromes?

The key question for the future, still unanswered by the responsible federal, provincial and territorial ministers, is: "Who must account publicly for what responsibilities, to help prevent repetition of deaths and harm in Canadian use of blood and blood products?"

The answering starts with the Canadian ministers of health. Canadian standards for blood safety and for having a safe supply of blood available are the responsibility of the overall regulator, the federal Minister. This Minister sets and enforces the safety standards that Canadians expect. These are not standards to make life easier for those with blood responsibilities, including supplier corporations. The standards for citizens' access to blood and blood products are negotiated among federal, provincial and territorial health ministers. This is because the access standards involve the aims of federal funding agreements under the federal *Canada Health Act*, and involve provincial governments' own political policies in making blood and blood products readily available to citizens through provincial hospitals.

In the case of blood in the 1980s, upholding the precautionary principle was not just a fairness imperative; it was a statutory requirement of federal ministers under the *Food and Drugs Act*. The principle implies that blood-related corporate managements and boards and government officials and ministers are obliged to inform themselves adequately for their decision-making. No barriers stand in the way of people with important responsibilities informing themselves to a reasonable standard of diligence before they act. Citizens can legitimately regard as negligence the failure of authorities to inform themselves for their duties.

The first area of answering is for compliance with the law. The federal Minister's control duty is to ensure that public servants carry out the safety intent of the *Food and Drugs Act*. It is also to ensure that corporations – including the Red Cross and its successor – comply with the intent of the law. The *Act* applies both to government's own safety regulation diligence and to the performance of corporations, hospitals and other entities involved in the manufacturing, distribution and use of blood and blood products. All were subject to federal government control in the 1980s – and still are.

Public answering should have told Canadians whether safety control was adequate. In particular, the responsible authorities should have been reporting whether they were:
- complying with the precautionary principle and the law
- adequately informing themselves to decide:
  - what risk to thrust on blood recipients
  - the consequent safety performance standards needed
  - how to account usefully and publicly for the decisions
- giving adequate and timely public notice, for public challenge, of intended risk acceptance and performance standards
- meeting the safety standards that the federal Minister of Health had decided
- protecting employees of conscience trying to get their superiors to reduce the blood risk.

So long as the Red Cross and other pharmaceutical suppliers had anything to do with products coming under the intent of the *Act*, the federal Minister of Health had the statutory power to control their actions, and should have accounted for that duty. Regardless of weak or missing answering requirements in legislation, all authorities involved in blood had a fairness obligation to Canadians to report their action intentions and reasoning, their performance standards for vigilance and protection diligence, how well they were succeeding in protecting Canadians during the crisis, what they were learning, and how they were applying what they had learned.

Ministerial accountability

Federal ministers have not been required to make public assertions about their perform-ance. For example, the *Food and Drugs Act* is silent on the question of the federal Minister of Health answering for his or her regulatory responsibilities. The same is true for the *Department of Health Act*, which governs the Minister's responsibilities for the depart-ment. There is simply no current requirement for a health minister to answer publicly for his or her diligence in safety. Annual reports to Parliament to explain departments' in-tended and actual accomplishment are prepared by civil servants but the contents don't go to the bone. The Minister simply signs a public-relations transmittal note at the front. This lack of adequate answering for responsibilities leaves citizens with only the two op-tions of blind faith or seeking redress after harm has been done.

Canadians received no accountings from federal health ministers to give them critical information. With respect to their duty, ministers did not report whether they:
- knew the blood contamination risks and feasible means of reducing hazards that had been pointed out by blood scientists in the medical- scientific community
- knew the extent to which the directing minds of the Red Cross were ignoring the precautionary principle in their blood decisions
- decided the standards reasonable for the Red Cross to meet, conveyed that expec-tation authoritatively to the Red Cross, and asked the corporation's Board to tell the Minister whether Canadians were getting that standard in Red Cross opera-tions
- decided, on the basis of what was feasible in hazard reduction, the level of risk to accept in the public interest through the blood donation and manufacturing stages
- undertook the action needed to reduce the hazards, which included not only ad-equate public warning but also identifying contaminated or suspect blood and stopping its distribution
- produced the needed public reporting on performance from all those subject to the *Food and Drugs Act*, including the Minister

Canadian ministers of health have yet to publicly account for the discharge of their responsibilities.

Senior civil servants' accountability. Ministers' reporting to Parliament did not tell MPs whether senior civil servants in the Department of Health, with respect to their duty:

- ensured that they knew the blood contaminants and possible effects in blood and blood products used for transfusions, knew the available contaminant tests and screening methods, and knew the implications of Canadian inaction
- protected employees of conscience who were ringing alarm bells within the Department and the Red Cross (Of the directors in the Red Cross, those who expressed concerns – over a dozen – were apparently fired or forced out during the 1980s. There is no auditable trail in the Canadian federal government to show who fails or refuses to act on professional or scientific concerns or advice given them – for example, the reasoning given by the scientific and professional experts doesn't stay attached to briefing documents going up the line to the minister)
- determined whether the Red Cross's board, CEO and senior doctors were upholding the precautionary principle to the standard intended by the *Food and Drugs Act* and regulations
- made recommendations to the Minister for regulating the Red Cross at the first sign of safety problems
- ensured that the Minister knew his or her statutory duty and approved or rejected the views and reasoning of Department officials on the safety control measures that they felt it was the Department's duty to impose
- told blood recipients their risks from transfusions and blood products and told the public at large what was going on (which would have disclosed the lag in action by Departmental officials as well as the Red Cross)
- acted properly on information on plasma safety given to fractionators by their raw material suppliers such as the Red Cross (the use of U.S. prison blood is an example)
- ensured that US corporations could not ship to Canadian corporations, including the Red Cross, contaminated blood that had become worthless in the United States because of the precautions already being taken there
- above all, ordered the Red Cross to stop shipping blood known to be contaminated or suspect.

It has not been determined who, as between ministers and senior civil servants, caused the five-year delay in the promulgation of the early 1980s revised regulations for biological drugs. Nor has it been determined who, either explicitly or tacitly instructed the Executive Director of the Canadian Blood Committee to destroy the 1982-89 tapes and minutes of the Committee.

Red Cross Board accountability. With respect to its duty, the board of the Red Cross gave no public answering telling Canadians whether it had:

- ensured, in its governance role, that Red Cross operations in blood distribution demonstrably applied the precautionary principle
- informed itself to a standard Canadians could reasonably expect of it in blood safety, and acted promptly and effectively on the information
- understood the intent of the *Food and Drugs Act* as it logically applied to the Red Cross as a manufacturer, and the obligation to comply with the intent of the Act and regulations
- knew whether reasonable safety standards were being set and met by Red cross officials – for example in response action through the use of feasible surrogate tests for hepatitis C
- above all, made sure that the board's management control system for the Red Cross was adequate to ensure that blood risks were:
  - identified at the highest possible level of accuracy and dealt with to a reasonable standard of due diligence
  - communicated in a timely way to the regulator, blood recipients and Canadian users and potential users

The Krever report includes one instance of a blood-risk concern at a 1995 board meeting. The concern was about the lack of distribution of Red Cross information pamphlets, but seemed focused on the legal liability of directors and officials. The Red Cross's attitude contrasts starkly with a 1982 statement by Dr. Johanna Pindyck, director of the New York blood program responsible for 700,000 units of blood a year. Quoted in the Krever report, she said:

> We know we're going to incur extra cost in running the (surrogate testing) program but we think the cost-benefit ratio ($2.40 per unit of blood) is satisfactory.... We think we can protect 7,000 to 10,000 people a year in the New York area and, over a five-year period, that adds up to a significant number of people....

It is simply not credible that a board of a corporation like the Canadian Red Cross would buy the proposition from their staff that if people in the U.S. were getting hepatitis C from blood, Canadians were not. Or that the Red Cross would have to "test the tests," when the reliability of the surrogate ALT test for detecting hepatitis C in transfused blood was no longer in question.

Commissioner Krever notes, "The Red Cross's internal committees that decided to reject surrogate testing lacked both the expertise and information necessary for appropriate decisions." We must not infer that no one was responsible for the committees' competence and diligence. We must ask who had management control responsibility for ensuring that the corporation's advisory committees had the necessary ability and motivation. The Red Cross board had that responsibility.

Since the blood operations of the Red Cross affected the public in life-or-death ways, its Board had an obligation to answer to the public for the discharge of its responsibilities, not just answer to the health ministers' Canadian Blood Committee that funded its blood operations. The Red Cross's external answering for its performance was the obligation of the Board. Yet the only persons answering in public and before the Krever Commission for the 1980s Red Cross performance were the Red Cross CEO and officials lower down.

Neither the Krever Commission nor Canadian journalists dealt with the responsibilities and accountabilities of the board of directors of the Red Cross as an issue in its own right. The legacy of this is the absence of legislative debate in Canada on the composition, responsibilities and accountabilities of the board of the national blood agency replacing the Red Cross.

But more important than the Red Cross board's motivation in its decision-making is the fact that the ultimate safety regulators, the federal Ministers of Health, failed to do their commonsense duty under the governing legislation and allowed the Red Cross board to distribute lethally-contaminated blood. Without adequate public answering from those ultimately responsible for safety – the health ministers – no one can claim that preventable human destruction won't happen again.

Endnotes

[1] I am indebted to Dr. Michèle Brill-Edwards for critiquing this case.

[2] Commission of Inquiry on the Blood System in Canada, *Final report*, Ottawa, Canadian Government Publishing, 1997

CASE 2

The Westray Mine

What Happened

On the 9th of May 1992 the Curragh corporation's Westray coal mine operations in Nova Scotia killed 26 miners in a methane and coal dust explosion. This happened only eight months after the mine's official opening.

The mine was unsafe: the deaths were preventable. This meant that the responsible directing minds hadn't done their jobs, which in turn means that they hadn't been telling Nova Scotians their intentions for safety and the state of Westray safety. If these people – the responsible ministers of the Crown and the Curragh board of directors – had been required to report their intended and actual performance for mine safety, the citizens of the province could have forced them to take the steps needed to prevent miners being killed.

The Westray miners, not unionized and working in an area of high unemployment, feared losing their jobs if they pushed safety concerns with mine managers who were pre-occupied with constant start-up problems in applying new technology in a coal seam rated as one of the most volatile on the continent. Making the mine safe meant falling further behind production targets that were unrealistic for the site. If the miners had left Westray for work at another mine, they felt they would be have been turned away as malcontents.

During the commission of inquiry by Justice K. Peter Richard of the Supreme Court of Nova Scotia, a United Kingdom mine consultant described Westray as "an absolutely unbelievable disgrace" for such a small mine operating for such a short time, and noted that one week's work by Curragh could have eliminated the lethal conditions. [1] Nova Scotia's mine regulations were shown to be inadequate for Westray's coal seam hazards and Curragh's technology, and the provincial government was shown to be ineffectual in safety regulation. The miners saw the government inspectors as intimidated by their own hierarchy, backing away from shutting down the mine and being worried about repercussions from Nova Scotian government ministers focused on getting federal funding for Westray and on political reward for economic development.

Mine inspectors, finally taking significant action on the mine danger that had been well known to them, served a formal order on Westray 30 April 1992 to clean up the coal dust immediately. The Westray general manager's apparent response was an intention to install a sprinkler system. Nine days later, with nothing changed, the mine blew up.

Despite a lengthy official inquiry that was unable to get senior company management to testify, and concurrent ineffective attempts by the Nova Scotia Crown Prosecutor to lay criminal charges against the Curragh mine managers, the Nova Scotia ministers of the Crown and Curragh's board of directors have yet to be held to account for the miners' deaths.

The responsibility for the mine's safety lay with the executive government of Nova Scotia. This meant the responsible ministers of the Crown having the statutory duty for workplace safety – not their lower-level departmental civil servants. The board of Curragh Resources Inc. was accountable both to the miners and to the public for Westray safety, but it was the ministers' statutory responsibility, as the regulators, to ensure that the corporation's directing minds operated a safe mine. The purpose of regulatory law set by legislatures is to install fundamental rules: our society is set up to have corporations respect what government tells them to do in carrying out the intent of legislation. But when the government gives them no orders or fails to ensure their compliance with the law, corporations do what they want.

Coal mine operation and safety risks are well known, through the history of Springhill and the hundreds of mine accidents Nova Scotia's past. The decision of federal government ministers to supply federal funds for Curragh was central in launching a mine having high safety risk and likely low profit expectations. Critical success factors for safety and potential profit had been assessed by senior civil servants in Ottawa because of the ministers' intentions to fund the corporation, but ministers decide what they want. As it was, the Curragh board of directors offered the mine for sale within two months of opening it.

The accountability aspects are taken from Commissioner Richard's inquiry report on a "predictable path to disaster," as the Commissioner put it, and from media sources. As we saw in the case of lethally-contaminated blood, the killings stemmed from three things.

First was the failure by provincial and federal ministers, the Curragh Corporation's board of directors and their respective officials, to apply the precautionary principle to Westray's safety. Mine regulation law in Nova Scotia reflected this principle to some extent, but the ministers didn't enforce the law. Instead of thinking, "We won't allow a mine to operate without reasonable assurance of safety," they seem to have thought along the lines of: "Let's go ahead until someone who we can't easily dismiss convinces the public that the mine is so unsafe that the probable repercussions for us mean that we had better halt the operations until the hazards are fixed."

Second was the ministers' failure to have a management control system within the Nova Scotia government ensuring mine safety. The control function is to ensure that the basic elements critical to mine safety are working at all levels, including dealing with politically driven pressure and corporation profit priorities. The control system needed for the precautionary principle would have dealt with not just the mine operations at Westray but also with :

- how the balance between corporate cash flow and safety decided by the Curragh board of directors and top management signalled the attitudes, intentions and conduct for safety in Westray that company managers were to take
- how the ministers' political aims in economic development and appearances would affect the quality of their departmental officials' review of mining plans and the quality of on-site safety assessment by the government's mine inspectors, and the resolution of officials in confronting their ministers

The third element was the lack of public answering before the fact by ministers and the Curragh board, for their safety-related responsibilities. As in the blood disgrace, adequate, timely and validated public answering for key responsibilities would have given the public a heads-up on what was going on. This could have helped to force safety performance to a standard. Nova Scotians lacked answers to basic questions, but the right safety questions were not being put to those having the directing-mind responsibilities. Commissioner Richard's report was silent on what public answering is needed from those with workplace safety responsibilities, even though the inquiry mandate given him invited such recommendations. (See Chapter 6)

The extent of a government's regard to workplace safety is affected by the political aims of its ministers, which include being seen to produce jobs. It is also affected by ministers' attitudes toward corporations – whether from their personal ideology, political donation expectations or expectation of some kind of future reward from the corporate community. Yet, as we saw in the blood deaths, Canadians by and large continue to place blind faith in corporations, ministers of the Crown, civil servants and legislative assemblies, and simply hope for the best.

Fairness to Nova Scotia miners and their families in mine safety is a policy decision made by the ministers comprising the executive government of Nova Scotia, which has supreme power over mine safety in the province. But if the concern for safety and needed control isn't there, only Nova Scotians can install it in their ministers. Fairness in safety includes upholding the precautionary principle, regardless of the extent to which the principle has been legislated for workplaces. A minister's duty starts with his or her statutory duty, but common sense adds to it.

In mine safety, the Nova Scotia government had two ministers responsible for its regulation: the Minister of Natural Resources and the Minister of Labour. Ultimate responsibility for mine safety meant responsibility for the quality of government's management control over safety. Nova Scotia ministers of the Crown had full power to require corporations to meet the intent of the Acts governing mining, and to meet the intent of safety regulations and directives under those Acts. Ultimate responsibility also required ministers to understand their workplace safety responsibilities and their obligation to answer.

The divided statutory responsibilities of the Minister of Natural Resources and the Minister of Labour predictably – and perhaps intentionally – diffused responsibility and accountability. Commissioner Richard reported that he couldn't tell for sure who had what mine safety duty because officials from Resources and Labour gave conflicting testimony on who was responsible for what. But this simply meant that the ministers and their deputy ministers had the responsibility to get together to ensure that their mine engineering and safety inspection units collaborated to get the regulator's job done properly. From this would come any needed amendment to the law and regulations to create a sensible cohesive accountability framework for workplace safety, and timely answering by mining corporations.

In his November 1997 inquiry report,[2] Commissioner Richard did not make clear for Nova Scotians what he thought the responsible ministers' specific statutory duty was for Westray mine safety, and whether the ministers had discharged their safety responsibilities. Concluding that inspectors down the line didn't do their duty (something not new to the miners' families) was less important than telling Nova Scotians the reasons why they didn't.

Centuries of injuries and deaths in Nova Scotia mines provided the necessary learning.[3] Nothing constitutional nor any convention prevented Nova Scotia ministers of the Crown from doing their statutory and commonsense duty. Their job was to properly inform themselves through an effective safety control system and to enforce the precautions that the intent of the law told them to enforce.

Government ministers, senior civil servants and the Curragh corporation Board all had responsibilities for installing the needed control systems to ensure safety. The government's control system not only tells those who need to know what is going on, but also causes unsafe workplaces to be fixed or shut down. As in the case of contaminated blood, when the directing minds fail to inform themselves and fail to apply the precautionary principle, they are open to a charge of negligence, regardless of whether these two responsibilities have been specifically legislated or precedented in law. This is because these responsibilities are imperatives for fairness in society and the responsible authorities know it.

If we don't require people in authority to answer publicly for their responsibilities, we should not expect them to put the public interest before their own. No one appeared to have answered to anyone, let alone to the public, for the mine's safety. Internal operations reports filed by government inspectors and mining companies aren't the same thing as adequate public answering by corporate and government ministers for their intentions and actions in workplace safety. Ministers answering questions in legislature Question Periods meet no standard of public answering, and corporate directors currently report only on financial matters.

Workers on their own can't be expected to track down the corporate directing minds and spell out for them – and the company's shareholders – the duty of the board of directors to ensure workplace safety and the board's obligation to answer publicly for it. That is the job of the regulating executive governments. Nor can workers be expected to spell out to a legislature the performance and answering standards for ministers and public servants in regulating workplace safety. That is first the job of the ministers, who should be required to invite knowledgeable challenge of their proposed standards, and second the job of the legislative assembly, which sets the standards in law. Because the obligation to account publicly is unassailable, unions have the power to exact it if their leaders choose to do so. But at the time of the Westray explosion the miners were not unionized, and unions thus far don't appear to be working on standards for public answering by corporate boards and regulators.

The Missing Public Answering

The issue in Westray is who remains accountable for 26 preventable deaths.

Nova Scotians received no answering from the responsible ministers telling them whether, with respect to their duties, the ministers had:

- informed themselves, to a standard reasonable for their safety responsibilities, about:
  - the actual risk in the mine
  - the ministers' own duty under the law
  - the adequacy of the safety regulations and compliance with them
  - what stood in the way of civil servants having the competence and motivation to act and report all the way up the line
- given adequate and timely public notice, for expert and public challenge, of their intended risk acceptance and performance standards
- complied with the intent of Nova Scotia law
- ensured inspectors' timely reporting to their superiors, and superiors' reporting up to the ministers, on:
  - the degree of Curragh's compliance with the intent of the law and safety regulations under the law
  - the validity of Curragh's reporting on its compliance
- ensured that the inspectors and their superiors were competent and motivated and

protected such that the ministers would know the true situation at Westray, whether ministers wanted to know or not

- removed barriers standing in the way of officials doing their jobs and protected employees of conscience trying to make workplaces safe
- ensured that the law and regulations and the departmental safety control system were working as intended
- ensured mine operators met the site-specific safety standards that the ministers had the duty to set
- ensured that, if the mine operations continued to be unsafe, they would back their senior government officials in shutting it down

In our provincial and federal legislatures, ministers respond to Opposition questions but no one could argue that this effectively holds ministers to account. Questions on Westray addressed to the responsible ministers in the Nova Scotia Legislative Assembly appear to have been specific, but only about particular incidents such as frequent roof falls up to the time of the explosion. MLAs would not typically ask ministers questions that go to the bone, such as: "What are your specific safety standards for the Westray mine?" "What would you say are your responsibilities for knowing the actual safety in Westray and using your power to act on the information?" "What authoritative direction have you ordered be given the Curragh corporation to ensure miners' safety, and when did you give it?"

At the time the miners were killed, Nova Scotia's legislation appeared to be silent on ministers' obligations to answer publicly for mine safety beyond ministers' ritual annual reports to the Legislative Assembly on their departments' operations as a whole. The legislation may still be silent. Commissioner Richard's comments on ministers do not deal with their obligation to answer for their responsibilities.

As to the ministry officials, there was no apparent accounting to the Nova Scotia legislature on the duties and performance of the responsible senior civil servants. This would include reporting whether the deputy ministers, at their level of responsibility, had:

- told their ministers the level of Westray danger and what the ministers' statutory duty was
- sorted out with their ministers the respective duties and answering obligations of each responsible ministry
- informed themselves adequately for their own duty as deputy ministers
- determined the adequacy of the Nova Scotia mine safety regulations and placed before ministers both needed amendments and the ministers' statutory duties supporting the amendments
- ensured that mine inspectors and their supervisors were competent and were re-

porting the state of Westray safety fully and fairly up the line to the deputy minister

- told Curragh corporation top management the corporation's duty for the Westray mine under Nova Scotia's mining-related Acts and regulations, and under any relevant federal legislation
- asked for adequate and timely performance reporting from Curragh on its compliance with the intent of the regulations as they applied to Westray, and advised their ministers on what to do if the compliance reporting was not given or was inadequate
- overall, ensured that the responsible ministers and their ministries had a cohesive management control system that either made the Westray mine safe or shut it down

In December 1997, writing on the release of Commissioner Richard's Westray report, Nova Scotia journalist Ralph Surette summed up the underlying integrity issue for all provincial governments and the federal government. He criticized the Commissioner's report for not dealing with how ministers use their power, but he also laid out what Canadians as a whole apparently hadn't realized: that senior civil servants not only go along with ministers' wants but anticipate them:

> But couldn't we also say that (Albert) McLean and his superiors were doing what was demanded of them – that the context in which they operated required that they override laws they were intended to uphold? After all, did one pipsqueak inspector really have the authority to make trouble for, and even shut down, the pet project of the premier of Nova Scotia, backed by the prime minister of Canada, and designed for political effect in the 1988 election?…. There need be no direct order given from the political level. With time and usage, the limits are understood.[4]

Senior departmental officials know what a minister doesn't want to be told if it would require the minister to make decisions that he or she doesn't want to make. Since ministers have many issues on their plates, senior officials have much better information on particular responsibilities, especially in safety matters and feasibility in safety protection. That is why senior civil servants brief their ministers.

So long as ministers can successfully claim not to have known something important (civil servants call this "plausible denial"), and no one asks them whether they had a duty to inform themselves, they may be able to duck public blame when a key government duty hasn't been done. Surette's message that civil servants accommodate their ministers' wants includes not informing ministers when there is tacit agreement that this isn't to be done. The job of deputy ministers in the public interest is to carry out the intent of laws and legitimate policy direction. But it is also to tell ministers what their statutory duty is and what ministers must know to do their duty. Commissioner Richard did not deal with the duty of the deputy ministers to ensure that their ministers knew exactly what was going on and thus could not say that they didn't.

What ministers need to know depends on what they are responsible for. The statutory duty for workplace safety lies with the ministers, but since the Nova Scotia law left mine safety responsibilities divided between two ministers, the deputy ministers involved had the commonsense duty to understand the intent of the law, sort out a division of departmental responsibilities and accountabilities that ensured no gaps, and get the ministers' confirmation of which minister had what responsibility. Even without ministers' approval, the deputy ministers had the responsibility to get on with the business of keeping mines safe and to make sure that a coherent management control system for ensuring safety was in place and working across the departments. That was within their control.

Control monitoring for safety starts with the inspector level but extends up the line to the point where departmental management control responsibility and safety accountability meet and often clash with the political aims of ministers. Civil servants are to work for the public interest in applying the intent of the law. The most senior civil servants therefore had the duty to know Curragh's inaction on safety and, if it persisted, to give the ministers their written reasons for shutting down the mine. If the ministers refused permission, at least the deputies' intentions and reasoning would be on the record. The deputy ministers would then have the option of bringing their concerns immediately to the public, resigning to do so if necessary. A senior civil servant is not expected to disagree publicly with minister's political policy, but giving a safety heads-up where lives are at stake is something else.

Commissioner Richard's report doesn't tell us that the deputy ministers sorted out the responsibility-sharing, ensured no serious gaps and ensured miners' safety to the extent of deputy ministers' powers and duties delegated by ministers. He did not deal with the question of senior department officials' accountability. Nor did he propose which departmental officials had what obligation to answer to whom, for what responsibilities in performance reporting within the departments and up to the minister and externally.

Inspection officials' actions reflect the standards of the deputy ministers who determine the reward systems in their departments. If ministers didn't want to command Curragh top management and were in effect sending that signal to the company over the heads of the deputy ministers, that was something the deputy ministers had a duty to confront. Said the Commissioner, "Thus the stage was set for Westray management to maintain an air of arrogance and cynicism, knowing that it was not going to be seriously challenged" (by government).[5]

As to the mining company, the Board of Directors of Curragh Resources has never been held to account. A corporation's board of directors has the legal responsibility and public answering obligation for what the corporation does. The mining licence was issued to a corporation called Westray Coal Inc., but the board members of the parent company Curragh remained the publicly-accountable directing mind.

Commissioner Richard concluded that in decision-making, Curragh's board was in effect Clifford Frame, who was both its chairman and CEO of the company. Thus the Commissioner did not come to grips with the issue of the responsibility and public answering obligations of the members of the Curragh board of directors. Since the legislated duty of a corporate board is to supervise management, the words "board members" rather than "Westray," or "Frame", or "Curragh" would locate corporate accountability more usefully.

Regardless whether the Curragh decisions were made by Clifford Frame, it was the responsibility of the board members – especially the company's officers – to understand what constituted reasonable information for good governance, obtain it, and act on it. Unless board members recognize their self-informing responsibility and publicly account for their duty, they can act like innocent bystanders, claiming the "plausible denial" used by ministers of the Crown.[6]

There was no apparent answering by the Board of Curragh Resources telling the government safety regulator – let alone the Nova Scotia public – whether the Board:

- knew the state of Westray mine safety – not just its production, costs and viability
- ensured that Curragh's management control system ensured that mine managers met the company's safety standards approved by the Board and complied with the intent of safety legislation in the jurisdiction of each mine.

The Nova Scotia government's mining regulations were out of date for Curragh's mining technology (the "continuous miner" machine and its methane sensor), but the safety intent of the legislation was not, and apparently new safety technology was available.[7] A corporate board must regard compliance with government safety regulations as the minimum – not maximum – responsibility. Nova Scotians may legitimately ask if the Curragh board members reviewed mine management control, which included mine safety control, and whether they were aware of the Westray risks and the available new safety technology.

The board members had the obligation to decide the company's diligence standards and therefore the safety standards for Westray, and to have had a management control system at the board level that ensured that adequate safety standards were met. Their control system would tell them whether their safety standards were being carried out at Westray, and their obligation to act included making sure that their directions were carried out. And what they knew, they could report. They had the obligation to know enough about Westray to be able to assert to Nova Scotians the actual risk in the mine, as they saw it, and the quality of their management control over safety.

To the extent that an on-site manager puts planned production before safety, the Curragh board members were responsible for the conditions that permitted it or encouraged it. They had the power and duty to know the mine management's ability and motivation, and the legal obligation to supervise management. Being simply a panel of advisors to Clifford Frame is not an acceptable discharge of directors' duties when safety is a major responsibility.

Members of the Board of Curragh were not asked or made to state to the inquiry Commission what they thought their duty was in knowing Chairman Frame's intentions (and, therefore, the mine manager's) for the trade-off between production and safety. Nor were they asked to state what they knew about Westray safety, when they knew it, and what decisions they took.

Commissioner Richard's report suggests that the Curragh board members were only in the background somewhere, without visible involvement in the quality of management control over mine safety. Neither the inquiry report nor journalists' reports deal with the Curragh board members' decision-making about the level of mine safety. Since the board members were not required to give testimony in the inquiry, their decisions affecting the quality of corporate management control for safety have yet to be disclosed.

Allen Martin and Joe MacKay, each of whom had a brother killed in the explosion, summed things up when the hapless Nova Scotia Crown prosecutor threw in the towel in July 1998 and announced the curtailment of manslaughter and criminal negligence charges against Curragh officials.[8]

> We all know that they were negligent in many, many ways and we all know
> who is responsible and who is responsible for regulating the mines. It's not
> reasonable. (Martin)

> They let experts pick this thing apart and say, 'Well, maybe it started here,
> or maybe it started there, or maybe over there,' and they're not willing to go
> in and prove there was too damn much gas and too much dust in that
> damned mine. (MacKay)

The families of the 26 miners must have thought that prosecuting Westray officials should have been shooting fish in a barrel. Legal ploys and obstructions to justice are one thing. But Commissioner Richard did not satisfactorily explain to Nova Scotians the statutory duties of ministers of the Crown and how this can be made to mean something. Nor did he deal with the duties and answering obligations of the Curragh board of directors, for which he didn't need brand new company law. Thus no one with central responsibility has been held publicly to account.

The underlying issue exemplified by Westray has yet to be dealt with. It is the question of how citizens can more accurately predict what directing minds – ministers of regulating governments and corporation boards of directors – are apt to do or fail to do that allows deaths and injuries. Requiring adequate public answering before the fact for authorities' intentions and performance standards is a necessary first step.

Citizens' groups must make elected representatives account for their responsibility for requiring executive governments both to act and to account to prevent harm in the workplace.[9] In addition to long memories for election time, it will take relentless holding to account by public interest organizations formed specifically to require elected representatives to install satisfactory performance and answering standards for workplace safety and to ensure that these standards are complied with.

Unions are uniquely positioned and equipped to exact accountability reporting by corporate boards and managements. The reporting would publicly disclose what the corporations' own standards are for workplace safety and whether they met them. Unions would then validate the reporting. This is not telling the boards how to do their jobs. It is simply requiring them to explain something – publicly.

Citizens' groups must require legislators to install in law the requirement that corporations and government regulators each report the performance standards they intend for themselves for workplace safety and whether they met them. The law must ensure that the standards authorities propose are publicly challenged and that independent audit validates the fairness and completeness of the performance reporting on whether the accountable directing minds are meeting the agreed standards.

The question is: will citizens continue to allow their elected representatives to ignore their commonsense duty to install in law safety performance and answering standards for ministers and corporate boards, and enforce them? It is up to citizens whether to allow "economic development" and investment returns for a few, and a limited number of jobs, to come before safety. If citizens truly want workplace safety they must face up to instructing their elected representatives and ministers.

And if the responsible ministers say, "We have good workplace safety compared with other countries," Canadians should note the ploy. For example, 3600 miners dying in mines in the Ukraine in the last decade (including the 45 in the Zariadko mine in August 2001 – grotesquely repeating the 50 deaths from methane explosion at the same mine in 1999), and more than 80 miners dying in the Longshan tin mine in China in July 2001[10] have no bearing on what Canadians have a right to see in workplace safety and public answering for it in Canadian circumstances.

Endnotes

[1] *Globe and Mail*, 17 January 1996, p.A1

[2] *The Westray Story: a Predictable Path to Disaster*, Report of the Westray Mine Public Inquiry, Province of Nova Scotia, 1997

[3] For example, in the Springhill Collieries, 424 men and boys died between 1881 and 1969 (Roger David Brown, *Blood on the Coal*, Lancelot Press, Nova Scotia, 1976, p.57)

[4] Ralph Surette, "The Larger Lessons of Westray are Obvious, But Unmentioned," *Halifax Mail-Star*, 12 December, 1997

[5] Richard report p.606

[6] For example, in an article, the executive vice-president of Curragh at the time of the explosion, who was also a director, said, "…Curragh's board, and many Curragh managers were kept in the dark about many things, as Judge Richard noted." (Adrian White, "Westray: Directors Did Their Job," *Globe and Mail*, 5 February, 1998, p. B2)

[7] See Dean Jobb's *Halifax Chronicle-Herald/Mail Star* article: "Sensor Prompts Westray Re-think," 14 November 1998, p.C2

[8] Martin is quoted in the *Globe and Mail* 1 July 1998, p.A4, and MacKay in the *Globe* 2 July, p.A5.

[9] Ed Finn describes how little attention Canadian governments and legislators pay to deaths and injuries in the workplace ("Cost of Carnage in the Workplace is Staggering", *Ottawa Citizen*, 24 July 1996, p.A11). And as an editorial in the UK's *Independent* pointed out, commenting on everything from Creutzfeldt-Jakob Disease to ferry groundings, "We no longer choose to take risks; we have them thrust upon us." (The *Independent*, 28 March 1996, quoted in the *Ottawa Citizen* 23 April 1996, p.A11)

[10] *Times Colonist*, 21 August 2001, p.A9 and *Guardian Weekly*, 16-22 August 2001, p.6

CASE 3
The Herald of Free Enterprise

What Happened

Suddenly, still in daylight at 6 pm on 6 March, 1987, the large British car ferry *Herald of Free Enterprise*, with 540 people on board, sank off Zeebrugge, Belgium.

The description of what happened, why it happened and the subsequent events is taken from the book *Zeebrugge: Learning From Disaster*, written by Stuart Crainer for the Herald Charitable Trust that was set up by the families of the 192 drowned.[1] The Trust wished to have the learning applied from what happened before, during and after the event. The account shows the lack of public answering by corporate directing minds and the weakness of the legal system as a means of redress and of producing learning.

As described in *Zeebrugge,* the facts are simple. The bow doors of this "ro-ro" (roll on, roll off) car ferry were still open as the ship headed out to sea from Zeebrugge, taking in more and more water onto the car deck as it progressed to normal speed. The ship design, known to be unstable, made the car deck like a large plate of water that tips if not kept level. The bow of the ship was still down from the weight of the water ballast taken on to speed dock loading. The ship lacked a high-speed pump that could have emptied the ballast while the crew cleared for sea to make the tight schedule that the company's profit targets required.

The doors were not visible from the command position in the ship, but there was no simple warning light telling the captain that the bow doors were open. These had been in existence since the 1970s, and were required in all ships built after 1984. Ferry captains had requested them for the ships without them, but apparently had been turned down.

Within three minutes from the time the captain noticed the ship starting to heel, about a mile off Zeebrugge, the ship was on its side, on a sand bank, killing 192 of the 540 passengers and crew. Without the sand bank the dead would have been many more.

The *Herald* conformed to existing ship design conventions and safety regulations for such ferries. Yet naval architects deemed the ship "unacceptably vulnerable," in that it would not stay afloat long after an accident. It was, therefore, unsafe by any reasonable standard of management control for safe operation of ferries.[2] In 245 incidents involving ro-ro ferries worldwide between 1978 and 1988, 5300 passengers were killed. This made traveling by such ferries ten times as dangerous as traveling by air.

The owner, P&O European Ferries, had taken over the ferry as part of the Townsend Thoresen operations that it had purchased only six weeks before the sinking. It is not clear what attention was paid during the coroner's inquiry and subsequent court proceedings to the nature and extent of P&O's risk assessment of Townsend's safety assurance practices during P&O's financial purchase investigation.

The Crainer account sums to more than the issue of corporate concern for profit as opposed to meeting feasible safety standards in ship operations. The account deals with the relative concerns for profit and safety of corporate executives, marine professions and government departments, and also with who had what commonsense responsibility for passenger and crew safety. But, like the Canadian disgraces of lethally-contaminated blood and the Westray coal mine, it prompts the question whether lawyers and judges understand (or choose not to understand) senior corporate management and governing-body responsibility and accountability.

The Management Control Issue

Locating responsibility for management control, which includes safety control, was key in the *Herald* case. As the Herald Charitable Trust stated in the preface to the Crainer account,

> Directors find that they can defend themselves against legal action by claiming that this or that "was not my job" – even when they had clearly failed in their responsibility to make it someone's job – or that no one had told them what was going on.[3]

Issues of governance of corporations and the responsibilities of directors and senior management in the *Herald* case were "all but ignored." No member of corporate senior management ashore, or of the board of directors, was formally found responsible or accountable for anything. Board members of corporations don't consider safety their own responsibility, and the court judgment following the coroner's inquest allowed this avoidance of responsibility.

In the mid-1950s a noted English judge, Thomas Denning, later Lord Denning, wrote in his judgment in a corporate case that the management and board of a company "represent the directing mind and will" of the company. He used the analogy of the brain controlling the body.[4] Since the board directs management,[5] the boards of Townsend Thoresen and of P&O had the commonsense responsibility to know the incidence of ro-ro ferry accidents and the inherent instability of the ships, and to act with diligence on that information to protect passengers to a feasible standard. The directors had the duty to have in place a management control system that ensured safety beyond mere compliance with inadequate transport department regulations.

If the directors' obligation is simply to meet existing regulations,[6] the buck is passed to the regulators who propose the standards to their ministers. Regulations mean compromise with industry, to an extent not known by the public, and the resulting regulations become lowest common denominators. Ministry officials write regulations to propose to ministers, but they keep in mind what the ministers want or don't want as obligations for the business community. If corporations can make the public think that government regulations are as good as it gets in safety, boards escape having to state their own feasible safety standards. A retired Canadian lawyer, commenting on the UK Channel ferries, said, "Passengers have to make their own risk assessments."

As a Canadian example, the 1985 mission statement of the British Columbia Ferry Corporation adopted by its board of directors is commendable:

> The mission of the British Columbia Ferry Corporation is to provide effective, dependable and safe coastal ferry transportation services in the most efficient manner possible.

Thus the service is to be safe, which is a recognizable performance standard. The statement doesn't talk about simply striving for something.

But the replacement Mission Statement, set out in the Corporation's 1999-2000 Annual report, backs away from a standard:

> At BC Ferries we are committed to satisfying customer and community needs for a safe, reliable and sustainable ferry service.

> We strive to build on our tradition of excellence in ferry service, one in which employees and citizens take great pride.

The shift is from stating that a standard will be met (the service will be safe and dependable) to a striving statement that doesn't say how safe or dependable the ferries will be. The second sentence says nothing.

The public statement on the bulkhead at the main passenger entrance in the *Spirit of Vancouver Island*, the Corporation's biggest ship, reads:

> At BC Ferries, passenger safety is our highest priority. In every way, we adhere to the safety regulations established by the Canadian Coast Guard – regulations that either meet or exceed all international standards.

But the management for the *Herald of Free Enterprise* met authoritative regulations, too. This adherence assertion in the BC ship gives no information on what Coast Guard and international safety assurance standards provide or don't provide. It is an assertion of compliance, which doesn't tell passengers what the corporation's board intends to meet as its own safety standards for its ships in BC coastal circumstances, including harbour and docking work.

The Court Case

The coroner for the inquest into the *Herald* deaths, Richard Stuart, ruled that the Townsend directors were too remote from what happened for their evidence to be important for the inquest and for them to be accused of gross negligence. In this he was backed by three judges of the Divisional Court of the High Court responding to the families' attempt to overturn the coroner's decision.[7] So much for these officials' grasp of directing-mind control responsibilities and accountability.

Ignoring the coroner, the coroner's jury came to a decision of unlawful killing. As the *Daily Mail* then observed,

> It's been laid down in law that the people responsible in such matters are those directing the minds and policy of the company. Develin and Ayers were responsible for the safety of the company fleet. If a system of positive reporting had been introduced, this disaster would not have happened.[8]

Following the coroner's jury verdict, the Director of Public Prosecutions ordered police to carry out a criminal investigation into the deaths. P&O European Ferries (Dover) was charged with corporate manslaughter, the charge for unlawful killing. Apparently this had been used only once before in the English courts, in the 1960s, and was unsuccessful. As the Crainer account noted, "It was the first time that the directors of a company had stood trial in an English court for allegedly killing people by their reckless conduct though they were absent from the scene of the deaths." Although the Crown Prosecution Service termed the charge an untested part of the law, [9] the Crainer account is a litany of what auditors would call "lack of due regard" in performance that would appear horrific to the average person reading the book.

The trial judge, Mr. Justice Turner, instructed the jury to consider only the evidence presented within the courtroom, three and a half years after the event, and to ignore the coroner's inquest and the previous Court of Inquiry report that had diagnosed an "infection of sloppy management."[10] The prosecution stated to the jury on the opening day of the trial:

> The Crown's case is that the capsizing was avoidable and that each of the defendants that you are trying, the seven humans and the company, is responsible for the deaths that occurred because their behaviour or conduct was reckless or grossly negligent. The guilt of the company can only be established by the guilt of a directing mind. Hence, if you find one of those mentioned have committed the offence of manslaughter in the capacity of a person managing or directing the company, then the company likewise should be found guilty of the offence of manslaughter.[11]

As Crainer states the process in the English court, the prosecution's argument meant that to find the company guilty of a criminal offense someone qualifying as a directing mind had to be found not only grossly negligent but also reckless. Recklessness required the person to have either not recognized or disregarded an obvious and serious risk that a ferry would sail with its bow doors open. Ship captains called by the prosecution – all on P&O's payroll – said that they hadn't recognized the bow doors risk, yet the report of the earlier inquiry into Townsend ship deaths had noted that "By the autumn of 1986 the shore staff of the company were well aware of the possibility" (of a ship sailing with its bow doors open). In fact records showed that five ro-ro ferries had gone to sea with their bow doors open.

The judge concluded that if the company's ship captains called to testify saw no risk, no one ashore should be expected to. Said Turner, "We have heard a weight of evidence to the effect that experienced seaborne personnel never thought for a moment that, with the system in force, there was any risk of that event happening."[12] If the judge was accurately stating the view of ferry captains at large, it raises the obvious question why the command position warning lights – not expensive – were being installed in ships in the 1970s and required in ships built after 1984.

The "system" the judge was talking about was a ship operation practice convention in a particular company, not a precautionary system for preventing drownings. The "weight of evidence" was not independent expert evidence, and the captains called as witnesses don't seem to have been challenged on their risk assessment ability or asked whether they understood the purpose of control systems.

The judge, apparently oblivious to the concept of management control and the precautionary principle, concluded that the bow door risk didn't qualify as obvious or serious. Because an assistant bosun regularly closed the bow doors with no incidents, captains occupied with meeting management's efficiency expectations may well not have thought about the risk daily. (The captains called to testify were presumably not the same ones who had requested the warning lights in the wheelhouses.) But a control system for safety answers the question, "What about assurance for the *next* sailing?" The systems heads-up had been given to company management – and to captains – by the earlier Court of Inquiry report that described management as sloppy.

Less than a month into the case the judge ordered the jury to acquit P&O.

We see here warnings to citizens similar to those arising later in the Canadian blood and Westray mine inquiries. From the Crainer account, the trial judge's grasp of directing-mind responsibility for the management control system that drives the safety system appeared weak or non-existent. Yet citizens – not just the relations of those killed – grasp it clearly. Moreover, P&O's assertion that it met the government's regulations (meaning that is all a company need account for) appeared to influence the judge in telling the jury to acquit P&O.

For citizens, the prosecution got it right in arguing that to show that the risk was foreseeable by a reasonable person is all it takes to decide whether the bow-door risk is an obvious one.[13] "Reasonable person" in this case applied to those with safety responsibility – the company top managers responsible for safety and the board members, who had the control responsibility to satisfy themselves that the company's safety control processes were effective. It was not the assistant bosun. The board's control responsibility, in view of the known instability of such ferries – kept that way for greater profit – was to know the effect of de-stabilizing water flooding an internal deck. This marine risk had been known since a troop ship sank because of it, in the mid-1800s. The board's responsibility was then to ensure that the company's safety control system compensated for the risk. But that which was obvious to any person who thought about it was apparently ignored by those who had specific responsibility to think about it and who had the power to act to limit the risk.

From the Crainer account the prosecution failed to deal with the safety record of the ro-ro ferries and called no expert independent witnesses, such as Sealink captains. Thus the jury failed to learn what could reasonably be expected from modern-day board and management in applying the precautionary principle to its control systems for marine safety.

As Crainer puts it,

> With more than 20 counsel in attendance, the court seemed to be concerned with containing – rather than fully exploring – issues of immense importance. The jury were continually excluded because of legal wrangles.[14]

"The case has proceeded as I envisaged it would within its own tiny walls," said Justice Turner. With the jury excluded, the judge amazingly concluded:

> There is no evidence that reasonably prudent marine superintendents, chief superintendents, or naval architects would or should have recognised that the system gave rise to an obvious and serious risk of open-door sailing.[15]

The judge then directed the jury to acquit those named: the two most responsible company directors, the deputy chief marine superintendent, the senior master and the ship captain – but not the named first officer and assistant bosun. The prosecution then dropped the charge against these two. The fact that the judge kept the first officer and assistant bosun on the hook says that the judge saw no control responsibility up the line. (Canadians can ponder "tiny wall" thinking when they assess the public inquiry into the mid-2000 deaths in Walkerton, Ontario from lethally-contaminated municipal water.) As Maurice de Rohan of the Herald Families Association stated after the acquittal: "The real issues were not focused on in court. We had a lot of legal language and technicalities. The issue in our minds was to ensure that corporate responsibility went to the top level of the company."[16]

For a judge to rule out the relevance to the trial of a board's management control responsibility, he or she would have to know what management control is, why it exists and who is responsible for it. The U.S. federal court did not miss the control responsibility issue in its 1994 verdict in the *Exxon Valdez* case, that the Exxon corporation was reckless about the operation of the ship.

Two issues were never on the table in the *Herald* court case: the issue of how the value system of the directors governs the CEO's and managers' attitude and actions toward safety throughout the corporation, and the issue of what the board's commonsense responsibility and accountability is for the quality of management control over safety. The board either places safe ship design and feasible safety standards first or places profits first. Corporate public statements about safety coming first are to be regarded as simply appearances statements until independent audit of control systems suggests that feasible safety does indeed come first. Statements saying that each individual captain is responsible for everything simply say that corporate managers and board members are responsible for nothing but profits.

The Crainer account shows a trial detrimental to corporate public answering. The trial judge appeared to fit directing-mind responsibility to his perception of the issue at stake. In instructing the jury on the definition of "obvious" risk as it applied to how management perceived serious safety risk, the judge chose a definition that exonerated the accused. A further disturbing question is why the directors were charged with criminal conspiracy, requiring a high level of evidence, rather than criminal negligence, a charge that might well have succeeded. [17] Thus an important question for citizens, as we saw in the Canadian inquiry into contaminated blood, is whether inquiry trucks are being purposefully driven into the ditch – either through the inquiry mandate or charging decision at the outset, or in contrivances and predictable legal wrangling. Another concern is who lawyers really work for.

One clear message from the *Herald* trial is that citizens must find a way to flow around legal processes that won't expose the quality of corporate management control affecting people's lives and who is responsible for them. The gulf is widening between the public's perception of justice and the law profession's legal systems that are not legal justice systems. Those seeking justice through the courts are thoroughly outgunned by the legions of expensive defence lawyers. The ability and motivation of prosecution counsel is a question mark, and judges are trained only in legal processes – or as the families of the *Herald* victims put it, "legal niceties." Judges are not trained to help produce public answering for intentions and reasoning. Chapters 6 and 11 raise the question of performance standards for judges.

In the case of the *Herald of Free Enterprise*, if corporate boards were forced to publicly state their own management control standards, which include their safety control standards, citizens could compare what the boards assert with what safety forums of knowledgeable mariners, independent marine professionals and seasoned travelling citizens at risk recommend as achievable standards. Public debate, facilitated by elected representatives, would show what is an acceptable set of performance and accountability reporting standards for a particular industry.

The answer is not in "socially desirable" speeches in legislative chambers, or in bureaucrats writing regulations. It is citizen instruction to elected representatives on what to change in the law. It is stigmatization of board members refusing to account publicly and adequately for their responsibilities and their intended and actual performance. It is also compulsory education for judges in what modern management control means in terms of directing mind responsibility in the public interest.

The Law Commission, Britain's official law reform body, issued a consultation paper in 1994 on "involuntary manslaughter" and asked for informed comment on its provisional proposals. The section on corporate liability drew heavily on the P&O case. [18] On the question of whether a risk is obvious and serious, the Commission suggested that "the question should more properly be whether the company should be aware of the risk, because it is the company which is in a position to do something about it." The Commission proposed a "special regime" to deal with corporate liability for manslaughter and suggested two criteria:

- that the company ought reasonably to have been aware of a significant risk that its conduct could result in death or serious injury
- the company's conduct fell seriously below the conduct that could reasonably be demanded in preventing that risk from occurring or in dealing with it if it did occur

The ultimate outcome of this initiative, measured by actual significant changes in the law for corporations, will tell UK citizens much about their chances. For example, the meaning of "conduct" for a company must include the adequacy of its board-directed control systems for safety, not just actions of individual managers and employees. Keeping the focus on individuals below the board and CEO levels has traditionally been the means for responsibility avoidance by those ultimately in charge. Yet it is they who decide the risks the public is to take. Moreover, directing minds receive social honours no matter what had happens on their watch. Law that talks about responsibilities of "the company" is talking about intentions of identifiable, responsible and accountable human beings. This means that, to locate responsibility and the public answering obligation, "the company" must be clarified for all to mean its ultimate directing mind, which is the board.

The Missing Public Answering

The public had not been told by the boards of either Townsend Thoresen or P&O:

- the extent to which the members of the board of directors had informed themselves about:
  - the actual risks associated with ro-ro ferries, given their design and ship design history going back into the 1800s
  - given that knowledge, their own commonsense governance duties in management control for safety
- the board's intended trade-off between profit and feasible safety
- the safety standards and safety critical success factors for the fleet (including accountability reporting within the corporation) that the board had approved as part of the board's management control system for the operation of the ferries
- whether the board's control system was working to the standard that the public is entitled to see met

Following the drownings, it does not appear that the P&O board reported to the families of the dead and to the public what they had learned from the deaths and how they had applied their learning. The public has the right to the same scope of answering from the government regulator, who is the responsible minister and his or her ministry. But in future, citizens and unions must demand this public answering from both corporations and the regulator, and validate the answering.

Endnotes

[1] Stuart Crainer, *Zeebrugge: Learning From Disaster*, (London, Herald Charitable Trust, 1993, funded by the Joseph Rowntree Foundation)

[2] The Royal Institute of Naval Architects issued the following statement in March 1988:
"The ro-ro passenger ships now in service, despite their full adherence to the laws and regulations, are unacceptably vulnerable in the event of a collision." (Peter Spooner, *The HFA Story 1987 - 1994* (Herald Families Association, London, 1994, p.16)

[3] Crainer, op. cit., p. xiv

[4] *H.L. Bolton (Engineering) Co. v. T.J.Graham & Sons Ltd.* , [1957] 1 Q.B. 159 at 172, [1956] 3 All E.R. 624 at 630 (C.A.)

[5] See Chapter 13 on the accountability of governing boards

[6] A P&O spokesman said, of a 1995 U.K. House of Commons Transport Committee report on cross-channel safety, stemming in part from the *Herald of Free Enterprise* and other accidents, "We comply with all legislation, both national and international, and there is

nothing to suggest that our ships are anything other than safe." ("MPs Claim 70% of Ferries Are Unsafe." *International Express*, July, 1995)

[7] Crainer, pp. 92-93

[8] *Daily Mail*, 20 October 1987, cited in Crainer, p.94. (Jeffrey Develin was the Townsend director responsible for safety and Wallace Ayers was the group technical director responsible for ship design and improvement. Crainer, p.50)

[9] Crainer, pp.96-97

[10] Crainer, p.98

[11] Crainer, p.98

[12] Crainer, p.99

[13] Crainer, p.100

[14] Crainer, p 101

[15] Crainer, p.101

[16] Crainer, p.102

[17] Dr. Edgar Gold, QC and master mariner, "Lessons in Corporate Responsibility: Learning From Disaster?," p.16 (paper given in Copenhagen in 1996 on the implementation of the International Maritime Organization's International Safety Management Code).

[18] Peter Spooner, *The HFA Story*, Herald Families Association, London, 1994, pp. 5-6

CASE 4

The Court Martial[1]

As in the earlier three cases and the citizen audit illustrated in Appendix 2, the purpose of this case example is to show why people in senior authority must answer publicly for the discharge of their responsibilities. Senior military officers are not exempt.

Background

Lieutenant Commander Dean Marsaw joined the Canadian navy as an Ordinary Seaman but was quickly commissioned from the ranks. His many commendations as a submarine commander included high marks from the tough UK submarine training "Perisher" course and a salute from a US admiral in training exercises with Marsaw's 1950s Oberon Class diesel boat, the *Ojibwa*.

Crew members felt safe with Marsaw as skipper, perhaps more so than with other captains. But Marsaw was hard on his crew in maintaining action readiness at all times, to the extent that he was thought of as a martinet. Like many officers, he was following the style of his role models in the navy. He was never criticized by his superiors for being harsh on subordinates; in fact he was praised for his performance. The citation for the recommendation for Marsaw to receive the Meritorious Service Cross read: "He has always been highly regarded for showing particular concern for his men and his job." Through the performance of his boat he became the top submarine commanding officer in the fleet. His file supported this and he was due to be promoted to Commander. For his part, Marsaw loved the navy and trusted his superiors, believing in the integrity of top command.

Partly in response to the new "results oriented" atmosphere of the time, the standards he set for his submarine's fighting prowess and safety were probably higher than Canadian admirals were expecting from other officers. Thus Marsaw's competence standards could have dismayed some officers and men joining his crew if they were not used to his level of discipline. Because his boat was uniquely always ready for war-level action he was the first called upon for exercises, but his crew was likely unhappy with constant exercises and being away from home. At no time was Marsaw ever told of any leadership problem. If he had been too harsh, it was the management responsibility of his superior officers – especially in view of his outstanding seamanship performance as a commander – to have detected that early on in his command role and given him leadership counselling.

As LCdr Marsaw's family explained it, shortly after he left his submarine in October 1993 to head Canada's first submarine officer's training course, a Halifax *Chronicle-Herald* reporter, a former naval Sub-Lieutenant, told Halifax naval officials that he intended to write an article saying that the *Ojibwa* was unsafe under LCdr Marsaw's command. The navy's public affairs office rejected this allegation as baseless because of LCdr Marsaw's record of outstanding seamanship, something the reporter ought to have known.

The reporter apparently then telephoned crew members at their homes to try to support a story of abusive conduct by LCdr Marsaw as a commanding officer, and for alleged improper behaviour during a mess dinner in the submarine in December 1991. The reporter alleged that sometime during the evening Marsaw had pushed a cigar tube into the anus of an inebriated British submarine officer on exchange. The evidence suggests that the reporter told naval officials that he would write a story on this, including a claim of navy cover-up of the alleged event, even though parts of the article would be comments from people who weren't present at the alleged event and who were seen as bearing grudges against Marsaw. The reporter produced his story to the *Chronicle-Herald* and an edited version appeared next day.

Marsaw's superiors, ignoring the consistent praise they had given him throughout his career, did not stand behind him to force validation of the reporter's allegations before letting the story get out. If the might of the Canadian federal executive government can be thrown at the commissioners for the blood and Somalia inquiries, it can be applied to a Halifax newspaper. Instead, Marsaw's superiors disassociated themselves from him.

As processes against LCdr Marsaw rapidly took on a life of their own, he was painted in the media – and allowed to be by military top command and the Minister of Defence – as simply an unfeeling too-harsh officer rather than as an outstanding seaman, despite his long list of career commendations. The admirals went with the media flow, but Marsaw was told not to speak to reporters.

The reporter's story triggered a series of events that led to LCdr Marsaw being charged, court martialled and convicted by the end of 1995. The Court Martial Appeal Court quashed the conviction two years later, but a brilliant naval officer who had revered the navy and trusted its top command was wronged, his naval career permanently smashed and his mental state ultimately crippled.

The conduct and motivation of the newspaper reporter appears not to have been examined, including his relationship with officers later called as prosecution witnesses in the court martial, and with an officer who had failed the Perisher course (meaning that he couldn't expect to command a submarine) and with whom Marsaw had had an altercation. The Halifax Chronicle-Herald had its legal counsel attend with intervenor standing at the court martial appeal.

At the time Canadian newspapers took up the allegations against Marsaw, the disclosure of the killings of Somalia civilians by soldiers of the Canadian Airborne Regiment peacekeeping force were causing public revulsion. The Department of National Defence (DND) correctly perceived that the public thought officers were being protected right up the line. This perception could have caused the Defence Minister's advisors and/or military top command to offer an officer in sacrifice – but not an army officer. The colonel who was the Assistant Judge Advocate General (AJAG) most active in the charges against Marsaw was apparently involved in writing the Somalia Rules of Engagement.

In 1993 the then Director General for the military's public affairs branch wrote a memo to the Chief of the Defence Staff (CDS) suggesting that the department "provide a 'strawman' set of themes and messages" to counter negative publicity for the army from Somalia.[2] If, given the Somalia and other revelations, Canadians think that their government and military couldn't possibly do such things, they probably think the tooth fairy exists.

The question never asked of the CDS and Minister of Defence, who are responsible for performance in the military, is how top command could conclude that a rising star in whom the military had invested a million dollars in training could suddenly have a "substandard leadership style" overnight. Another obvious question never asked is what the CDS and Minister did to inform themselves properly about what was going on. Senior Defence officials do not account publicly for the extent to which they inform themselves for their decisions – as Canadians saw in the public inquiry into the Somalia killings. But neither of these management responsibilities would be given attention if the agenda of the Department of Defence was to sacrifice LCdr Marsaw.

No one in the Department, including the Defence Minister at the time, answered publicly for their responsibilities for ensuring fairness. Had these officials publicly accounted, to an answering standard that Canadians have a right to see met, and had their answering been validated, what happened to LCdr Marsaw probably would have been prevented.

Applying the precautionary principle raises a fundamental question about justice in LCdr Marsaw's case, and in many others: How would the Chief of the Defence Staff and Minister of Defence have demonstrated to Canadians that the processes causing Marsaw's court martial outcome were fair, when:

- there is no public answering for the fairness of the conduct of military officers involved in charge-laying and in court martial processes
- courts martial are more processes for discipline action operating under "command influence" than processes for producing justice[3], which means that military pros-

ecutors are free to create at the outset of a court martial an "atmosphere of guilt" that helps to produce the outcome top command wishes

- those who officiate in such processes – the senior line officers laying the charges, the Judge Advocate General (JAG), the senior military officers acting as court martial judges and the JAG's officers assigned as judges, prosecutors and defence counsel – are all under the command of the CDS and are therefore subject to a career reward system in an organization controlled by the CDS and the Deputy Minister?

But the questions go beyond military command thinking in peacetime. It is generally said in the military that the Chief of the Defence Staff at the time of the Somalia revelations, General Jean Boyle, a relatively junior general, was promoted to the military's top command position over other candidates of greater stature and tacitly expected to "take the fall" for Somalia. There, the overall issue was the Department of Defence's failure to have had a control system preventing soldiers who are trained to kill from being assigned to a Somalia peacekeeping mission inadequately trained and overseen for that role. But the immediate issue was the cover-up of what happened, both in Somalia and in the military's appearances damage control. This means that political agendas can drive decision-making in the Canadian Forces when political outcomes are sought by Ministers, senior officials and top command, and subordinates carry out their agendas.

Responsibility and Control for Fairness in the Military

The issue in the earlier horror stories was public safety. The issue here is responsibility and accountability for fairness and justice in the military. Management control in the Marsaw case meant the control system of the federal executive government, operating in the military, needed to ensure that personnel are treated fairly and justly when accosted with allegations.

Fairness responsibility was ignored in the gross injustices done to Donald Marshall, David Milgaard, Guy Paul Morin, Thomas Sophonow and others by the civilian police and prosecutors. The motivation and competence of the officials involved were the main issues in the harm done to those men, and the same holds in the case of LCdr Marsaw.

As the ultimate directing mind for the military, the Minister of Defence has the duty to have in place a control system throughout the Canadian Forces that ensures fairness and justice. We must not confuse utterances of top command with actual evidence of fairness. In the first place, this means having the function of the Judge Advocate General independent of top military command. Process control standards include honesty safeguards and prevention of "command influence" overriding officers' duty to ensure fairness. Conduct standards apply not only to senior officers' own decision-making, but also to their governance of the conduct of units such as the Military Police, who gather the type of evidence they are told to gather.

As it is, the Minister of Defence cannot demonstrate that we have a legal justice system for the military as opposed to a command-run discipline process within the military, cloaked in legal trappings.

Below the level of Minister, the obvious control questions are: Who was responsible for what fairness control processes? Did they inform themselves adequately for their decisions? Did they uphold the precautionary principle in their decisions? The question, "Did they do their duty?" isn't useful, since officers define duty as serving the intentions of their superiors and, in a peacetime politicized senior military cadre, this means too often anticipating and serving the wants of ministers.

Defence ministers have never been asked to report specifically how they are discharging their overall control responsibility to ensure fairness to all Canadian Forces personnel. The most senior officials involved in the Marsaw case – admirals, the Chief of the Defence Staff and the Deputy Minister of Defence – have never answered publicly for their responsibility for the destruction of LCdr Marsaw.

The Charges, Court Martial and Aftermath

Canadians can reasonably expect the Department of National Defence to have had processes that adequately validated the Halifax newspaper reporter's allegations about LCdr Marsaw. This would include identifying the motivations of the reporter himself. The corporate aim of newspaper articles is to sell newspapers, and articles that are sensational or that create conflict sell more newspapers than articles that do not. DND officials knew this. Fair assessment of the allegations would also have had to rule out the possibility that those officers and crew members unhappy with LCdr Marsaw were the only ones sought out by the reporter. The assessment would also have had to rule out the fact that submarine personnel were not volunteers, and that some crew members didn't meet Marsaw's standards of seamanship for war simulation and boat safety and were perhaps not prepared to shift from the comfort zones that the navy's training had allowed them to develop.

There is no available evidence that the navy's proper rejection of the reporter's and accusing officers' first allegation – that LCdr Marsaw's submarine was unsafe – was followed by DND assessment of the reporter's and accusers' credibility and motivation in the second round of allegations. Thus the officer accusers, unchallenged, were later able to successfully testify against Marsaw at the court martial. An audit of DND's decision-making would have addressed whether DND was simply "shafting" Marsaw, as a CBC's Fifth

Estate TV documentary on LCdr Marsaw put it in October 1996.

Having allowed the media stories to take off across Canada, the military laid charges against LCdr Marsaw. In the military, the person who must lay a charge leading to a court martial is the officer's superior officer. This was Marsaw's naval Commanding Officer (CO) at the Maritime Warfare Centre, who refused to lay charges when presented with the evidence. But while this officer was absent in Europe on military business, the Assistant Judge Advocate General (AJAG) for the area presented his evidence to the Acting Commanding Officer, an air force officer who wouldn't know submarine operations standards. He laid charges.

Commanding officers rely on the advice given them by their specialist staffs, which should be accurate and unbiased. So they normally do not examine all statements given by all witnesses. Yet the summaries that are produced by the military's legal personnel, and trusted by COs, are instrumental in COs making their decisions.

When a CO intends to charge someone, Queen's Regulations and Orders for the Canadian navy instruct the CO, after the charges have been laid, to prepare a Synopsis of matters relevant to his or her decision. This is done whenever a higher military authority will have to deal with the charge. But it is permissible for a CO to delegate the drafting of his Synopsis. In Marsaw's case, however, the Acting CO stated to Marsaw that he decided to lay his charges after discussion with the area AJAG and after dealing with the Military Police report. Because the Police report comprised interviews of up to 150 people, it is possible that the Acting CO didn't read it and relied on the AJAG's use of it, as well as relying on the AJAG's synopsis. The AJAG interviewed crewmen apparently after he had read the Police report, which meant that he was free to choose which crewmen to interview, according to who said what in the Police report.

There is evidence to suggest that the AJAG's Synopsis contained significant errors and didn't accurately reflect the statements of several witnesses. Several of these were clearly prejudicial to LCdr Marsaw. A subsequent review of the Synopsis by an officer in the Military Police at National Defence Headquarters raised questions about the accuracy of the Synopsis, but senior officers took no apparent action. Under naval regulations, a Synopsis is not to include any reference to "opinion or character of the accused." Yet the court martial prosecution's main ploy was to attack the character of Marsaw, based on the Synopsis.

There is no visible control process preventing an AJAG from both counselling a CO to lay charges and writing the Synopsis for the CO.

The Synopsis for Marsaw was dated the day he was charged, 19 July 1994, suggesting that it had been written before the charges were laid. The same day, Marsaw's Unit Personal File was taken from the Base Orderly Room to an office in the Maritime Warfare

Centre. There his file was purged of all letters of commendation.

The Assistant Judge Advocate General counselling the Commanding Officer also advises the responsible area commander, who is the CO's superior. In Marsaw's case this was Vice-Admiral Mason, Commander, Maritime Command in Halifax. He would then decide whether to convene a court martial. Inexplicably, the admiral, soon to retire, shifted his court martial decision responsibility to his army maritime counterpart. The commanding general of land forces in the area, Major-General McInnis, was already in the process of retiring, with a retirement fanfare costing enough public money to make the headlines.[4] Like the air force officer who charged Marsaw, the general would have known little about submarine fleet operations. Admiral Mason's reasons for transferring his responsibility were not made known and the land forces general, also likely counselled by the AJAG, chose to court martial LCdr Marsaw.

The AJAG, expected by his mandate to provide unbiased, objective legal advice to commanders before charges are laid, later took on the role of Assistant Prosecutor in the court martial. This sequence of involvement of the AJAG, for which his superiors were responsible, put him in a position of influence that he should never have had.

The Judge Advocate General function in Canada's military cannot be considered impartial or independent as those concepts are interpreted by civilian courts. As noted earlier, the court martial process in armed forces is still viewed more as part of the discipline process than a justice process. Senior officers serving on courts martial are not only untrained in law(the trial Judge Advocate is a lawyer); they also have their own career progress to think about. Success in large formal organizations means pleasing one's superiors, which has nothing necessarily to do with justice or the public interest. This motivation is even more even more likely in peacetime military organizations. Thus, in military courts, the precautionary principle – having reasonable assurance that fairness is safeguarded before proceeding with an intention – dictates the highest order of control to ensure fairness, not just the carrying-out of procedures.

The precautionary principle also dictates that no important information or briefing should be relied on without a reasonable check of its validity. There was no evidence of answering obligations for anyone for ensuring that both the charging process and court martial process were fair. The military had no apparent interest in checking on the AJAG's motivation or competence in counselling the senior line officers.

The Judge Advocate General's office also supplies a Judge Advocate for a court martial, who sits on the panel and has the responsibility for keeping the process honest and instructing officer members on inferences they shouldn't draw. Thus, for the Marsaw court martial, the Judge Advocate General (JAG) not only supplied the Judge Advocate, the Prosecutor and the Assistant Prosecutor (who had been instrumental in the charges being laid), but also supplied Marsaw's defence counsel. And the JAG, a career military officer, is himself under the command of the Chief of the Defence Staff: he doesn't report to a judiciary body. Despite having a role established by Parliament, the JAG and his office's court martial operations are not independent. They can reasonably be described as an arm of the military with a non-military label.

As LCdr Marsaw's family understands the facts, in addition to his file being stripped of his career commendations, an investigation report by a chief petty officer in Ottawa on possible coercion of witnesses by the Military Police was made a classified report. Key defence witnesses willing and/or wanting to be called were not called by LCdr Marsaw's defence counsel, who apparently led him to believe that the evidence against him was so weak that this wasn't necessary. One such witness was a Royal Australian Navy submarine commander who earlier had been with Marsaw in his boat as an observer. Although he made himself available to the court martial he wasn't called, so the panel didn't know that he would have refuted certain videotaped testimony by a crew member. Although apparently interviewed, the British naval officer allegedly the cigar-tube victim of LCdr Marsaw was not called as a witness.

Other witnesses told the Marsaw family that they were dissuaded by their superiors from testifying on Marsaw's behalf. Military Police intimidated witnesses through thuggish behaviour that should not have been tolerated by any self-respecting Canadian Forces officer being interrogated. This was clear to anyone, from the video footage of the Military Police interrogations screened in CBC's TV documentary.

It was not until mid-1997, after Marsaw had been destroyed, that two crew members realized they had independently given the same testimony to the Forces' investigative unit before charges were laid. Had it been used, the testimony of either would have been virtually fatal to the charge against Marsaw.[5]

In a 1997 visit to LCdr Marsaw's brother Roy, himself a former naval officer, one of the former *Ojibwa* crew members read for the first time the Military Police Report account of his own interview by them. He was horrified to see that important information he had given the Police was omitted from the report. Had the information been used in the court martial, it would have cleared Marsaw of the cigar-tube charge. The crew member recalled that the interview had been recorded, and even described the tape recorder. Yet the preamble to the Military Police report said that no recording was made of the interview.

Roy Marsaw arranged for the crew member to meet with a Department of Defence investigative official to point out the omission. In February 1998, Mr. Marsaw received a letter from the Acting Judge Advocate General, stating that the official had met with the former crew member and that the crew member was "invited to document what he considered to be misconduct or improper behaviour...." That letter effectively put the lid on this evidence. No former crew member could have been expected to push for an audit in the Department of National Defence that would expose to Parliament and the public what really happened.

When the accusations against Marsaw arose, the military didn't ask people to document their suspicions. They assigned a team of Military Police and sent out investigators. Yet when a former crew member raises a question first hand about the validity of Military Police reporting, the military makes it the responsibility of the former crew member to provide the evidence of unprofessional conduct. The disheartened crew member couldn't possibly re-produce his evidence, since he didn't run the tape recorder nor did he have a copy of the tape. He didn't even have the opportunity to sign the Military Police report of what he said, as a check on its validity. And he never saw the report that emerged until it was shown to him years later. Moreover, in the stonewalling atmosphere of the Somali-disgraced military, he could expect intimidation or suppression tactics and would be alone in challenging the military.

Thus by mid-1997 the Marsaw family knew the full extent to which LCdr Marsaw had been, as the Fifth Estate program put it, shafted, but were exhausted, both emotionally and financially. Senior Defence officials knew this.

The court martial process ended in late 1995 and LCdr Marsaw was convicted of five of seven charges, including the cigar-tube charge and of abusing his crew. Immediately after the court martial decision, Vice-Admiral Mason sent a message to the fleet and to others under his command, commending the decision. Astonishingly, for someone at his rank, he trumpeted that 43 witnesses had spoken against LCdr Marsaw and only 10 in his defence. Yet the crucial questions of the validity and reliability of the 43 witnesses' testimony, and who was not called, stared the admiral in the face. The fleet never knew that important defence witnesses were not called and that important evidence, like the former crew member's testimony apparently suppressed, were not presented by LCdr Marsaw's military defence counsel.

Within 10 days of the court martial verdict, the traumatized LCdr Marsaw was ordered back to his base despite his civilian doctor's advice that he was not fit to return that soon. He had learned that he was facing precipitous discharge and loss of pay, yet this is apparently unheard of immediately following a court martial. Marsaw had earlier been told that the administrative process for discharge and pay stoppage would take about twelve months. His civilian doctor was suspicious that making him return the base was a move to have him sign papers to get him out quickly. The navy declared his medical leave exhausted by the end of January 1996, yet extensions of leave are common.

LCdr Marsaw appealed the court martial decision but was also determined to achieve an independent inquiry into the processes that led to the charges against him. Marsaw undertook a fast in January-February 1996, under doctors' surveillance, to test his endurance for a hunger strike that he was contemplating to try, to achieve an independent inquiry of what had gone on. Neither he nor the military made any public announcements during that time.

The available evidence suggests that the navy wanted Marsaw in a military hospital, where doctors' decisions could be expected to be less independent. Military doctors sought out the required civilian doctors' certification for admittance but were refused in no uncertain terms. Marsaw may have been traumatized but was still mentally competent. The apparent aim of the navy through 1996 was to have Marsaw declared medically unfit for what he was expert in doing. When the civilian doctors thwarted that approach, the navy turned to its administrative processes such as Career Review Board processes.

The October 1996 CBC Fifth Estate TV program on Marsaw finally placed important questions before the general public. But the navy had closed ranks against Marsaw, declaring him in effect the enemy.[6] On the anniversary of the court martial verdict, Marsaw launched his hunger strike to try to achieve the independent inquiry he sought. Following the court martial, the admirals had reduced LCdr Marsaw's rank to Lieutenant. Marsaw ended his hunger strike 28 November when top command and the Minister, realizing he would likely die, gave him the acting rank of Lieutenant Commander pending the decision of the court martial appeal court.

In a 29 November message to the fleet, Vice-Admiral Mason said:

> Let me be very clear – I disagree with his (Marsaw's) methods, and consider the entire process of publicly holding the justice system hostage unnecessary. I rely on all commanding officers and individuals in leadership positions to provide for the widest possible dissemination and full understanding of this message.

The fleet wasn't told the criteria for a "justice system."

On 20 November, as Marsaw's hunger strike became medically serious, Vice-Admiral Mason had written a dismissive letter to Marsaw stating that an appeal from the court martial would supply what Marsaw wanted. The admiral said at the end of his letter, "You achieved magnificent results operationally. I am sad that you and we have come to this." Yet it was Admiral Mason who had management control over what happened to Marsaw, and who has never had to account for his actions.

People across Canada linked to LCdr Marsaw's Halifax support group had voiced their anxiety about his condition and what had been done to him. When, for example, the Alliance for Public Accountability wrote 21 November to the Acting Chief of the Defence Staff, Vice-Admiral Murray (General Boyle having left in the fall of 1996), Admiral Murray replied:

I can assure you that it is not my wish to see anyone suffer in the manner chosen by Lieutenant (Navy) Marsaw. I also very much regret the pain that this action is causing his family and friends. However, I must also emphasize that Lieutenant (Navy) Marsaw's primary demand of an independent review will occur through the Court Martial Appeal Court, an independent panel of three civilian justices from the Federal Court of Canada or the superior courts of the provinces. Further, under the rules of the Court martial Appeal Court, Lieutenant (Navy) Marsaw can seek to have new evidence heard.

The 29 November 1996 message by Vice-Admiral Mason to all those under his command stated, "There has been no commitment to conduct an inquiry into the Military Police," and went on to say:

I am confident the court martial appeal process will provide the independent review that LCdr Marsaw has sought. It is important that all members of Maritime Command realize that the navy is determined that this case be concluded in a court of law and not in the court of public opinion."

The statements of both these senior officers about Marsaw's appeal are misleading. They both knew or should have known that the inquiry Marsaw sought wasn't possible through a court martial appeal process. Appeals are trials of trials, not an examination of the fairness of authorities' actions culminating in court martial. Since an appeal from his court martial was automatically available to him, LCdr Marsaw's attempt to bring about an independent inquiry (Admiral Mason's word "review" was not the same thing) was obviously to achieve something more than an appeal court's examination of whether Marsaw's court martial met legal-precedent criteria for a fair court martial trial process.

Marsaw wanted an honest examination and explanation of what had happened to him and why, and suspension of the court martial sentence until an outside competent examination had been carried out. The admirals would have known that a "competent independent inquiry into the situation" (the words attributed to LCdr Marsaw by Admiral Mason in his 20 November letter to Marsaw) could expose the systemic causes of what happened to Marsaw.

The appeal court in September 1997 overturned the decision of the court martial panel. Immediately following, Mary Lou Finlay of CBC Radio's "As It Happens" interviewed LCdr Marsaw's appeal counsel, Jim Connors. She asked him the central question: whether what had happened to Marsaw was unusual or the result of something systemic. Mr. Connors replied that he couldn't tell because the court martial appeal was confined to points of law. There were other points of issue, he said, but only some could be raised.[7] Connors was saying in effect that an appeal heard from a court martial can't be expected to expose an unjust process leading to a court martial. This presumably means that if important testimony or evidence that should have been presented in the court martial had been suppressed or withheld, the evidence could not be introduced in a subsequent appeal. Neither a court martial nor an appeal from a court martial would examine the interlinked processes in the military that determined what happened to Marsaw, let alone the motives. The admirals would have known this.

There is no evidence that the Minister of National Defence at the time of the court martial, Douglas Young, was interested in checking the briefings likely supplied to him by the CDS and JAG against the valid views and relevant facts held by LCdr Marsaw's family and support groups. When a member of the Halifax support group sent evidence to Minister Young about LCdr Marsaw and the role of the local admiral, the Minister's staff sent the letter back unseen by the Minister, under an asserted technicality.

The Message of the Appeal Court Decision

The judges of the Court Martial Appeal Court heard Marsaw's appeal in late June 1997 and gave their decision in September. One example of several will illustrate why they quashed the court martial verdict.

Appeal counsel for LCdr Marsaw cited specific sections of prosecution's testimony from the court martial transcript as evidence of competence shortcomings and/or questionable motivation on the part of the JAG's officers conducting the court martial. The JAG colonel for the military asserted that this was unfair – that the appeal court judges should take an "holistic" approach to what the court martial prosecution put forward. Yet it is obvious that any "holistic" approach to evidence would have included identifying the motivations, abilities and external constraints of key officers responsible for the processes applied to LCdr Marsaw. The military would not have wanted this in the court martial. Moreover, the prosecutor's "holistic" view would not likely have included the evidence of LCdr Marsaw's superior performance in his submarine's fighting prowess and safety, logged in his file by his superiors but stripped out before the court martial. Properly examined, this would have called into question the military's motivation for court-martialling Marsaw.

The JAG's military defence counsel assigned to LCdr Marsaw in the court martial could not have been expected to bring out critical responsibility issues and facts at the senior officer level. Annual Personnel Evaluation Reports must be presumed to be as influential for JAG officers in their motivation as they are for other officers in the Forces. Of the court martial Judge Advocate, LCdr Marsaw's appeal counsel said at one point, "We can't know what was in the mind of the Judge Advocate."

In setting out a litany of prosecution ploys in the court martial, Marsaw's appeal counsel made it clear that the JAG prosecutor, at the outset of the court martial, mounted a general character attack on Marsaw. The prosecutor's claims of poor leadership (apparently using different criteria from those Marsaw's superiors had used for his commendations) were not relevant in a trial designed to re-create reality to arrive at specific facts about specific charges. The court martial transcript showed that the prosecutor maintained this tactic throughout the court martial and reinforced its effect on the panelists in his sum-up. The four senior officers on the panel, not being lawyers and not being alerted by the Judge Advocate on the panel (who would have known what the prosecutor was doing, and why), couldn't be expected to know what was being done to them.

The appeal court was satisfied that the military prosecutor's tactic, probably not allowable in a civilian court, likely succeeded in creating an "atmosphere of guilt" in the minds of the members of the court martial panel. Earlier, in the gathering and processing of testimony used against him, it was clear that LCdr Marsaw had no protection from the authorities converting someone's comment, "He was disliked by some" into the assertion, "He was widely disliked."

In civil courts, where the lawyers' objective is to win, an even playing field is presumed. In a letter to the editor during Marsaw's hunger strike in November 1996, one retired admiral, Fred Crickard, asserted that courts martial are even playing fields:

> Defence and prosecution both had their day in court, a judgment was laid down and sentence awarded. Due process was followed. And for people to suggest this was a show trial to show that a senior officer can get clobbered, that to me is sensationalist.... What would have been done had this not been brought to light and no due process had taken place? Wouldn't you call that a coverup?[8]

Ignoring, for the moment, senior officer thinking such as "If the military's processes concluded that X happened, then it must have happened," neither this former officer nor any of the other retired senior military officers writing letters to editors in the year following the court martial would have been able to credibly assert to the public the motivation and ability of those in charge of "due process." LCdr Marsaw's appeal counsel convincingly showed that he hadn't stood a chance in the court martial.

What is allowed as part of the game to win in civilian courts becomes a disgrace if allowed in a military court. This is because the Judge Advocate General has total control over all aspects, including how the charging and convening officers are briefed; what evidence is used and not used; whether his subordinate, the court martial prosecutor, conditions the environment of decision of the senior officer panelists; and whether the trial's Judge Advocate adequately counsels the panelists on "collateral matters" introduced by the prosecution to win.

Courts martial were created for wartime conditions. Citizens haven't the evidence to assume that military officers with legal training but operating within the command control environment of the military will think and act counter to tacit or explicit expectations of their superiors. Nor can the public assume that senior line officers assigned as courts martial panelists can detect subtle prosecution ploys and are totally independent of the aims of a top command having career fate control over them. If conscientious line officers take umbrage at this proposition, it doesn't alter the risk to fairness in the existing structure.

As Halifax journalist Ralph Surette said of senior bureaucrats anticipating and serving ministers' wishes in the case of the Westray coal mine, "The limits are understood." That being the case in a civilian bureaucracy, the chances in the military are surely higher. All it takes is an agenda set at the top.

The navy put out its own spin the same day as the Crickard letter, through Commodore Cogdon, Maritime Command Chief of Staff. Cogdon officially wrote to the editor of the *Ottawa Sun* to counter both the CBC Fifth Estate program and an article in the *Sun* by Peter Worthington supporting Marsaw. In a classic example of the senior officer mind, Cogdon recited all the charges against Marsaw to make sure *Sun* readers knew them, and then implied that the charges must be infallible simply because they appeared on someone's charge sheet. Like Admiral Crickard writing about courts martial, Cogdon ducked the question of the fairness and validity of "due process" at the stage of charging.

It is reasonable to infer that fairness for a submarine commander in some corner of the navy at the rank of Lieutenant Commander was not a priority with admirals running an agenda known only to themselves at a time of citizen disillusionment with the military because of Somalia. A bewildered LCdr Marsaw, his family and the public didn't know what the agenda was. The revelations in the court martial appeal about what was done and allowed to be done to LCdr Marsaw in the court martial itself point to the need to discover top command's motivation in charging Marsaw and proceeding unfairly in the court martial.

The court martial process was handy because, once launched, the words "court martial" produce the psychological baggage attaching to the word "court," i.e., by definition the result must be fair. Yet it is a process of the military, operating under command influence. Given that those who made themselves aware of what happened to LCdr Marsaw concluded that he was wrongly court-martialed, the admirals would certainly have known that something wasn't right.

There is no evidence that the Minister of Defence ensured that fairness was the first criterion of the Chief of the Defence Staff, Deputy Minister of Defence, Judge Advocate General and admirals. Nor is there evidence that the Clerk of the Privy Council, responsible for ensuring ethical conduct by all senior federal public servants – military included –

took an interest in what was happening to LCdr Marsaw.

Nor is there evidence of any learning intention by the military. A naval press officer gave the following comment after the appeal court quashed the court martial verdict:

> I don't think this is an embarrassment to the navy. The appeals court did its job and it is part of the military justice system. There is a system of checks and balances that is there to be used. We were happy last fall when LCdr Marsaw ended his hunger strike last year and chose that option.[9]

This is a typical military spin statement. The civilian Court Martial Appeal Court is an external check on military processes; it is not part of the military's own processes. The appeal check in the "system of checks and balances" is only to be called upon if the military's own trials fail to be just. And the press officer's "option" attributed to Marsaw was chosen by top command, not Marsaw, who wouldn't have ended his 1996 hunger strike without the military backing off its "go to Hell" stance.

Note that an appeal court can only overturn a court martial verdict; it cannot restore the stature of a Forces member that the military has smashed and intends to keep smashed.

The sum-up in credibility is that LCdr Marsaw throughout was consistently highly intelligent, rational and articulate. Senior officers – and indeed ministers – seemed to be unable to cope with someone with Marsaw's integrity and sense of justice other than through exercising their power. A classic example was the Prime Minister's and Defence Minister's public denunciation of the 1997 Somalia Commissioners' report, with their refusal to appoint the recommended inspector general for the Canadian Forces, and their refusal to make justice-related inquiries and military processes independent from command influence. Status does not mean stature in the military, any more than it does in politics.

Other failures and denials of military responsibility in other areas disclosed in 1998-99 underscore the need for adequate public answering from the military and from their Minister. Alternating decrees and "leave it with us" assurances from senior military officers and accompanying fog from the Minister suggest that military top command intends to guard its autonomy and concede no public answering obligations, and that the Minister sees no need for top command public answering to Parliament and the public.

The Missing Public Answering

Despite the 1997 Somalia Commission report, the federal executive government has no process for accounting to the public for the discharge of its responsibilities for fairness and justice in the military. The following are simply the military equivalent of answering expectations that the earlier horror stories showed as necessary to achieve fairness and justice. It is a lengthy list, but we have no public evidence that Minister and top command have standards for their performance and answering.

With respect to their duties, at no time have Ministers of National Defence told Parliament or the public:

- the specific performance standards for military top command that the Minister requires to be met to ensure fairness to military personnel of all ranks
- the actual performance of senior officers, compared to the Minister's standards
- the reporting that the Minister exacts from the CDS and senior officers which, when validated, tells Ministers whether military command is meeting the performance standards for fairness set for them by the Ministers
- the extent to which the Minister at the time informed himself to carry out his duty to govern:
  - senior officers' intentions for those under their control
  - the ability of senior officers to grasp what Canadians would regard as these officers' fair responsibilities and accountabilities

In the specific case of LCdr Marsaw, the Ministers did not tell the public:

- the navy's performance standards for safety and seamanship that other submarine officers and would-be submarine commanders were used to
- the Department of National Defence's performance standards for validating the Halifax Chronicle-Herald reporter's allegations about Marsaw
- DND's performance standards for the Judge Advocate General and the Assistant JAG in upholding the precautionary principle, for:
  - ensuring competence, objectivity and fairness in the advice and conduct of JAG officers assigned to the Marsaw case
  - identifying possible significant influences acting to have LCdr Marsaw charged and dealing with them
- DND's performance standards for the officer directing the Military Police, for:
  - ensuring objectivity and fairness in its work and reporting
  - identifying and dealing with external influences affecting its work and reporting
- DND's performance standards for the Halifax admiral in charge of Maritime Command for upholding the precautionary principle in informing himself fully and fairly for his responsibility to:
  - validate the Military Police reports and their convergence with the Synopsis
  - assess the motivation and competence of the Acting CO who charged LCdr Marsaw
  - assess the AJAG's objectivity in his advice to the charging CO and to the Maritime Command admiral

- why the Maritime Command admiral removed himself from his responsibility to take the decision on whether to convene a court martial for LCdr Marsaw, at a time when both he and the general to whom he passed this decision were about to retire from the forces
- what courts martial are and are not, in mandate, independence and required competencies (especially when Forces members choose JAG officers as their defence counsel)
- the criteria used to select senior officers as the presiding officers in a court martial
- the DND performance standards that would prevent senior officers from misrepresenting to the Minister and public at large the purpose of LCdr Marsaw's hunger strike, which was to achieve an independent competent inquiry into what was happening to him

There is no available evidence that defence ministers require the CDS and Deputy Minister to regularly report to the Minister:

- the performance standards these officials have in place to ensure fairness to all those in the Canadian Forces
- who accounts to whom for compliance with the standards
- whether the standards are being met
- how the performance reporting has been validated.

In an attempt to get the military interested in its public answering obligation, the Alliance for Public Accountability wrote to the Acting Chief of the Defence Staff, Vice-Admiral Murray, in March 1997. The Alliance asked him to explain the CDS's responsibilities and answering obligations for ensuring fairness in military processes that could lead to courts-martial or decisions about the careers of those charged, including their discharge on deemed medical unfitness grounds.

A designated colonel wrote back to say that the CDS was responsible for "ensuring the overall fairness of military processes" and to that end gave orders, recommended statutory and regulatory changes and was a redress authority. The colonel went on to say that the Forces had "instructions which…create fair processes for reviewing the conduct of any service member." But none of the colonel's responses on responsibility dealt with control assurance: whether issuance of instructions can by itself be expected to ensure fairness, and which military processes could be asserted to actually ensure fairness. The colonel's response was silent on the CDS's answering obligations. Since the Somalia Commissioners' report, the Minister of National Defence has set out no visible answering standards for senior officers.

The Alliance also wrote a briefing letter to the new CDS, General Maurice Baril, in September 1997, offering him assistance in "identifying what would constitute reasonable public accountability standards for DND." Another Colonel wrote back to say that Gen. Baril would "deal with all accountability issues as they arise." Presumably this meant, in bureaucratic language, that the new CDS would deal with damage control when he had to, but was not offering to account for his and his officers' fairness duties – that is, reporting their performance standards and whether they were meeting them. For example, the answering by senior officers throughout 1998-99 for disclosures of medical-related conduct by the military can best be described as inept spin.[10]

Summary

There is no evidence that DND conduct in the case of LCdr Marsaw met performance standards for fairness and answering that Canadians have the right to see met.

There is no evidence suggesting that the Minister of National Defence, Clerk of the Privy Council, Deputy Minister of National Defence, Chief of the Defence Staff or the responsible admirals even had performance and control standards – let alone adequate standards – governing the structures, processes and conduct applied to LCdr Marsaw.

Nor is there evidence that the two Ministers involved had ever formally satisfied themselves, as the ultimate publicly-accountable directing minds for the Department of National Defence, whether standards were in place at the time and were being met. Neither Minister Young nor Minister Eggleton stated to Canadians their view of the control standards for fairness in the military that the Minister of National Defence has the duty to install and maintain.

Lacking standards set by ministers of the Crown, military top command appears to operate by whim. But the most senior officers have the opportunity to earn back the level of trust that the public and the ranks in the Forces had given them on blind faith until the Somalia revelations. The Marsaw case clarifies the need, but at a terrible cost to him. Trust can be earned in part through full and fair answering, independently validated.

— — —

For Canada's new phase of submarine operations, LCdr Marsaw could have expertly advised the Auditor General of Canada on the accountability reporting Parliament has a right to expect from the Department of National Defence for testing out and keeping up its four Upholder class diesel-electric submarines purchased from the Royal Navy in 1998. The Department's reporting (which would be audited) would assert whether the Department is meeting reasonable standards for safety, readiness and performance, and competence in technical maintenance. But the Minister and top command would have fought the idea.

Endnotes

[1] This case is based on the February 1997 briefing document of the Alliance for Public Accountability sent to the then Minister of Defence, Douglas Young, pointing out the need for an audit inquiry into the court martial of LCdr Marsaw. The Alliance's briefing document was copied to the Acting Chief of the Defence Staff, the Deputy Minister of Defence, the Clerk of the Privy Council, the Chair of the House of Commons Standing Committee on Defence and Opposition party Defence critics. Following the court martial appeal but before the Appeal Court's decision in September 1997 quashing the court martial verdict, the Alliance sent a follow-up briefing in July 1997 to Arthur Eggleton, Mr. Young's successor as Defence Minister. Neither of these briefings to the ministers was acknowledged by the ministers' office staff.

> Other text is based on documents and information supplied by the Marsaw family, and the author is indebted to Roy Marsaw for critiquing the text.

[2] *Ottawa Citizen*, 28 August 1996 p.A4

[3] Captain Kevin J. Barry, U.S. Coast Guard (Retired), "Reinventing Military Justice," *Proceedings*, July 1994

[4] See Chapter 10 on the accountability of military top command.

[5] Noted in a 26 September 1997 briefing letter from the Alliance for Public Accountability to the Chief of the Defence Staff, General Maurice Baril.

[6] For example, Commodore Cogdon wrote an intimidating letter to Roy Marsaw in March 1996 about the family's letters to newspapers.

[7] CBC Radio, 10 September 1997

[8] *Ottawa Citizen*, 20 November 1996, p.A4

[9] *Globe and Mail*, 12 September 1997 p.A3

[10] See Chapter 10

CHAPTER 2

What Public Accountability Means

Public Accountability

Public accountability means the obligation to answer publicly – to report, to an acceptable standard of answering, for the discharge of responsibilities that affect the public in important ways. This concept is based on the 1975 report of the Independent Review Committee on the Mandate of the Auditor General of Canada. The review was chaired by J.R.M. Wilson, FCA, who had just retired as senior partner of Canada's mightiest auditing firm, Clarkson Gordon.

The Wilson report defined accountability as the obligation to answer for a responsibility conferred. For government reporting to a legislature, this definition has stood the test of time. The word "conferred" fits in the context of government's answering, but is too restrictive for accountability in society generally. The obligation to answer publicly arises as a fairness obligation whenever authorities intend something that would affect the public in important ways. Thus the obligation extends beyond answering for responsibilities formally or legally conferred. For example, if corporate boards were to forever report only what the law requires them to report to the public, and considering the lag time for the law to catch up with what citizens need – especially when corporations largely control what is enacted – citizens would remain forever ill-informed about boards' intentions and actions that would significantly affect the public in safety or fairness.

Responsibility is the obligation to act, and accountability is the obligation to report on the responsibility. These are separate obligations. The purpose of having authorities answer publicly for their responsibilities, before and after the fact, is to let citizens make reasonably informed decisions about the safety and fairness of authorities' intentions. When citizens are reasonably informed they can act to commend, alter or halt authorities' intentions. This means that citizens have more control over what affects them. Well enough informed, citizens as a whole usually make fair decisions. As George Washington put it in a 1796 letter:

> I am sure the mass of Citizens in these United States mean well, and I firmly believe they will always act well, whenever they can obtain a right understanding of matters....[1]

The right to know what authorities intend that would affect us and why they intend it stems from a mix of common decency, reciprocity, mutual respect, "do unto others" and other aspects of fairness But all we do now, in effect, is to submit pleas to (or fight with) authorities who in turn are not made to explain their intentions. Answering is also needed to know authorities' performance. Important answering must be validated, whether by public interest organizations or professional auditors, or both. Thus the answering requirement is also to help citizens decide their trust in authorities.

Adequate public answering is central to society working properly. As pioneers in the subject Day and Klein put it,

> It is a tradition of political thought which sees the defining characteristic of democracy as stemming not merely from the election of those who are given delegated power to run society's affairs... but from their continuing obligation to explain and justify their conduct in public.[2]

Those who don't want citizens to think of accountability as a simple, powerful concept giving citizens more control will immediately say, "But if accountability is to serve the public interest, what's the public interest? No one can define it, so how can anyone propose general standards of accountability?" This is like saying that we have to have extensive research into health care delivery before health ministers can make basic resourcing decisions to reduce hardship for the ill and their families. Or that a city has to undertake development of performance measures (taking years) before council and staff can account for their performance.

We all know what the chronically ill and others needing extended or rehabilitation care go through, and what they need. And citizens can ask municipal councillors to state their own and their staffs' existing performance standards, judge whether they are adequate and, if not, write the performance standards that citizens reasonably think can and should be met. The same for health care, at all levels of responsibility.

We can say that an intention serving the public interest is an intention that increases or maintains fairness in society, in the sense of fairness in the distribution of benefits and burdens. As to the definition of what is fair in a situation, we don't have to be a carpenter to tell if a door jamb is crooked: any honest jury can roughly assess whether something proposed is fair. But the public's decisions about fairness require the information to make them.

The essence of the public answering obligation is the requirement that authorities, when what they propose would affect citizens in important ways, will disclose their intentions and their reasoning, their performance standards, and their actual performance and learning. And they are to meet reasonable standards of timeliness, fairness and completeness in their answering. We don't have this answering requirement in either our laws or conventions, but since Magna Carta there has been nothing stopping citizens in democracies from installing it.

To install public answering to a reasonable standard, citizens must agree on what it means. At present we have a variety of notions of accountability that keep the concept unclear. Newspaper editorials and articles usually confuse responsibility with accountability, and journalists don't see their job as helping to bring about public answering . Academics get right the idea that the purpose of accountability is to prevent abuse of power, but then they claim that accountability is "complex." This allows them to write about it in ways that don't offend the executive government branches that fund them, and to keep producing notions of what accountability includes or doesn't include without having to say what accountability *is*. Worse, academics don't propose how citizens can bring about adequate public answering.

Holding to Account

Holding fairly to account means exacting from decision-makers the information we need to assess both the implications of their intentions and the effects of their actions; equally it means doing something sensible with answering given in good faith. Holding to account supersedes blind trust in authorities, helping us to head off decisions leading to harm and injustice.

The requirement to answer before the fact says: "Please explain your intentions and why you think they are fair, and tell us your own performance standards for your responsibilities." The requirement to answer after the fact says, "What do you think resulted from what you did, and how have you applied the learning you gained from it?"

Holding fairly to account means that we don't hold people to account for results or outcomes they can't control, and it means that people holding to account, such as opposition parties in legislatures, do not seize on honest reports of lack of success to blame for self-serving purposes.

Holding to account can't be achieved if we leave it to auditors and other examiners to tell us what those with the responsibilities should have been reporting themselves. Auditors serve the accountability relationship, but they stand outside it. Nor does it mean establishing who is to blame for something. And it doesn't mean public interest organizations and individual citizens working after hours to dig out information and submit access to information requests to get information that authorities should have reported in the first place. Whistleblowing in the public interest is an accountability issue when courageous employees feel compelled to give the public the information that those with the senior responsibilities should have given, but wouldn't.

"Political accountability" is fuzzy, because to most people it means politicians subjecting themselves to citizens' assessments of their performance after the fact, as in elections. But used in the correct sense of the answering obligation, political accountability means government ministers reporting to elected representatives in a legislative chamber, and answering fully and fairly in response to fair questions put to them. Legislators then decide what confidence they have in the ministers. But in the English parliamentary system, this usually means only ritual exchanges in Question Period, while challenge and confidence votes in the assembly are expected to change intentions only with minority governments. Regardless, the first minister wields so much power in controlling ministers, governance appointments, rewards and punishments, and the way public money is spent, that "elected dictatorship" is an apt description of our system.

"Legal accountability" is useful if it means the requirement to answer as part of a contract. But accountability doesn't mean answering questions in a court or inquiry, or trying to identify what happened after harm has been done. Apart from contractual answering requirements in law, neither political nor legal accountability means fair and timely public answering for intentions and reasoning, performance standards, results and learning applied.

Why We Must Hold to Account

We need evidence before we can properly place our trust in authorities' ability and fairness. A large part of the evidence we need comes from their answering. A high standard of validated public answering reduces uncertainty about people's intentions. When we have a better idea of what authorities are likely to do, we have a better chance to control outcomes. This idea applies equally to employee trust in managements and boards of directors and to citizen trust in institutions such as executive governments, courts, corporations, central banks, police and the military. It applies equally to the trust of Southern countries in the intentions of Northern country governments, banks and corporations who currently have the power to adversely affect the fates of Southern country citizens.

Most people's ideas of answering in an accountability relationship is that it happens after the fact, like year-end financial reporting. This is understandable, but the most important answering from authorities is explanation of their intentions and their reasoning, and that kind of answering comes before the fact. When it is validated as far as possible, before-the-fact answering lets citizens judge the fairness of what authorities intend. It lets us publicly challenge them. Then we can commend or move to alter or stop what they intend.

Answering before the fact must include authorities' intended performance standards, because these clarify their intentions. Answering after the fact means authorities state what happened as a result of their actions, what they learned from their effort and how they applied that learning.

Citizens want to be able to predict what authorities will do and not do. When we are uncertain we lose trust and put on the brakes. When authorities answer before the fact, we tentatively set our level of trust in them. Later, validated answering for results and learning lets us adjust our prediction confidence, which means the level of trust we place in the authorities for the future.

Hitlers gain power when citizens who feel uneasy about political developments feel unable to act because they and their families might be stigmatized or personally harmed if they spoke out. The same is true in government departments and large corporations when employees keep silent about what they see going on. Whistleblowers who risk their own ruin usually do get ruined, because they get no support from the citizens at large who benefit from their courage. Worse, other employees willingly take direction from superiors to work on the whistleblowers' destruction.

What we need are self-regulating processes, installed in the law, to help limit harm by authorities and help bring about greater fairness in society. It is not just a matter of installing confrontational "checks and balances." That gives us only fighting by the few in the form of lobbying, adversarial court injunctions to stop something, and court processes for redress after harm has been done.

Making authorities answer publicly for their intentions and performance is a useful first step, because the requirement to answer publicly qualifies as a self-regulating influence. When the directing minds of governments and private and public sector corporations intend something that would affect us in important ways, or when interest groups push for some kind of gain for themselves, they have an obligation in fairness to explain the outcomes they intend, for whom, and explain why their intended outcomes should be seen as fair.

"Affecting the public in important ways" means that, being aware of authorities' action intentions and the probable outcomes, we may well take different decisions and action than we otherwise would.

Sociologist James D. Thompson pointed out that organizations seek to control their environments, rather than be controlled by them, and if they cannot control their environments, they seek to buffer them.[3] We can think of enough examples to know that this proposition applies equally to businesses, government departments and other organizations, regardless of their tasks or who the stakeholders are.

When we speak of an organization doing something we mean the identifiable persons governing or directing the organization, whom we call its directing mind. Accounting to stakeholders – those affected by what the directing minds intend – reduces an organization's autonomy because it gives the stakeholders information they can use to exert influence. Yet good public answering that builds trust can earn greater freedom of action for decision-makers in the long run.

Harm such as the blood and Westray mine deaths and injuries can happen even with public answering by authorities. So can deaths from inadequately-regulated drugs licencing, or staff cuts in hospitals. But the chances of harm are smaller if the responsible authorities tell citizens their performance standards, and citizens have those assertions audited. Citizens can then act to endorse or alter the standards. For example, government officials charged with safety regulation have a fairness obligation to tell us the extent to which they apply the precautionary principle in their work. Regular, timely and validated public answering gives us in-time control. Courts come into play when there is no preventive answering before the fact, and harm is done. Their task is then to identify fact and blame, and the nature and means of redress. When the answering rules are missing, we get lapses in the precautionary principle and reluctance by responsible officials to immediately report an emerging danger, not only for a lethal coal mine but also for something like public water supplies in the Walkertons and North Battlefords.

In the federal government a notable case was the exposure in the Canadian House of Commons in early 2000 of the federal executive government's deployment of a large job-creation fund before the 1997 election. It was a classic example of ministers not answering publicly for their intentions in spending a billion dollars of public money, and not answering for their own standards for the integrity of the spending decisions. This case is dealt with in Chapters 8 and 9.

Opposition Members of Parliament sensed the accountability issue was important, claiming that the main intention for the spending across political ridings was patronage for vote-getting, not investment to lower unemployment. But Parliament has no rules or conventions in place for exacting adequate answering from government ministers, and MPs had no coherent process for pursuing the issue as an accountability issue.

We might try rewards as a means of influencing authorities' conduct, but this isn't a self-regulating influence. And if corporations can directly or indirectly offer government decision-makers whatever it takes to have them put corporate interests first, the reward approach won't protect the public interest. We can reduce harm, unfairness and injustice if we can make the conduct of authorities more self-regulating.

The requirement to answer publicly is self-regulating because it exerts a significant effect on the conduct of those who must answer. We already know that business managers who must report their profit goals and intended effort pay more attention to producing profit. For the same reason we can expect elected and appointed officials of government and those directing corporations to make fairer decisions if we require them to state publicly their intentions and reasoning and their performance standards, and, later, their results and learning. After all, who would want to publicly state achievement intentions and performance standards that aren't commendable? And if authorities mislead us about their intentions and performance they can be found out and exposed as liars. It is true that, in some cultures, wealthy people as owner-managers may not care about public loss of face if they are held to account and found out, but our politicians, corporate board members and executives of public companies likely would care.

The public answering requirement is unassailable because it tells no one how to do his or her job. Who gets what in society stems from political processes, but the public answering requirement simply obliges people to explain something to all – before and after the fact. The requirement is politically non-partisan because no political party in its right mind would say that citizens shouldn't be adequately informed. And public answering adds no significant cost. To do their jobs properly, decision-makers must know the implications of what they propose and how they will carry it out. They must also know their results and the learning they need to apply. What they know, they can report.

A valid priority in academic research is to identify the societal cost of having poor or no answering before and after the fact. Most requests for information under Canadian Access to Information legislation can be attributed to inadequate public answering. Misleading answering – or none at all – leads to low trust in our institutions, and that leads to access demands. The cost of dealing with access requests is significant when we count in the time and effort spent by staff of an accountable organization instructed to defeat the purpose of the access request – an example being the Somalia case.

Applying the Precautionary Principle to Accountability

Requiring adequate public answering applies the precautionary principle that we know from risks in food safety and environmental protection. In essence, the principle says that we don't proceed without reasonable assurance that it is safe to do so, and, if we are unsure, we err on the side of caution. It is the opposite of authorities going ahead unless some person or group conclusively proves it is unsafe. The precautionary principle is embodied in the citizen concern about sale of unlabelled, genetically modified foods (GMF), and the authorization of their production. The range of decisions disregarding the precautionary principle runs from the fatal U.S. *Challenger* space shuttle launch to the loss of the North Atlantic cod fishery. In the horror stories of Chapter 1, authorities disregarded the principle. They were not ignorant of it.

Today we must apply the precautionary principle to the intentions of all authorities. We must have authorities publicly demonstrate that they have informed themselves sufficiently about the implications of what they intend, and that what they intend would not lead to harm. When we apply the principle we see immediately that we have been allowing reverse onus – the practice of requiring that citizens prove that politicians' or corporations' intentions are unsafe. This is quite the opposite of citizens requiring the authorities to provide reasonable assurance that their intentions won't lead to harm. Allowing authorities to shift the answering obligation from themselves to those who should be holding to account spells the end of citizen control of outcomes.

Coupled with reverse onus is the aim of corporations to have us think that our tolerance of risk is unacceptably low.[4] This saves corporations from having to give assurances about the safety of what they wish to produce as products. It would also save governments, as the regulators, from having to control the safety of products to a feasible standard. We see this happening now, with government political parties increasingly allowing corporations to police themselves in food, drugs and other responsibilities without public answering obligations. This can be expected to increase political donations from the corporate community, but it puts citizens at much higher risk. Citizens' expanding boycotts of genetically modified foods may be temporarily effective from country to country, but if the safety tolerances are relaxed in the law, citizens will eventually be taking more and higher personal and environmental risks across the board. The higher the risk that citizens accept, the greater the corporations' profits.

Applied to public answering, the precautionary principle tells us, for what authorities propose to do, "No disclosure of risks, intentions and reasoning and the extent of the authority's self-informing, no decision taken to go ahead." The principle says for performance, "No reporting of performance standards, management control and actual performance, no contract." If citizens have to make their own risk decisions, they must know more about the risks.

The precautionary principle also implies that we must identify and hold to account those who make the decisions: the real directing minds – the people who make or authorize the decisions producing important outcomes for others. If we are unhappy with the service of a restaurant or dry cleaner, we can hold the owner-manager to account. We can ask a simple question: "What is your own service performance standard, and do you think you've met it in this case?" If the service is delivered by a government department, we can ask a similar question of identifiable managers – if we can identify them and reach them.

But for the policy issue of what needs or wants our governments appear to be honouring, and for what groups in society and in what priority, we must hold the government's directing minds to account. The same holds for corporations. The public interest becomes important when safety or fairness imperatives conflict with the financial interests of corporate managers and owners – who constitute only a small part of the corporation's stakeholders.

Corporation managers answer within the corporation for the quality of their service delivery, but the corporate directing minds must answer publicly for their control responsibilities in supervising management, and for the extent to which their intentions serve the public interest. Within a company the directing minds are the identifiable board members – not just the "board of directors" as a collectivity. In local government they are the councillors whose faces we probably know well, and in provincial and federal executive governments they are the ministers of the Crown we so often see interviewed on news broadcasts. These are the people who must answer to the people they affect.

A property developer may apply to a city's planning department to build a housing project or office complex, but identifiable councillors (and perhaps provincial ministers as well) approve or disallow it. Hospitals close, and staffs are reduced from decisions actively made by health ministers and premiers, not by "restructuring commissions" spin-portrayed as bodies acting independently from the minister who in fact appoints them and gives them their marching orders. International trade agreements may be signed by trade ministers, but the directing minds are the countries' prime ministers and finance ministers.

The Westray mine inquiry let the responsible provincial ministers of the Crown responsible for mine safety off the hook, condemning only lower-level mine inspectors. We saw similar escapes by identifiable directing minds in the cases of the *Challenger* space shuttle, the *Herald of Free Enterprise* and the Canadian disgraces of Somalia and lethally contaminated blood. In none of these horror stories did the accountable directing minds adequately and publicly explain their management control intentions and performance standards, even when their decisions were to affect people in terrible ways.

Doing what we have always done – simply giving authorities statutory powers and duties – isn't enough. While the precautionary principle demands that we tell our authorities to state not only their intentions and reasoning but also how well they inform themselves for their decisions, we must go beyond that. We must have authorities state the performance standards they set for themselves and for others they supervise. If years of analysing two world wars has shown that the competence of politicians and generals was less than we would have expected, what evidence do we have in today's world to presume that the ability and motivation of people behind cabinet and boardroom doors is any better?

No other obligation of authorities is as fundamental yet so disregarded as the obligation to answer. Unless we require the right people to answer before they act, validate what they report and act on what they say, we will continue to invite decisions producing harm and injustice.

The Components of Reasonable Public Answering

We will never eliminate deception, but we can at least require authorities to tell us:

- what they intend to bring about, for whom, and why they think the outcomes they intend are fair – that is, who would benefit and who would pay, and why they should
- the extent to which they have informed themselves for the decisions they make
- what they specifically plan to achieve and their intended performance standards
- who would answer to whom, for what, if their proposals were to be accepted
- later, the results from their effort, as they see them, the learning they gained and how they applied that learning

Citizens can – and must – validate the fairness and completeness of the reporting, just as external auditors do for corporate financial reporting.

Because people in authority want certain outcomes for themselves and others, the most important part of answering is disclosure of intended outcomes – who would be affected, how, and why they should be. We owe this core component of public answering to University of Toronto Professor Emeritus Ursula Franklin, who pointed out in her 1989 Massey Lectures:

> Much clarification can be gained by focusing on language as an expression of values and priorities. Whenever someone talks to you about the benefits and costs of a particular project, don't ask "What benefits?" ask "*Whose* benefits, and *whose* costs?" [5]

We must ask authorities to make this clear for both the short and longer term. We can ask for authorities' intentions and reasoning to be laid out in a simple equity statement made available for public challenge. (This statement is described in Chapter 5.) For important proposals, equity statements answer the "who" questions, explaining the intended outcomes, for whom, and providing a basis for holding decision-makers to account. For example, no such statement was provided to Canadians by the federal Trade Minister when the terms of OECD's proposed Multilateral Agreement on Investment (MAI) were exposed in early 1999. Yet the government had the information to provide it (See Appendix 1).

The second component of authorities' answering before the fact is reporting the extent to which they have informed themselves to make important "who" decisions. The self-informing obligation was set out by the CCAF-FCVI (formerly called the Canadian Comprehensive Auditing Foundation), a research and education foundation for governing bodies, management and auditors. Effective governing bodies

> know what constitutes reasonable information for good governance and obtain it.[6]

Again, to use the MAI as an example, it was clear that Members of Parliament didn't have the information they needed to supply to their constituents a credible equity statement for the MAI as support for how they would vote on what transnational corporations intended through the MAI. Each province's obligation to learn from the blood disgrace (and, failing to heed that stark lesson, Ontario's Walkerton) and to face up to the precautionary steps needed is part of government responsibility to obtain reasonable information for good governance and apply it.

When managers report to a governing board or to employees, and when a governing board reports to organization members and externally to the public, or when an executive government reports to a legislature and to the public, answering before the fact says:

> These are the outcomes we intend, for whom, and why, and here are our specific achievement objectives and performance standards. Do you have a problem with them?

Outcomes are results, not outputs. For example, good health, safe workplaces and fair societies are outcomes. Well-staffed hospitals and effective health promotion are means for producing intended outcomes in health. As with US President Kennedy's decision to put a man on the moon, we start with the agreed outcome and work back. We mustn't confuse people's statements of intended activity with statements of their intended achievement, because intended activity can be simply busywork for appearances. Thus government intentions to "update," "promote," or "facilitate" aren't statements of intended accomplishment forming a basis for holding to account. Effort is not accomplishment, let alone effort only for appearances.

Public challenge of authorities' action intentions simply reflects what Peter Drucker said more than thirty years ago: "Without dissent, you don't know what the problem is." If the public answering and validation process is carried out reasonably well, the intentions of people in power who are motivated by greed and self-interest will be made visible, as can the intentions of those in power who uphold reciprocity. The validation-challenge process invites those authorities who intend to be unfair to concede the fact.

The next most important reporting before the fact is reporting the performance standards that authorities intend for themselves and for those whom they supervise. These include the quality of their control processes (called management control) that cause to happen that which should happen and cause not to happen that which shouldn't. Performance standards clarify whose needs are to be honoured, and how. They also help clarify the ability and motivation of those with the responsibilities, and how they plan to cope with external constraints.

Knowing authorities' performance standards allows us to track how well they are carrying out agreed aims. For example, a public interest organization can ask a person or body having a safety regulatory duty: "What are your performance standards for upholding the precautionary principle and reaching an informed decision, as regulator, on whether product X should be licenced or banned?" This is a legitimate question that requires a public answer.

Then comes reporting after the fact. This answering says:

> These are the results of our effort, as we see them, and why they are different from what was intended (if that is the case). This is the learning we gained and how we applied it, and this is what we plan to do in future. Is it what you had in mind?

Answering for results and learning allows us to judge overall how well those in authority carried out their duty. But to assess performance fairly, we have to know what authorities think is within their control and how they are coping with external constraints beyond their control. It is fair to have the accountable report, but it is also fair that they be given the protection to report what they think stands in the way of their planned achievement, and how they are coping with the external constraints.

When we require the accountable to report the use they made of what they learned, this implies that they learn. Today, authors and consultants work with managers to make organizations "learning organizations" and to have learning valued as much as the current year's profits. They argue that the ability of people in organizations to learn quickly and respond quickly will influence organizational success in the future. But simply exhorting the creation of learning organizations doesn't suffice. There is enough agreement on the nature of learning in organizations to require that diligence standards for learning be forged, accepted and accounted for. To sustain and improve performance, governing bodies must know what works in their organizations. Therefore, governing bodies can be asked to assert publicly whether their organizations have met learning standards reasonable in their circumstances. And if managers account for what produced good performance, their successors will find it harder to disregard or dismantle this answering practice.

The large public interest organizations have the collective power to create the climate of opinion to bring about adequate public answering. Regardless whether these organizations champion accountability, citizens can simply ask their respective elected representatives to make basic expectations for answering the law. Legislation is key because executive governments and corporate directors have to obey the law. Auditors report on compliance with the law (or if they don't, they can be asked to do so), and citizens can require their elected representatives to ensure that the law is complied with. These are reasonable expectations for authorities' answering. Chapter 5 discusses the issue of legislating public answering expectations.

Fair and complete answering can be expected to earn public trust, but we mustn't forget that how we act on information reported to us is important. If we don't deal responsibly with answering given in good faith, it won't be given twice.

Validating the Answering

Public trust in authorities has to be earned. It doesn't come automatically with the office. That is why we must validate authorities' public answering. And that is why we have professional audit of corporations' published financial statements. Audit's main purpose is to assess the fairness and completeness of answering given in an accountability relationship. It is not to give the accountability reporting for those with the responsibilities. Professional audit is called for when the validation of reporting requires a high level of rigour. But in governments, where departments and agencies are not accounting adequately for their intentions and results and are not being made to, auditors serving legislators must audit government performance direct. This means giving legislators the departmental performance information that departments and agencies themselves should themselves be giving. But because accountability is politically neutral, it is reasonable to ask legislative auditors to propose the public answering standards for ministers and officials beyond financial results. Chapter 5 also comments on audit.

Why We Lack Public Answering

We don't have public answering standards in our national constitutions because our laws are drafted by people in power, and people in power don't like the idea of having to answer publicly. In our parliamentary system, governing-party ministers propose the laws that their party majority then passes in the legislature. At their level, ministers have been accountable only within the rituals of their legislative chambers.

If the ministers of any party in power were to intend adequate public answering by institutions for important responsibilities, someone would quickly point out that it should apply to ministers first.

Authorities realize that full and fair public answering shares power, and people in authority who enjoy power tend not to want to share it. The rarity of genuine public consultation before politicians' decision-making illustrates this. The problem is that those having power in government control the means of installing the answering requirement in the law, and those with power in organizations control the organizations' charters and by-laws that instruct the organization's officials on their answering obligations. Few if any organizations have rules requiring their executive bodies to answer fully, fairly and regularly for its intentions, performance standards and accomplishment, let alone learning. And government's rules for incorporation don't ask for it.

Government-party legislators don't propose what ministers don't want proposed. The opposition legislators either haven't caught on to the power of the public answering obligation or shy from the idea that it would apply to them if they were in power. As citizens, we haven't set standards for our elected representatives; we have simply elected them. We give them power and then leave them alone until harm, injustice or gross waste happens. But then the government uses its power to defeat challenge in the courts and uses limitless spin to defeat challenge through the media. Since we send no one to jail when preventable harm or unlawful acts happen, why should the accountable account?

We continue to give people responsibility and the power to act, but we don't make them answer for their responsibilities. Instead, when harm occurs we demand more regulations, more audits, and generally more "checks and balances." Then we act freshly surprised when these are ignored. So we add still more regulations. Thus authorities feel no pressure to install answering standards.

At least two types of barrier stand in the way of installing public answering by authorities. One is the predictable resistance of authorities to account, and the second is citizens' failure to demand it. Reasons for citizen failure include lack of understanding of what public answering is and what it can achieve, but they also include undue deference to authority, and apathy.

Knowledgeable observers of political and corporate organizations haven't included in their writings the need for public answering and made a case for it. The large activist organizations tend to do what they know best, which is awareness-building and fighting. And as a response to authorities' intentions, defiance is only defiance; it doesn't propose who should have what responsibility and answering obligations. However, authorities will answer if a climate of public opinion forces elected representatives to force it, and certainly if the law requires it. Once authorities start answering, it can be worked up to an acceptable level.

Some people in authority (for example, very senior civil servants convinced of their good intentions and competence) think that they needn't account to the public. They may well be performing in exemplary ways, but unless they publicly account for their intentions and their performance in the public interest, there will be no check on either their ability or motivation and, therefore, no evidence for public trust in them.

But it still comes down to citizens themselves. The underlying barrier to adequate public answering is summed up in Pogo's observation: "We have met the enemy, and he is us." Citizens having sufficient initiative can understand what public answering means and how it can help increase safety and fairness in society. They can cut through authorities' fog and deception ploys. They can act to exact answering, even if they act in only a modest way. But to have accountability work in society, we have to overcome centuries of citizen conditioning in deference to authority, and we have to overcome citizen apathy.

Citizens' groups still write to authorities deferentially, in the language of supplicants, yet these same citizens pay the salaries of the authorities who work for them. Citizens' groups write, "We would be grateful if you would consider…" instead of writing, "We think it reasonable that you tell us …" Part of the deference problem is cultural, evidenced in class structures that reinforce deference and supplication. Yet the British don't hesitate to apply the word "sleaze" to politicians' actions. Canadians don't, perhaps because doing so would mean that they would have to do something about it.

Somewhere along the line the leaders who had stature through their courage, deeds and thinking began to lose their power in society to people who acquired social status through their wealth, political skills or opportunism. Today we have the dangerous situation in government where status, which is appointed authority, takes precedence over and even drives out stature, which is respect earned from expertise and integrity. This is happening in the departments where citizens rely on professionals and scientists, such as in health, fisheries, agriculture and the environment.

Decisions on health and safety regulation are now being made by officials who are appointed to further ministers' agendas and who have no stature in health protection and whose motivation is unknown to the public. A simple example is the federal executive government appointing an assistant deputy minister from the Department of National Defence (where supplier industry relations are important) to head the government's Health Protection Branch responsible for safety in drugs licencing.

As well, professionals and scientists outside government having uncertain or declining stature succumb to the anticipation of status appointments and other rewards. They don't object when an executive government or a corporation simply decrees that a product or process is safe, or that a "new role" is needed within government for a research agency or for a prevention responsibility that would have the effect of gutting the prevention capability.

Citizens who give undue deference to authorities may grumble at what authorities do, but they accept it. An example is the federal Minister of Defence getting away with truncating the inquiry of the credentialled and independent commission investigating the killing of Somalians by Canadian soldiers. This was done when the inquiry was starting to track up to the responsibilities of the Deputy Minister of Defence and Minister. Later, the successor Minister and the Prime Minister simply decree, with equal success, that the Commissioners' report got it wrong. They knew the Canadian public would be patsies.

Citizen denial is also a syndrome. Citizens may not want to face the possibility that those in authority don't know what they are doing or are wrongly motivated. For example, older Canadians who remember what honour and standards are may not want to lose respect for the most senior ranks of the Canadian military. They find it difficult to accept that senior officers could operate by whim in peacetime. Disillusionment is even harder to accept by those within the Forces, who expect their leaders to be models of integrity and to resist politicization. The ranks have always put their faith in top command under the contract, "be loyal and we will look after you." Then they find that top command is suddenly cutting personnel to reduce costs, through medical criteria designed by the military. They see their top general in the twilight of his command taking a public fall for the Prime Minister, and inept appearances spin by officers when failure or sub-standard performance is exposed.

Some of us may want to maintain blind faith in political leaders, perhaps preferring them to be "often wrong but never in doubt." Then, when we are faced with our leaders being wrong-headed or ill-intentioned, we blame – but only after the fact, when it is safe – and we take no responsibility ourselves for preventing harmful intentions by those who work for us. One problem in holding government to account is that a large number of citizens are directly or indirectly employed by the various governments and their agencies. Their tendency may be not to rock the boat. The number of citizens totally independent of government payrolls, contracts or funding influence is less than we would think.

Trust in authorities' fairness and competence must be based on evidence, not deference or denial. So long as we are unduly deferential to authority, we will never achieve adequate public answering. A reality check would be: "What *evidence* do I have that that officials X, Y and Z are competent and soundly motivated to serve the public interest in their work? What *evidence* do I have that they are not motivated primarily by personal gain in money and status, either immediate or in prospect?" Even without this check, citizens comfortable with deference don't have to cancel it entirely in asking for adequate public answering, because all that is asked for is explanation. When our job as citizens is to combat erosion of standards and deal with globalization risks over the next decades, undue deference, blind faith and empty blaming are equally obsolete and equally dangerous.

Perhaps the most difficult problem is apathy. Some citizens, perhaps most, would rather leave problems to others or not even think about the duties of authorities unless it had an impact on them personally. We see this inside organizations as well, when employees fail to support their fellow employees of conscience blowing the whistle to try to maintain integrity.

Still other citizens unabashedly serve only their own self-interest and expect others to do the same. These people refuse to support common sharing of community costs such as medicare, and may even lobby against it. Public answering isn't useful to them because they wish only to work the system for themselves. Rather than do anything to help fix medicare or public school quality, they would rather pay for private supply for health care and education – for themselves – but only because they are well off. We therefore need adequate public explanation of how medicare and school systems can be maintained as the fairest and most economical approach for all.

Still another concern is that if answering is given in good faith, those with the duty to hold to account and to receive the accountings – legislators and citizens – will realize that they have to act responsibly on the reporting. It will be easy to tell if the response of those holding to account is sensible. Backbenchers in a legislature, feeling impotent as it is and perhaps thinking that, having no power to act on honest answering, they would be quickly "found out" as impotent by their constituents, may shy away from asking for honest and complete answering. As we have seen, the provincial and federal legislatures have never examined the adequacy of the accountability arrangements for the Canadian Blood Services that replaced the Red Cross in national blood distribution.

Since the reasons why we don't have adequate public answering are an obvious subject for research, the obvious question is why academics and research organizations haven't undertaken it.

The foregoing needn't be a bleak picture if we understand the purpose of adequate public answering, which is to make us better informed and to be able to better predict what authorities will do for us or to us in the future. Even if we care nothing about greater fairness in society, we should want greater predictive ability. Validated public answering shouldn't be hard to achieve, once citizens decide they want it, because authorities have no argument to put up against it. The public answering requirement holds up a mirror that says to citizens, "This is what's going on; is it what you had in mind?" The democratic process then allows citizens to act or not act.

When enough citizens at large and public interest organization leaders understand why adequate public answering is important, we can get going on it.

Citizen response to public answering is not just to commend, alter or halt what is proposed. It is also to ensure that the law includes fundamental rules that set and clarify not only authorities' responsibilities but also their public answering obligations. These rules are not to be broken without the consent of the public, and must cover how the most important answering is to be validated. Rules for answering and validation must be written to head off deception and spin, and can be drafted for clusters of responsibilities by public interest organizations knowledgeable about those responsibilities – and the deception practices used by authorities.

Summary

Answering the question "Who is accountable to whom, for what?" clarifies responsibilities, reduces uncertainty and helps identify gaps in important responsibilities for safety and fairness. If we accept the argument that the requirement to answer influences the conduct of authorities, and that adequate public answering allows us to increase our control of what goes on, holding fairly to account will fundamentally change the relationship between citizens and people in authority. Through practice in holding to account, citizens will increase their competence in their duty to oversee authorities.

This doesn't mean that we must all get involved with every intention affecting the public in important ways. We can ask public interest organizations, unions, churches and journalists to act for us in having authorities publicly answer the "who" questions. The "who benefits and who pays" assertions of people in authority can be publicly validated by people who understand the issues. Elected representatives and corporate directing minds will soon get the message about full and fair disclosure of their intentions and reasoning. Publicly-challenged statements of the fairness trade-offs implicit in important proposals will then point to the course of action citizens ought to endorse.

When There Is No Time...

If the situation calls for action to stop something and there is no time to develop accountability levers to protect safety, justice and fairness, citizens must reach for the best activist strategy they can find and get at it with all the force they can muster. Concurrently, however, activists need to understand why they have to fight and should start work on getting adequate public answering in the areas they are concerned with. Otherwise harmful intentions will only repeat later, in some other issue, or even repeat for the same issue, under a different guise.

Endnotes

1 Letter to John Jay, 8 May 1796

2 Patricia Day and Rudolf Klein, *Accountabilities: Five Public Services*, London, Tavistock, 1987, p.6-7

3 James D. Thompson, *Organizations in Action,* (New York, McGraw Hill, 1967)

4 For example, the Fraser Institute in Vancouver brought to its 1999 Ottawa conference "Junk Science Junk Policy" a Lecturer from England's Aston Business School to argue the point.

5 Ursula Franklin, *The Real World of Technology*, (1989 Massey Lectures, Toronto, CBC Enterprises, 1990.) p.124

6 "Principles of Effective Governance," CCAF-FCVI, Ottawa, 1994

CHAPTER 3

The Language of Deception

Deception[1]

Deception by governments and other institutions is now a culture: most questions put to them are met with spin. Deception disables citizens for their scrutiny duty, thus allowing institutions to serve their own interests. The institutions, through their appointed masks, use language as a potent weapon against reality and so against being made accountable for actions and omissions running counter to the public interest and their own official responsibility. Elected and appointed officials placing self-interest before the public interest use language to deny, obstruct and confuse. While the directing minds for deception are arrogant, their masks are compliant.

Deception means imposing a false notion, idea or belief that causes ignorance, bewilderment or helplessness.[2] It means purposefully misleading, creating false appearances, deluding people or otherwise obscuring the truth, as in spin. It doesn't mean innocently misleading.

Through the use of language, deception conditions the misled not to challenge what the directing minds want to do.

Sissela Bok argues that a lie is any intentionally deceptive message that is stated.[3] Lying forms part of deception, but deception is broader. Deception practices can include people in authority simply decreeing something and counting on their status to cause it to be accepted, or using their resources and influence to discredit someone challenging their intentions, or causing divisiveness in groups organizing to challenge them. But imposing false beliefs is generally done through language that lulls or creates false impressions, as in spin-doctoring for the public at large. Or it can be done through spoken language that tricks, lulls or confuses us.

As Bok notes:

> In law and in journalism, in government and in the social sciences, decep-
> tion is taken for granted when it is felt to be excusable by those who tell the
> lies and who tend also to make the rules. Government officials and those
> who run for elections often deceive when they can get away with it and
> when they assume that the true state of affairs is beyond the comprehension
> of citizens.[4]

Bok was writing in the 1970s. Today citizens are likely to grasp the implications of the
true state of affairs as well or better than ever, but they can still back away from the truth.
The task is therefore to first make the truth visible. Whether citizens want to know the
truth, and what they would do if they had it, are questions that must also be faced. The
belief by authorities that they can get way with something has probably become stronger
as citizens tolerate ever-increasing deception while not realizing why the precautionary
principle must be applied to answering. The moment we apply the precautionary principle to what authorities say, we are likely to come away with a different take on what they
say.

The present ease and speed of communication, far from helping clarity and sense, has
created a glut of verbiage, most of it perhaps unrealized and institutional in origin. This
makes it easier for politicians to obscure their meanings, so that they can deny on Monday
what they said on Friday. Lawyers are praised – and paid – for amorality and legal niceties
that increase confusion about who is responsible and accountable for what. They serve
their clients, but not necessarily the public interest. Lawyers and other professions avoid
the accountability question for themselves.

Deception includes authorities falsifying or withholding important information that
should be provided to the public. Without "a right understanding of matters," citizens
can't make sensible decisions about authorities' intentions that would affect them in important ways. Deception erodes the answering obligation because the citizens who should
exact public answering for particular responsibilities are lulled or tricked into thinking it
isn't necessary. (The fostering of deception by citizens' using supplicating language is discussed in Chapter 14 on holding to account.) Since deception is the opposite of answering, it follows that holding effectively to account can limit deception.

Unneeded secrecy is also a means of deception. Valid needs for secrecy exist, as in
national security or for a cooking recipe in honest business competition. But those in
authority are helped in deception if the scope of secrecy can somehow be extended to
cover up incompetence, disregard of the precautionary principle, unfair or illegal decisions, and plain wrong policy from being cavalier about being adequately informed. Thus

in the Canadian parliamentary system, much information in government can be made secret by calling it a cabinet document. But it is also fair to expect that opposition parties, media and some interest groups may not responsibly use information on cabinet deliberations that amounted to legitimate sorting-out of political options.

Language Defeating Accountability

Truthful language can earn trust, but what we read or hear can also suggest the need for an immediate deception audit. When used by a Churchill, language can inspire, motivate and even raise people's ability. Today it is more often used to anaesthetize us so that we fail to question what should be questioned. This was George Orwell's central point in his writing about the use of language by authorities. As George Woodcock put it in his radio biography of Orwell:

> Orwell was really insisting on the idea that tyranny thrives on the manipulation of truth, of the twisting of the truth. And the twisting of the truth also means the twisting of the language, the making of language inexact, because if your language is evasive, it is possible to defend what is otherwise indefensible.[5]

Authorities who choose language to evade responsibilities and answering obligations use different strategies for different situations. When they are confident of not being challenged, they may simply decree. Or when they are not so confident, they may use euphemism that suggests something is not as bad as it actually is and, therefore, need not be examined. They may use language that lulls the listener into thinking matters are being taken care of and, therefore, to feel no discomfort or guilt by not acting. Or it can be righteous language, intended to bulldoze the listener into submission. Or language that tricks the listener. These tactics are helped when examiners asked to inquire into events causing harm use language in their reports that pulls punches, whether through euphemism or deference.

Language that simply decrees. In using decree to avoid answering, a person of status but not necessarily stature simply pronounces instead of answering for responsibilities, expecting his or her status to produce acceptance. The example cited in Chapter 2 was the Canadian Minister of National Defence and the Prime Minister publicly dismissing the report of the commission inquiring into the killing of Somalians by Canadian peacekeeping soldiers. The ministers assumed that their positions would render them exempt from answering for their responsibilities and decisions, and allow their decrees to go unchallenged.

When an Ontario education minister says that a major province-wide high school curriculum "has been properly planned" yet the curriculum won't be available before June for a September school year, the minister is counting on ministerial status to make the assertion credible.[6] A typical form of decree statement is a government official saying about a safety concern in the news, "Public safety is not compromised at this time. We're dealing with it using various strategies[7]

A more subtle form of decree-as-answering is a Saskatchewan government official saying, "We take seriously their (nurses') concerns," in effect saying, "Leave it with us" and telling the public to accept the motivation and ability of the government on faith. Not conceded is that raw political power forced the government to do something about nurses' pay and overwork.[8]

In a legislature, arrogance can be a minister or first minister uttering a partisan banality rather than properly answering a legitimate Opposition question. The lack of legislature rules requiring ministers to answer, let alone usefully, combines with obedience in the government majority benches to allow patronizing non-answers by ministers.

Another type of arrogance is an authority making a public statement reckless as to its validity. An example is the Minister of National Defence, announcing a new Judge Advocate General in 1998, saying to the press that the military will now have "a system more accountable, open and fair across all ranks."[9] At the time he made this statement, the Minister knew that public trust in top command was at an all-time low; that evidence of adequate answering and change of thinking at the top was critical to rebuilding public trust in the senior military; that the Judge Advocate General he was appointing was not independent of top command; and that he had refused to appoint an Inspector General for the Canadian Forces, as the Somalia Commission had strongly recommended. This meant that the Minister's assertion said unabashedly to Canadians, "You accept anything and never hold us to account, so here's one more in your face, just to remind you of who's boss."

Language that distorts. Straight lying to distort is one thing, but a recent example of distortion is the portrayal of the American military's July 2001 missile interception exercise as successful. This was important to the military, because the first such test failed. But the "successful" hit was rigged. There was a helpful guidance beacon on the target that obviously wouldn't be there in an actual situation.[10]

Language that lulls. Authorities with public answering obligations can choose language that lulls people into not holding to account for what actually happened. The most common form is euphemism, and the most notable example of recent years is "ethnic cleansing," invented to have mass murderers perceived as cleansers. We all know that the term means genocide, which means mass murder, not just the idea of unlawfully evicting people and stealing their property on the grounds of cultural antipathy. Cloaking murder with the virtue of cleansing diverts us from identifying and holding to account the directing minds of mass murder. We didn't even hold journalists to account for why they accepted the term "ethnic cleansing." In mid-1999 we still heard "cleansing of villages" by radio journalists reporting on Bosnian Serbs.[11]

Canada's own leading euphemism is "tainted blood," used to describe lethally contaminated blood distributed by an unregulated Canadian Red Cross in the 1980s. Journalists lacked the courage to adopt a term that could point to authorities' responsibility, even as people were dying. They didn't even use the term "contaminated," as the French did. The earlier Canadian media use of "tainted" was more honest. It was used for an episode of poorly-inspected canned tuna reaching grocery shelves, with some of the product simply being discoloured. Now we get "tainted letters" (anthrax).

Euphemisms are everywhere:

smart bombs (meaning Gulf war bombs lauded for their technology in reducing harm to citizens but which didn't work)

collateral damage (meaning civilians killed)

outplacement and **downsizing** (meaning firing workers)

we're doing better (government talk about creating jobs but with no mention of an achievement standard being met)

tamper with files (meaning documents were destroyed)

the guidelines weren't clear (meaning public servants broke obvious fundamental rules)

liberalization of trade (meaning our lives are to be ruled by the large corporations)

communication (meaning corporations' published financial statements accounting for financial performance)

the intercept was not achieved (meaning that an anti-missile weapon simply didn't work)

practical shooting (meaning combat-simulation target shooting by civilians shooting at human-image targets)

critical care by-pass (meaning the hospital's emergency unit will refuse ambulances)

incident (meaning accident or performance failure)

bolster arrest powers (meaning introducing sweeping unprecedented 'preventive arrest')

Lulling language suggests that authorities are acting responsibly, the problem is in good hands and everything reasonable is being done. This language counts on the perceived legitimacy or expertise of the speaking authority. It ranges from U.S. President

Ronald Regan, as Commander in Chief, saying to Americans after the U.S. marines were killed in their camp in Lebanon, "I take full responsibility" (as if the President were significant in the quality of security management control for U.S. military bases) to a Canadian government spokesperson saying of farmers, "We have one of the best safety nets in the world for farmers" (meaning that 90% of the government contingency fund is for 10% of the farmers).[12]

Language designed to reassure but give no commitment is often given away by statements of empathy ("We share your concern"). Or the commitment is to activity rather than achievement. Thus a minister responsible for prisons says, "It would be silly of me to say that there are no drugs in the prisons. What I'm saying is that I'm addressing it,"[13] as if this response were more informative than the minister reporting that he showed up for work that morning.

Or the head of the Canadian Blood Services saying, in response to criticism that the operations of the new agency replacing the Red Cross are still not visible, that operations are "running smoothly,"[14] and are focused on "best practices."[15] This reports nothing about the agency's own standards for blood safety. Members of governing boards for such agencies who say, "We have to challenge ourselves" are worrisome.[16]

Another form of accountability evasion asserts high moral dedication to make the speaker appear beyond reproach. An example is a chemical corporation executive appearing before a Canadian Senate committee examining the safety of bovine growth hormones who says, "I look at myself in the mirror each morning and feel ok."[17]

Or the strategy is to cause a self-congratulatory mood that takes media and citizen attention away from the lack of answering for the real reasons for an outcome. An example is the federal Minister of Finance pronouncing a large government surplus, likely understated at that, produced by slashes in health and other social expenditure: " Canadians can be proud. This is their victory."[18]

Lulling terms include "harmonizing" (meaning that standards drop to the lowest negotiated international common denominator); "going forward" (in closing a mine)[19]; an International Olympic Committee senior official's reassuring "Recover, re-group and move on"[20] (meaning that it's questionable whether the underlying conditions allowing corruption will be dealt with); or an authority announcing a "full independent inquiry " (without saying what "full," "independent" and "inquiry" mean).

Language that denies. Denial has the trappings of decree. The most common example is, "No decision has been made." Yet the process of conditioning the environment of decision among the decision-makers is likely complete and all that remains is the announcement. A classic example is the OECD's proposed Multilateral Agreement on Investment, whose provisions would overturn core social, health and environmental protection policies in the hitherto sovereign countries that were to be parties to the agreement. Opponents in parliamentary committee meetings were told, "Since there is no agreement (yet), you have no case." Had the proposed terms been agreed, it would have been too late to challenge them.

Language that sounds plausible but isn't. Seemly plausible language must be examined. For example, during the 1999 Olympic Committee scandal, a governing-board member of an Olympic-related body said, "I placed my faith in the executive committee....I would like to have had more information and been able to ask more questions."[21] Yet members of governing bodies have the obligation to inform themselves adequately, and the power to demand the information. If they cannot get the information, they can resign and publicly say why.

The accountability evasion can be subtle. When a government document like the United Kingdom's Citizen's Charter for the UK income tax department says, "Citizens have the right to expect..." it sounds boldly accountable – until we realize that the legitimacy of citizens having expectations is axiomatic. The assertion not given is what the minister and senior officials of the department actually commit to achieving. Or a government may say, in an assertion attached to its annual financial statements, "We have systems in place designed to..." This is quite different from saying, "We have systems in place that..." The first statement is a statement of intention as a "socially-desirable response." The second statement, not given, would be a statement of actual achievement in control.

Language that righteously attacks. One example is a United Kingdom defence minister responding in July 1999 to British generals publicly discounting the effectiveness of NATO air strikes in Yugoslavia: "We achieved our aims; we're in there now.... I would have thought they would have been (supportive) rather than carping on the side."[22] In Canada we had the Prime Minister in May 1999 charging that an Opposition member in the House of Commons who questioned a connection between a minister and a corporation purchasing contaminated blood from Arkansas jail donors in the 1980s was "making a mockery of democracy to reach that far into the past."[23] Regardless whether there had been a connection, the executive government's own blood inquiry commission into contaminated blood reached even further into the past.

Language that exonerates. Language by independent examiners that has an exonerating effect doesn't help. For example, the title of the Nova Scotia public inquiry report on the Westray mine deaths is "The Westray Story: A Predictable Path to Disaster." The title tends to translate life-and-death responsibilities into a story. It doesn't suggest that the

Commissioner's report will be an instructive briefing for citizens laying out who, in the Commissioner's view, caused what; who was ultimately responsible and accountable; and what it takes for Nova Scotians, through legislation and holding relentlessly to account, to prevent needless workplace deaths in the future.

Similarly, a commission examining sexual abuse cases of Canadian Aboriginal children in church-run residential schools states its purpose as "exploring the tragedy" (of the abuses)[24]

The words "disaster" and "tragedy" suggest acts of God, not authorities' performance failures and questions of motivation. A seaworthy ship, ably-captained, crewed and navigated, sinking in sudden and unpredictable lethal weather can be called an act of God. So might schizophrenia, in striking the hundredth person. But preventable coal mine explosions and abuses of children are not.

Another style of exoneration language takes the form, "Because of X, the authority could not do Y" when X is wholly within the control of the authority. Thus Britain's National Health Service is reported as "starving for lack of resources,"[25] when the resources allotted to the Service, relative to politicians' wants such as spending public money in support of arms sales, are entirely within the control of the executive government. Another example is Commissioner Krever commenting in his blood inquiry report that the Canadian federal government's Bureau of Biologics resource limitations prevented it from doing its job when the resource allocation within the Department of Health was entirely controlled by the Minister and Deputy Minister. (See Chapter 6).

An auditor general may report that internal control in a particular unit or department of government was "weak," but go on to say, "therefore the department could not..." This logic lapse exonerates, because the quality of control within the department was entirely the decision of the department's top management.

If the reporting style of an audit office uses headings of the type, "X could be improved," it lets the accountable department management off the hook, since virtually any performance can be improved. It fails to tell legislators and the public whether a reasonable performance standard was met. Or an auditor general may describe an executive government's accounting practices as "acceptable but not appropriate." What needs to be said in the same breath is that the legally-allowed accounting practices of the government permit financial deception; that the particular practice used likely misled the legislature; and that the law should be changed to force the most useful reporting for the legislators' decision-making.

Language that fails to locate accountability. The most common type of unhelpful language holds things to account rather than identifiable human beings. The obvious examples are "The government should…" or "the corporation should…." This diverts attention from the identifiable directing minds of the executive government and the members of the corporation's board of directors.

The most familiar accountability deflector is "the system." When we say "You can't beat the system," we mean that we haven't tried to identify the directing minds and hold them to account. But "system" can also be used by the accountable to evade accountability. Thus a federal Justice Minister is allowed to say about Donald Marshall, David Milgaard and Guy Paul Morin, each wrongfully imprisoned for more than a decade, "Our justice system can make mistakes."[26] The harm done to these men (and many other persons wrongfully convicted) means that we don't have a justice system, we have only a legal system. The statement further implies that the Minister is not responsible for turning the norms of the legal profession, police and courts into a justice system operating to a standard that citizens have a right to see met.

Deception tactics. Recognizing the following tactics for particular events or issues can help us to recognize others:

Change the scope. In this, the written or spoken response to a complaint or enquiry reverses the dimension. A specific question about the discharge of an important responsibility produces a well-sounding but empty generalization – such as, "We have 4500 people in this organization; we can't oversee everything." But a general and open-ended request for information is answered by a minutely detailed description of the smallest component part of the subject. In either case the responding person claims to have answered but has done no such thing.

Rewrite the question. Here the response follows a restatement of the question in terms favourable to what the respondent wants to say. This is the usual practice for government ministers in a legislature when the minister answers a question not asked, such as praising a government activity when the Opposition questioner has asked whether an achievement standard was met, or trumpeting an achievement (to thunderous backbench applause) in a political area not asked about.

Pretend the problem is new and ignore what's been agreed. An example is the federal Health Minister saying in January 2000, "If we had the wit to invent Medicare, we can find the will to save it."[27] This ignores the far-sightedness and political will of Tommy Douglas, the Saskatchewan premier who brought it about, and the will of the majority of Canadians, who have repeatedly demonstrated that they want medicare kept and improved.

Create a cooling distance. The objective is to separate the responsible persons from the cause of the complaint. The third person passive works admirably, as does repeated reference to time past. We move from, "I failed to meet an ethical standard," to "I made a mistake," to "Mistakes were made"[28] (omitting the what, when, by whom and why).

Invoke due process. Challenge of an authority's performance and decisions taken is met by the assertion that due process was followed. Given that a process was followed, whatever came of it must be right. Or, someone publicly pointing out an outrage is criticized for not using due process when the fairness of the due process hasn't been demonstrated and is held suspect by the public.

Hide the reason. A favourite of bureaucrats and consultants wanting a minister to spend money for something, and to have interest groups support it, is simply to say, "There is a need for..."

Use the passive voice. This hides the accountable decision-maker, as in "It was felt that..."

Convey helpless goodwill. The idea is to express willingness – even eagerness – to meet the questioner's wishes, but regretfully allow that the subject is too complex for a speedy answer or that another related inquiry process must be awaited first.

Invoke "positivism." This takes the well-known form of, "Lets put it behind us," or, "Lets move on." This means that attribution of harm to underlying causes need not be identified so as to ensure that the harm doesn't happen again.

Use a buzzword generator. The idea is to put together nice-sounding fog words or sentences to give the appearance of political achievement, such as "creative practical solutions to a changing world."[29] Or earnestness: "We have a good foundation and we're working very hard to build on that foundation."[30]

Appeal to modernity. The British Labour Party seized control of the words "new" and "modern" in its election campaign language to characterize Britain under a Labour Party, thus making the Conservatives "old" and "traditional."[31] But "new" was used by Canadian federal Health Department officials in their 1998 PR meetings with stakeholder groups on their "Transition" program apparently aimed at weakening federal legislation governing the Health Minister's responsibilities for protecting the health of citizens. Since the existing legislation satisfactorily directs the Minister in protection of Canadians, "transition" must mean something leading away from what is satisfactory. Yet officials characterized the existing legislation as a "1954 Dodge" – meaning that by definition the law couldn't be satisfactory or be efficiently consolidated.

Create a straw man. This shifts attention from a fundamental problem to one that is lesser or not relevant in the face of the real problem at issue. An example is a radio reporter concluding that comments made in Alberta by the federal Health Minister on Alberta's Bill 11 for privatizing health care "will do nothing to improve relations between Ottawa and Alberta."[32] The real issue is Canada-wide, and of much greater importance than whether a federal executive government bickers with a particular provincial one.

Capitalize on people's deference tendencies. This takes the form of a profession or governing body saying, "Leave it with us; it is an internal problem and we will fix it," when the problem is part of a syndrome that will only be fixed by an external force putting a gun to the head of the institution governing body or profession.

Suggest that considering something means answering for performance. A person in authority may say, "One should be mindful of..." but not intend answering for how he or she dealt with the considerations to be kept in mind.

Pass the buck. When there is no escape in spin language for something that happened, the message is that it is someone else's responsibility. For example, Canada's Prime Minister blamed the military when he failed to attend the funeral of Jordan's King Hussein in February 1999. The other heads of state got there, making the absence of the Prime Minister a national embarrassment. "...they [the military] couldn't take me there in time,"[33] said the PM. The Chief of the Defence Staff predictably accepted the blame, but it was the responsibility of the Prime Minister's staff, knowing the King was seriously ill, to have had a workable contingency plan if the Prime Minister decided to ski at Whistler. And it was the responsibility of the Prime Minister to have the staff that would tell the PM what needed to be done to ensure his attendance, and what would happen if he didn't make sure he was there.

At a more serious level for learning, the blame-someone-else testimony in the Ontario public inquiry into the Walkerton water contamination earned the public label "the blame game." Since the Walkerton deaths, as in blood and Westray, were a case of failed management control that includes safety control, the provincial executive government was the identifiable directing mind for the adequacy of the water safety control within the province – and still is.

Hiding the responsibility itself. For every important responsibility there is accountability. The simplest way to avoid being held to account is to keep silent on the bases for holding to account, and hope no one puts them before the public. Thus authorities don't state fully and fairly, or not at all:

- the outcomes they intend, for whom and why,
- their intended specific achievement and performance standards,
- their actual results, as they see them, and
- the learning they gained and how they applied it.

When this disclosure avoidance succeeds, those who don't accept the outcomes can only confront and blame, limited by their own resources for overturning a result or seeking redress.

Regular Deception Practice

Deception practice comes in many Ds: decree, deny, deflect, disown, divert, disguise, dissemble, distort, delete, delegate, delay, defer, divide, denounce, discredit, defame, and others. In a 1997 workshop on the culture and pattern of deception in institutions, the Alliance for Public Accountability opened discussion on deception using denial, delay, divide (and conquer) and discrediting as common practice. For example, the most obvious practice in discrediting is to label an employee of conscience who exposes a wrong or safety protection failure, or who questions senior management's motivation, as merely a "disgruntled employee." The basis used for the "disgruntlement" charge is that the employee hasn't risen in the organization. But promotions only go to those who go with the flow.

The Alliance's workshop included as deception the withholding of accountability information needed by citizens to assess an institution.. For example, an authority may say, using the change-of-scope ploy, "Our public answering fully meets the requirements of the Canadian Institute of Chartered Accountants." But reporting only financial results won't tell us about directing minds' compliance with the law, let alone their action intentions and reasoning, their key performance standards, their actual performance or their learning. Citizens may then think that this important information couldn't be all that important.

"Deny" also means, as well as denying fact or motivation, denying access to important information. Withholding information is clearly deceptive in the case of legislation introduced by government. For example, the federal government hasn't told Canadians that its environmental protection laws are weak in part because having weak legislation avoids jurisdiction confrontations with provincial governments. The federal legislation for species protection initially debated in early 1999 was pronounced by critics as being worse than useless because it contained no mandatory habitat protection – most habitats being on provincial land.[34]

Records are key. An important deception indicator is lack of adequate records management, because well-kept records locate responsibility and answering obligations and thus help with accurate attribution of cause.

The practice of deception includes the directing minds for deception cloning like-minded persons within the institutions, and intimidating all but resolute whistleblowers. Those who stand for truth and disclosure are first told that they are simply being stupid about what they stand to lose in rewards. But if they continue to resist, or threaten to speak out, they are quietly labelled the enemy and dealt with as such – losing their status and offices and being accused of what the military call conduct to the prejudice of good order and discipline. The others see what happens and keep their heads down. Hear, see and speak no evil: Survive.

Then, those compliant in the institution's ranks produce the language of deception for the masks, the people who make presentations at conferences or respond to the press. Like the corporate executive, they look themselves in the mirror and see only dedication and integrity. And if over half the citizens in a country like Canada depend on government for their livelihood in direct or indirect ways, they can be expected not to question executive government practices as much as they should.

The agenda of the directing minds for deception could include any or all of the following:

Paving the way:
- Ensure appearances come first: condition the public's perception, paying for it from program funds and calling it "communications."
- Engage consultant spin doctors for the language chosen for legislators and the public.
- Carefully select the organizations to declare as the stakeholder organizations to be consulted.

Dealing with opposition:
- Identify which important individuals in opposition to an intention have power, as opposed to simply passion, and design strategy accordingly. A common successful ploy is to co-opt a leader from a potentially-opposing activist organization by showering her or him with special attention, such as private meetings with a minister and status as a special adviser ("The Minister needs you.").
- Identify the wants of prominent citizens' organizations who would otherwise be part of opposition and give them something that can be expected to reduce their opposition effort.
- Declare general public consultation, but make the notice time allowed for citizen-group response too short to allow a proper challenge – and do this in the summer, when people are on holiday.
- Identify groups whose leaders are personal supporters of the politicians or other directing minds for the agenda and make sure those groups are in the consulted stakeholder group. They can be counted on to chip away at others trying to get to the bone or hold to account in the meetings.

- Actively promote reverse onus: make citizens prove a concern.
- Use legislation wording to defeat the public will. Legislation processes are kept within the legislature and are under government majority control. For example, when Albertans say that they don't want private hospitals, the government can have its legislation allow new surgical facilities that keep patients in overnight, i.e. private hospitals.
- Legislate several major changes at the same time. This will ensure that citizens' organizations can't effectively challenge them all.

Running the agenda:
- Generally, diffuse or deny responsibility and claim external constraints.
- Offer no public answering except generalities, but if forced to answer, claim that financial reporting norms for businesses and governments suffice for public answering.
- When major harm happens and the attribution of it could be dangerous, have the matter go before a court or public inquiry. The public will accept the claim that this prevents the accountable from answering until the inquiry has reported. "Let the inquiry do its job." No one will think of calling for an audit instead.
- Hide officials whose actions have been or could be exposed as counter to the public interest, or simply unlawful: promote or transfer them.

Deception can be achieved simply through withholding of information, but for the most part it is achieved through language. Its purpose is to alter perception to lessen public control over what people in power intend to do. There will always be deception, but the indicators are not difficult to recognize. Once deception has been identified, the task is to understand the motivation of those who produced or allowed it, and to understand its effects in terms of safety, fairness and justice.

Before deception can be capped, the syndrome and the methods used must be understood and their effects put before citizens for their reaction. Given that fellow citizens would tell us that they don't want deception, we can develop and circulate indicators that can be used to publicly identify deception. University students would be good at the project. We can call the indicators Institutional Deception Indicators. Those scoring high on the indicators get public attention from the deception squads.

Endnotes

[1] The late Leo Demesmaker contributed greatly to this chapter.
[2] Webster's Ninth New Collegiate Dictionary (1991)

[3] Sissela Bok, *Lying: Moral Choice in Public and Private Life,* Vintage Books 1989 (Pantheon 1978)

[4] Ibid., p.xvii

[5] Canadian Broadcasting Corporation, January 1984

[6] CBC Radio 4 March 1999

[7] CBC Radio 15 July 1999, Department of Transport official responding to a report of inspection staff shortages and morale problems in DOT

[8] CBC Radio 12 April 1999 on the Saskatchewan nurses' strike.

[9] CBC Radio 12 March 1998

[10] "Missile Test Succeeded - With Help from Sensor," Globe and Mail, 28 July 2001, p.A10

[11] CBC Radio 2 June 1999

[12] CBC Radio 7 October 1998

[13] CBC Radio 1 June 1999

[14] CBC Radio 16 July 1999

[15] CPAC TV 29 September 1998

[16] Ibid.

[17] CBC Radio 7 December 1998

[18] CBC Radio 24 February 1998

[19] CBC Radio 13 September 1999, Minister's statement on closing of the Devco mine.

[20] CBC Radio 17 March 1999

[21] CBC Radio 9 May 1999

[22] CBC Radio 7 July 1999

[23] CBC Radio 25 May 1999

[24] CBC Radio 23 March 2000

[25] CBC Radio 25 February 2000

[26] CBC Radio 26 August 1998

[27] CBC Radio 27 January 2000

[28] CBC Radio 1 October 1999, on the Japanese nuclear accident

[29] CBC Radio 29 August 1999, coverage of the NDP national conference

[30] CBC Radio 25 October 1999, the federal Agriculture Minister on support for farmers.

[31] Maurice Saatchi, "Why Labour Makes Britain Feel Good," *Daily Telegraph*, reprinted in the *Ottawa Citizen* 6 December 1997. p.B3

[32] CBC Radio 10 March 2000

[33] CBC Radio 9 February 1999

[34] CBC Radio 30 March 1999

CHAPTER 4

Twelve Principles of Accountability

Holding to account gives us greater control over what authorities do that affects us. If we want adequate public answering to help ensure fairness, we need to agree on standards for the answering, but these standards should be based on a set of organizing principles of accountability. General principles are the basis for specific answering standards for different types of responsibilities of concern to different groups of people – for example, health, education, social justice and the environment.

We already have conventions to guide public reporting of corporate and government financial results. Formalized financial reporting has been the norm for over a hundred years. Accountants and auditors call the reporting conventions generally accepted accounting principles. Their purpose is to limit management whim in the reporting of financial results. But in matters of fairness, we have yet to introduce principles for the answering obligation.

For example, in the corporate world, current law instructs corporation directors only to act "with a view to the interests of the corporation."[1] This isn't necessarily the same thing as acting in the public interest. The issue of patented genetically engineered foods is a case in point. In answering, the law asks directors to publicly report only financial information. So we need to forge principles and standards for answering for the fairness of authorities' intentions.

From the examples in the previous chapters of what can stem from the lack of public answering, the following 12 principles of accountability and of holding to account suggest themselves. Principles are written as principles, not exhortations. Therefore they don't take the form of "Authorities should…" which is only an exhortation.

The public accountability principle

Every responsibility that affects the public in important ways carries with it the obligation to answer publicly for the discharge of the responsibility.

It makes no sense to assign important responsibilities to authorities and then allow them to act without attaching the self-regulating influence of answering to the public. Without answering, we are left with only fighting to stop something and/or blaming after the fact. We have no evidence to suggest that authorities will answer adequately on their own initiative. The obligation to answer is simply an obligation in fairness – one that is reasonable to expect.

With institutional deception already pervasive, we can't expect people in authority but having no answering obligation to put the public interest before their own wants. If we are lucky they do. Nor can we expect subordinates to refuse to go along with their superiors' self-serving intentions.

The precautionary principle

We apply to authorities' intentions in all responsibility areas the precautionary principle we apply in safety and environmental protection.

That is, we require authorities to demonstrate, through validated public answering, that what they intend will not lead to harm or unfairness. We do not allow authorities to make citizens prove that the authorities' intentions are harmful or unfair. Authorities have the added responsibility to show why an intention significantly affecting the public is really needed: that it satisfies public needs and not just certain people's wants.

The principle of coherence in assigned powers, duties and accountabilities

Public answering obligations attach to each power and duty of authorities, in sufficient rigour to tell the public whether the powers and duties are being discharged in the public interest.

Powers, duties and answering must be in balance. It is not good enough to legislate powers and duties for governing bodies without adding the answering requirement. By the same token, duty is empty without the authority to carry it out, and it is unfair to hold a governing body responsible for something that is beyond its power to control.

The principle of identifying the directing mind

To make accountability effective, those holding to account identify the directing minds answer-

able for what a government, corporation or other organization intends to do, actually does or fails to do.

Holding fairly to account will succeed only if citizens hold to account the real directing minds: those who determine the intentions and actions that are the subject of concern. The blood, Westray and *Herald of Free Enterprise* cases illustrate the tendency of examiners to limit blame to levels below the directing minds. If we hold to account only those at lower levels and fail to deal with the persons ultimately responsible for the intentions and needed control, we should not expect improved safety, fairness and justice.

The principle of self-informing duty

People in authority whose responsibilities affect the public in important ways inform themselves for their decision-making to a self-informing standard that citizens have the right to see met.

Self-informing implies that authorities will know reasonably well what information they need for their duties and obtain it and, to the extent called for, will validate the information they get. They will not simply use whatever information is given to them. The self-informing principle implies, "No self-informing to a standard reasonable in the circumstances, no decision taken."

The principle of answering for precautions taken

For the responsibilities they control, authorities answer publicly for the extent to which they apply the precautionary principle in their own decision-making.

This includes answering for obtaining reasonable assurance that it is safe or fair to proceed before proceeding, and for what precautionary action they took if the assurance of safety or fairness is uncertain. The principle implies that authorities don't make citizens take risks that are feasible to avoid.

The principle of intentions disclosure

People in authority who intend action that would affect the public in important ways state publicly the outcomes they wish to bring about, for whom, and why they think the outcomes they intend are desirable and fair. They also state their own performance standards and the standards for those whom they direct, which clarify their outcome intentions.

Without full and fair answering before the fact, citizens have no way of knowing whether they should commend, alter or stop authorities' intentions. The equity statement explained in Chapter 5 structures public answering for intentions and reasoning.

The principle of corporate answering for fairness

The directing minds of corporations answer publicly for the extent to which they serve the public interest as well as the interests of the corporations' management, owners and investors.

It is reasonable that corporate boards of directors publicly explain how they are serving the public interest when their intentions for corporate action could reasonably be deemed to affect the public in important ways in safety, health, social justice or in environmental impact. It is also reasonable that those responsible for governing and for regulating corporations publicly report the extent to which their supervision meets the intent of the precautionary principle.

The principle of performance disclosure

Authorities disclose their achievements or lack of achievement through adequate public answering, which is given by those responsible for the achievement objectives, performance standards and actual performance.

It is reasonable to expect people in authority to report promptly the results of their actions, why results were not as intended if that is the case, the learning they gained and how they applied it. Performance reporting reflects what is fairly within the control of those accountable and includes reporting how external constraints are being coped with.

The principle of answering by those responsible

Those with the responsibilities give the answering, not someone else such as subordinates or external examiners such as auditors, inspectors, inquiry commissioners, ombudsmen or others.

It is reasonable to expect the directing minds themselves to account for their responsibilities. External examiners stand outside the accountability relationship. It is not acceptable that the directing minds leave the answering obligation to subordinates – as when government ministers don't themselves account to parliamentary committees for their control responsibilities. Those directing minds responsible for holding others to account answer for their knowledge and supervision of those others' actions.

The principle of validation of answering

Important answering for intentions and reasoning, and for results and learning, is validated by knowledgeable public interest organizations or professional practitioners, or both.

In the case of corporate financial reporting, external auditors attest to the fairness and completeness of the corporation's financial reporting. This is simply the precautionary principle applied in business affairs. If the business community does not accept corporate financial reporting without validation, it follows that citizens should not accept on faith the fairness and completeness of reporting by directing minds of institutions for intended and actual performance that significantly affects the public.

The principle of the wages of abdication

To the extent that citizens abdicate their responsibility to install public answering standards and hold fairly to account, they give tacit approval to the abuse of power and they reduce their civic competence.

The idea of citizen duty is not prominent today, in part because of the erosion of standards in society that has led to mushrooming institutional deception and media conversion of virtually all information for citizens into entertainment. Yet it is surprising how many people know Pogo's "We have met the enemy, and he is us." The realization must have stuck.

The accountability principles proposed here are to help citizens decide whether public answering obligations make good sense, and to decide whether they will do anything to help install it for all authorities.

Endnotes

[1] See Chapter 12

CHAPTER 5

Basic Standards for Public Answering

Standards

A standard is something established by authority, custom or consensus as a model or example – a means of determining what something should be. It is a criterion for assessing conduct. In organizations, standards are reasonable expectations for the level and direction of people's effort and their accomplishment.

Standards are judged by their usefulness and reasonableness; they can't be simply someone's specifications for the behaviour of others – what someone would like to see in others as their own preference. Political correctness is about people's specifications replacing standards. The test is whether a claimed standard is in the public interest. If it isn't, it isn't a standard.

The now-commonplace expressions "dumbing down" and "situational ethics" indicate standards decay. We see no labels being coined for strengthened standards. While leaves decaying in a forest serve a useful purpose, decay in standards of conduct leads to harm and fosters deception. It reduces citizens' incentive to hold authorities to a reasonable standard of performance, which in turn allows further harm and deception. Those who deny that standards are generally decaying in society would be hard pressed to give the evidence. Personal bests in sports may be rising, but so is the use of drugs to artificially enhance performance. Manners survive from a fundamental need for norms that make people comfortable with each other, but manners don't produce the control diligence that prevents deaths, injustices and corruption.

Standards have eroded in a wide range of responsibilities:

- In a country church an annual fall service is marred by the constant noise of several small children in the balcony section voicing their discomfort. The minister can hardly compete. The parents of the children, perhaps oblivious to what they are asking of other parishioners – or perhaps not – don't quiet their children or take them outside, even temporarily. Those in the choir and congregation, many of whom are elderly and for whom this particular annual service is special, simply grit their teeth.

- The hierarchy of the Anglican Church is seen by senior members of its congregations to be jettisoning the *Book of Common Prayer* and replacing it with the *Book of Alternative Services* on the grounds that young people who are wanted as church members can't relate to the transporting language of the King James Bible. The concerns of the seniors were summed up by Alan Bennett: "All must be flat, dull, accessible and rational….the logical end of rewriting the Prayer Book being that serious-minded congregations would worship in Nissen huts."[1] Apparently no one in the hierarchy thought of the alternative of raising the intelligence and capacity of the young to be moved spiritually.

- The owners of Ottawa's Chateau Laurier, perhaps not so grand as the Chateau Frontenac in Quebec but one of the pillars of Canada's national cultural and political memory and venerated by travellers, decide that it should be re-named the Chateau Laurier Fairmont. This is to attract more American and other tourists. Thus the Chateau's name would become a hotel industry equivalent of the *Book of Alternative Services*. Ottawans' public outcry shelves the intention for the time being, but the point is why the intention got as far as it did.

- Random House's dictionary now bestows on "disinterested" the meaning of uninterested as well as impartial. Thus mediators can now be uninterested as well as impartial. A standard for accuracy in communication – something that can help prevent wrong outcomes – erodes because those we expect to protect communication standards abdicate their leadership role.

- Increasing violence pushed on TV is unabashedly asserted as entertainment, so the media companies can evade upholding the precautionary principle in safety.

- Misleading published financial statements no longer bring stigma or punishment as self-serving accounting becomes increasingly accepted.

- An assistant deputy minister of the Department of National Defence is given the same position for the federal Health Protection Branch, a post once held by doctors. The safety criterion of medical experience in health protection is replaced by experience with client industry.

- In his final statement before the 1990s blood inquiry commission, the Canadian federal government's legal counsel scorns the judge carrying out the inquiry. Later,

154 Liberal Members of Parliament, ignoring a fundamental standard of fairness and Justice Krever's recommendation, obediently vote down compensation for pre-1986 victims of hepatitis-contaminated blood.

- Senior civil servants used to serve the needs of the public interest. Now they appear to serve the wants of their political masters. "The limits are understood": the expectations needn't be spelled out for the civil servants.

- Health ministers and first ministers no longer hold to the standard of medicare that Canadians agreed would be delivered. Rather than produce publicly-funded universal medicare to the publicly expected standard through feasible government management standards, ministers refuse to do what Canadians told them to do. They pretend that medicare must now be re-invented as something less – something that would wind up serving the private sector at public expense.

When we see nothing but lowered standards everywhere, we stand out oddly if we maintain our own. We may then feel anxious and lower our own standards, pushing out of our minds Shakespeare's "to thine own self be true." This forces us to lower the expectations we hold of others, to the point where we concede that the expectations we once thought were sound and influential mean nothing.

Yet, in public responsibilities, a standard implies conduct reasonably expected that ensures safety, prevents injustice or otherwise produces a public benefit of some kind. That is why citizens who try to maintain standards must ask those with the responsibilities, "Would you kindly tell us your own standard?" Standards crumble because we don't challenge their erosion, and successive people in authority, in the abdicating language of "choice" and "lifestyle," cease to understand the importance of standards in society.

If standards are important, public answering for responsibilities must meet reasonable answering standards. If it doesn't, the answering (if given at all) can mislead, successfully putting spin on responsibilities that weren't discharged. The best way to visualize no answering standard is to think of Question Period in our legislatures. Sometimes the legislators' questions hold to account, and sometimes the government gives reasonable answers. But in the main it is a ritual of partisan rhetoric or inept questioning met with arrogance and fog.

Holding to account makes visible the standards not only of those with responsibilities but also those with the duty of holding to account. Saying about people's responsibilities, "Well, I sure hope they…" says that we don't intend to hold accountable people to account.

We often hear the statement, "We've come a long way." Listen carefully to what is being said. Is the speaker saying that a praiseworthy attainable standard was met? And if someone says, "Our government's senior civil servants serve the public interest better than the civil servants in other countries," the question to ask is whether these officials are meeting performance and answering standards reasonable to expect in the circumstances of their own country, not in someone else's country.

For any intention affecting the public in important ways, we must require the responsible decision-makers to tell us their intentions and reasoning and to meet reasonable standards of fairness and completeness in their answering. Adequate answering means that the answering meets a public interest standard of informing reasonable to expect in the circumstances of the person or authority giving the answering. It tells us whether authorities are fairly intentioned and know what they are doing.

To judge the adequacy of answering, we need to agree on a simple set of answering standards that will fit most circumstances. We can then ask our elected representatives to install the standards as law in their respective jurisdictions.

Six Basic Standards of Public Answering

The following answering standards reflect the principles of accountability proposed in Chapter 4.

For all proposals that would affect the public in important ways:

1. *Authorities state, for public challenge, what they intend to bring about, for whom, and why they think the outcomes they intend are fair.*

This standard requires the central "who" question to be answered publicly, whether by political parties, government departments and agencies, corporations or other institutions. It is the "who gains, who loses?" question for authorities' intentions, although some decisions are truly win-win. When authorities proposing something are required to answer two specific outcome questions, we can then challenge the fairness and completeness of the authorities say about their intentions and reasoning, to know what is really at stake. The questions are:

> "Who would gain, how, in the short and longer term, and why should they?"

and,

> "Who would bear what costs and risks, in the short and longer term, and why should they?"

Larger public interest organizations will have the knowledge to challenge and publicly validate what the authorities say in response. The answers to the "who" questions can be structured in a relatively simple equity statement, described later, which is a fairness impact statement that emphasizes the who as much as the what.

2. *Before taking a decision to act, or to authorize others to act, authorities report publicly the extent to which they have informed themselves for their decisions.*

The expectation that governing bodies will know what constitutes reasonable information for good governance and obtain it is a fair standard, not just an ideal. Authorities haven't had to answer publicly for the adequacy of their self-informing, except perhaps to a court if charged with negligence. Yet the self-informing duty is axiomatic whenever a government's or governing-board's decision affects the public in important ways. So is their obligation to inform themselves to the standard implied by upholding the precautionary principle in their decision-making.

In safety risks, we still don't know to what extent the federal Ministers of Health and members of the Board of the Canadian Red Cross informed themselves about blood distribution risks in the early 1980s. Nor do we know how well the responsible Nova Scotia cabinet ministers and mining company board members informed themselves about the likelihood of miners dying in the Westray mine. But Nova Scotians should have been told, in time to have caused precautionary action if they put safety before the promise of miners' wages.

At the level of local government, council members are unlikely to report to the community, before they vote on a contentious property development application, how well they informed themselves about the proposal's effect on the community and environment. Examples range from inner city protection of community to the mid-1990s Bamberton housing development proposal for Vancouver Island's Malahat that involved provincial ministers, to China's and India's dam projects and displacement of millions of people. There is no reason why governing bodies shouldn't give this public accounting.

3. *Authorities state publicly what they specifically plan to achieve, and their intended performance standards for the achievement.*

When authorities state intended outcomes in only general terms, such as "a healthier population," it doesn't provide a basis for holding to account for achievement. We need specific achievement statements, such as "Type A strokes will be reduced by X% by the year Y and the rehabilitation rate increased by Z% as measured by (the agreed standard indicators)."

Since achieving an objective requires accountable authorities to meet performance standards, those with the duty to hold them to account must know the performance standards. Authorities' statements of their performance standards clarify their intentions. For example, health district performance standards for strokes might include, "No one needing stroke emergency care will be more than two hours from a competent hospital stroke unit and first-hours emergency advice will be constant on a publicly-known help line," and "Hospitals designated to treat stroke victims for rehabilitation or extended care will have pain specialists to call on who are knowledgeable in stroke aftermath pain, at the state of the art in means of restoring limb functioning, and sufficient in number that stroke victims get the recovery treatment they have the right to."

Included in authorities' performance standards would be fundamental rules that no one is to break, such as compliance with the law. In the case of the civil service, the fundamental rules would include rules for probity and prudence.

4. Authorities state who would answer publicly for what, and when, if their proposal or authorization were to go ahead.

The requirement to make clear who would answer for what should affect our acceptance of authorities' proposals, because if the answering for this is weak, the "who" intentions may be suspect. Without this clarification we would be accepting authorities' actions on blind faith. (Note that in asking who would answer, we use the conditional. If we say, "Who will answer…" we signal acceptance of what authorities intend, leaving "how" as the only issue.)

After the fact:

5. Authorities state the results from their effort, as they see them, and why they were different from their stated intended results, if that is the case.

"Results" doesn't mean simply production or outputs; it means some kind of change in end-state or condition that is in the nature of an outcome. It means that an intended difference is made to something. Reporting results as the authorities see them must cover both intended and unintended effects. The results must be stated in a way that allows them to be compared with the specific intended achievement and must include explanation of significant differences between intended and actual results. To set our confidence in authorities for the future, we need to know which results are attributable to whom. We also need to know what stood in the way of planned achievement, and how authorities coped with external constraints.

A special case is withholding public answering for government intentions and action in the name of national security. If information is to be kept from the public as a matter of national security on the argument that it is for the public's own good, the public should decide the criteria the executive government are to use.[2] There must then be an independent oversight body assigned to report whether the government abides by the criteria.

6. Authorities state the learning they gained and how they applied it.

In setting answering expectations for authorities, public answering for learning applied hasn't even made it to the drawing boards. Yet the directing minds of every organization affecting the public have a fairness obligation to learn from what they did or authorized and apply their learning. What they learned, they can report. Refusal to answer publicly for learning applied is not a good sign in judging the future ability and motivation of a government or other organization affecting the public.

Although general standards for authorities' learning responsibilities may not yet be agreed, each accountable authority can state its existing standards and report against them. The requirement to report learning applied will produce a self-regulating effect.

The Equity Statement

Programs and projects affecting the public can be initiated by authorities, such as an executive government intending policy change in levels of health care. Or they can be proposed by others who apply to the authority for approval, such as a municipal by-law amendment proposed by a property developer, or a corporation seeking a government subsidy or change in regulations.

We need a simple means of structuring proposals for public challenge before authorities' decisions are taken. But it must be rigorous enough to tell the public what the proponents intend, for whom, and their reasoning. The proposal statement should the answer to the question of who would benefit from what an authority intends, and who would bear the costs and risks, and why. As well as political fairness issues, this includes safety and environmental protection. For example, what is often the case in "development" projects is that those who get the benefits don't live where the impact occurs, and those who live there are the ones who pay.

We can call such an explanation statement an equity statement (EqS). The fairness issue of who would get what benefits and who would pay must be brought out and debated, not confined to back rooms of politicians, bureaucrats and corporate executives. The main purpose of the equity statement is to make visible, for public inspection, the fairness trade-offs implicit in any major proposal. Answering the "who" question helps us tell whether the only needs intended to be honoured are those of the proponents.

The purpose of the equity statement. For each significant proposal, for legislators' and public scrutiny, the proponents can reasonably be asked to draw up a statement that meets the answering standards proposed earlier, that is, to specifically state, in their view:

- who would benefit, and why
- how they would benefit, immediately and in the future
- who would bear the costs and risks, and why
- what the costs and risks would be, immediately and in the future
- who would answer publicly, for what, and when, if the proposal succeeds

In city council development application approvals, for example, councillors can make it a rule not to decide contentious property development applications without a publicly-challenged equity statement. The statement would be audited and signed off by city staff for its fairness and completeness in setting out the proposal's affect on the community and the environment. A summary equity statement would be backed up by information accessible by those wanting to examine the proponents' reasoning in greater detail.

A corporate board can require the same. For example, a CEO may recommend that the corporation acquire another company. An equity statement for the proposal, rigorously examined by the board, should help bring out CEO ego-based motivation if that is a main element.

At the provincial, state or national level, making publicly visible the underlying policy intentions and reasoning is vital to citizen understanding. For example, focusing on the quality of the delivery of government services doesn't address fairness policy – the decision of whose needs the policy would honour and whose it would not. Confining the public's attention to aspects of the delivery of the service diverts attention from the underlying issue of the fairness trade-offs intended. The equity statement goes to the bone on fairness policy by making visible who gains and who loses, and the reasoning for it.

To legislators having information overload, and therefore too little time to think, accurate statements of executive government's intentions are more important than descriptions of past activity, or financial statements after the fact.

In regular decision-making in approving programs and resolving equity issues, governing bodies have a diligence obligation to be reasonably informed on the matters that come before them. They therefore need pertinent information in a succinct, useful form for the issue, whether it's for a proposal to launch or stop a program or project, or make a major change where safety, fairness, community values or the environment are involved. The equity statement structures this information.

For elected representatives, the equity statement makes a succinct briefing document. It doesn't replace existing means that politicians use to assess issues; it augments them. Using the statement meets an informing standard that citizens can reasonably expect to see met by governing bodies. Politicians can ask their civil servants to develop equity statements for important proposals identified through public consultation. And if an important proposal is already on the table, the proponents' equity statement for it can be set out for public consultation and reaction.

This isn't a complicated idea. Bare-bones equity statements can be drafted on the back of an envelope. On big issues, citizens are entitled to reasonably complete equity statements that can be presented in half a page in a newspaper. Once elected representatives are satisfied that the equity statement has been challenged, and identifies the trade-offs fairly, and that no major effects are missing, it can be used for making decisions.

The scope of an equity statement can easily be extended to become an ongoing "one-stop" reporting document that includes reporting on all the answering standards introduced earlier. An expanded equity statement can make visible not only authorities' outcome intentions and reasoning, but also their specific achievement objectives, their key performance standards, their actual performance results and their learning gained and applied. It can also be continued over a project or program life cycle, giving governing bodies and stakeholders the complete story for their control.

As the basis for legislators' scrutiny of programs of government departments, the statement can be broadened still further, to show for each program or project the authorities' intended performance standards for each of fairness, efficiency and compliance with the law, and to report whether the standards have been met.

Applied to government programs and policies, equity statements combined across departments would clarify for parliamentarians the fairness issues and show serious policy gaps or overlaps. They would show whether policies that should be coherent are in fact coherent, show whether policies are at cross-purposes, and whether some people seem to gain consistently while others lose. In each case where joint government action is intended, the responsible or lead government (for example the federal government in health) would draft the equity statement for challenge by other government jurisdictions and by citizens' groups.

If government ministers and civil servants say they are already producing what equity statements would show, they can produce the information that they claim is equivalent, and say why it is as useful as the information structured through equity statements.

Publicly-challenged equity statements could focus issues sensibly and help to structure public debate. Example issues are a governments' intentions with respect to medicare, key provisions of intended international trade agreements, the existence of tobacco companies, or media corporations' continued violence on TV.

In each case, successive rounds of public challenge increase the accuracy of the equity statement in setting out the fairness trade-offs in what is intended, and their relative weighting. Stakeholders can then decide for themselves whether what an authority intends is fair and in the public interest. The requirement to disclose longer-run benefits and costs and whose they are could help prevent short term or expediency-based decision-making.

Equity statements serve as a basis for holding both proponents and elected representatives fairly to account for what is ultimately decided. If a publicly-challenged equity statement points clearly to a certain course of action but the elected representatives decide something else, their constituents can ask them why they decided as they did. Requiring equity statements to be produced for public issues and to be accessible through the Internet would allow us to be better informed about trade-offs before making our views known to our elected representatives.

Most important, if the decision-making authorities won't produce equity statements for public challenge, citizens' groups and public interest organizations can produce their own and publicly ask the authorities to state publicly what they think is wrong with them.

The rule is that whoever proposes an action affecting the public in important ways attaches an equity statement to their proposal. This provides the basis for checking out the proposal with the public. If the issue is very important, challenge can include independent professional audit of the assertions and estimates in the equity statement. The statement can be divided into elements that are the responsibility of elected representatives (the fairness issues) and those that are the responsibility of management (efficiency and most compliance issues).

The equity statement isn't rigid. As times change, the definitions of "fair," "benefit," "cost," and "risk" change, as do the stakeholders involved. But without such a statement and its validation, stakeholders can only guess whose needs are intended to be honoured and whose are not, and what the proponents and decision-makers in authority mean by key terms that they use. Moreover, having to present an equity statement to the public forces proponents to be up to date on the thinking and research that underpins or refutes their reasoning. Public interest organizations challenging the statements will be.

The main components of successful decisions are quality and acceptance. A good decision not accepted by stakeholders may have no effect, and an accepted decision could be wrong and harmful.[3] The key to public acceptance of proposals is good understanding of the reasons for them. Unexplained reasons lead to suspicion of motives. Equity statements, validated through public challenge, can help produce better decision quality and acceptance.

Using the equity statement. An everyday decision about the use of land in a municipality can illustrate the use of equity statements.

> It is reasonable to expect a property developer, filing a development application that will significantly affect a community, to demonstrate that the

proposal is compatible with the intent of the official plan for the area; to state who would benefit and how; and to state who would bear what types of costs or risks from the development and why what is proposed is reasonable.

If the city is reluctant to ask the developer to state publicly what he or she wishes to bring about – that is, to account to the community – members of the community can take the initiative and draft the equity statement. But they need to draft it with as much fairness as they would demand from the developer. Then, the community representatives, councillor for the area and developer sit down to discuss the main elements of the statement and the weightings, and challenge it for benefits and costs left out.

The developer has the obligation to make clear in the equity statement what the property use is to achieve, and all parties involved assess the impacts on the community – including how a good development idea can be improved upon through ideas volunteered by stakeholders.

City staff and the area councillor satisfy themselves on the fairness and completeness of the statement as a basis for the planning department's recommendation to council and for the councillors' vote on the application. If the application is important enough to call a public meeting, the equity statement serves as a basis for the community's discussion.

The area councillor states his or her own position to the community, with the reasons. If, for example, the application is contrary to official plan intent, city staff and the councillor would advise the developer that an official plan amendment application is needed, not just a by-law amendment, let alone a minor variance application.

Based on benefits and costs that were subject to public challenge through the equity statement, residents and developer alike can judge the fairness of the staff recommendation and the ultimate voting by council members.

Another example is a provincial government ordering that a city close a number of schools for cost-saving purposes. This gets parents up in arms and pits them against each other as the local argument centers on which schools will close. But did any group representing parents and present and future school children publicly say to the executive government – and to the city school board if it was apparently willing to carry out the government's intention – "You will close *no* schools until you give us validated evidence, in a usefully structured statement backed by reliable demographics, why your intention is in the public interest, and we have had a chance to challenge your statement and lay our assessment of it before the public." The group can then attach its own equity statement for the proposed closings and ask the government to state its view of the fairness and completeness of the group's statement.

At any level of government, when the executive is involved in the decision about a program or project, civil servants review the draft equity statement, make it as valid as they can, and sign off on the statement for fairness and completeness of the trade-offs involved – to the extent they know them – before the elected representatives deal with it.

The public control rule is simple: no publicly-challenged equity statement, no decision taken by the responsible governing body on the intended action.

Whether the proposal for a major change comes from government or the private sector, journalists can help by asking authorities for bare-bones equity statements and by asking those in authority – city councillors, corporate boards or government ministers – whether they think their equity statements are fair and complete as a basis for taking decisions. Journalists can identify the most important types of information that should be in the statements, seek to extract the missing information from he proponents and distill it to workable length for their readers. In cases of suspected patronage or conflicts of interest, reporters can have a field day with the "Who benefits?" questions.

Intentions Needing Equity Statement Disclosure

The range of authorities' intentions across the planet that call for publicly-challenged equity statements is huge, but if the statements were required, those affected by the intentions would soon learn how to figure out the basic fairness trade-offs and what's missing from the statements. As George Washington said, citizens will make sensible decisions if they are reasonably informed. What has been missing in benefit-cost assessments that governments claim they already producing is the information we need on the "who" questions: who benefits and who pays – and for how long.

Considering obvious examples in the use of natural resources, what would a rigorous, publicly-challenged equity statement have explained to the several million citizens of Toronto about the development plans to wall off their downtown lake waterfront with condominiums? What would it have explained to British Columbians about the Bamberton land proposal on lower Vancouver Island, or clear-cut logging? What would it have explained to Prince Edward Islanders or Skye residents about the bridge proposals? Or to the Dutch, about freight railway tracks across the Netherlands from Rotterdam into Germany, or the Australians for their car racing track in park land? Or the merits of an intended huge dam in China or India?

In health, publicly-challenged equity statements would give Canadians a better picture of government intentions to privatize health care or dismantle the federal regulatory functions for drugs and food safety. Such statements would also make clearer the "who" answers for issues ranging from gun control to fairness in income tax policy. Perhaps the best example of a needed equity statement in Canada is the central political issue: the proposal that Quebec separate from Canada. What happened leading up to the 1995 Quebec Referendum wasn't debate – the proponents on each side simply raised bogey-men. Benefits, costs and risks brought out were presented to the public in bits and pieces. And there is more to the issue than leaders' personalities, elites' power ambitions and mass spillings of emotions in Montreal squares.

Neither separatists nor federalists have proposed to the citizens of Quebec a clear statement of who would benefit from the separation, how, immediately and down the road, and who would bear what costs and risks, immediately and down the road. If the proponents know the answers, they can report them for public challenge. Benefits and costs as citizens see them are not solely economic, and can be stated so that all understand them. The citizens of the rest of Canada also need the equity statement information to help them better grasp what is at stake. Federalist leaders can present their equity state-ment for continued union, and separatist leaders can present theirs for separation. Dura-ble compromise can result if citizens – not the power seekers – see net benefit to staying in the marriage.

If a newspaper series laid out for us equity statements for the Quebec separation pro-posal, dismantlement of medicare, changes to legislation and the drift to becoming the next state of the US, we might then see more clearly what we are letting happen. The fact that people in other countries both envy our country and think we are civicly incompetent in our management of it should tell us something.

Again, if those with the responsibilities refuse to set out equity statements and our elected representatives refuse to ask them to, public interest organizations can develop the statements themselves to lay out for the public the main elements of the fairness issues. Through Internet networks they can link up with other organizations to produce equity statements for important issues and steadily make their use a standard in democracy.

As an example, Appendix 1 proposes the basics for an equity statement – in this case for certain provisions of the OECD's 1997 Multilateral Agreement on Investment. The appendix is not the result of thorough research into the MAI; those with expert knowledge could flesh out the statement to make it complete and accurate enough for formal public challenge. The example is simply to show the types of information that can be usefully summarized for citizens for any proposal important to them. A more accurate MAI equity statement should serve as a way of scrutinizing re-engineered MAI clones that will relentlessly come down the tracks over the next decades.

Auditing the Answering

The purpose of audit is to answer the question, "Is the answering given fair and complete?" Audit started centuries ago with validation of adventurers' profit reports from trading enterprises. It progressed to today's external audit of corporations' published financial statements, but we must now apply audit to public answering for safety, health, social justice and environmental responsibilities. In most situations where citizens have concerns, public interest organizations can take the first cut at auditing the quality of answering before deciding whether to call on professional auditors.

The auditors' word "assurance" is tricky, because those responsible are to give the performance assurances (the answering for their responsibilities), not the auditors. Auditors attest to the fairness and completeness of the types of assurances given that lie within their realm of attestation competence. They report, in their professional view, how valid and reliable the assurance assertions are. Professional auditors' attestation scope is quite limited at present, because the scope of authorities' statutory accountability reporting is so limited. But professional auditors can expand their expertise to attest to whatever accountability reporting is required, if it is required.

Auditors should not only attest to the fairness and completeness of accountability reporting; they should report to stakeholders what the scope of authorities' answering should be if none is being given.

Important answering by authorities must be validated, whether by citizens or professionally. If not, we will be operating on blind faith. If authorities know that their answering won't be publicly validated, they have no incentive to report fully and fairly. We then get unfettered spin and deception.

Legislating the Obligation to Answer

When we are serious about people's rights and obligations, we legislate them unless we can rely on the common law to ensure them. Since we have no common law on public answering and shouldn't wait for it, we must install legislation requiring decision-makers in authority to answer publicly and adequately for the discharge of their responsibilities.

This means legislating minimum public answering standards for those whose decisions affect the public in important ways. Thus far, however, legislation applying to authorities is a collection of powers, responsibilities and restrictions for specific people and classes of people – all having to do with the obligation to act or not act. The requirement to answer, and to a standard, has been missing. The public answering requirements that do exist in legislation are usually confined to the production of after-the-fact financial statements, which say nothing about fairness intentions and results, and requirements for annual reports on the "activities" or "affairs" of the organization. Activity is not necessarily effort in the public interest, and effort is not accomplishment.

We can't simply rely on courts for redress after the fact. Courts and the legal system are invoked when people fail to act as they should. But that is costly and the legal system produces uneven results. We must legislate public answering to make agendas and reasoning clear for public inspection before the fact, that is, before harm can occur. Legislating answering standards is non-partisan and can prevent whim in people's answering for their responsibilities.

There have been encouraging signs. For example, the 1993 *School Act* of Prince Edward Island states that the Minister shall

- define the goals, standards, guidelines, policies and priorities applicable to the provision of education in Prince Edward Island...
- establish expected outcomes and standards of performance and assess the extent to which outcomes are achieved and standards are met... and
- establish an accountability framework for the school system...

Note that the Act's "shall" rather than the usual "may" requires the Minister to set standards and meet them. The words are not simply "promote," or "encourage" in these provisions. Reasonable criteria for the accountability framework can be identified to satisfy the school constituencies, those running the schools, the Minister and departmental officials. The Auditor General can then report to the legislature how well the criteria serve the purpose, and whether those accountable under the framework are answering to a reasonable standard.

Another good example of initial public answering legislation is Saskatchewan's 1993 *Health Districts Act*. The Act provides that each health district board is to hold two meetings a year which the public can attend. At one of these meetings the Board is to present an operating and expenditure plan for the next fiscal year and

> ...a report on the health status of the residents of the health district and the effectiveness of the district health board's programs.

For those familiar with Canadian law, this is a significant advance. The Act requires the accountable board to report on its effectiveness direct to the public, not just internally to the Minister of Health.

The underlying issue, however, is the power of local and regional health boards to set and produce adequate levels of health services to citizens, and to have the executive government send the needed public money into the communities to do it. Provincial ministers of health have confined those powers to themselves, leaving citizens to think that regional boards of health have more power than they actually have. Legislation must, therefore, ensure that the ministers' and boards' respective powers, duties and accountabilities are in balance and clear to the public.

Reporting to Prince Edward Island's Legislative Assembly in 1995 on the province's Crown corporations' accountabilities, Auditor General Wayne Murphy wrote, "The legislation should be limited to the requirement to report and the minimum standards to be met."[4] This recommendation applies to all governmental responsibilities, everywhere.

Basic Standards for Legislation

The following specific standards are reasonable and feasible:
- Legislatures formally state to the public their expectations for public answering within their jurisdictions.
- Ministers of the Crown, immediately they are sworn in, each report to their legislatures (which means reporting publicly) their interpretation of their statutory powers and duties and their statutory and commonsense public answering obligations. This is the first indicator for legislators' confidence in the minister.
- All executive bodies (ministers and governing boards) overseeing departments, branches, corporations and agencies of government and entities controlled by government, and those bodies overseeing municipal and regional corporations and the entities they control, regularly and publicly account for the discharge of their responsibilities.
- The accountability reporting obligation applies to all entities and public bodies that receive, directly or indirectly, a significant part of their funding from the public purse. There are no excluded entities.
- The overseeing governing bodies meet standards of public answering reasonable to expect for their responsibilities, which include holding fairly to account all entities they oversee.
- Governing bodies answer for fairness, efficiency and compliance with the law. (where fairness responsibilities include safety, health, justice and the environment)
- When the precautionary principle applies in governing bodies' responsibilities, their public answering includes their compliance with intent of the principle. (Contaminated blood and water in Canada are examples)
- Governing bodies' answering includes reporting the extent to which they inform themselves for their decision-making. (This means that governing bodies will manage their information to a standard.)

- Governing bodies report what they plan to bring about, and why, their specific achievement objectives and key performance standards, their actual results as they see them, and the learning they gained and how they applied it. When what they plan to do would affect the public in important ways, they explain publicly their reasoning for their intended action through equity statements or their equivalent.
- Bills introduced in a legislature have attached to them the sponsoring minister's or legislator's publicly-challenged equity statement or equivalent, whenever stakeholders can reasonably expect legislators to use such a statement for their decisions on the Bill. This statement of explanation of the Bill's intention becomes part of the public record when the Bill becomes law.
- For each Bill, the legislature's auditor gives to the legislature committee dealing with the Bill his or her opinion whether the government's reporting of the Bill's intentions and reasoning has met reasonable standards of disclosure in public answering. The auditor also reports whether the Bill's provisions for public answering by those who would be given important responsibilities under the Bill meet a reasonable standard of public answering. (These are politically-neutral matters.)

Installing Answering Provisions In Regular Legislation

We have several ways to proceed in legislating public answering, but a wrong way is to start with augmentation of financial reporting. The idea instead is to start with a clean piece of paper and identify the most important responsibilities of government and other governing bodies requiring public answering. Based on their experiences with missing public answering, public interest organizations can work together to draft the public answering needed, by whom and when, for the issue areas they are concerned with. They can then present the draft legislation to the appropriate elected representatives for their response. This is explained in Chapter 14. The process mustn't be rushed such that legislatures and local government councils quickly vote on self-serving proposals put forward by the executive to pre-empt debate sound standards of answering.

As to accountability provisions in Bills, each Bill introduced into the legislature should contain a standard accountability reporting section, with a title such as "Accountabilities," setting out who is to answer to whom, for what, and when. Another issue is "shall" versus "may" in legislation on authorities' responsibilities. The difference is obvious if, in the Prince Edward Island legislation above, the section were to read, "The Minister may establish an accountability framework" rather than "The Minister shall establish..." There are reasons for "may" in legislation, but when the responsibility should be a "shall," it should say "shall." And drafting ministers' responsibilities in the style, "The Minister is concerned with" won't do. Acts authorizing ministers to do something "if it is in the public interest," must include a provision requiring the minister to disclose the criteria for deciding whether something is or is not in the public interest.

Legislation must require our elected representatives in executive positions to understand what constitutes reasonable information for good governance and obtain it.

At the local government level, residents often lose on community-protecting issues because developers and their lawyers do their lobbying during working hours. To do the same, citizens either have to get time off work or use their vacation time. Councillors must be made by law to answer for obtaining adequate information on issues going to council.

In addition to requiring intentions and reasoning to be visible and clear, legislation in each jurisdiction must require authorities to publish their performance standards for serving the public interest and to tell the public whether they lived up to them.

An Example of Feasible National-Level Accountability Legislation

The highest level of legislated public answering is at the level of a country's constitution. A written constitution with a clear structure for amendments makes it reasonably simple to show what public accountability law might look like. Since the Constitution of the United States fits the bill, we can use it to illustrate an accountability amendment, and the reasoning for it.[5] The basic reasoning for a 28th Amendment to the Constitution comes from America's own George Washington, cited earlier – if citizens have a "right understanding of matters," they will make sensible decisions. "Right understanding" can be obtained in large measure from adequate public answering. The reasoning for the law can be set out in a preamble.

A Proposed Public Accountability Amendment to the United States Constitution

Whereas:
1. The Constitution of the United States is designed to serve the interests of the people and sets forth the nation's fundamental laws.[6]
2. The Fathers of the Constitution in 1789 expected the needs of the nation to change and thus envisioned Amendments.[7] An example is the 19th Amendment, ratified in 1920, giving women the right to vote.
3. Citizens must be informed for their civic duty to ultimately oversee their elected representatives, administrators and judiciary at every level who are responsible and accountable for regulating fairness in society.
4. The implications of legislative, administrative, judicial and business power in to-

day's world require that those in authority affecting the public in important ways inform themselves adequately and make clear to the public the outcomes they intend, for whom, and their reasoning. This allows citizens, through due process, to commend, alter or halt authorities' intentions.

5. Public accountability is the obligation to answer publicly for the discharge of responsibilities affecting citizens, and holding to account means that citizens exact fair, complete and timely answering from decision-makers in authority. This leads to greater public trust in the authorities.

6. Adequate public answering is of such importance in achieving a fair society that the public answering obligation must be made part of the law of the land, which means being embedded in the Constitution.

7. An Amendment to the Constitution establishing fundamental rules for public answering would support the intent of the Constitution's existing provisions. For example, Article 2, requiring that the President "from time to time give to the Congress Information of the State of the Union," reflects early constitutional accountability intent at the Presidential level.

8. An accountability Amendment would complete the needed balance of authorities' powers, responsibilities and answering obligations. Clarity of all three is necessary to judge the diligence of those in authority. The *Government Performance and Results Act* of 1993 is an example of a specific set of public answering obligations for those directing departments and agencies of the federal government.

9. Those with the obligation to account are the identifiable persons (elected or appointed) who constitute the directing mind and will of the entity whose actions are subject to public answering. It is therefore identifiable people who account, not a "government" or a "corporation."

10. Because the obligation to answer tells no one how to do their jobs, yet exerts a self-regulating effect on the conduct of people in authority, a public accountability amendment to the Constitution could be expected to:
   - reduce deception by authorities and reduce citizens' time, stamina and funds spent on lobbying and fighting,
   - limit legislation or executive orders benefitting only a few,
   - improve elected representatives' understanding of intended actions, outcomes and means and, ultimately,
   - improve citizen respect for and cooperation with authorities, and the development and deployment of the nation's human resources.

Therefore, AMENDMENT 28 could be drafted to read as follows:
   Section 1. Citizens of the United States significantly affected by the intentions

and decision-making of persons in elected and appointed authority have the right to full, fair and timely disclosure by those persons, and have themselves the responsibility to act fairly on answering given in good faith.

Section 2. Persons directing the affairs of any level of government in the United States, or directing the affairs of business enterprises operating in the United States, have the duty, when the action they intend or control would significantly affect the rights, safety or well-being of citizens, to publicly disclose before the fact the outcomes they intend, for whom, and the reasons; their performance standards for bringing about the outcomes; and, later, the results of their performance.

Section 3. The Congress shall have the power to enforce this Article by appropriate legislation.

A similar law can be drafted federally for Canada.

A Specific Role for the Senate of Canada

At the federal government level, the Canadian Senate can make a significant contribution to public accountability. In its regular review of proposed legislation introduced in Parliament, senators can specifically task themselves to assess the adequacy of the public answering provisions in each Bill coming before them. As the public increasingly realizes the need for standards for public answering, "sober second thought" would take on revitalized meaning.

Collectively, senators have the range of knowledge to assess whether proposed public answering provisions in a Bill permit responsible governing bodies, Parliament and the public to hold fairly to account.

The parliamentary record can show the Senators' decisions and reasoning, as a basis for earning credibility with the public in serving accountability. By putting the non-partisan issue of public answering ahead of partisan politics, and developing public-interest criteria for the adequacy of answering provisions in legislation, Senators would help build public respect for the Upper Chamber.

Endnotes

[1] Alan Bennett, *Writing Home*, London, Faber and Faber, 1994, pp.352-3

[2] Sissela Bok, op. cit.

[3] Norman Maier, *Psychology in Industrial Organizations* (Boston, Houghton Mifflin, 1973)

[4] *Report* of the Auditor General to the Legislative Assembly of Prince Edward Island, February,

1995, para. 2.12

[5] The example was introduced in the accountability course seminar of Dr. Ernest Pavlock, 20 March 1999, in the graduate school of business, Virginia Tech Northern Campus

[6] *The Constitution of the United States With Explanatory Notes*, U.S. Information Office, 1987

[7] As James Madison put it in 1787, "In framing a system which we wish to last for ages, we should not lose sight of the changes which ages will produce."

CHAPTER 6

The Limits to Public Inquiries

As used here, the term "inquiry" includes inquiries commissioned under inquiries Acts and what people think of as "judicial inquiries" or "official inquiries" of various types that are wholly or largely governed by processes established and run by the government and legal profession. "Public inquiry" can be a misnomer, because experts having useful information don't necessarily obtain standing with an inquiry commissioner to tell the public what they know.

The term "commissioner" is used here for public inquiries because it directs attention to the role of the person conducting the inquiry rather than his or her judicial title. A judge hearing evidence in a court and giving a decision has a different role from that of a commissioner engaged for a specific task by ministers of the Crown.

Driving the Inquiry Truck Into the Ditch

The evidence from the blood and Westray inquiries raises the disturbing possibility that authorities, seen in retrospect as callous about the harm they could have prevented but doing anything to avoid blame, are permitted to take on an attitude of distancing themselves almost psychopathically from the people and families suffering the harm. And there is no limit to the amount of public money authorities will spend to suppress or deflect blame.

The purpose of this chapter is to show why public inquiries won't suffice if the logical objective for an inquiry into harm is to identify who had what responsibilities and answering obligations, whether the obligations were discharged, the reasons if they were not, and what must be done to prevent harm in the future. The chapter will propose that audit is a more effective way to deal with responsibilities, at least at the outset. Public inquiries fail citizens for several reasons.

Inquiry commissioners give the reporting that should be given by those accountable. On the opening day of hearings for the Commission of Inquiry on the Blood System in Canada in 1993, Commissioner Horace Krever said he would make "findings of fact," not conduct a witch hunt, and would not be concerned with civil or criminal liability. He went on to say, "the focus of the Inquiry is to determine whether Canada's blood supply is as safe as it could be and whether the blood system is sound enough that no future tragedy will occur." This may sound logical, but with the Commissioner's acceptance of the scope of his inquiry, the federal executive government successfully shifted its own obligation to publicly report its performance for blood safety in Canada – past, present and committed for the future – onto the shoulders of a commissioner. Having commissioners give the answering that the responsible and accountable government owes the public doesn't advance public answering. Inquiries let authorities off the answering hook.

The federal executive government knew something that most citizens didn't. The person who has long had the supreme power and duty under federal law to ensure that the blood supply in Canada is as safe as it can be is the federal minister of health. Given that responsibility, the minister has the obligation to report to Canadians his or her safety intentions and performance, so that citizens can judge whether they are being well served. The moment the federal government successfully engineered someone else to report after the fact on blood safety, the Crown was relieved of the obligation to answer for its intentions and protection performance. It wouldn't matter whether the person assigned to report were an inquiry commissioner, the Auditor General of Canada or a federal ombudsman (if we had one). When those with the responsibilities account, we need someone to assess the fairness and completeness of what they say. That is an audit task.

People will say, "But we don't trust answering by a minister: that's the very reason we want an inquiry." We want the truth, but we have never asked ourselves whether inquiries do the job. If we don't ask federal and provincial ministers to publicly answer for their responsibilities, they escape scrutiny because inquiries commissioned by ministers don't examine ministers. We are then saying, in effect, that accountability doesn't matter for ministers.

The ministers' validated answering would give us valuable information on how well they informed themselves for their duties, what they knew and when they knew it, and why they acted as they did or failed to act. Audit of their answering would tell us whether an inquiry should be commissioned and what its scope should be. The audit tells us how much trust to place in them in the future, and in those senior civil servants who advise them. When someone else reports on their behalf, we will never know the ministers' or civil servants' minds.

Ministers set the inquiry mandates. Commissions of inquiry are commissioned by ministers of the Crown, advised by the senior civil servants who report to them and whose futures and rewards are controlled by ministers. Senior civil servants administratively and financially control the work of inquiry commissioners who report to the ministers who engaged them, even though their reports are public.

Ministers are politically forced to commission inquiries, but because inquiries so often deal with responsibilities of ministers and senior civil servants, the precautionary principle warns us that we should assume that the mandate drafting will be influenced by what ministers and their senior civil servants don't want as inquiry outcomes. Inquiry staff and lawyers for the parties involved accept the scope limitations and may not even think through whether the inquiry truck is being headed into the ditch. Or they may accept the structure because it is part of their own profession's practice to do so.

Most of us tend to believe that once an issue goes before a court or public inquiry, a sound process kicks in that will produce the truth and result in justice being done. The evidence clearly doesn't support this assumption in any jurisdiction. But still we blindly trust – though with a sense of unease. When we have a personal stake in an inquiry and find that the process comes up short, and further discover built-in obstacles to justice that we didn't know about until the legal proceedings are closed, we don't know what to do about it. We then find that the executive government fails to act to produce fair redress, let alone fix the underlying causes of the harm.

We must accept that there are tacit expectations for commissioners, and we know the tendency of ministers to protect themselves as an ilk, past and present, regardless of political party affiliation. We know less and less the motivations of senior civil servants because they haven't been accounting publicly for their intentions and performance.

Therefore, we need to know more than we do about the independence and competence for the task of those appointed to conduct inquiries. This is no different from the need to know more about judges assigned to decide major cases in the courts dealing with safety, public policy and corruption – and to know more about the way judges are assigned. The appointment of judges is not discussed publicly with respect to their way of thinking and the possible effects of executive governments' ability to influence their later careers, appointments and rewards. Ministers and senior civil servants can be expected to select commissioners who pass muster with the general public but who are not likely versed in identifying and laying out control responsibilities. Few if any will have publicly reported that a minister didn't do his or her statutory duty and that people died because of it, and if any judge had, he or she wouldn't be appointed again.

The blood inquiry was commissioned under the federal *Inquiries Act* by ministers of the Crown and senior civil servants of the federal executive government. Had the victims' families and groups decided the nature of the inquiry, they would have mandated it to tell them the underlying reasons why their loved ones died or had their lives wrecked, and who, from health ministers on down, had what responsibilities and whether they discharged them.

Under the federal *Inquiries Act*, the commissioner serves "at pleasure." This allows ministers to close down an inquiry. Inquiries are thus controlled overall by the executive government.

For the blood inquiry, the federal ministers and their civil servants had the power and opportunity to ask Commissioner Krever to report on matters that go to the bone, such as:

- Who had what responsibilities in Canada in blood risk identification and response, and who failed to do what, and why did they fail in their duty?
- What was the control system implied by the federal health protection law, or needed in common sense, that would have helped to prevent harm, and what control and answering is needed to help prevent harm from happening again?
- What was the needed regular public answering for intended and actual performance that would have told legislators and the public about emerging risks and the extent to which the precautionary principle was being applied?

Instead, the ministers told Commissioner Krever to "review" the activities of "the blood system in Canada" (although including review of blood-related interest groups and other countries' experiences); to make recommendations for current safety in an interim report; and, in a final report, to make recommendations for "an efficient and effective blood system," including roles and responsibilities of organizations.

A "review" instruction does not ask a commissioner to identify the respective responsibilities of each of the federal executive government and the Red Cross and the respective safety-regulation responsibilities of senior civil servants and their ministers, or to report whether the responsibilities were discharged. And an inquiry confined to "systems" means that the commissioner is not asked to identify for citizens the motivations and abilities of the identifiable people having the key responsibilities. The commissioner is therefore not likely to identify and report underlying causes or syndromes. But unless we know the underlying causes, we can't fix the problems and install the right precautionary duties and public answering obligations.

A system is not accountable: identifiable people are. A system is governed by the motivations of the key people responsible for the system, by their abilities and the organization structures they create, and by whatever expectations for how they are to deal with external constraints. Commissioner Krever was not asked to identify the motivations and abilities of the directing minds of the federal and provincial executive governments, the Red Cross and other blood products corporations. His mandate could produce something about people's abilities, but even that can be lost in "getting the facts." Commissioner Krever's mandate also lacked the important "any other matters" mandate that Nova Scotia ministers gave to Commissioner Peter Richard for his Westray mine inquiry.

By contrast, the Westray inquiry mandate was more useful. It was set by Nova Scotia ministers under the province's *Public Inquiries Act* and the special examiner provisions of the *Coal Mines Regulation Act*, but the Commissioner was asked to "inquire into, report findings and make recommendations" in several areas of responsibility "in relation to which (matters) the Legislature of Nova Scotia may make laws."

The ministers asked the Commissioner to make recommendations, not just to the Governor in Council (the lieutenant governor and ministers of the Crown) but also to "the people of Nova Scotia." Ministers effectively invited the Commissioner to propose what the province should legislate to help prevent future needless workplace deaths and injury – law that could make ministers and corporate directing minds account publicly and to a standard for their intended and actual performance for workplace safety.

Equally important, the Commissioner was asked to make recommendations respecting

> …all other matters related to the establishment and operation of the Mine
> which the Commissioner considers relevant to the occurrence.

This provision to report has the same intent as the wording in Canadian federal and provincial law directing auditors general to report matters of significance. They are asked to bring to the legislatures' attention anything that they think is significant to the legislatures' decision-making in its scrutiny duty. This includes, but is not limited to matters specified in the audit Acts. The intent of the provision invites auditors general to report as well, to the extent evidence can support it, underlying reasons for government performance failing to meet standards reasonable in the circumstances. Taken as a whole, the wording of the ministers' commission invited Commissioner Richard to show Nova Scotians how to hold to account for future mine safety.

The federal executive government works differently. In August 1999, the government lent an RCMP inspector to the military to investigate the destruction of an on-site military doctor's warnings placed in soldiers' medical records following their exposure to toxic substances when deployed in Croatia. This was use of an inquiry mandate to keep control of the inquiry in the hands of ministers. The inspector reported to the military top command, not to RCMP top command. Military control would have been lost if the Minister of Defence and the Chief of the Defence Staff had chosen independent forensic audit by the RCMP itself, or by the Auditor General of Canada.

Legal obstructions are predictable. If an inquiry looks to be grinding relentlessly toward the question whether ministers and senior civil servants did their duty, ministers can halt the inquiry, as federal ministers did with the Somalia inquiry. The ministers were betting on Canadians to accept this, once the initial media flurry of indignation was over. Sure enough, when the cabinet and Privy Council Office terminated the Somalia inquiry, Canadians accepted it.

In the case of blood, once Commissioner Krever was instructed to examine "the system," the next aim of the federal executive government, shared by the Red Cross, was to block the Commissioner from naming in his report the directing minds that he viewed responsible for the contaminated blood. This would help keep the focus on "systems." Thus we had the delaying legal wrangling and court challenge under Section 13 of the *Inquiries Act*.

Commissioner Richard's Westray inquiry had its own delays: three years of it. First, the constitutionality of the inquiry itself was challenged by Curragh mining corporation officials all the way up to the Supreme Court of Canada. But at about the same time that Curragh launched this challenge, the RCMP commenced criminal charges against the on-site Westray mine managers. This created the same kind of problem that we saw in the Krever blood inquiry. In Canadian legal practice, a public inquiry mustn't compel testimony by people that could hurt their chances if they are charged with a criminal offence. For that reason, full-scope testimony in a public inquiry might adversely affect the success of a criminal prosecution or cause it to be stayed. In other words, a public inquiry cannot identify blame if there are criminal charges not disposed of, yet many occurrences leading to public inquiries involve actions that are criminal under the law, such as document-shredding.

We seem to have to choose between public inquiries and criminal charges. The Supreme Court of Canada allowed the Westray inquiry to proceed, but at the cost of a complete inquiry and with no assurance that the criminal charges would bring justice. When criminal charges are launched, the Crown can be inept in pursuing them. Citizens are no longer as trustful of the RCMP in investigating and laying criminal charges as they once were. In announcing the Westray inquiry in 1992, the Nova Scotia ministers did not make clear to the public how the scope of a commission of inquiry would have to be restricted in its usefulness if the Crown were to lay criminal charges.

Moreover, the executive government can withhold or delay giving up information, as we saw in the case of the blood inquiry.

The executive government can hold the commissioner in contempt. Canadians must understand what the executive government expects its lawyers to do. In the Krever inquiry, instead of acting in the public interest and dealing head on with the federal Health Minister's precautionary duty under the intent of the *Food and Drugs Act*, the federal government lawyers' final submission at the close of the Commission's hearings was sarcastic in tone and sufficiently specious as to be deliberately insulting to the Commissioner.

The government counsel's summary document[1] makes over a dozen misleading assertions, reasonably seen as arrogance. Five will illustrate.

- Commissioner Krever was simply witch-hunting for individual fault and unfortunately did not understand the difference between accountability and the blaming of well-intentioned, public-serving Canadians through his "scapegoating"
  (As if blameworthy officials are unconnected to accountability, and victims and their families had no right to know who was responsible for the harm done, whether the responsible officials were in fact well-intentioned and serving the public interest, and whether officials and ministers were negligent in discharging the duties for which they were accountable)

- The central "defining" issue was not organizational fault but the "interrelationships within the system," meaning constitutional "frameworks" and "political relationships"
  (As if the accountable federal health minister's statutory supreme regulatory power and precautionary duties, made the law to protect citizens, did not exist)

- The Canadian Blood Committee of health ministers and officials, funding the Red Cross in the 1980s, had no power as a committee, had no reporting obligation to the federal government and therefore had no obligation in blood contamination
  (As if these ministers of the Crown, as the Blood Committee's directing minds, were impotent, when ministers are the supreme power in government)

- the federal government was not involved in or responsible for anything to do with the blood system apart from footing half the bill for the Blood Committee's secretariat costs
  (Again the vague "government" is used rather than "minister," to deflect attention from the federal health minister's supreme statutory powers and duties to regulate blood safety).

- "Officials and Ministers of the federal Crown were accountable in a very direct and continuous way for their decisions throughout the critical period" because Question Period in the House of Commons adequately held ministers to account for blood safety, and therefore government officials too. If there had been a problem, said the government's lawyers, MPs were well enough informed as parliamentarians to have asked the right questions

(As if Question Period were regarded by a single adult Canadian as effective in holding to account, and parliamentary committees having government-member majorities would diligently and objectively examine ministers' duties).

Using these and their other claims, the government's lawyers asserted that no one could have been be in charge of what the Red Cross did and that regulation of it was unnecessary. Therefore, there could be no such thing as government performance not meeting a statutory and commonsense standard. Therefore, there could be no suggestion that identifiable ministers of health and departmental officials had failed to do their regulating duty. Therefore (finally getting to the ultimate legal strategy aim of the government lawyers), there could be no legal liability by the Crown, ministers or senior officials.

The astonishing thing about the government's 40-page submission summary is not so much the litany of straw-man statements distorting responsibility and accountability. Nor is it that the document reflects thousands of hours of civil servants and high-priced lawyers being paid from the public purse. It is that these people made their statements unabashedly on the record – as if obediently only intent on "winning" against citizens and their families whose lives were wrecked by attributable and actionable negligence. The lawyers' conduct must be considered to have been encouraged or ordered by those who controlled them: the federal ministers of the Crown and their top civil servants. Yet those who had directing-mind control haven't answered for their responsibilities. The claim that the government lawyer's conduct was "simply part of the game" illustrates the grotesque situation we have in expecting justice in legal processes that are not legal justice processes.

And in the case of the Somalia inquiry, when the Commissioners' truncated inquiry report was published, the new Minister of Defence, together with the Prime Minister – neither having credible understanding of military management control responsibilities – simply decreed that Commissioners Létourneau, Rutherford and Desbarats had got it wrong.

Inquiry Mindsets

Legal thinking focuses on blame and redress, not on control responsibility and answering. The processes in court cases and inquiries are owned by the legal profession. The focus is, therefore, battle over what happened, related to blame and redress, and simply "winning" for the lawyers. The profession's court processes were labelled by the frustrated families of those drowned in the *Herald of Free Enterprise* in 1987 as "legal niceties." Missing from inquiries about safety responsibilities is what really counts: whether the precautionary principle was upheld by the directing minds and the necessary management control systems installed to uphold it; whether anyone answered to anyone for their responsibilities; and what needs to be done about each of these two imperatives to prevent harm in the future.

Commissioner Krever's report did not make clear that all federal government health officials act as extensions of the Minister: that ultimate responsibility for what they do or fail to do lies with the Minister who, while not expected to know what goes on daily throughout his or her department, is responsible and accountable to Canadians for the quality of control system governing the officials to whom the minister delegates the power to act.

The report attributed no sub-standard performance to:
- provincial health ministers and provincial health ministry officials,
- federal health ministers and senior departmental officials as the safety regulators, and
- the directing minds of the Red Cross and supplier corporations,

all of whom were responsible for operations that they knew or ought to have known were becoming lethal. Ministers had no impediments to their safety control, had they informed themselves about what was happening and exercised their control power.

Commissioner Krever could have produced a report more useful to victims and their families, public interest organizations and citizens at large if he had said, on the first day of public hearings:

> My inquiry will not be a witch hunt, nor is it intended to be grounds for civil or criminal liability. But since I am commissioned to report on the blood system affecting many lives, I see the central task as identifying the key safety responsibilities involved and who had them, and whether these responsibilities were discharged and accounted for in a timely manner by those with the responsibilities.
>
> The precautionary principle required adequate control systems to detect and restrict health hazards. The scope of my inquiry will therefore be based on the following questions, on which I shall separately report:
>
> • Who had what statutory and commonsense safety control and performance obligations for blood safety, from the ministers of health on down?
>
> • Who had what answering obligations for their performance?
>
> • Were these performance and answering obligations met, and, if not met, why not, and what were the evident results?
>
> • What were the underlying causes?

- What do Canadians need as timely and validated public answering for key responsibilities in the future, and who must give it, to prevent as much as possible repetition of harmful outcomes from the use of blood and blood products?

The same type of opening statement would have usefully guided citizens in the Westray inquiry. These scope areas are more relevant to citizens looking for answers than the arrays of data and information in inquiry reports. There is nothing preventing a public inquiry commissioner from taking such an approach – or publicly refusing the commission if blocked in this scope.

Environmental protection lawyers understand that upholding the precautionary principle is a duty for decision-makers in authority, but other lawyers involved with other public responsibilities don't seem to. The blood and Westray inquiry reports don't make the precautionary principle a line of inquiry in its own right, even though it drives people's safety responsibilities. And there is nothing stopping the legal profession from learning what is meant by management control and adequate public answering and respecting these obligations in their work, be they barristers or judges.

In the case of Westray, the precautionary principle starts with the assumption that business corporation management fundamentally puts profit before everything else. That is what corporation managers are paid to do, and we shouldn't expect something else. Their objectives and strategies are predictable. Yet Commissioner Richard devoted 50 pages of his inquiry report to management problems *within* the mining company – something inquiry reports can't be expected to fix – as opposed to reporting to Nova Scotians what is needed in Nova Scotia legislation to help govern the conduct of the directing minds for workplace safety. Commissioner Richard did not examine the Curragh board members' responsibility to control what their managers intended to do and did do.

The Westray Commissioner's "all other matters" mandate allowed the Commissioner to apply precautionary responsibility to Curragh's board as well as to ministers. His mandate allowed him to:

- propose the responsibilities of corporate boards of directors for workplace safety and the needed corporate control systems

- conclude the extent to which timely, adequate and validated performance accounting to the public by corporate boards and managements could prevent workplace deaths

- propose the minimum public reporting

The Commission staff knew that Canadian companies Acts follow the 1950s Denning judgment confirming the board of directors as the "directing mind and will" of the company. Therefore the Commissioner could have set out Curragh directors' responsibilities and answering obligations, as he saw them. A supplemental brief to the Commission by the United Steelworkers of America asked the Commissioner to recommend that directors' failure to maintain an "appropriate standard of occupational health and safety in the workplace" be made a criminal offence, and that Nova Scotia law "prevent such individuals from hiding behind the corporate veil when their corporations violate health and safety legislation."

In response, the Commissioner recommended instead that the federal government

> institute a study of the accountability of corporate executives and directors for the wrongful or negligent acts of the corporation and should introduce in the Parliament of Canada such amendments to legislation as are necessary to ensure that corporate executives and directors are held properly accountable for workplace safety

and that the province of Nova Scotia

> review its occupational health and safety legislation and take whatever steps necessary to ensure that officers and directors of corporations doing business in (the) province are held properly accountable for the failure of the corporation to secure and maintain a safe workplace. [2]

The Commissioner appears to have missed the point on answering for prevention of harm. What legislated standards of performance do we apply to decision-makers for upholding the precautionary principle and what timely public answering for their intended and actual performance do we require in the law?

Commissioner Richard did not propose basic responsibilities and accountabilities of corporate boards for workplace safety, or deal with the definition of "wrongful." For example, it should be wrongful or negligent in law for a company board to fail to demonstrably apply the precautionary principle and to fail to have in place adequate management control systems producing safe operations where workplace safety is an obvious major consideration – such as in mining, construction or public transport.

Nor did Commissioner Richard explain what he meant by "held properly accountable." If he was thinking of answering in courts of law, he misunderstood what public accountability is. Courts attempt to re-create reality after the harm has been done. Public inquiry commissisoners may use the term "accountability," but they don't tell us what they mean by it.

Public inquiries don't tackle directing-mind control responsibilities. Inquiry commissioners seem reluctant to tell citizens what they think ministers' regulatory statutory powers, duties and answering obligations are. In neither the blood or Westray inquiry reports do we see clear sum-up statements under an appropriate heading, such as:

The Powers, Duties and Answering Obligations of Minister X

In my view, Minister X had the power to....

He had the duty to....

At the time, although the Minister had no statutory duty to report A or B to the public, in my view he had an obligation in fairness to tell the public..."

In the Westray inquiry report we see over three pages on the notion of "ministerial responsibility," which is about government ministers' relationships with legislative assemblies. Bureaucrats and academics seem to carry on endlessly about "ministerial responsibility" without dealing with the adequacy of a minister's public answering obligation. Nova Scotians, the people to whom the Commissioner was reporting, were surely more interested in who was ultimately responsible for safety in the mine than in descriptions of hoary notions about how parliaments operate. They wanted to know who, exactly, was responsible for the deaths of the 26 miners and what they did or failed to do that led to the killings.

Commissioner Richard's report examined events leading up to the explosion and dealt with Westray's operations, including provincial ministers' promotion and funding of Westray; what mine inspectors failed to do about Westray; mine managers putting production before safety; and how mining regulations should be strengthened. His report wasn't on what the ultimate directing minds – the ministers and the Curragh board members – did or failed to do to prevent workplace deaths, and was silent on answering obligations.

The Commissioner didn't nail down for Nova Scotians the statutory and commonsense duties of the directing minds responsible for workplace safety and then report whether, in the Commissioner's view, they did their duty. And if not, why not. Provincial and federal public-purse funding of the mine, described in his report, was not a statutory duty of ministers; preventing miners' deaths was.

The Westray inquiry dealt with competencies and apparent attitudes of mine managers and inspectors within government departments, but not with what caused that motivation and conduct: the expectations of the directing minds. Nova Scotians must know those critical influences if they are to fix the underlying problems. If the Commissioner intended to omit them, he should have stated at the outset why he was excluding them. Miners and their families, backed by the citizens of Nova Scotia, might then have forced underlying cause to be formally part of the inquiry scope.

While Commissioner Richard uses report headings of "Duties of," for various departmental officials, he has no such sections for the safety control duties of the ministers in whose names the officials acted. He doesn't deal with the specific statutory duties of the responsible ministers as the overall controlling minds for Westray safety, their responsibility to publicly delineate their own and officials' duties, and whether, in the Commissioner's view, the responsible ministers discharged their duties.

The Commissioner instead discusses responsibilities of "the Department of Labour." He doesn't say, "Minister of Labour." It was the *Minister's* statutory duty to ensure safety from coal dust and methane explosions. In concluding that a department didn't do its duty, the Commissioner failed to point out that this meant the Minister didn't do his duty to have the department carry out the responsibilities that are statutorily assigned to the Minister. Civil servants act in the name of a minister of the Crown, who lawfully delegates his or her power to them. But delegation means having someone else carry out something faithful to the intent of the person delegating; it doesn't mean giving autonomy and shedding responsibility.

Talking only about a "department" diverts attention from holding each minister to account for ensuring a control system that has each department's officials working cohesively with each other to make sure Curragh either complied with the intent of the legislation or saw its operations shut down.

No one would dispute the Commissioner's contention that ministers didn't understand their statutory responsibilities. The question is whether it was reasonable for Nova Scotians to expect the responsible ministers to have learned their statutory obligations in prevention of workplace harm and done their duty. Some obvious questions arise:

- Should the ministers responsible for mine safety have known, in view of Nova Scotia's mine accidents and explosions history, whether Westray presented a significant safety risk?
- Would the ministers have had the power to apply the precautionary principle and identify, before Westray started to produce:
  - the likely tendencies of company officials, in their trade-off decisions between production cash flow and safety, in the face of constant start-up problems
  - the particular level of risk and feasibility of Westray, given the geologically-hazardous structure of the coal seams in the area and available studies on those problems, the intended new technology for the mine and whether existing regulations covered the technology
  - the ability and motivation of mine-related provincial civil servants, from deputy minister on down, and the barriers standing in their way of doing a diligent job for miners and Nova Scotians at large?
- Was it within the power of Nova Scotia ministers of the Crown to ensure that they

had a control system in place telling them whether people's obligations for mine safety were being carried out?

- Under the axiom, "If you know it, you can report it," was it within the power of the responsible ministers to regularly report to the Legislative Assembly whether they were meeting the intent of their statutory duty for workplace safety, and Westray in particular in view of its high profile and the known dangers?

The answer to all these questions is yes.

Commissioner Richard states in his report:

> The fundamental and basic responsibility for the safe operation of an underground coal mine, and indeed of any industrial undertaking, rests clearly with management.

This misleads in two ways. Within the corporation, the fundamental and basic responsibility for mine safety rests with the overseeing board of directors. Management operates to the values and standards the board of directors set, whether it is a mining company, an English Channel ferry company, the Canadian Red Cross or the Toronto Hospital for Sick Children. But the rules that corporate boards are to meet are the responsibility of ministers of the Crown. As the statutory regulators, ministers set the safety standards that corporations must meet and are responsible for ensuring that corporations comply with them.

Nova Scotians surely wanted to know what Commissioner Richard thought the duty of the ministers was; whether he thought they had done their statutory duty; and what it would take, in the Commissioner's view, to prevent responsibility failures in the future. They wouldn't have expected pages of commentary on "ministerial responsibility."

In the section of the Commissioner's report on recommendations, the only recommendation about ministers proposes a "program" for ministers that would include studying the British parliamentary responsibility system. It would offer "guidelines" for ministers, with ministers having "access to" advice on the nature and the extent of ministerial responsibility in specific situations. This proposes no standards that ministers can reasonably be expected to meet. It in effect says, "Lets just have ministers study something rather than make them answer." If mere study was expected, then ministers would be better made to study what it took to make English and Welsh mines safe, and what exists in Nova Scotia's culture allowing mine risk that may stand in the way. Justice Richard did not suggest that ministers, before commencing their ministerial duties, undergo mandatory instruction on their statutory duties and legal liabilities from someone other than their subordinates, who know what ministers don't want to hear.

Commissioner Richard reported on the competence of government mine inspectors and company mine supervisors, and offered technical proposals for more mining regulations involving mine ventilation and the like. But his recommendations, from 600 pages of inquiry, did not deal with fundamental issues central to citizens being able to hold ministers of the Crown and corporate boards to account for workplace safety.

Inquiry commissioners' reluctance to deal with the precautionary principle and ministers' and boards' responsibility to uphold it can lead to inadvertent exoneration of directing minds. For example, in the blood inquiry, Commissioner Krever reports, under the heading, "The Limited Resources of the Bureau of Biologics":

> The Bureau was unsuccessful throughout the 1980s in its efforts to secure the level of funding needed to discharge its functions effectively.... The inadequacy of resources not only limited the bureau's ability to extend its regulatory reach, but also affected its performance of the regulatory functions that were directly within its authority.[3]

This implies that once Bureau officials exhaust their initial allotted resources, some uncontrollable external constraint takes over. Not so. Given that the blood hazard was known and mushrooming, the head of the Health Protection Branch could have shifted resources into its Bureau of Biologics. Failing that, the Deputy Minister of the Department could have done so. Failing that, the Minister could have, within his or her funding. Failing that, the Minister could have found the money in some contingency fund of the government, or by obtaining "volunteered" resources from other departments or agencies through prime-ministerial marching orders in a cabinet meeting. A cabinet attitude of deregulation and privatization at the time is entirely within the control of ministers. Safety erosion is not an act of God.

Similarly, regulatory power lies with the Minister of Health, not the Bureau. Only if the Minister were statutorily restricted from regulating blood operations for a health hazard would the Minister's Bureau of Biologics be restricted from acting.

The blood and Westray reports tend to leave the reader with the impression that the problems lie in the middle and lower levels of management. Commissioners don't make clear for citizens that it is the ministers in governments who are responsible and accountable for the control systems needed for safety, and for how well they work. Ministers not only have the duty to inform themselves; they have the power to do so.

Had their inquiry not been terminated, the Somalia commissioners' inquiry would have progressed to the minister level. But they started with the facts of what happened in the field, with the Canadian troops' murder of the Somali teenager Shidane Arone not being disputed. They didn't start with the directing-mind control responsibilities of the Minister of National Defence, deputy minister and the Chief of the Defence Staff at the time.

Starting with the directing-mind responsibilities for control, and the types of control for peace-keeping reasonable to expect, the commissioners might have identified the values, abilities and motivation of ministers and top brass. This would have helped predict the control needed for Somalia – for example, the adequacy of peace-keeping training for the Canadian Airborne Regiment, and on-site control within the Regiment. This would also have armed the commissioners to assess the likelihood of cover-up tendencies of senior officers, given the fact of records destruction.

By abruptly disbanding the Regiment, the government avoided dealing with who had what overseeing responsibility for the ability and motivation of the Regiment's soldiers and officers. And terminating the inquiry allowed ministers and military top command to get away with falsely portraying the Somalia inquiry Commissioners as witchhunting and blaming the troops for the syndrome.

Commissioners don't deal with the self-informing duty of directing minds. Commissioner Richard states in his Westray report:

> Having criticized Cameron (Minister of Industry, Trade and Commerce Donald Cameron, later Premier) for his conduct throughout the development stage of the Westray project, I must carefully note that my criticisms cannot be construed as evidence of any sort of complicity in the many defaults and oversights that led to the terrible event of 9 May 1992. There is no evidence that Cameron was ever told by his staff that the Westray mine was poorly or inadequately planned, poorly or unsafely operated, or operated in contravention of the *Coal Mines Regulation Act* and the *Occupational Health and Safety Act.* [4]

This too, misleads. There is a difference between complicity, in the sense of participating in an ill-intentioned decision, and failure to do one's statutory and commonsense duty. If we buy the proposal that a minister is off the hook because he wasn't told something (the "plausible denial" ploy), we excuse the minister from taking the initiative to inform himself to do his duty. The question is whether all ministers with mine responsibilities informed themselves well enough to do their jobs diligently in the public interest, as ministers of the Crown. This includes whether they instructed their deputy ministers to tell them what they should be aware of, to do their statutory duty. If ministers tend to shoot messengers, the deputy ministers' guild can sort that out.

The same holds for federal ministers responsible for blood safety.

Commissioners fail to deal with authorities' answering obligations. Unless specifically prohibited by their commissions, inquiry commissioners are not prevented from making recommendations for public answering by authorities for the discharge of their responsibilities. Good regulatory law sets fundamental rules for people's conduct. But regulations must universally include the answering requirement. At present they don't. Neither Commissioner Krever nor Commissioner Richard recommended legislation that would protect ministers from themselves and do the same for departmental and corporate officials. Commissioner Richard simply stated an axiom in his consolidated recommendations – that the aim of the provincial legislation should be to protect miners.

While he made a recommendation for legislation for corporate executives and directors, Commissioner Richard didn't explain what he meant by "held properly accountable." He lets Nova Scotia ministers off the hook in provincial legislation by passing the buck to a federal parliament that failed to deal with blood safety responsibilities and denied the redress that Commissioner Krever recommended, and to a federal department that worked against Commissioner Krever.

Moreover, if Commissioner Richard and his counsel had in mind federal companies Acts amendments, they would know that these would apply only to companies incorporated under those Acts. If federal law is to be amended to strengthen the control and answering duties of boards governed by provincial legislation, it would seem to require Criminal Code amendment. Commissioner Richard made a process recommendation, but stated no diligence or answering standards for corporate directors to meet – which his inquiry work would have allowed him to do, at least for the board's workplace safety responsibilities.

Without hindrance, inquiry commissions can lay out basic provisions for legislation and safeguards for its drafting that would:

- require ministers to uphold the precautionary principle in their regulations and action,
- require ministers to install the management control and answering systems that would ensure government does its regulatory job and that corporations comply with the intent of the law,
- require boards of directors to install within their companies management control and answering systems that produce safe products and workplace safety, not just systems "designed to" protect lives, and
- state who must answer publicly for what, and when they are to report.

As learning from the Westray case, Nova Scotians can require their law to say that a designated minister be responsible and accountable for workplace safety and they can install specific and clear public answering obligations for safety. The law should specify the public answering required for the adequacy of safety performance standards under the minister's control, and the minister's answering for whether the standards were met. Prince Edward Island's 1993 *School Act*, described in Chapter 5, is a good start in legislative practice. In the case of mining, the answering would be from the corporations' boards to the responsible regulating minister, and from the minister to the Legislative Assembly, workers and the public.

Commissioner Richard states:

> It is obvious that legislative change will not, of itself, ensure that future coal mining in this province will be carried out with safety as the paramount consideration.

and that:

> Attitudes must be directed toward safe mine production....[5]

This is true, but the passive voice doesn't tell Nova Scotians whose attitudes and conduct must be altered, in what order, how they would be changed, and who has the responsibility and public accountability for the altering. Nor does the Commissioner propose that ministers publicly report the level of workplace safety actually achieved. The board's answering must include assertions about its application of the precautionary principle, the corporation's own safety control standards and whether they are being met, and its compliance with the intent of the law.

But no accountability legislation and no teeth will be produced unless citizens themselves instruct their elected representatives. Passing the buck to the federal government for legislating corporate board responsibilities isn't the answer. Federal parliamentarians have done nothing yet to ensure public answering for future blood safety, and they don't impede corporations' profit aims. For his part, Commissioner Krever could have proposed the performance and accountability legislation needed to ensure that provincial and federal ministers of health do their duty and answer to the nation for the performance of the blood agency that is under their supervision.

The work of inquiries, done diligently, will tell commissioners the answering needed, and from whom. To the credit of the Somalia inquiry commissioners, their executive summary of their June 1997 report states:

> Leadership in matters of accountability and an accountability ethic or ethos have been found seriously wanting in the upper military, bureaucratic and political echelons. Aside from the platitudes that have now found their way into codes of ethics and the cursory treatment in some of the material tabled by the Minister of National Defence on March 25, 1997, the impulse to promote accountability as a desirable value or to examine seriously or improve existing accountability mechanisms in all three areas has been meagre.

There also appears to be little or no interest in creating or developing mechanisms to promote and encourage accurate and timely reporting to specified authorities, by all ranks and those in the defence bureaucracy, of deficiencies and problems , and then to establish or follow clear processes and procedures to investigate and follow up on those reports.[6]

Unhelpful Inquiry Reporting Practices

While Commissioner Richard's report seems better organized for the reader than Commissioner Krever's, the practice of inquiry reports omitting a subject and name index must end. It prevents the reader from telling what isn't covered in the report. More important, it partially defeats the very purpose of such reports by making it difficult for citizens to judge gaps in commissioners' examinations or to trace responsibility and answering obligations by particular people or groups of people.

Citizens should be able to go direct to indexed text sections – for example, "The Statutory and Commonsense Duty of Nova Scotia Ministers of the Crown," or "The Statutory and Commonsense Duty of the Company Board of Directors." Or, under "Accountabilities," we should be able to find who the Commissioner thought had what performance answering obligations, to whom. Citizens need to be able to go beyond description and who did what and when, to see who had what important responsibilities and whether they discharged them and answered for them.

As another practical matter, public interest organizations are called on within hours of a report's release to give their views on the report. Without a good index they can hardly even skim a lengthy report to assess the adequacy of the inquiry for important issues. They get one "sound bite" opportunity with impatient media, and then the well-briefed ministers wade in with the spin they want to put on the report. If inquiry commissioners give reasons for not having an index, these must be challenged. Whoever is assigned to build the index will be providing a great service to the public and the cost would be minuscule in the total cost of the inquiry.

Secondly, to be useful to citizens, inquiry reports must go to the bone in cause and effect and what it will take, by whom, to overcome syndromes. Nova Scotians could fairly view the first 46 of the Westray Commissioner's 74 recommendations as a technical appendix, because they are relatively detailed requirements for mine operations. Of the remaining 28 recommendations, 11 are on the structure, tasks and staffing of the two departments involved and 14 are about legislated regulations and practices – but not the legislation of duties of directing minds and their public answering obligations for their responsibilities. The remaining three recommendations, about ministers and corporations, have been discussed: they don't put forward answering standards.

Centering the inquiry report on operations, inspection and regulations is an emphasis on policing that can divert attention from how ministers and corporate directors must answer to the public for their workplace safety responsibilities. It can also divert attention from citizens' and opposition legislators' obligations to make ministers account adequately.

A government should not have to call a commission of inquiry just to revise its mining safety regulations. At the time the Westray mine was proposed, in a volatile area and with major new technology, the Nova Scotia government could have engaged a small team of specialists – including experts from the UK and US – having professional stature and independence from the minister' and mining company's influence to speedily draft publishable basic safety control standards for coal mine development and operations. Given the province's mining history, Nova Scotians would surely have been willing to pay for it. Citizens can't be expected to assess the technicalities of mining operations, but they can certainly tell their elected representatives to legislate adequate workplace safety standards and public answering obligations

Governments Can Ignore Inquiry Recommendations

In public-relations damage control for what they see coming from an inquiry, ministers can create diversions. One such was the speedy "study" of the military by consultants engaged by the Minister of National Defence, concurrent with the Somalia inquiry. If meant as a diversion, it failed.

As we saw in the blood inquiry, government ducked its answering by creating a "new" agency, the Canadian Blood Services, before Commissioner Krever could issue his report. This was done with a flourish, even before the agency's name was settled, to lessen people's attention to the inquiry recommendations. Federal, provincial and territorial health ministers proclaimed the "new" agency as being different from the existing operations and fixing everything that Commissioner Krever could possibly come up with.

The health ministers chose silence on their own control obligation for the agency's safety performance, silence on their expectations for the agency's board of directors' performance and public reporting on their safety and blood-tracking standards, and silence on independent audit of the board's performance reporting beyond audit of the agency's financial statements.

The government didn't have to state responsibility, control and answering standards for the new agency because it could predict that the inquiry recommendations wouldn't set expectations for them. The government could also predict that legislatures, journalists and citizens at large wouldn't seize on those issues.

Once an inquiry report is public, an executive government can simply put spin on the report recommendations, ignore them, or stall their implementation. In our parliamentary system we lack a body with power to cause recommendations from inquiries to be promptly implemented, or to have challenged recommendations speedily, independently and expertly critiqued and the resulting beneficial proposals promptly implemented.

The obvious body to supervise ministers' action on inquiry recommendations is the legislature. But in the case of blood, for example, the government-controlled House of Commons Standing Committee on Health and Welfare had produced a report to the House in 1993 euphemistically titled "Tragedy and Challenge: Canada's Blood System and HIV." The MPs concluded that the Canadian blood system "did not respond to the HIV/AIDS challenge as quickly as it might have," and MPs adroitly didn't include hepatitis C harm in the report title. The report didn't determine "the precise reasons for the delay." The Committee ducked underlying cause, and the words "might have" are as unhelpful as an auditor saying "Management could have done better in…" In majority governments, legislature committees, through their governing-party chairmanship and membership majorities, will be given marching orders to support whatever the ministers want or don't want.

In 1998, rather than initiate a House of Commons oversight committee for implementing the Krever recommendations, all Liberal MPs in the House, including a weeping doctor in their ranks, rose obediently to vote down the compensation to pre-1986 Hepatitis C victims that was recommended by Commissioner Krever. The victims' hardships were caused by early 1980s ministers not doing their statutory duty – something the current ministers didn't want exposed, so loyal backbenchers prevented it. The Opposition benches were united in the vote, but couldn't carry it without at least some Liberals voting with their consciences.

In any case, Opposition parties are unlikely to risk causing a government to fall over failure to implement inquiry recommendations. Ministers would explain the implementation stall in the House of Commons such that the Opposition, lacking the evidence to refute what ministers claim, would be on soft ground in later fighting an election on that particular issue.

For their part, journalists haven't reported what the federal government has done or has failed to do in blood safety, and what the Nova Scotia government has done, if anything, to prevent future harm in workplace safety and whether the government appears to be meeting a reasonable standard for prevention.

Thus far we have blindly assumed that, once everything is laid out as "findings of fact" by an inquiry body appointed and mandated through "due process," the governments and organizations that either caused or allowed harm will surely fix what's wrong.

Standards for Public Inquiries

The weaknesses of inquiries suggest fundamental rules that can be legislated through the Inquiries Acts or their equivalent:

1. Inquiry commissioners will:
   a) report, in the view of the commissioner(s), who had what self-informing and performance obligations in the public interest that were reasonable in their circumstances and whether these standards were met;
   b) identify, to the extent possible, underlying cause and effect;
   c) recommend who in future should account to whom, for what responsibilities, and the basic standards for this reporting, and
   d) report any other matter that the commissioner(s) deem of significance to the public in the discharge of people's responsibilities affecting X.

2. Ministers commissioning an inquiry will formally report to the legislature their compliance with these scope directions.

3. Ministers commissioning an inquiry will state to the public how the inquiry's scope and commissioner's powers relate to and are reconciled with the possibility of criminal charges being laid, citing examples of such problems in the past and how the particular inquiry will get around them.

4. All civil servants at or above the level of director who advise superiors or ministers in commissioning inquiries will state in a publicly-accessible record what they each recommended as inquiry scope to serve the public interest.

5. Inquiry commissioners will include in their public statements at the outset of the commission:
   a) their reporting objectives with respect to the important responsibilities and accountabilities involved in the matters being inquired into: and
   b) the extent to which they are satisfied with the scope of the mandate given them.

   For example, a commissioner can report to the public at the outset of an inquiry:

   > To prevent this sort of thing repeating in the future, what I think you need to know is A, B and C. Given the mandate I have accepted, all I can expect to tell you is X, Y and Z. I will push the envelope as much as I can, but you are forewarned that this inquiry, commissioned and governed by ministers, may give you nothing more.

6. Each inquiry report shall have an index that will tell the reader, in addition to the usual information given in a subject and name index, where to find the significant issues, responsibilities and accountabilities involved and who, in the commissioner(s)' view, had those responsibilities and accountabilities.

The Alternative of Audit

In cases of apparent failed performance, if citizens are to know who had what performance duty and answering obligations, and whether these obligations were met, those assigned to report this – and the likely underlying causes – must be experienced in those areas of inquiry. Lawyers, judges and parliamentarians are not. It is time to consider independent professional audit as the first resort rather than the public inquiries we have thus far relied on but which fail to tell citizens what they need to know and don't recommend public answering obligations.

Citizens trust that public inquiries, usually headed by members of the judiciary, will examine the right thing in the right way in the public interest and make useful recommendations. But citizens relate more to the scope of audit, which deals with:

- whether people's performance met a reasonable standard, including control responsibilities
- what caused performance failures, to the extent the audit can determine it
- how the accountability reporting needs to be fixed if it is inadequate

Political intent has to be audited by citizens and legislators, but responsibilities and accountabilities are matters regularly dealt with by professional audit. Audit can bypass the quagmires of straw-man arguing, posturing and legal obstructions that cripple inquiry commissioners. Audit reports can also help train journalists to ask and report on the questions of greatest concern to citizens.

Unless his or her mandate prevents it, an inquiry commissioner can take an audit approach. But this means a learning curve for people coming from the legal profession, and we have no accountability processes in place for their learning.

Several advantages are apparent for examinations instead by auditors general. It doesn't matter whether the auditor general carries out the inquiry and reports to the legislature, or does the audit work for a committee of the legislature taking on an investigative duty. Private sector auditors can be engaged by auditors general to do examinations in special or technical areas, under the auditor general's control.

1. Audit provides a disciplined assessment and reporting of whether people met performance and answering standards.

Auditors are professionally trained in determining whether reasonable performance and answering standards have been put in place and met. In their audits and reporting, auditors general identify commonsense management responsibilities – not just statutory obligations that may omit fundamental responsibilities and generally do omit adequate public answering obligations. As we saw in Chapter 2, the requirement to answer publicly for the discharge of responsibilities exerts a self-regulating influence. But when things go wrong, we need to learn the underlying causes. Auditors can reasonably be expected to explain underlying cause to the best of their ability and of that of experts they can call in. An audit report doesn't preclude criminal charges being laid.

2. Audit is an inquiry discipline applicable to all accountability relationships.

Critics of auditors general argue that giving the legislative auditor power to examine anything beyond financial statements and probity in government spending leads to auditors getting into policy-making. But in serving accountability relationships, the auditor simply expresses a politically-neutral professional opinion. It is whether answering given to the legislature is fair and complete, allowing legitimate decision-makers and stakeholders to do their duty in holding to account. Where there is no answering, auditors report whether observed performance in a department or agency meets a reasonable criterion.

The policy intrusion charge conveniently omits the fact that reports of auditors general simply say that the legislators are not getting adequate information to make sensible decisions. But if no one is required to report adequately on their performance, the auditor must shift to expressing an opinion on whether those accountable met performance standards reasonable in their circumstances. This is called direct reporting. If, in the auditor's view, those accountable haven't met reasonable performance and answering criteria, the auditor can be expected to say why. In their reporting, auditors general take into account limits to elected representatives' experience in assessing performance and answering obligations.

3. Audit is independent.

The staffs of auditors general are trained in objective inquiry and are independent of both executive government and corporate business interests. They report to the legislative assemblies, not to the ministers of the executive governments. The scope of their statutory inquiry and their reporting of their conclusions is determined by what the auditor general thinks the legislature needs to know to do its duty. It is not to be determined or limited by ministers and senior civil servants. And because auditors general have statutory mandates, ministers cannot shut down their audits.

4. Auditors engage the expertise they need and tap relevant sources of knowledge.

Auditors general can acquire whatever expertise is needed for their inquiries, and can consult knowledgeable people without the problems of "standing" in public inquiries.

For example, at the outset of Commissioner Krever's blood inquiry, Dr. Michèle Brill-Edwards, MD (who until her resignation in January 1996 was the senior physician in drugs licensing in the federal Health Department's Health Protection Branch) was and still is a leading expert in federal Health Ministers' statutory duties in drugs regulation. That includes blood. She offered her regulatory expertise and inside knowledge of the 1982-1996 period and events to the Krever Commission, but was not asked for her views. Without being asked by the Commission, she couldn't make public certain information important for the inquiry. It is unlikely that an auditor general would have ignored this expertise in a performance audit of blood responsibilities.

5. Audits avoid lengthy legal warfare.

An auditor general, armed with information access and subpoena power appropriate to the audit, will have no more power than a court to have people make auditable statements. But an auditor general wouldn't have to act in sea of contentious lawyers. If getting needed information for the audit did grind to a halt because of legal-process obstructions, the auditor can at least establish publicly who had what responsibilities and accountabilities, and what the available audit evidence suggests about who met or failed to meet their obligations and why. When they have gone as far as they can in serving accountability relationships, auditors general can at least put up signposts to legislators to guide further inquiry by those holding to account.

6. Audits are less expensive than judicial inquiries.

Audits don't attract legions of lawyers with enormous fees. The total cost to Canadians of the legal processes and wrangling in the blood, Somalia, Westray inquiries and other provincial and federal inquiries of the 1990s is a huge amount, not yet known by citizens. Yet it's unclear whether these inquiries actually achieved anything in changing performance and public answering, let alone durable change. The same might be said of audit reports not acted upon by legislative bodies, but citizens will find the audit approach and results more understandable as a basis for holding to account, if the audit went to the bone.

The aim is prevention in the future, not just redress, and that means control assurance. The adequacy of control is an audit concern. There is nothing stopping legislators from asking their auditors general to act, reporting to the appropriate legislative committee, instead of turning to public inquiries as the first and only option.

Endnotes

[1] Summary submission of the Attorney General of Canada
[2] Richard report p. 601
[3] Krever report p 135

[4] Richard report p.64
[5] Richard report p.646
[6] Somalia Inquiry Commissioners' Report, Executive Summary, p.ES-17.

PART II

The Public Accountabilities of Important People

CHAPTER 7

Accountabilities
and the Role of the Crown

People Are Accountable, Not Entities

People given the authority to do things that affect us include elected representatives, civil servants, judges, members of governing boards, and people in organizations such as professionals, academics and journalists. All people in authority are identifiable.

We have already seen that we haven't set adequate rules of conduct for authorities, let alone answering obligations. So we operate on blind trust. Then, when we discover that officials intend things we don't want, we fight or simply recriminate when something bad happens. No one goes to jail for lethally contaminated blood or lethal coal mines. No senior civil servant lethal to ethics in the civil service gets fired. No judge over his head in giving a decision that fosters abuse of corporate or government power is allowed to be publicly criticized. Back-bench Members of Parliament on the government side, lacking power but not willing to concede it to their constituents, simply obey their party leaders or, if in Opposition, question ineptly in ritual Question Periods.

Part of the problem is that we help shield people from answering to us for their intentions and actions by not identifying who has the responsibility. We talk only about organizations – governments, corporations, courts, professions, universities and so on. We don't identify and examine the conduct of the individuals who direct them. We say, "the Cabinet," which is a body with no legal power or obligation. We don't say, "the responsible Minister of the Crown" who has the statutory duty and signing authority, and therefore liability. We say "the Hospital." We don't say, "the Board of Trustees," let alone "the members of the Board." For example, all public answering by the Canadian Red Cross in the Krever blood inquiry was given by the CEO whose duty, wrote Commissioner Krever, was to assist the Board.

Moreover, once people form "boards," "cabinets," "courts," "professions" or "independent review committees," a veil drops and we are asked to accept whatever they decide as being the result of "due process." If a decision is decreed to be the result of due process, it surely must be sound. The meeting was held. The minutes were taken. The decision was made by people with status. It therefore must have been a well-motivated and competent decision. No questions can be raised about the extent to which the decision-makers informed themselves, what their credentials were for making the decisions, what criteria they used in what relative weighting, or whose interests each decision-maker at the table was really serving. It's considered in bad taste to suggest that the intentions of people as authorities or governing body members may be self-serving or serving the wishes of undisclosed clients.

But the precautionary principle says that we must see the evidence of good intention and competence. This means setting fundamental rules of conduct and fair achievement objectives for people in authority, having them answer publicly and adequately for their responsibilities and, where warranted under the precautionary principle, validating their answers.

Since people with power are not used to sharing it, the immediate response of some will be that having to publicly answer for their responsibilities is a straight-jacket that would hinder them in doing their jobs, and constitute an insult to their dedication. But we have seen that answering is simply explanation, and what decision-makers need to know to do their jobs, they can report. That being the case, if authorities won't account to the public and make their intentions visible, the precautionary principle entitles citizens to assign risk to authorities' intentions until their validated answering lessens the risk.

Statements of proposed accountabilities for important people clarify their responsibilities, and validation of their answering tells us what risk goes with placing our trust in them. Therefore the framework for discussing the public accountability of each group of people in the following chapters will be a statement of what they should answer for. Discussing people's accountability by type of issue – for example, workplace safety, justice, health, education, the environment and the transnational corporation problem – would be useful, and could lay out who should be accountable to whom, for what responsibilities. But this would amount to a large encyclopedia of issues and accountabilities. Moreover, an issue-based approach would be repetitious because the responsibilities and answering obligations of people like elected representatives are common for many public issues.

But before we get to the accountabilities of specific groups of people, we should identify the role of the ultimate regulator in our parliamentary system, which is the Crown. This is because the ultimate regulation of everything in society lies with the Crown, which for practical purposes is the government Executive. Legislatures make the laws, but they are actively controlled by the Executive when there is a government majority. The courts have veto power over the Executive if its actions contravene the law as the courts see it, yet the prime minister appoints the judiciary. Hence the expression in our parliamentary system, "elected dictatorship." However, ultimate constitutional power is vested in the Crown – the Queen – to whom, constitutionally, the Prime Minister and other ministers are advisors.

The Importance of the Crown in Public Accountability

The meaning of the Crown. In our constitutional system the Crown means the Queen as sovereign, not in her personal capacity. It doesn't matter that the Royal family is portrayed in the media for the most part in their personal capacities. The importance of the Crown in our Constitution doesn't hinge on the sovereign being a role model – although King George VI and Queen Elizabeth were indispensable as such during the United Kingdom's ordeal in World War II, and Queen Elizabeth II is greatly respected. It is that the Crown is the person ultimately able to act for citizens if government ministers – her ministers – intend something dreadful. An apt observation is attributed to Lord Menuhin:

> The Monarchy commands a loyalty owing nothing to power. Power must always be partisan: it belongs to money or to the military, to Republican or Democrat, left or right, capital, labour or bureaucrat – to those in power. To have a non-power above power seems to me to be the ultimate safeguard.

In our parliamentary system the "executive government of and over Canada" is vested in the Queen, represented in Canada by the Governor General and in the provinces by lieutenant governors, each of whom acts on the advice of ministers of the Crown. The Executive in Canada is the Crown, acting on the advice of the relevant incumbent ministers of the day.[1] That is why Acts of Parliament begin with: "Her Majesty, by and with the advice and comment of the Senate and House of Commons enacts…" Our system is known as a constitutional monarchy. As a matter of course, ministers decide how the Crown will exercise her executive power. For example, orders in council are Executive decisions made on the recommendation of the responsible ministers. Only the Crown has the legal authority to implement action flowing from decisions made by responsible ministers.

Similarly, to have legal force, legislation must be enacted by the Queen, acting through the governor general or lieutenant governor, as the case may be, with the advice and consent of the Senate and House of Commons (or of the relevant provincial legislature).

The ministers comprising what is called the cabinet are the Crown's principal advisors[2] and are the directing mind of the party in power. The cabinet consists of the prime minister and the ministers that he or she appoints as ministers of the Crown. This is a group itself having no capacity or authority to make decisions carrying legal force, but it is the political directing mind:

> The Cabinet, in fact, is the final body for co-ordination and negotiation, bringing around one table the Ministers responsible for all the multifarious activities of government and at the same time responsible for reflecting the views of the significant groups in the various parts of the country.[3]

But it is the Crown, acting on the advice of ministers, that has the legal accountability and authority to make regulations and spend public money appropriated to the Crown by the legislature.

Thus ministers wear three hats: (i) as ministers of the Crown they have the responsibility to advise the Crown to do Executive acts; (ii) as leading members of the House of Commons/legislatures they have the power to propose legislation to Parliament/legislature; and (iii) as members of the House of Commons/legislature they have the right to represent their constituents and the public at large in legislation proposed to be enacted.

Federally, for example, a minister or first minister may want to confer certain benefits from the public purse to certain people. But it is the responsible minister, as a minister of the Crown, who decides whether to write the cheque, and for how much, keeping within the *Financial Administration Act* and Parliament's money appropriation votes. It is these ministers of the Crown who are individually accountable for compliance with governing legislation, legality of spending and value for money from the cheques they cause to be issued.

Yet we now have a strange thing at the federal level in Canadian executive government. No one uses the word "Crown" any more unless it is absolutely necessary to use it in a legal document. As a substitute, the term "government" doesn't specifically locate accountability. In the public mind, "government" can mean the system of administration, the Executive, the bureaucracy, the majority party in the legislature, or indeed the whole parliamentary decision system.

If it is made politically incorrect to use the correct term for the fundamental mechanism overseeing the legality of ministers' actions, soon no one will remember that the term "Crown" signifies legal authorization for ministers' intentions. Decisions made in a cabinet room then become the accepted legal authority, even though cabinet decisions have no legal authority on their own. The reasoning for cabinet decisions and the extent to which ministers inform themselves adequately for a decision isn't visible to the public, and public answering for the decision quality isn't given. As George Orwell put it, "Once the language is perfect, the revolution will be complete" – meaning that removing the significance of "Crown" and replacing it in Canadians' minds with "Cabinet" as the legal authority gives ministers absolute power.

Canada seems to lack people who make it their business to ensure that the term "Crown" is protected and used as it should be used, and that its crucial constitutional and day-to-day legal significance is kept before the public. With no protection of "the Crown," ministers are likely to move to dispense with the Crown's signature required to make politicians' intentions the law.

One of Canada's recent governors general, on leaving office, remarked for his successor that governors general have no authority and exercise only moral suasion to encourage things.[4] Were this statement true, it would mean that the prime minister has complete dictatorial power, not just virtual dictatorial power as he or she does now.

The constitutional safeguard is that governors general and lieutenant governors, being agents of the Queen, are the people who hold the executive authority, not prime ministers. The prime minister may decide what will be proposed to the Queen or her representative by ministers, but ministers have power only to the extent that the governor general or lieutenant governor, on the ministers' advice, consents to what ministers propose. The fact that the Queen and her representatives are not expected to thwart the political intentions of governments by withholding consent or dissolving a parliament (thus creating political trauma) doesn't alter the Crown's power. Under a constitutional monarchy the safeguard against governing politicians' abuse of power is always there.

The late Governor General Roland Michener recounted his thorough awakening to his constitutional power to a friend, years after the 1970 "October crisis." Prime Minister Trudeau wanted greater legal power following the murder of a Quebec minister of the Crown by political terrorists. Michener said, "When Trudeau walked into my bedroom for my signature, I realized I was Commander in Chief of Canada."[5]

The constitutional safeguard is always there so long as there is a Crown as the ultimate constitutional protecting power for the legality of what government intends. Those wanting a republic should answer the question, "What safeguard against the abuse of power by politicians would replace the Crown as a constitutional protection device?" The fact that the young support the monarchy [6] likely indicates their suspicion of politicians' intentions. Americans are experienced in controlling abuse of power through checks and balances, however imperfect these may be. Canadians are not, because of our different system. Our suspicions about dispensing with the Crown likely parallel those of the Australians, who in 1999 turned down the proposal for a republic having a head of state appointed by politicians.

The constitutional monarchy as a safeguard for citizens works only so long as the Queen's representatives have the "right stuff" not only for their responsibility to warn, but also to ask about the legality or fairness of what ministers intend and to exercise their ultimate constitutional authority to decline to approve it, should it ever come to that. But there is nothing preventing the prime minister of the day or a provincial premier from proposing to the Queen as her representative someone who is sufficiently popular with the people but who can be expected not ever to question what ministers intend in the orders in council they bring for signature. Once signed by the Queen's representative, orders in council are the written intentions of the executive that ministers carry out.

Currently missing is the means for the Queen's representative to tell whether an intention of ministers in an executive order submitted for signature is lawful and doesn't create an abuse of ministers' power. In practice this check on ministers falls to the central agencies of government, upon whose work the Governor General relies. But, like J. Pierpont Morgan's lawyer, central agencies may be expected to tell ministers how to do something, not tell them that it cannot or must not be done. Governors general don't maintain an independent office to check the legality of intentions, which may be why judges of the Supreme Court have the authority to sign orders in council in the governor general's absence. But a problem arises when such an order in council later becomes the subject of litigation landing in the laps of the same Supreme Court judges.

A Specific Task For the Crown

The Crown is in a unique position to do a great service for citizens, and as a champion of democracy, by undertaking an important function in public accountability. The supreme constitutional power of the Crown happily coincides with the fact that the public answering obligation is an imperative in democracy, politically neutral, and doesn't tell anyone how to do their jobs. This means that the Queen and her representatives can, unassailably, and with the certain support of the public, withhold consent of a Bill that clearly affects the public in important ways but which has no provision stating who will answer to the public – and to what standard of answering – for the discharge of the powers and duties that the proposed Act would confer.

For the same reasons, the requirement for adequate public answering provisions in Acts can first be advised by the Senate in its regular review of Bills. It doesn't matter whether the Bill is initiated in the Senate or House of Commons. As already noted, the accountability check would be a solid role for the Senate and one bound to help overcome the current negative public stereotype of that body. It could even save the Senate's existence.

Given Senate and House of Commons scrutiny of the adequacy of public answering provisions in a Bill, and public knowledge of how well Parliament dealt with them, the Governor General should not have a problem with the Bill. But if the Governor General sees that the House of Commons and Senate have not produced adequate answering provisions by any standard, the Governor General could make her or his misgivings public by not readily signing the Bill into law. Legislators likely would not be able to withstand the dissatisfaction of citizens, if alerted by the media to the Governor General's concern. The felt accountability of governors general for their diligence in this role should be palpable, since citizens taking seriously their rights to public answering will look to the Governor General.

The same holds at the provincial level. For example, in the public outcry over Premier Mike Harris's late 1990s Bill 160 giving the executive power to decide what teachers in Ontario would do, thousands of citizens telephoned, wrote or sent emails to the Lieutenant Governor asking her not to sign the Bill.[7]

This is not a case of governors general misusing the Crown's ultimate constitutional power to thwart a legitimate political aim, however wise or misguided they may think the aim. We have already seen in Chapter 1 why the answering obligation is absolutely necessary and politically neutral. Lord Menuhin's "non-power" is there for a purpose. We can apply it safely and actively in the public interest.

Endnotes

[1] Halliday, W.E.D. "The Executive of the Government of Canada," *Canadian Public Administration*, September 1959, p.229. The constitutional function of ministers as advisors to the Crown has been more recently supported by Sir Robert Rhodes James, *A Spirit Undaunted: the Political Role of George VI*, (Abacus, London, 1998). Sir Robert had been Clerk of the United Kingdom's House of Commons for a decade, and later a Member of Parliament

[2] Halliday, p 231

[3] Halliday, p.232

[4] Governor General Romeo LeBlanc, *Ottawa Citizen*, 2 October 1999, p.A3

[5] Personal communication.

[6] *Ottawa Citizen*, 3 November 1999, p.A15

[7] Michael Valpy, *Globe and Mail*, 27 November 1997, P.A25

CHAPTER 8

The Accountability of Elected Representatives

Elected Representatives' Responsibilities

Elected representatives are the highest order of public servant, responsible for fairness in society. They are ultimate regulators, elected to intervene in society to make it work. They protect people from themselves, through legislation ranging from municipal by-laws to federal laws. They help ensure justice and fairness in citizens' opportunities. They regulate the distribution of benefits that society generates. They authorize international relationships, and they deal with natural disasters. Because this work is so important – and also because we pay their salaries and pensions – we have the right to see our elected representatives meet reasonable standards of performance and answering in overseeing executive government and legislation.[1] Yet we haven't even set performance standards for those running the government – the ministers.

Something happens when newly-elected representatives enter a legislative assembly, eager to work for fairness as each of them views it. They immediately yield to the processes of the assembly – processes for voting discipline and for maintaining conventions in challenge and debate. But these aren't processes for exacting adequate answering from executive governments. Because assembly processes in the parliamentary system are governed by ministers through the governing-party vote and majorities in each parliamentary committee, and through ministers' powers to award perks, parliamentary processes serve the wants of the senior ministers and are changed only to the extent that ministers allow it.

The parliamentary system gives the first minister (prime minister or premier) awesome dictatorial power. He or she appoints all ministers and all civil service heads of the departments of government, and has effective control of the appointment of judges and parliament's auditor general – even officers of parliament, through the government's majority. Scrutiny of government operations by legislative committees is limited: when their inquiries start going to the bone, the government majority in the committee heads it off. They don't have to be told.

Simply because legislatures represent "due process," we have tended to think of them as effective means of holding governments to account. We therefore we haven't thought it our right to set performance standards for our elected representatives and set fundamental rules and performance standards for our legislative assemblies to ensure that they serve the public's needs rather than ministers' wants. The current rules for assemblies aren't designed to ensure that ministers adequately inform themselves, speak honestly, exact adequate answering from their departmental officials and answer to the public for what they know and intend. Nor do we have performance standards for members of the assemblies at large. Citizens turn out in decreasing numbers to elect their representatives and then (except perhaps for municipal councillors) leave them alone and simply hope for the best until the next election.

An astonishing revelation happened in one of Peter Gzowski's television programs in early 1999. He was interviewing the Neilsen brothers, movie actor Leslie and ex-parliamentarian Erik. Gzowski played a short video clip of former deputy prime minister Neilsen, years earlier, answering an Opposition question in the House of Commons. The question was whether a cabinet minister colleague had met ethics standards. As the clip rolled, Neilsen muttered to himself, "Liar." Gzowski was amazed. Neilsen explained that loyalty to his political party had to come before truth in what he had said to the House, and this was one reason why he later left politics. He said 95% of politicians are liars, and people simply no longer believe politicians. His advice to aspiring politicians was to have it made before they entered politics, because "You can't stay honest."[2]

At the level of backbench Member of Parliament, the entire body of government Members voted in April 1998 to deny compensation to the pre-1986 hepatitis C victims of contaminated blood – making obvious the reluctance of obedient government MPs to know and act on the truth.

In an early 1990s study by the office of the Auditor General of Canada on control in the federal government, an outside advisor and former MP, Professor James Gillies of York University's graduate business school, told the office team that the best thing the Auditor General could do was to report to Parliament – and therefore to the public – that Canadians couldn't expect MPs to be motivated to ask about management control in government because the MPs were impotent, and knew it. Another seasoned MP, Alan Redway, who had been a minister, told the study team that MPs have to pretend to their constituents that they have power. Opposition legislators can cause media flurries, but they haven't brought about fundamental change.

The combination of the personal aims of ministers who have no effective answering obligations, the impotence of backbench legislators and the battered-wife syndrome of citizens' perpetual acceptance of government's agendas, "decrees" and spin makes adequate public answering necessary. Once we make answering and its validation the law, we can individually decide whether to do our civic duty in responding to the answering, or abdicate.

The precautionary principle says that we must assume that executive government will, if it can, put appearances first but will also seek to eliminate, by whatever means, liability that could arise if ministers fail to do their statutory duty. When ministers seek to turn over their responsibilities to corporations, they want citizens to think that the ministers would no longer be responsible and accountable, when constitutionally they remain so no matter what responsibilities they try to shed. Meanwhile they portray themselves as defending existing policy set by the citizens themselves – such as medicare.

We have to be serious about this. How do we tell whether a relationship amounting to a state of war exists between executive government and the majority of citizens who want core protection policies to stay in place? What do the citizens of the Walkertons of Canada have to say for themselves when they elect a party whose ministers appear to have dismissed the precautionary principle and government's duty for testing water, and deaths ensue? Will a public inquiry make a government do its duty thereafter?

Legislators can be as well-informed about executive government intentions and likely effects as they collectively choose to be. Nothing stops legislators from being sovereign in their own assemblies in their scrutiny and decision-making. And nothing stops governing-party members from resisting the tacit commands of party bosses to carry out ministers' wants and prevent their ministers from being held to account in the assembly.

For government's regulatory protection responsibilities, can legislators say they know what goes on in the departments? Do they know whether the officials to whom scientists and safety inspectors report champion staff professional concerns about risk and safety feasibility up the line to the point where ministers' intentions to satisfy industry are confronted? Does a regulatory department's director say to a scientist or workplace inspector, as a Morton Thiokol vice-president apparently said to a company engineer protesting the politically-pressured fatal launch of the *Challenger* space shuttle, just hours before lift-off, "Take off your engineer's hat and put on your manager's hat"?[3]

If the elected representatives in the governing party can please their ministers by helping them abdicate their statutory responsibilities, why not do it? And if they can abdicate their own duties by handing over government's responsibilities to corporations while still retaining their salaries and pensions, why not do it? In a society where standards are crumbling, why not indeed? If standards are falling, what do legislators gain by holding fast themselves?

If we don't set performance and answering standards for our elected representatives and exact full and fair answering from them, we can't tell whether they are betraying the public interest behind the scenes – especially ministers. If we install the responsibility and answering standards, braying by obedient government backbenchers will be exposed for what it is, because all will have to account to their constituents for how well they hold the executive to account. And to make fair decisions as governing bodies, elected representatives must inform themselves to a standard reasonable for the types of decisions facing them. They will have to be prepared to publicly explain their reasoning to their constituents.

Here is a test, using health as an example. Can Canadian Members of Parliament demonstrate to their constituents, and could citizens assert to their neighbours, that the following assessment by an MP is wrong?

> The government is involved in a full-scale retreat from the role of government as regulator when it comes to drugs, food, water, blood, organs, tissues, sperm banks, medical devices, and so on. The closing of the drug research bureau, the gutting of the food directorate, the intimidation of scientists concerned about bovine growth hormone, the evidence of Nancy Olivieri of drug company influence over the drug approval process, the absence of research on the long-term effects of genetically engineered foods, the decision to lump food promotion and safety inspection into one agency – all of these are examples of the government retreat from health protection and of the industrial hijacking of health.

> It is an insidious agenda of moving this country away from the do-no-harm precautionary principle to a risk-management, buyer-beware model. The onus is being shifted away from the manufacturer to prove safety and onto the public to prove harm.... The Liberal government is playing Russian roulette with the lives of Canadians in order to reduce its own liability and to release corporations from responsibility. Instead, Canadians pay with their health and even with their lives.[4]

What does it mean for citizens if everything in the above statement is true? How do we even start to find out the truth if we don't ask our elected representatives to make government and other authorities answer for their intentions and responsibilities and validate their answering?

In health, for example, an equally important question is whether the directing mind for the federal government's health responsibilities is the health minister or the industry minister. The industry minister's job is to help produce healthy corporate profits, not healthy citizens, and trumpeting new technology as the answer to everything, including health issues[5], distracts people's attention from fairness decisions made behind the scenes in government.

Elected representatives need to be helped by mandatory public answering if we expect them to grasp what goes on. In the Chapter 1 horror stories, none of which involved corporate assault on our national core policies, the Canadian legislatures were ineffective in preventing harm and failed even to produce redress. If legislators left on their own can't even ensure people's safety, we have no assurance that they will be effective in protecting what citizens have installed as core social policies in their countries. In legislating the labelling of genetically modified foods, for example, good law can be fatally flawed if it doesn't require the minister to publicly state, before the fact, the reasoning for each ministerial exemption.

At the global level, Isabel Hilton summed up the major fairness problem in a May 2000 article in the *Guardian Weekly:*

> The advocates of untrammelled global free trade argue that this is all to our benefit. We are wealthier, better fed, better housed and longer lived than at any time in history. And the past two decades have delivered an extraordinary rate of growth that has lifted millions out of poverty. Free market purists argue that all the ills the process has produced can be cured by further liberalisation.
>
> The demonstrators in Seattle last year and on the streets of London this week – and those who quietly cheer them on – say that's not the whole story. The counter argument was thoroughly made at Seattle: that the cost of this economic growth in environmental terms is unpayable, that the political price is too high, that the power of the global corporations, which are the prime beneficiaries of the system, is too great, that the huge disparities in wealth that the process has produced is immoral. For most people the argument is not whether there should be capitalism or not. It is: what kind of capitalism? What degree of rapacity can I accept for the benefits I enjoy?
>
> ...Globalisation of trade has generated the globalisation of protest – the internet allows movements to build critical mass – as they fight against the Multilateral Agreement on Investment or Monsanto's terminator gene. But so far it has failed to create a global political ground on which the terms and conditions of capitalism can be negotiated. Until it does, the discussion will

stay in the streets.[6]

Discussions will likely stay in the streets until we install simple ways to force visibility of the real agendas of governments' directing minds and their reasoning for the outcomes they seek.

But for France, the 1997 proposed Multilateral Agreement on Investment (MAI) of the Organization for Economic Cooperation and Development (OECD) may well have been adopted by the OECD member countries, despite activists' good work. As we have already found with the North American Free Trade agreement (NAFTA), on which the MAI was based, national governments would in effect sign over to transnational corporations their countries' sovereign power over core policies for food and health, education, employment, environmental protection and other responsibilities. By committing the country, they would override local government policies. Other trading countries would then be expected to sign on, or be punished.

In Canada the prime minister and finance minister, because of their executive power, could decide the MAI issue for Canadians and simply pass it through Parliament , using their majority in the House of Commons. Federal parliamentary hearings on the MAI, hastily thrown together, amounted to endorsement not only by the government majorities in the committees but also by corporation-supporting opposition members.

But there was no evidence that Members of Parliament had read the draft Agreement and understood what was at stake for Canadians.[7] Canada's Trade Minister at the time, Sergio Marchi, having full access to all the facts and intentions, wasn't asked by MPs or by the large activist groups to lay before Parliament and Canadians an equity statement for the main MAI provisions. It would state who the government thinks would benefit, how, and why they should benefit, and who would bear what costs and risks, and why they should – immediately and down the road. This public information is still needed for the MAI proposals to show what its successor proposed agreements will be aiming for.

Activist groups in several countries mounted cohesive strong protests against the MAI, unprecedented in scope because of the Internet. Many more Canadians became alarmed than we would have expected. But no organization with a powerful podium demanded that the national governments who govern the OECD require that secretariat to produce, along with its draft Agreement, equity statements for the MAI's main provisions. Had the OECD been made to do this, the governments of each of its member countries would then have been expected to disclose this information to their legislators and citizens, for challenge. Had this been done, the national legislators of each country would have been accountable for debating the "who gains, who loses" issue. The MAI intentions might then have been debated in a logical, structured way in the legislative chambers and not, as in Canada, within a government-controlled parliamentary committee. The committee simply received certain groups arguing their different views but didn't identify and debate in a structured way the MAI's intended outcomes in terms of who would gain and who would lose, and why they should.

The question is, who answers publicly for the intentions behind trade agreements, so that citizens in all countries can grasp the fairness trade-offs and whose needs or wants would be honoured, and why? If the transnational corporation directing minds expect countries to subordinate their core national policies to corporate owners' and managers' profit aims, the legislators in each country are accountable for explaining why citizens should or shouldn't go along with it. The Appendix I equity statement example deals with this disclosure issue for the MAI.

An example completely within Canadians' control is Alberta's Bill C-11. In May 2000 the executive government of Alberta created provincial law permitting privatization of hospital services. Bill C-11 was something a majority of Albertans didn't want. They saw it as the first step of a tacit aim to dismantle medicare as Canadian national core policy and not, as provincial premier Ralph Klein portrayed it, an Act simply starting debate on how health care should be managed in future. Rather than taking responsibility for fixing the way governments deliver health care and publicly stating the performance standards needed by their governments to do it cost-effectively, the health ministers and premiers generally appear to be turning health care over to the private sector. They know that their legislative majorities will let them do this and, as well, make the public purse pay the additional cost of the private sector's profit margins.

The Alberta provincial legislature made Bill C-11 the law without the executive having to produce a publicly-challenged equity statement as a basis for the legislators' decisions and for Albertans to judge the motivation and competence of their legislators. Federal Minister of Health Allan Rock ultimately conceded that the Alberta law didn't contravene the federal *Canada Health Act*. But he showed no intent to change the federal Act to prevent health care in Canada from becoming simply a product to be handed over to American corporations under the North American Free Trade Agreement. The Canadian federal government hasn't told Canadians whether it has already given over to the provinces effective control in health and environmental protection, which is perhaps why it blusters in both these responsibilities yet insists on nothing.

The majority of Canadians wring their hands, not wanting medicare dismantled but not knowing how to keep our own national policy.

In view of the Alberta health law, coming six years after the federal government's signing of NAFTA in 1994 (which a majority of Canadians opposed), we cannot assume that activist efforts and minority legislators alone can stop determined executive governments from giving business profits top priority and installing trade agreements that override the law of their own countries.

When we shift from decisions that can make or break a nation to parliamentary scrutiny of day-to-day government operations within a country, we find no discussion of the self-informing and control duties of parliamentarians for ensuring that government complies with the law and decided policy.

Compliance involves two types of responsibility. In its broad sense, compliance means producing what is legitimately asked for. The accountability question is, "Did you achieve what you were asked to achieve, with due regard to fairness and value for money?" The health protection and medicare abdication issues can be viewed as compliance issues if the doctrine of legitimate expectation is applied to what Canadians expect their legislators to maintain as policy. In administrative law, legitimate expectation doesn't prevent policy change that is produced through legitimate political process, but it requires adequate hearings and public consultation if established policy is to be jettisoned. Shedding medicare and health protection is being carried out by executive governments as a "tell and sell," not by genuine consultation with the people. Citizens' valid concerns about dismantlement may, therefore, be actionable in the courts.

But compliance in government operations also means conformity to fundamental rules of conduct. In this sense, compliance includes meeting the intent of laws, including laws governing ministers' duties. It also means meeting commonsense standards of prudence and honesty. Legislators must install fundamental rules for the conduct and answering of executive governments and civil servants, to keep these people law-abiding and serving the public interest. In addition to their fairness decision-making in setting laws, elected representatives have the control responsibility of making executive government answer for compliance.

Efficiency in government means using resources well to produce intended results. Efficiency includes economy, which means getting the quality of resources one needs at the least cost. Both compliance and efficiency are fairness issues, but they are important enough in their own right to require elected representative attention. Efficiency is largely the job of civil servants, but elected representatives have the duty to approve the standards of efficiency that citizens can reasonably expect for government operations, ensure that these standards are visible and met, and ensure public reporting of the level of efficiency actually delivered. This holds federally, provincially and municipally.

A well-known example of ministers not discharging their self-informing and control responsibilities was the February-June 2000 furor over the federal government's 1990s management of a billion-dollar group of grants and contributions programs housed in the federal government department now called Human Resources and Development Canada (HRDC). Here we will focus on ministers' responsibilities and accountability for management control – causing to happen that which should, but also causing not to happen that which shouldn't.

The Accountability Issue in HRDC

The Ministers' responsibilities. The Human Resources and Development Department (called Human Resources and Development Canada) made grants in the late 1990s of about $1 billion. These were dispensed through several programs for jobs creation, job training, disabled people and Aboriginals. The state of management of the programs was made public by a 1999 departmental internal audit report that repeated more forcefully what 1991 and 1994 internal audits had already reported to top management about the Department's programs.

The government calls project funding either a grant or a contribution. The usual difference is that contributions require recipients to meet certain terms and conditions, and thus invoke accountability reporting by the recipient, and compliance auditing, while grants are amounts in effect to be placed on doorsteps with no strings attached. In the case of HRDC, neither the government nor the media made clear which of the $1 billion jobs-creation money was grant and which was contribution, and therefore whether the control implications were different for each. But even with grants there needs to be public assurance beforehand that the money will be spent for the purpose. Here we will use the only term used by the media: grants.

Before the fact, the responsible minister should have publicly reported the government's achievement objectives and reasoning for creating the billion-dollar fund, and the control standards it intended over the funding decisions for the thousands of anticipated project applications. Many of these came from demonstrably effective community and other organizations, some from political-appearances motivation and some from opportunistic sharks who suspected that money was being given out simply for the asking.

During and after the fact, the government should have reported what was being achieved by the projects for the amount spent. The quality of the public answering helps tell us the extent to which the billion dollars was thought out and spent constructively in the public interest or simply thrown at the issue of what to do after the federal government cut back people's unemployment insurance eligibility and coverage.

What seems clear for the HRDC grants was that a jobs-related project application was to be submitted only in regions where unemployment exceeded a threshold rate (12%, later lowered to 10%), and the local MP had to approve it, which was likely automatic. But HRDC could override an MP's disapproval. The original eligibility criterion of 12% unemployment rate for a region was relaxed by HRDC officials to approve higher-unemployment "pockets" within a region – except that not all MPs were told this. The project grants, in total numbering 40,000 to 50,000, ranged individually from a few thousand dollars to several millions.

The various accountability aspects in this HRDC example emerge from over 150 newspaper articles on the affair from February to June 2000,[8] excluding reported police investigations for some projects. The purpose of the example is to show, from a welter of facts, parliamentary questions and various people's observations reported in the media, why we need legislators to set and enforce rules for adequate answering from ministers. A full explanation of the responsibilities, accountabilities and conduct of the significant people involved in the HRDC affair would need a book on its own. It would need *Hansard*, parliamentary committee minutes and government documents for illustrations of control failures, questions asked and what accountable people said or refused to say.

The affair and the thousands of public comments on it illustrate the problem facing citizens trying to understand an executive government's motivations and actions, and whether they serve the public interest. What has been missing in all the press reports, letters to the editors, comments by academics and former civil servants, and House of Commons questions and frustrations, is a logical framework of responsibilities, fundamental rules for control and public answering in the public interest. The facts of an HRDC cluster of programs, or any other political program, can be organized by a framework of responsibility and accountability which can guide holding to account by elected representatives.

An obvious public answering issue in the HRDC affair is whether the grants helped the organizations receiving them to do productive work. This is a value for money issue. The government conceded that it didn't know. The government's political aim in the grants could have been to create temporary and durable jobs, but it could also have been to sway votes in ridings narrowly held by Liberals or where Liberals had a chance of winning in the 1997 federal election coinciding with the timing of the HRDC programs – or both. The government repeatedly decreed that the funding had created 30,000 jobs without giving the evidence for the claim, yet said that it lacked the information to report on the grants made riding by riding. The opposition parties repeatedly claimed the $1 billion was a political slush fund.

The furor started with a 1999 internal audit report stated as completed in early October 1999 but released to the public by the Minister of the Department, Jane Stewart, on 19 January 2000. The government requires completed departmental internal audit reports to be made public. Interim audit reports are accessible through access to information requests.

The internal audit sample was 459 projects, representing $200 million of funding across 27 programs, run by seven directorates in HRDC. The 1999 report included the following audit observations:

- 15% of the projects were approved without application forms
- 66% lacked rationale for the funding
- 97% lacked financial background checks on the recipient
- 25% lacked description of the activities to be supported
- 72% lacked cash flow forecasts
- 46% lacked estimates of the number of participants
- 80% lacked evidence of monitoring to know the projects' results

The audit report excluded the question of influence exerted on Department officials by MPs and ministers in funding projects in their ridings.

In summary, most of the projects examined lacked adequate evidence to support the spending of public money at the stage when government cheques were written, and were not tracked to see if the money was well spent.

Given the department's own audit reports of 1991 and 1994, the 1999 review and the federal Auditor General's repeated observations on financial control in government over the decade, the fair inference is that the lack of control diligence was purposeful at the minister level. And there is no available evidence that the senior civil servants setting up the programs countered such a signal given them: weak value for money control can't be called political policy that civil servants must carry out. But "the limits are understood."

The issue is not just citizens shrugging their shoulders. As a sole-proprietor Ottawa barber put it at the time, "The government gets GST (Goods and Services Tax) from me on my supplies and my rent – on all my big expenses – and then I pay it again on what I get for haircuts. Then the government throws away a billion dollars of what it takes from us." He paused and then said, "It breaks the spirit." When asked if he had thought of organizing others like himself to do something about it, the barber said, "I can't. They'd get me."

To fix something, we have to know the underlying cause. When the underlying cause is a policy intention by politicians that is not in the public interest, the only body with the mandate to identify and react to executive government intention is the legislature. Given that governing party members support the executive, right or wrong, the scrutiny work falls to the Opposition. In the HRDC case, the Opposition couldn't get answers to fair questions about what ministers intended, and did or failed to do.

The HRDC example illustrates accountability issues that must be dealt with by citizens and elected representatives alike.

Ministers' self-informing and answering duties. Successive ministers responsible for HRDC and its predecessor departments have never told the public the extent to which they informed themselves about the adequacy of value for money control in the department – control that ensured that the $1 billion was "used as intended, spent wisely and produced the desired results," as Auditor General Denis Desautels summed up the issue to the press at the end of March 2000. If the ministers intended to inform themselves about control, the department's own audits and reviews throughout the 1990s, coupled with the auditor general's observations on control in government departments, stared them in the face.

Specific cases about what ministers should have known and when, such as in contaminated blood, Westray, Walkerton and the Al-Mashat case,[9] make adequate self-informing a central duty of each minister of the Crown. It is the minister's responsibility to set the level to which he or she wishes to be informed by the departmental management head (the deputy minister), and the minister's responsibility to ensure that this happens. Each minister should publicly account for the extent to which they obtain the information they need to do their statutory and commonsense duty. But it is the job of the Clerk of the Privy Council, as the head civil servant in government, to set basic rules for deputy ministers for informing their ministers, such that the minister can't plead plausible denial.

Thus, for a Watergate-type question put to a minister, "What did you know and when did you know it?" the response, "I was briefed on November 17" may seem plausible as the time the minister would have become aware. But "When did you know it?" isn't good enough, because Minister Stewart answered in the passive voice. Saying "I was briefed" avoids disclosing whether the minister sought out important governance information on her own initiative. "I was briefed…" is not the same answer as the following, which wouldn't likely be given by any minister in the absence of fundamental rules for ministerial responsibility and answering:

> As to how I informed myself, as soon as I became Minister of the Department, and because of my experience with audit findings in my previous department, I asked the deputy and assistant deputy ministers what problems there were in responsibilities A, B and C (the department's key responsibilities). I was told D, E and F, and I checked the validity of this as best I could from internal audit reports and other information. I then ordered X and Y to be done in people's responsibilities, and Z for their answering, and made sure that this was done. I reported to the Department-related committees of the House what I was doing, and why.

By the same token, questions to ministers about self-informing should be couched in terms of standards that citizens have a right to see met, such as:

> What did you do, and when, to inform yourself accurately whether departmental responsibilities A, B and C were being carried out diligently?

Getting fair answering from the executive government. In the HRDC case the ministers' answers were the most important, because the ministers set the value for money and fairness control processes. (Expectations for civil servants' answering follow in Chapter 9.)

Answering is for the discharge of a responsibility. The person in a government department having ultimate responsibility for control is the minister. This means that the person who answers to the legislature for the adequacy of management control within a government department is the minister, because he or she has control over the civil servants who do the controlling. The prime minister, advised by the Clerk of the Privy Council, has the responsibility for supplying the minister with the right deputy minister as the administrative head of the department and the accountable manager of the control system.

Here we need to refer back to Chapter 4 and Sissela Bok's definition of lying: any intentionally deceptive message that is stated. A minister's straight refusal to give an answer to a fair and legitimate question is rejection of the question, not lying, even though it is arrogance. But once a minister responds, it logically follows that the Bok definition applies. This is especially important in the case of a minister or prime minister, whose status means that many people will accept his or her answer as valid simply because the person has the status of minister of the Crown. In the HRDC case, much of the ministerial answering was answering of questions not asked, and so far off fair answering that it amounted to a refusal to answer. But, since it was given publicly as an answer in the sure knowledge that it wasn't a fair answer, it fell within the Bok definition.

The accountable minister of record for the main period of HRDC control failure, Pierre Pettigrew, simply rejected questions put to him. He decreed to a gullible press that the rules of Parliament prevented him from answering for his past responsibilities. The "Pettigrew defence" was publicly refuted by former Prime Minister Joe Clark, who told the media that ministers can answer – and have done so in the past – if they agree to do so. But even this fails minimum standards of required public answering. Who else is protected by what amounts to a statute of limitations that could be only a few months if ministers are shifted to other portfolios?

Prime Minister Jean Chrétien decreed that the problems affecting the Department were minor because only 37 cases in the 459 sample were being further audited at what amounted to a forensic level of examination. This was sufficiently reckless as to the truth and the implications of the cumulative internal and external audit reports that it fell within the Bok definition.

Minister Stewart, who had taken over HRDC in August 1999, responded to questions in the House of Commons but said, for example, "We know where every cheque has gone." This ducks the central question whether they should have been issued, and deceives because it attempts to give the impression of value for money diligence in authorizing the cheques. Saying at the same time that "The (internal) audit did not say there was political interference" deceives because it suggests that the question of political influence was part of the scope of the audit, when the Minister knew it was not.

Examples of the Minister's answering in the House of Commons include the following:

> Opposition MP to the Minister (three times asked):
>
> How much of this $1 billion of spending was not supported by proper evidence?

> Response by the Minister (three times given):
>
> We're looking for administrative deficiencies and fixing them.

> Opposition MP to the Minister:
>
> How much of the $1 billion was paid out in overpayments and advances?

> Response by the Minister:
>
> Our administrative practices have to be improved.

> Opposition MP to the Minister:
>
> Doesn't the audit mean that we need an independent inquiry?

> Response by the Minister:
>
> The audit tells us that we have administrative deficiencies in our management of grants and contributions. As you look at the action plan, you can see that we take this situation extremely seriously.

As to the contentious point of when the Minister first became aware of the HRDC problems, in view of the fact that she consistently maintained that it was not until 17 November 1999:

> Opposition MP to the Minister 9 February 2000:
>
> Would the Minister of HRDC please advise the House on the exact date on which she was first advised of the problems that were uncovered by the internal audit of her department?

> Response by the Minister:
>
> I received a briefing on the full internal audit on November 17.

The next day the question was:

> Would the Minister have Canadians believe that she didn't know there were problems in her department until the date of November 17?

> Response by the Minister: What I will confirm is that the final internal audit that looked at the seven program, grants and contributions in my Department as we have shared with the House over and over again was presented to me in its entirety on November 17

Parliamentarians would assume that the Deputy Minister or other senior official aide would brief the Minister instantly, considering that the explosive audit report needed instant public damage control. It is not credible that the audit observations were new to the Minister as late as October 1999. But the issue being pursued by Opposition MPs wasn't a month's time discrepancy; it was whether the Minister had lied to the House about when she knew of the extent of the control failure. As to when the Minister knew, auditors don't present surprises to audited management. Auditors give progress reports and draft observations along the way. Thus it is unlikely that the minister knew nothing until November 1999 – especially in view of the available earlier audit reports in the Department, and the Minister's familiarity with internal audit as the minister's "intellectual bodyguard."

On the question of grants awarded in the Minister's riding,

> Opposition MP to the Minister:

> Were all 301 MPs informed about the flexibility in the way the unemployment figures could be juggled to qualify for the TJF-CJF grants,[10] or was it only ministers who were made aware?

> Response by the Minister:

> "Mantra" (the word used by *Globe and Mail* columnist Hugh Winsor to describe the Minister's response)

The pattern is clear. When a minister is fairly asked, "What did you know about report X and its implications, and when did you know it?" the response is, "The sun is shining." In fact the popular CBC TV program, "This Hour Has 22 Minutes" twice aired a skit satirizing this very type of response. The famous television coverage of the seven tobacco company CEOs answering to a US congressional sub-committee included the same attempt – except that the legislators could and did require the CEOs to finally answer the specific questions asked.

The Minister surely realized that responding to parliamentarians in the February-June 2000 period by not answering questions, or answering questions not asked, would be seen as arrogance – but arrogance not fatal to the public's confidence because the ministers expected the affair to blow over. Read by the public as lying, however, misleading ministerial responses aren't that safe – unless the public doesn't care. In the HRDC case, it is more likely that the media and the public, including the Ottawa barber, simply didn't know what to do about it.

The answering issue isn't simply whether a minister was consistently giving responses apparently scripted by others, and whether the HRDC case was simply a matter of political warfare. Since answering shares power, refusal to answer is arrogance. Making intentionally deceptive statements as dismissive responses is even greater arrogance, whether viewed as lying or not. But when this is done in a legislative assembly, regardless of the chamber's rules allowing it, it amounts to contempt for the assembly and for the very purpose of a legislative assembly. It also affects important answering of senior civil servants questioned in parliamentary committees, because they take their cues from what their ministers say.

In a majority government with obedient backbenchers, ministers can refuse to account with impunity. This raises the question whether, in a minority government, given a minister's non-answering, the opposition would combine to bring down the government on a vote of non-confidence. The answer is, not likely. Current House of Commons rules don't require answering from ministers in Question Period and don't require the Speaker to ensure adequate answering.

Speakers don't see their role as requiring adequate answers to clear and fair questions in the legislature. They see their role as largely protecting the rights of all members of the assembly to be heard and to put questions.[11] But what good is this, when it's certain that a minister will refuse to properly answer a fair and clear question? If MPs wish Canadians to think that they serve public accountability, they must amend the rules of the House to require ministers to answer a fair question fairly. The judge and referee for what is a fair question is the Speaker. Since the Speaker is to be nonpartisan and the public answering obligation is politically neutral, it is a reasonable duty. If auditors can give professional opinions on what fair financial answering is, speakers – selected by the MPs themselves – can tell what fair parliamentary answering is. Both the House rules and the Speaker's selection are decided by the government's majority in the House. But citizens can cause their MPs (including the Speaker) to take seriously the comment attributed to U.S. Senator Everett Dirksen: "When I feel the heat, I see the light."

The breakthrough needed is acceptance by all legislators that adequate public answering is not someone's political policy; it is a needed universal and neutral governor for fairness.

An Initiative for Legislators

Legislators can reasonably be expected to install in their legislatures the requirement that members of the executive (ministers in the parliamentary system) will answer fair questions fully and fairly, or state when they will answer. Fundamental criteria for judging the fairness of questions and the fairness of the answering would be developed by the legislators themselves and exposed to citizens' groups for challenge. The criteria would then be given to the Speaker to use in regulating the assembly. This fundamental change in rules could significantly reduce appearances conduct, posturing, power-tripping and arrogance in the assemblies, and help them become forums in which ministers properly answer for their responsibilities.

Government MPs won't likely improve government answering themselves, through parliamentary evolution. Being obedient, these backbenchers will more likely support their ministers' stonewalling as part of the partisan game. But in the HRDC affair, Opposition members of the House acted with unusual cohesiveness in trying to get adequate government answering.

There is nothing stopping each party caucus from identifying an appropriate member to meet with counterparts in other parties as an Accountability Task Group, to set basic standards for government answering and, as well, basic standards for Opposition questioning.

To get around the predictable blocking of this initiative by an instructed government-member majority, such a group would comprise only one member from each party – someone who views accountability as nonpartisan. To get around prime ministerial media spin denigrating the idea of such a group ("That's the very thing Parliament itself already does"), those willing to create such a group would have to get the public behind them by setting out why an all-party accountability task group is needed.

The group would propose to MPs how reasonable accountability could be achieved in the House, installed by the Members themselves. The group would ask for challenge by the Prime Minister, ministers and Opposition party leaders but give no veto rights, and in any case make its conclusions and recommendations public. The group's report would also ask citizens to let their Members of Parliament know their expectations for House of Commons action on the report. If the Prime Minister issues orders that no such group will be allowed, the Opposition parties can do it on their own, based on their cooperation demonstrated in the HRDC case. But it is something that MPs must do themselves, not pass off for study by outside groups funded by government.

The difference between this approach and usual parliamentary reform activity is that the group's recommendations would not be watered down in a parliamentary committee dominated by government members, and would be presented to the public.

The sequence of the group's work would be roughly the following:

1. Identify reasonable answering standards for ministers and civil servants under the precautionary principle (including the protection standards for civil servants at the Director level and below) and the critical success factors for achieving adequate answering in the House

2. Identify current norms and extent of answering (While the HRDC affair is instructive, there are other examples as well, and examples in other jurisdictions)

3. Report how the present processes must be changed, through changes in rules for the House (both for questions put and the answering), augmenting the speaker's duty, and legislation giving statutory direction to ministers for answering adequately for their responsibilities.

Again we would hear, "But this isn't how Parliament works." Exactly. The point is that Parliament isn't working and, in the words of the Leonard Cohen song, "everybody knows." In fact, each minister and government-party MP can be asked to state publicly why this task should or shouldn't be undertaken. The same type of legislator group can be formed in each provincial legislature.

The Quality of Opposition Questioning

The MPs' questions cited above were good questions. But Opposition MPs mustn't lead with their chins. Questions such as:

> "When is the Minister going to do the right thing and resign?

and

> "How long was the Minister really planning to keep it under cover that she had actually bungled a billion dollars?"

aren't questions holding to account. They invite a minister to scorn them as simply partisan posturing and to seize the opportunity to make a partisan government statement that uses up the question time. No one is any further ahead.

Perhaps few MPs on their own could be expected to think of dead-centre questions such as the one put by Louis Desmarais in the early 1980s. As the Vice-Chair of the Public Accounts Committee and a former CEO of a major Canadian corporation, he asked his question of the new Deputy Minister taking charge of the two-billion-dollars-a-year Canadian International Development Agency. (The question fits for ministers as well, since they are ultimately responsible for the running of their departments.)

Desmarais asked, "What would you say are your most important management problems, and what are you doing about them?"

This is a nifty two-part question because it covers self-informing duty, ability to rank problems and control diligence intentions. The first part of the question asked the deputy to disclose his or her own ranking of management problems, which can then be publicly validated by those who know the operations – including the auditor general. The second part of the question required the Deputy Minister to make a diligence commitment statement, which also becomes subject to a credibility check by those who know the department – especially the employees of the department. What soon becomes clear is whether the accountable official knows the central underlying problems and is prepared to disclose them, and has an action intention that deals with causes of problems, not just symptoms.

Thus a minister's saying that she (courageously) disclosed an audit report that in any case had to be disclosed by the government's own rules, and that she had a "six point plan" approved by the auditor general to deal with control failure simply won't do. As a February 2000 *Ottawa Citizen* editorial put it:

> "Forgive us for being skeptical, but nothing in that "comprehensive plan" seems to be anything more than basic management practices required of all public servants under the existing *Financial Administration Act*."

Opposition members can make certain things clear for citizens. They can report whether "action plans" appear to be only processes for carrying on usual duties, and not processes that identify and deal with syndromes, underlying causes and accountabilities. They can report who should answer to whom, for what responsibilities, They can report the action needed and ask the minister to tell the legislature whether he or she agrees, and why.

In their report to the House of Commons on HRDC following committee hearings, the Department-related parliamentary committee cautioned against "overreacting" to the control failures. But as an Opposition member put it, "They (the government-controlled committee) liken it to a cold, instead of the serious cancer that we see." The dissenting Opposition members of the committee also accused the government committee members of failing to provide whistleblower protection for employees who wanted to bring damning evidence of departmental wrong-doing to the committee. Commenting on the committee's interim report in the House in April 2000, the Minister predictably said,

> "We have heard day after day the rantings and ravings of the Opposition on this issue. We have a program that we are implementing to improve our system."

Control Pretense in Government

A citizen's impression of the words "Treasury Board" suggests a function providing effective control over spending. And this branch of the federal government does have statutory control over departmental spending. The Office of the Comptroller General of Canada was in effect forced on the government in 1978 by Auditor General James Macdonell, in part because Treasury Board wasn't doing an adequate job in control and in accounting to Parliament. Having first ensured that the Comptroller General had no statutory mandate, the most senior civil servants patiently took over a decade to dismantle the function into a title only, now only an appendage to the title of the head civil servant of the Treasury Board.

The Treasury Board is held out as the manager of control in government operations. It once was, but the President (Minister) of the Treasury Board at the time of the HRDC disclosures , Lucienne Robillard, conceded that it was not enforcing fundamental rules. Yet the President claimed in April 2000 that the missing HRDC control was not "systemic" across government. She said she based this statement on what the deputy ministers in other departments told her. Her assertion wasn't supported by an independent knowledgeable body such as the Auditor General, and wasn't based on public assurances given to the President by the ministers in charge of the other departments.

The President added, "I would agree that we (Treasury Board) should have a more active monitoring role of control practices." But this vague statement was not a minister's commitment to meet a performance standard in control. Note the "should have" rather than "will take," as if Treasury Board had no power to act. Commenting on Treasury Board, Parliament's Information Commissioner, John Reid, said

> It is the organization in government that sets policies, but it has no desire and no intention of enforcing them to ensure departments are following the policies laid down.[12]

Given the HRDC revelations, Canadians were entitled to a non-partisan public statement from the Treasury Board Minister such as:

> I will henceforth exercise the powers of the Treasury Board provided by statute to exact the quality of management control across government that Canadians have the right to see attained. I will publicly state whether anything stands in my way in doing this, and report to Parliament annually the quality of control across government actually being achieved.

Significant signs of Treasury Board ducking enforcement of fundamental rules for departments and public answering were evident by the close of the 1970s. The clue was the new value for money audit mandate given by Parliament to the federal auditor general put into effect in 1978. It was forced on the government by political pressure from Auditor General Macdonell's reports, mainly his 1976 statement to the House of Commons that both the government and Parliament had lost, or were close to losing, effective control of the public purse.

The government purposefully didn't accompany the amended 1978 *Auditor General Act* with a corresponding amendment to the *Financial Administration Act* requiring departments and agencies to set and state value for money performance standards and publicly report their intended and actual performance. Treasury Board would then have had to oversee that statutory compliance. The Auditor General would then have had the logical role of attesting to the fairness and completeness of ministers' performance reporting.

Instead, the government had Parliament tell the auditor general to do, in effect, the departments' performance reporting for them, through the new comprehensive audit reports. They knew that the auditor general couldn't be everywhere at once, and knew that the departmental deputies and their ministers would fight adequate public performance reporting because it would force them to declare their performance standards. Moreover, the government's ducking of statutory answering by ministers and deputies left the audit office vulnerable to departmental senior officials saying, in Public Accounts Committee hearings on the new comprehensive audit reports, "The audit team meant well, but the poor souls unfortunately don't understand the environment of our decision-making."

Thus the federal government's own rules for management control across its departments and agencies amount only to internal guides (and likely only "best practices" exhortations) with the minister for the Treasury Board having no clout and the public having no assurance of standards enforcement in the public interest. Journalists covering the HRDC story could have pointed out for Canadians that the Deputy Minister and the two other senior officials of HRDC most involved in the control issue came from the Treasury Board.

Nothing stops Parliament from asking the Auditor General to give a professional opinion on whether the Treasury Board ministers, Clerk of the Privy Council and departmental ministers are discharging their responsibilities for management control in government to a performance standard Canadians have a right to see met. (And nothing stops the Auditor General from doing this on his or her own initiative.) The Auditor General can tell Parliament whether these people's answering for their responsibilities meets a reasonable standard of answering and is fair and complete. Reporting on the rightness or wrongness of political policy for programs isn't the job of an Auditor General, but reporting on control performance and the adequacy of government's public answering is.

For all programs funded by Parliament from public money, Members of Parliament can ask ministers and deputy ministers to show that:
- spending complies with the achievement intent understood by Parliament and meets value for money criteria reasonable for the nature and amount of spending for the program
- grants and contribution application processes, eligibility criteria, fundamental rules

and the performance standards for those involved are visible to all and are likely to produce fairness and value for money for each funding cheque written

- ministers are adequately told by their deputies the state of control:
  - what the ministers' duties are, as ministers of the Crown
  - the quality of their management control over funding
  - the effect of minister-ordered constraints on staff (such as the effect of large staff cuts)
  - whether their programs' critical success factors are being met for fairness and value for money
  - what difference their approved expenditures are making
- ministers are reporting fully, fairly and frequently to Parliament

the extent to which they think they:

  - met reasonable performance standards for ensuring fairness and value for money in expenditures they authorize
  - complied with the stated rules for issuing program money, reduced barriers standing in the way of departmental staff doing a better job, and produced the intended difference for the public money voted them by Parliament.

These are not pie-in-the-sky answering standards. Legislators can install them. We have seen what is needed in government control responsibility and public answering for public safety and health. The same goes for social program spending, and applies equally to provincial governments.

Reasonable Expectations for Elected Representatives' Duties and Answering Obligations

The Chapter 1 horror stories, together with the HRDC case, suggest that sets of basic performance and public answering obligations must be forged for elected representatives in all jurisdictions. These can be re-worked as experience with them dictates. The tasks of elected representatives are many and complex, but they have basic duties and accountabilities that need to be set out. Whatever is proposed has to cover most situations. And the expectations can't be stated superficially or they will be meaningless. Appendix 3 sets out basic duties and answering obligations for all elected representatives. Citizens have the right to see these expectations met.

Endnotes

[1] The May 2001 proposal for a 20% salary increase for Canadian Members of Parliament cited

the need for a salary comparable to those having equivalent types of responsibilities (to the extent that comparisons can be made) to "attract, motivate and keep" good people. But neither the salary commission's announcement nor the Prime Minister's response said what MPs could fairly be asked to achieve for their salaries and pensions. (CBC Radio "As It Happens," 24 May 2001)

[2] "Gzowski in Conversation," CBC Television, 13 March 1999

[3] Roger M. Boisjoly, "Personal Integrity and Accountability," *Accounting Horizons*, Journal of the American Accounting Association, March 1993, pp 55-69

[4] Judy Wasylycia-Leis, New Democratic Party health critic, "Who Controls Public Health Care?" *Hill Times*, 18 October 1999

[5] Without adequate public answering by the institutes funded for it and by ministers responsible for it, private data on Canadians, gathered ostensibly to help health research, can wind up in corporations' marketing divisions as data for targeting their products – mainly the drug companies.

[6] Isabel Hilton, "Attacking Goliath," Guardian Weekly, 4-10 May 2000, p.13

[7] An Ottawa anti-MAI activist, the late and respected Terry Cottam, in a pioneering accountability exercise, sent a questionnaire to Members of Parliament asking them how well they had informed themselves about the MAI. While few MPs responded – most of these from the NDP – it was evident that MPs in general looked to the issue leader in their party to tell them what position to take.

[8] Most of the articles were from the *Globe and Mail* and the *Ottawa Citizen* and some from the *National Post* and other papers.

[9] This case was about what federal ministers knew about the Immigration Department's 1991 acceptance into Canada of a former top official of Iraq's Saddam Hussein.

[10] The Transitional Job Fund used a regional unemployment rate criterion of 12% or worse; its successor Canada Jobs Fund used 10%

[11] James Jerome, *Mr. Speaker*, McClelland and Stewart, Toronto 1985, pp.33 and 55

[12] *Ottawa Citizen*, 3 April, 2000, p.A2

CHAPTER 9

The Accountability of Senior Civil Servants

The motivation of today's senior civil servants, which could be taken for granted in earlier times, is becoming less and less clear as more and more preventable horror stories call their motivation and ability into question. It may be because they enter the public service with "business ethics." Or they may see corporations as the only winners in society and quietly support them for their own future employment purposes. But if they feel that they must be loyal to their ministers before all else, and they tell themselves that they are powerless to block ministers' self-serving intentions, they can at least publicly propose the public answering, before and after the fact, that they think ministers should reasonably give. This is because the answering obligation is politically neutral.

It is unreasonable to expect civil servants to produce adequate answering from ministers, but the senior civil servants can make sure ministers know what their statutory duties are and what they think constitutes adequate answering by ministers to the public. Parliamentary committees are entitled to know the extent to which senior civil servants have instructed their ministers on ministers' statutory duties and answering, and what they have put up to their political masters as feasible policy options in the public interest.

Senior Civil Servants' Responsibilities

As a term for government employees, "civil servant" is more universally known than "public servant." And since elected representatives are servants of the public, using the term "civil servant" here avoids confusion in responsibilities. When we talk about civil servants, we need to distinguish those who get the work done from those who are more senior and who translate the statutory obligations of ministers and ministers' wishes into policy and actions that other civil servants carry out.

In a 1996 newspaper article, a Canadian civil servant reflected the prevailing concerns about civil servants. The first concern was what we think of as level of effort:

> Whether you produce results or not, the pay is the same.
>
> Whether you work hard or not, the pay is the same.
>
> Whether you care or not, the pay is the same.

The writer's second concern is what we can call the direction of effort:

> In most cases, we don't have an assessment system to measure the results of our work. In fact, some public servants don't even have a clear idea of the results they are trying to achieve. We may know the tasks we are supposed to do, but not why that task is required or how to assess whether it is producing the desired result, or whether it even needs to be done at all.

But the conscience side of effort provoked a more disturbing observation from the writer:

> And as long as you don't take a risk, or question too deeply, or speak the truth to power, the pay cheques keep rolling in....[1]

The blood and Westray inquiries, whether purposefully or not, moved the line of sight up to the civil servant Director level and above. As one civil servant described it, the Director shuffles the paper and is the filter between the levels who bring things about and identify the problems, and the increasingly-politicized administrative and policy levels of Director General, Assistant Deputy Minister and Deputy Minister. Since the government's protection scientists report to directors, and since those scientists are themselves increasingly less protected, we can assume that the motivation grey area lies roughly at the Director/ Director General level. But it is moving lower.

In the past five years a significant number of Fisheries and Health Canada scientists have made it clear where they stand, taking great risk. Their non-scientist superiors haven't. Is success defined as pleasing one's superiors or serving the public interest under the precautionary principle? We don't know where the other scientists stand because they haven't spoken out – perhaps because they know the public won't act to protect them. There may be a parliamentary committee inquiry into the concerns of the scientists who speak out, but without effective whistleblower protection the scientists are left to the wolves once the committees have aired certain issues (but likely haven't gone to the bone in underlying cause). Other civil servants choose to go with the flow, adopting the line of senior management, and move on upward as carriers of departmental groupthink such as, "Our client is industry," or "We must think of ourselves as partners of industry."

In June 2000 an interesting session took place in Ottawa at the Canadian Centre for Management Development, a supernumerary entity of the federal government. The subject was "Accountability – The Case of Government Scientists," under the general discussion topic of "Public Service Values and Issues." The case study simulation was a government scientist "who has just completed an experiment that shows a potential for serious problems with a product that was approved for production a few months ago." The approval was the regulatory department's approval. The scientist's superiors had called for internal peer review before any publication of the scientist's results, on the ground that one experiment still under review was not strong enough evidence to demonstrate risk, and that the department reversing its approval would injure its credibility.

As the case material put it, the "dilemma" for the scientist was:

> The scientist S feels accountable:
>
> • as an employee, to the government and department
>
> • as a scientist, to scientific peers and science itself
>
> • as a civil servant, to the public and its safety

The scientist and several colleagues seek to talk to their manager. The case material then asked what each of the scientists and his/her manager should do.

To its credit, the case wasn't written in a slanted way, but the session centered on values and ethics, rather than accountability as such.

In the summary discussion:

- The precautionary principle wasn't proposed as the prime criterion for scientific work and management's decisions. Although some suggested that the ethical imperative was to err on the side of caution, they didn't say how that would play out in the case
- No one raised the question whether the reward system in the department would produce or allow objective internal peer review
- No one dealt with the issue of a minister already publicly supporting such a product
- Although the Tylenol strategy of quickly clearing the shelves was mentioned, no one suggested that the strategy for the case study product would offset any departmental credibility problem
- Comments were frequent along the foggy lines of "The culture of policy-making and scientists needs to be integrated," and "A healthy organization in which dia-

logue can take place, and good communication strategies would go a long way to dealing with such problems."

- Discussion groups placed more emphasis on establishing the validity of the scientists' conclusions before going public than on the issue of the importance of disclosing a problem – noting the legal liability risk from the manufacturer
- No one raised the issue of ministers' wants versus the precautionary principle
- Some said that the government must decide whether the same people should be responsible for developing products and regulating their distribution.

With the case material was a Treasury Board glossy plastic card entitled "Dialogue on Public Service Values and Ethics." (which adroitly ducks whether the card is to be a guide, let alone an authoritative guide) In the section "Four Families of Core Values," accountability is listed as part of "Democratic Values" in society, not as part of core "'Traditional' Professional Values" or "'New' Professional Values." Yet Professor Kenneth Kernaghan, in a CCMD seminar a few years before, reporting on a survey he had done, listed accountability as being among the most highly rated values by the civil servants that he surveyed.

The June 2000 session could be summed up as a collective re-affirmation of the need for "dialogue." No one proposed that standards for upholding the precautionary principle, and for answering for doing so, be set for anyone.

The session also provided insight into the thinking of departmental personnel. A Privy Council Office participant at one table had been in the Health Protection Branch. This person asserted that the concerns of eminent researcher Dr. Nancy Olivieri about the Apotex corporation's drug deferiprone – concerns which the Health Protection Branch was trying to dismiss (See Appendix 2) – had been "refuted" by " credible science." Yet this civil servant couldn't possibly have supported her assertion. The importance of this "decree" strategy in blind support of the Branch was that the others at the table would likely have viewed her comment about Dr. Olivieri as authoritative.

No one, neither speakers nor participants, raised the issue whether disclosure of a risk by people qualified to recognize them constitutes adherence to public policy. This means that any rule or norm in a department preventing public disclosure of an identified risk is contrary to public policy, and is therefore null and void. If this is true for research agreements between researchers and corporations sponsoring research – and it is (see Appendix 2) – it is presumably also true in government regulatory department operations with statutory protection mandates, unless otherwise decided by Parliament.

Governments and civil servants exist to serve citizens. But the ability and motivation of senior civil servants to serve the public interest is no longer clear. They argue that their role is simply to carry out the policies of the elected representatives who form the government and set the policies. They may only grudgingly carry out some policy that they think isn't in the public interest, but we seldom hear of a senior civil servant resigning instead. Senior civil servants by and large accept as their working definition of "public interest" whatever their current ministers define it to be. But, federally at least, civil servants in the field at junior or middle rank may be more in tune with the aspirations and safety of citizens they are trying to serve in their department's programs than with a departmental headquarters that is more in tune with the ministers' political aims and ideologies. Politicization of civil servants means that they put anticipated ministers' wants before public interest needs. Politicization effects diminish with the distance from Ottawa.

Legislatures have avoided distinguishing the responsibilities and accountabilities of senior civil servants and ministers. The issue was termed by Ron Huntington, a member of the House of Commons's Public Accounts Committee in the 1980s, as "the crossover" problem for MPs trying to hold government to account.

It is obvious that deciding policies that honour some people's needs or wants and don't honour others' is the role of elected representatives, not civil servants. Yet the public can't tell what advice senior civil servants give their political masters because it's kept confidential. This means that citizens can't tell whether these senior officials place ministers' wants before the public's needs. Federal examples have been senior civil servants' failure to force regulation of the Red Cross's blood operations in the early 1980s, their closing of Health Protection Branch laboratories, and their effort to dismantle the *Food and Drugs Act* with the apparent intention of shifting statutory responsibilities such as food inspection from ministers to unaccountable others. Provincial examples are failure to protect the Westray miners, failure to protect water supply safety, and failure to prevent a misleading provincial budget from being issued.

In the blood and Westray cases, it wasn't clear whether senior civil servants told their ministers what the ministers' statutory protection duties were. Since statutory duty isn't partisan, it's reasonable that deputy ministers be expected to demonstrate the extent to which they have explained to their ministers what the law says about their ministers' duties.

The self-informing duty of the deputy minister is to know what is going on in the department, immediately brief the minister on significant problems, get approval for the corrective action that departmental officials think should be taken but which needed the minister's approval, and request any needed action by the minister to remove external constraints standing in the way of departmental staff doing their jobs.

There is a potentially worse problem. By the late 1980s, federal senior civil servants had ceased expecting their political masters to support integrity (witness books like Stevie Cameron's *On the Take*) but didn't take matters into their own hands – something they had the guild power to do. They may also have believed, with international trade agreements and the coming of "globalization," that the large corporations were going to hold the power in society. Therefore, serving corporations' aims promised better career opportunities. Today, with no public accounting by senior civil servants for their intentions and decision-making, we can't say that we know their abilities or their intentions. We can't tell who they serve primarily: the public's needs, their minister's wants or corporations' wants. If we respect the precautionary principle, we have no right simply to hope for the best. For example, a director general in the federal Health Protection Branch issued an internal memo in the 1990s referring to the drug industry as the Branch's client.

Regardless of existing conventions within government, in today's world it is reasonable that senior civil servants account to departmentally-related committees of the legislatures not only for their management responsibilities but also for the advice and policy alternatives they give ministers. It is reasonable because their advice is to be nonpartisan, and taxpayers pay their salaries and pensions. Arguments that this would destroy "ministerial responsibility" are even weaker than the ministerial responsibility "principle" itself.

Since civil servants control the means by which government produces justice and fairness in society, they also control the means of inflicting harm on groups and individuals who challenge the government too much for its liking. If public interest groups are too big to be crippled by the executive government, or if a lone dissenter or whistleblower has too much stature, government simply buys up the needed academics and other organizations to stress the government's line before the public. If one organization or person is against an intention of government, three "illustrious" organizations or academics can be found by senior public servants to "refute." Newspapers, seeking only news, score it three to one.

In the meantime, we have a simple way to find out who senior civil servants serve. Because of their knowledge, it is legitimate that they tell us what they think reasonable public answering from ministers is. Deputy ministers can reasonably be expected to place in a public record the standards they think are reasonable for the answering by ministers of the Crown to the legislature. This would be for ministers' responsibilities: ministers' understanding of their statutory duties, their intentions and reasons in policy or orders in council whenever what they intend would affect the public in important ways, and the performance standards they set for themselves and for the civil servants of their departments and agencies.

The deputy ministers will immediately claim, backed by the academics they fund, that such standards can emerge only from political debate on public accountability. To the extent that this proposal is debated in legislatures, the proposal will be killed off by government majorities obedient to the ministers because the deputies know too much about ministers' intentions and reasoning. Yet it is clear that the imperative of adequate public answering is politically neutral in a democracy (unless George Washington was wrong); that answering standards are neutral; and that civil servants are ultimately to serve the public that pays their salaries. If they don't, the public won't tolerate their salary and pension costs.

Since the deputies' day-to-day job is to protect ministers from themselves by insuring that ministers know their duty, deputies can be expected to set out the public answering obligation, as they see it, that logically flows from the ministers' intentions and actions. This has nothing to do with confidential advice to ministers and there are no laws against useful public answering by any authority. Any senior civil servant who claims the ability to execute policy but who claims not to comprehend what constitutes fair, non-partisan public answering by ministers for their intentions, reasoning and performance is only a technocrat.

When we see what the deputy ministers' guilds propose as standards for ministers' answering to the legislature (and therefore the public), we will see who they serve. At the federal level, the Clerk of the Privy Council, the government's most senior civil servant, would state the basic standards, with each deputy minister stating those tailored for his or her ministers' particular responsibilities. For example, ministers with safety regulatory duties would meet more rigorous answering standards than cultural policy ministers.

The Accountability Issue in HRDC

Let us return to the Human Resources Development Canada control failure as an illustration of senior civil servants' responsibilities and accountabilities. We don't know what the successive deputy ministers of the department and its predecessor department saw as their management control duty, or what they told or failed to tell the successive ministers of the department. Nor do we have evidence of what the Clerk of the Privy Council for the period under review for the 1999 internal audit report told senior civil servants about their control obligations. But the Privy Council Office likely takes swift control when appearances damage control is needed by ministers.

While the departmental minister has overall responsibility for the quality of management control in the department, the deputy minister is responsible for installing and maintaining the system to a standard that citizens have the right to see met – and to account for doing so. A deputy minister who doesn't do this wouldn't be able to answer the Louis Desmarais question cited in Chapter 8.

The general explanation from senior HRDC officials was that major staff cuts and decentralization at HRDC in the mid-1990s and government emphasis on "client services" were the main causes of the control failure – as if these were somehow uncontrollable forces. These reasons may sound plausible to a Grade 10 student. But the officials dodged the question of the responsibility of the deputy ministers, at the time the funding programs were set up, to brief the directing-mind ministers on implications and to demand that the ministers make the trade-off decisions and be prepared to publicly account for them. Moreover, in the early-to mid-1990s, civil servants across government who were in the field didn't see the emphasis on service to the public pushed at them by top management of the civil service as genuine.

Given staff cutbacks with the program under way, maintaining fundamental control rules for each grant would mean that the volume of grants would have to be limited. The deputy minister of record then had the responsibility to tell the HRDC Minister to make the trade-off between control and the volume of grants and be prepared to account for it, before the fact, to Members of Parliament.

HRDC's deputy ministers would have been aware of the messages of HRDC's own 1991 and 1994 internal audits and the Auditor General's reports to the House of Commons on control diligence across government. It is also reasonable to assume that the new deputy arriving in February 1999, Claire Morris, knew the scope and likely result of her Department's 1999 internal audit, since it was an audit of the control system for which she was now responsible.

But the attempt by Opposition MPs to hold to account and to know what the deputy ministers did and didn't do was made difficult by the Prime Minister. He had transferred the earlier HRDC deputy minister, Mel Cappe, to the role of Clerk of the Privy Council in January 1999, and he transferred the minister of record, Pierre Pettigrew, to a different portfolio in August 1999. Jane Stewart took over as HRDC Minister. In the parliamentary system it is page one in the book to transfer or promote civil servants and ministers when trouble brews; claim that they don't answer for earlier responsibilities; and then count on this not being challenged by parliamentarians or the public. The controller of transfers is the head civil servant, the Clerk of the Privy Council.

The trouble in the HRDC case started with questions in the House of Commons about questionable grants made by HRDC in the Prime Minister's riding. The evidence shows that by August of 1999, HRDC officials were preparing a public "communications plan" as damage control for the compulsory public release of the 1999 internal audit report, but didn't include public accountability as an issue. The August plan meant the new deputy minister would have known what was going on and could have been expected to brief the new Minister on the audit immediately the Minister arrived after the cabinet shuffle.

Regardless of Minister Stewart's own obligation to find out what was going on through her own questioning, and regardless whether she sought plausible denial or rejected it, the new Deputy Minister had the duty to immediately take her Minister through the implications of the audit findings. The Deputy Minister could say that the control failures didn't happen on her watch, but they happened on the watch of the person now the Clerk, and the Clerk has career control over all deputy ministers. Deputy ministers are obviously expected to help ministers with damage control, but the briefing obligation was to have the new Minister deal with the underlying problems created or allowed by the previous ministers.

HRDC officials asserted publicly that it was not unusual that neither the Deputy Minister of record nor his successor were formally told about the 1999 interim audit results because the interim audit results were incomplete and not even the auditors yet understood the scope of the problems. This isn't credible, given the evidence from the department's own 1991 and 1994 audits and 1997 review, all of which stared senior officials in the face. Also, the officials' explanation doesn't match with how the real world of auditing works. Interim audit reports that follow the fieldwork clarify the risk and effects from the samples audited. Most of the auditors' work after the interim report is usually spent on how the report should be fairly written when made public, and in coping with pressure by the officials responsible for the weaknesses to water down the report.

It is also the responsibility of deputy ministers to tell ministers how they (the ministers) affect the quality of management control. For example, ministers themselves can be expected to prefer weak control over grants because this allows them greater "flexibility." Similarly, it has been the ministers who, for decades, have hindered development of adequate cost accounting systems in government.

The central question in management control over the deployment of large amounts of public money is not just the lack of control over compliance and value for money, intended by ministers to allow them freedom (i.e., whim) in spending. The issue is equally the extent to which the most senior civil servants accept the "understood limits" to control in matters such as grants. To the extent that senior civil servants feel trapped between serving ministers' wants and the public's needs they can, as noted earlier, propose the public answering by ministers for their responsibilities and use their guild to protect themselves from the ministers – making the Clerk of the Privy Council deal with the ministers' objections to answering.

Former deputy ministers who argued in the media that the attention paid to the HRDC episode would "re-bureaucratize" the government adroitly failed to suggest what the minimum fundamental control rules and standards should be in the public interest, and who should answer to whom, for what responsibilities.

Civil servants' answering. The HRDC deputy minister for the period under review by the

Department's 1999 internal audit, and the deputy succeeding him in February 1999, gave the impression that they were not aware of the compliance and value for money control failures.

In a televised message to the department's 23,000 employees on the internal audit findings, Deputy Minister Morris said in part:

> My concern, therefore, is that these findings represent systemic issues across the department and point to program administrative practices that are clearly unacceptable.[2]

Missing from this message was the answer to the question, "But where were the deputy ministers who had responsibility for setting and enforcing the control standards?" The quality of control in departments is a function of the standards each deputy minister upholds and how the deputies deal with any external constraints that keep their standards from being met. In the HRDC case, the failure to meet reasonable standards in the grants spending was the responsibility of previous deputy heads. But the new Deputy Minister had the obligation to state to the 23,000 staff members how she was dealing with the underlying problems, not just the symptoms, and what she was doing to remove barriers standing in the way of staff doing a better job.

In public answering, we must assume that senior officials are expected to place protection of their ministers before being useful to Parliamentarians. Dispatched to a media briefing 1 February to clear up "factual misunderstandings" about the audit report, two senior officials of the Department simply repeated the HRDC Minister's public statements:

> It is not a financial crisis or scandal in any way, shape or form....The $1 billion is not missing. We know where every penny of that money went.

This statement isn't explanation of the reasoning for issuing the cheques or of how the money was spent by the payees. As to money missing, citizens would regard substantial unrecoverable payments wrongly made to organizations as money missing.

The officials' answering, mirroring the Minister, took the form of:

> Question: "Why was there no control over the spending of $1 billion of taxpayers' money, and how much was wasted?"

> Answer by the officials: "The sun is shining."

In the *Ottawa Citizen* in February 2000, journalist Jane Taber summed up the spin:

> Surrounded by pie charts and documents, the officials spent nearly two hours trying to explain the situation. They still haven't managed to explain what happened and how it could have happened and how much money

we're really talking about.

In a meeting of the House of Commons Human Resources and Development Committee in March 2000, Mr. Cappe stated that there were reasons but no excuses for the lack of sound management practices in the HRDC spending. Yet in the same meeting he said that the lapse happened because the Department became "too client-oriented and not enough taxpayer-oriented." While commenting that he had only an "inkling" of the lack of control, he didn't explain what he thought his control responsibility had been as the deputy minister. Interviewed in June 2000 in his role as Clerk of the Privy Council, Mr. Cappe said:

> Throughout the HRDC issue, there was never an allegation of malfeasance or impropriety against any public servants. It was all questions about recipients.[3]

This straw man ducks the question of the deputy ministers' responsibility for management control in their departments.

The HRDC case isn't a past tense issue, something limited to HRDC and only for a five-month media frenzy. It highlights a continuing government management issue. Moreover, because the issue is control over the dispensing of grants, the questions were clearly directed to the ministers and senior officials authorizing the cheques, not those who took advantage of the programs to receive cheques.

The Privy Council Clerk also said that the episode showed that civil servants are held to "ethical values of honesty and integrity to a level that is higher than the private sector." But when senior civil servants don't account to the public for their intentions and performance, and MPs can't get responses from them that sound credible, no one is actually being held to a visible set of values. And there is no available evidence that senior civil servants across government operate at an integrity level higher than private sector managers when there are no clear standards for their performance, their conduct isn't on public display, and they don't answer publicly for what they do.

Moreover, the Clerk didn't distinguish senior officials' responsibilities for control from the application processing staff. This is the same tactic that military top command used for appearances purposes in the Somalia affair: fuse top brass with the troops so that the questioning of motivation at the top is seen as questioning the diligence and integrity of the ranks.

The Clerk lastly stated his concern that tightening control could "re-bureaucratize" the civil service with more red tape. Yet he knew that the central issue is the lack of installed basic control standards for value for money, not the amount of red tape. A prominent former deputy minister, Arthur Kroeger, had said the same in a *Globe and Mail* article in March 2000, arguing that the result of the HRDC examination would produce only more administrative paperwork at the cost of service to the public. But he didn't say what the fundamental control rules should be and who should answer publicly for compliance with them. He further claimed that media attention on HRDC was not on results achieved, yet a major part of the Opposition criticism was just that: the department couldn't demonstrate the results of the grants.

Kroeger further argued that Opposition questioning in the House of Commons hadn't yielded a constructive outcome. Yet the ministers, who had the power to get away with it, clearly refused to account. He said Parliament had failed to give "guidance to officials" on the desirable balance between control and spending flexibility. But it is clearly the role of the executive government to say to the House, "This is the program we intend and the balance we plan between autonomy in spending and value for money spending control. Is it what you had in mind?" And by claiming that everyone is the loser from the HRDC affair thus far, this former deputy minister implied that no gains in insight have been achieved – which is clearly not the case if the lessons are about installing adequate answering from ministers, deputy ministers and other officials.

In summary, the claims by opposition MPs and journalists have been essentially that
- Ministers wanted the control over compliance and value for money for a billion-dollar set of programs to be weak, precisely because they were grants and therefore usable for political influence and appearances purposes as well as being productive in many other cases
- Ministers didn't tell the public that fundamental spending control rules were to be waived for these programs
- Senior civil servants let it happen
- Neither senior officials nor ministers produced, in their statements of intended activity, evidence that the underlying causes of sub-standard spending control were being eliminated
- Once the internal audit made the control failure public knowledge, senior officials helped ministers in putting out spin. As we have seen in health and safety, ministers can't do this without the help of willing civil servants at all levels
- Nowhere in any government statement has there been a clear statement on anything

It may be that neither ministers nor senior civil servants know how to deal with solid public exposure of their failure in performance. When pigeons in the mid-1900s experiments of the behaviorist B.F. Skinner didn't know what to do, Skinner observed that they simply pecked, randomly. The equivalent is possible in government and the military.

Citizens can fairly conclude, from the collective statements of current and former senior civil servants in the HRDC affair and in the horror stories described in Chapter 1, that federal senior civil servants

- do not wish to grasp the meaning of management control for safety and value for money (All control is to be regarded as "command control" and "coaching" is better)
- do not acknowledge the need for fundamental rules made known to all (There are no systemic problems in government)
- refuse to understand, let alone promote public accountability and answering standards in the public interest (It is very complex and requires extensive study)
- make no distinction between imperatives and "red tape."

These civil servants thus fail to dispel journalists' and citizens' impressions that they simply go with the political flow and ministers' personal aspirations. They can overcome this impression by adequate public answering that at all times lets us see who they are serving.

If we accept that politicians are responsible for the major fairness decisions constituting policy, and civil servants are responsible for the probity, efficiency and economy of the operations carrying out fairness policy intentions, we should be able to view civil servants as being political neutral. That being the case, the argument that civil servants mustn't answer to the public because everything is the minister's responsibility falls apart. Senior civil servants already answer to legislative committees for their efficiency and economy responsibilities. If civil servants' advice to ministers is truly non-partisan, then what the senior civil servants suggest to ministers can be fairly reported.

At the least, senior civil servants, with their knowledge of the programs, can set out for citizens what they think the public answering standards should be for ministers' intentions that would affect the public in important ways, and for the consequent results of policy and control intentions carried out.

Reasonable Expectations for Senior Civil Servants' Duties and Answering Obligations

The foregoing arguments apply as well to provincial and municipal senior civil servants. Citizens have the right to know what basic duties and accountabilities are reasonable for senior civil servants. Appendix 3 proposes a set that legislators can be asked to install in their jurisdictions.

Endnotes

1 Chris Day, Globe and Mail, 2 February 1996
2 *Ottawa Citizen* 29 January 2000, p. A10
3 *Ottawa Citizen* 18 June 2000 p. A5

CHAPTER 10

The Accountability of Military Top Command[1]

Background

Most people don't have a concept of the military's public accountability, one reason being that its senior officers have never accounted to the public. But the military have a special duty and accountability to citizens. In times of war, military leaders ask families to give up their youth to serve. Moreover, top command is formally accountable to the people, not to the political leaders. Its Commander in Chief is the Governor General – the Crown in Canada – who stands outside the agendas of politicians and whose constitutional function is anything but ceremonial.

The Chief of the Defence Staff (CDS), the head of the military, takes deployment direction from the Minister of National Defence, mostly from international developments, and is responsible for the effectiveness and efficiency of the three service branches – navy, army and airforce – collectively known as the Canadian Forces. The Deputy Minister of National Defence, roughly at a level equal with the CDS, looks after the civil service functions of the Department of National Defence. Forces readiness and capability and its peacetime function depends on political and spending decisions. Procurement (defence contracts) largely involves the civil service side. Funding for the military comes through the Minister.

Currently the role of Canada's military is unclear, as is the role of its reserves. Its permanent force numbers were drastically reduced in the 1990s from about 88,000 to 60,000. Thus, holding the CDS fairly to account for the Forces' fighting or peacekeeping capability has to take into account what top command can't control as political objectives set for the Forces, or the amount of money given to it by Parliament. Nor can the CDS control the competence and intentions of the Minister and Deputy Minister. Within government policy constraints, however, the capability, performance and conduct of all personnel in military competence, efficiency and fairness is within the control of military top command.

The mid-1960s unification of the three services, followed by the 1972 merging of the civilian staff with military staff, all in the aim of cost-cutting and reducing inter-service competition for funds, tended to erode the traditional loyalties to regiment, ship and squadron. Unification was easier than getting the three services to work together efficiently and cohesively. Today's parallel is happening with medicare: dump the system rather than take responsibility for maintaining it properly.

But the needed characteristics of a post-unification officer corps weren't developed. Unification and the introduction of federal bureaucracy into the services led to politicization of the officer corps, meaning increasing attention to the wants of ministers and public polls.[2] One result has been the perception of retired and serving officers that military officers responsible for the Somalia cover-ups were doing it to protect the interests of the then Minister.[3] This coincided with the executive government's diminishing regard for the military, while not defining its role as it affects internal morale, international stature and plain cost-effectiveness for the taxpayer. By and large the Defence Ministers haven't been leaders that the military can be proud of.

Good senior command performance in peacetime with no cold war isn't easy, because the military culture isn't good at self-analysis and doesn't tolerate dissent.[4] Yet, as the world's best-known management consultant Peter Drucker said three decades ago, "Without dissent, you don't know what the problem is." The widely-perceived refusal of today's most senior officers to accept responsibility, let alone to account, was made clear in the Somalia inquiry. While it is a product of the politicizing of the promotion process and the reward system of the military that emerged after unification, it is also a function of questionable ability and motivation in ministers of the Crown.

Standards may be falling in today's military chain of command, but military people in all ranks certainly know crumbling integrity when they see it. Taking responsibility doesn't mean simply trumpeting "I take full responsibility" as an empty appearances response, as US President Ronald Reagan said as Commander in Chief, about the US marines killed in their barracks in Lebanon. When leaders say they aren't responsible for something that they didn't know about, but it is clearly their self-informing control duty to know it, it makes the members of their organization feel ashamed.

Externally constrained as it may be, top command can still earn the respect of the troops and Canadians at large by exhibiting competence in whatever the military is assigned to do, by ensuring fairness within the Forces and by publicly accounting for the discharge of its responsibilities. Leaving aside the performance of ministers of defence, the almost monthly media revelations in the late 1990s of horror stories, and inept or misleading top command reaction, suggests that today's military leadership hasn't earned this dual respect.

What has been exposed is the failure of top command to develop respected leaders as role models, and to prevent politicization of senior officers who seem now to look more to ministers' wants and their own future corporate employment possibilities than to their troops' needs. A form of reconstruction receivership is needed for top command, accompanied by rules for adequate public answering by top command for the discharge of its responsibilities, followed by audit validation of its public answering.

How much evidence do Canadians need to realize that something fundamental and perhaps traumatic has to be done with the military to put it right?

Consider the following.

The Somalia Inquiry and Other Alerts

Commissioners Justice Gilles Létourneau (chair), Justice Robert Rutherford and senior journalism professor Peter Desbarats were asked to inquire into the 1993 torture and murder of a Somali teenager and other killings by troops of the First Airborne Regiment. When the Commissioners started to work their way up from inquiry at the field level to the level of top command, deputy minister and minister, the Defence Minister terminated the inquiry on the grounds that it had gone on too long and at too great a cost to the public purse.

This wasn't just political damage control by the Minister, Clerk of the Privy Council and the Deputy Minister to keep blame away from the top civilian officials. The senior officers in the Department who had responsibility for the management control system that should have sent the right troops, properly trained for peacekeeping, and the right field and unit commanders obviously didn't want to be exposed as incompetent in their control duty.

The following extracts from the Executive Summary of the report of Commission of Inquiry into the Deployment of Canadian Forces to Somalia sum up what went on, to the extent the Commission was allowed to uncover the facts:

> ...the systems in place were inadequate and deeply flawed; practices that
> fuelled rampant careerism and placed individual ambition ahead of the needs
> of the mission had become entrenched; the oversight and supervision of

crucial areas of responsibility were deeply flawed and characterized by the most superficial of assessments; even when troubling events and disturbing accounts of indiscipline and thuggery were known, there was disturbing inaction or the actions that were taken exacerbated and deepened the problems; planning, training and preparation fell far short of what was required; subordinates were held to standards of accountability by which many of those above were not prepared to abide...

Many of the leaders called before us... refused to acknowledge error. When pressed, they blamed their subordinates who, in turn, cast responsibility upon those below them. They assumed this posture reluctantly (and) only after their initial claims, that the root of many of the most serious problems resided with a few "bad apples," proved hollow...

...we must also record with regret that on many occasions the testimony of witnesses was characterized by inconsistency, improbability, implausibility, evasiveness, selective recollection, half truths and plain lies. Indeed, on some issues we encountered what can only be described as a wall of silence. When several witnesses behave in this manner, the wall of silence is evidently a strategy of calculated deception...

Evasion and deception, which in our view were apparent in many of the senior officers who testified before us, reveal much about the poor state of leadership in our armed forces and the careerist mentality that prevails in the Department of National Defence...

No matter how an organization is structured, those at the apex of the organization are accountable for the actions and decisions of those within the chain of authority subordinate to them...The act of delegation to another does not relieve the responsible official of the duty to account...It is the responsibility of those who exercise supervisory authority, or who have delegated the authority to act to others, to know what is transpiring within the area of their assigned authority...

(In response to the Commission's order to produce relevant documents) Key documents were missing, altered and even destroyed. Some came to our attention only by happenstance, such as when they were uncovered by a third party access-to-information request.... It is clear that rather than assisting with the timely flow of information to our Inquiry, the (Department of National Defence) adopted a strategic approach to deal with the Inquiry and engaged in a tactical operation to delay or deny the disclosure of relevant information to us and, consequently, to the Canadian public...

> Perhaps the most troubling consequence of the fragmented, dilatory and incomplete documentary record furnished to us by DND is that, when this activity is coupled with the incontrovertible evidence of document destruction, tampering, and alteration, there is an natural and inevitable heightening of suspicion of a cover-up that extends into the highest reaches of the Department of National Defence and the Canadian Forces.[5]

It was also clear to the federal Information Commissioner that defence department staff had deliberately and significantly altered information legitimately asked for by a journalist.[6]

And in mid-2001 the Forces Ombudsman, André Marin, stated in his annual report tabled in Parliament:

> There appears to be a concerted effort to keep us out of any real issue concerning the military police.[7]

Thus the arrogance seen in the court martial of LCdr Dean Marsaw continues. We have had other alerts about top command:

- The lieutenant colonel who had commanded the Canadian Airborne Regiment before its departure was transferred when he made the point that the Regiment wasn't fit. Regardless of his own responsibility to have produced a satisfactory regiment, the colonel's superiors were likely unwilling to tell their political masters that the Airborne wasn't up to the job[8]

- The put-about reason for the executive government disbanding the Airborne Regiment in 1995 was the public disclosure of amateur videos of paratroopers performing repugnant hazing acts and making racist remarks. But disbanding the regiment made it impossible to track cause and effect leading to the Somalia killings by the Regiment's troops

- General John de Chastelain, CDS at the time of the Airborne's assignment, submitted his resignation to the Prime Minister in January 1995, saying, "I bear the ultimate responsibility for the actions depicted in the 1992 and 1993 videos," and that the videos showed "serious failures in military leadership." General de Chastelain accepted the Prime Minister's wish that he not resign. Others with felt responsibility simply go ahead and resign if they feel they should. General de Chastelain was criticized by retired and serving military officers for not resigning when Defence Minister Collenette disbanded the Regiment.

- The succeeding CDS, General Jean Boyle, an air force officer appointed in January 1996 when David Collenette was Defence Minister, had headed the military's Somalia damage control strategy group and, later, the DND unit supplying information to the inquiry. He was generally thought to have been appointed ahead of other more suitable CDS candidates to take the heat for Somalia killings and cover-ups.

General Boyle stated in the inquiry that he couldn't be held accountable for things that he said he hadn't been told about and claimed not to know about which, he said, were done by subordinates who "lacked integrity and moral fibre."[9] These included action to prevent disclosure of important documents to the inquiry and to access to information requests in 1994, and shredding of documents that the inquiry commission had ordered be turned over to it. Yet General Boyle's earlier role would have influenced the degree of "moral fibre" in his subordinates, and his self-informing duty as the CDS and directing mind for the military's control systems required him to have that knowledge for such an important matter.

- Vice-Admiral Larry Murray succeeded General Boyle as Acting CDS after Boyle resigned in October 1996, discredited through the Somali inquiry. Admiral Murray was Deputy Chief of the Defence Staff at the time of the Somalia killings. He had been asked three times by the head of the military police, Col. Allan Wells, to send military police to Somalia without delay because two Somalis had been shot in the back. The colonel had his team ready the day after the shootings but Admiral Murray, despite knowing the nature of the killings, didn't give approval until five weeks later – something characterized by the colonel as stalling.[10]

- Col. Geof Haswell was court-martialled but acquitted for breaching military laws by a scheme to thwart access to information by changing the classification of documents to allow them to be routinely destroyed after 72 hours. Col. Haswell claimed that the scheme was approved by the top DND officers and officials. He was transferred in the fall of 1995, before investigations began into allegations that documents had been pulled and destroyed[11]

- Before the Somalia inquiry was launched, the Prime Minister had appointed the Deputy Minister of the Department of National Defence at the time, Robert Fowler, as Ambassador to the United Nations. Mr. Fowler did not testify before the Somalia inquiry. Nor did the Minister of Defence at the time, Kim Campbell

- Defence Minister Douglas Young, succeeding David Collenette in October 1996, four days before the resignation of General Boyle, terminated the Somalia public inquiry when the Commissioners started heading toward "allegations of high-level cover-up" pertaining to the Somalia events and to the control responsibilities of top command, deputy minister and minister

- Minister Young said in January 1997, "We know who pulled the trigger in Somalia" and that no Canadian believes that ministers, senior officers or senior civil servants "plotted, connived or were involved in the shootings of unarmed civilians or the beating of an individual to death in Somalia."[12] The Minister answered a question no one was asking. The issue was the responsibility of the Minister to have a senior command competent in management control and who wouldn't cover up what happened.

- Prime Minister Chrétien, in July 1997, on release of the Somalia Inquiry Commission's report, decreed that "there is no cover-up" in the Somalia disgrace. But the Prime Minister himself couldn't possibly know that there wasn't, and it's doubtful that he would have privately put money on his "decree."

- As their most important conclusion the inquiry commissioners, with their inquiry truncated, recommended an independent inspector general for the military, reporting to Parliament. This person would have broad powers to supervise the military justice system and ensure it was independent from top command, protect whistleblowers and investigate officer misconduct including failure to take control responsibility for subordinates.

  A new Minister of National Defence, Arthur Eggleton, appointed only weeks before the release of the inquiry report, rejected the commissioners' recommendation, simply decreeing that the Forces didn't need an inspector general "to constantly look over the shoulders of officers in the chain of command." He also asserted that the reports that Parliament gets from the Treasury Board, Auditor General and the privacy and access to information commissioners suffice.[13] The Minister knew that these constitute piecemeal information on various aspects of various responsibilities and don't give an overall management control picture for fairness, efficiency and performance answering. Neither the Americans nor Australians have difficulty with their system of inspectors general. The Minister further decreed that an ombudsman would suffice, knowing that an ombudsman would have a restricted mandate.

  Inquiry Commissioner Peter Desbarats observed that the Minister's response sent a message to Canada's military that it doesn't have to be accountable to civilian authority – that there won't be civilian control of the military.[14]

- Following release of the Commissioners' report, the federal government's Justice Department failed to support the Commission when one of the officers named in the Commissioners' report went to court to have the Commissioners' statements about him quashed. In her April 1998 decision, Madame Justice Reed of the Federal Court of Canada decided that the Commissioners' findings – that the officer had failed to adequately train the Regiment before going to Somalia – were "deeply flawed." The Justice lawyers hadn't filed evidence to rebut the arguments of the officer's lawyer – all of which, said Justice Létourneau, now back at the Federal

Court of Appeal, could have been refuted by the Justice lawyers.[15]

The result was predictable denigration of the Commission's findings through court processes where the government lawyers, having a duty to defend the Commission's findings, report in their careers to an executive government that didn't accept the Commission's work. We have no mechanism to tell us whether Justice Department lawyers operate under the notion, "the limits are understood." Judges such as the one who heard the case would likely say that they cannot question the motivation and diligence of the Justice lawyers. But observations such as "deeply flawed," made by a judge who couldn't know what went on as well as the Commissioners on aren't helpful to Canadians.

The question for Canadians is whether they accept this type of action by the government – using its Justice Department as it did against Commissioner Krever in the blood inquiry – being done repeatedly and with impunity.

The Court Martial of LCdr Dean Marsaw

Coming close on the heels of the Somalia revelations in the media, the pattern in the wrongful charging and trial of an outstanding submarine commander on contrived and deficient evidence suggests that there was a top command agenda behind it. (See Chapter 1 for the case.) Elsewhere, civilian police and prosecution "tunnel vision" was applied to wrongly convicted people because of the need for a conviction. It's plausible that a military equivalent of this tunnel vision formed similarly against an isolated submariner from the need to offer the media an officer sacrifice to help distract attention from the performance of army senior command related to the Somalia killings.

Evidence suggests that the military could well have decided that the allegations against Marsaw were enough to sacrifice him to balance the Somalia revelations, all of which were army. Other explanations – simple incompetence among all who helped with Marsaw's destruction, or even a kind of wolf pack frenzy – may be plausible but there still has to be a directing motive. The point is that the senior officers making the decisions at the time, CDS included, have never been asked to explain their savaging of an officer the navy had consistently and highly praised throughout his career.

Top command have never been asked what their own standards are for fairness in the military – including the processes of their courts martial, what their control responsibilities are for fairness protection, as they see them, and whether and why they think they meet control standards that Canadians can reasonably expect them to meet.

The following case further exemplifies control and accountability failure by military top command – this time for health.

The Case of the Medical Files

On 22 July 1999 the media brought to Canadians' attention the question of "tampering" with medical files of soldiers who had served in a peacekeeping role in Croatia in the early 1990s. It stemmed from information obtained by the then Reform Party's researchers. The senior on-site medical officer, naval Lieutenant Dr. Eric Smith, observing wind-blown bauxite and other toxic waste in the soldiers' encampment area, sent samples to the UN headquarters and a report to Ottawa, asking for an environmental specialist to investigate. Dr. Smith got no answers and no support. In 1994 he had sent a Medical Intelligence Report on his concerns about infrastructure and the setting-up of hospitals. Two months of effort produced not even a thank-you.

Having had no response and being concerned about the risk to soldiers of later respiratory problems Dr. Smith, back in Canada at the end of 1994, drafted a memo for the medical files of up to 1200 soldiers. It commenced with the statement: "This member has been exposed to bauxite and related PCBs (from blown transformers at the destroyed mine) for six months while in Croatia."

Dr. Smith's memo was put into the soldiers' files under the authorization of his battalion commander, whose own instruction memo stated that Smith's memo was to "ensure pensionable coverage in the event of future health problems".[16] At this time of "downsizing," there was evidence that the military was using medical reports to move people out. Dr. Smith's memo subsequently came to the attention of officers who asked him to reword it. Alone, under pressure and suffering from stress disorder, Dr. Smith complied, and his May 1995 final version was changed, for example, to read "potential individual exposure." That was supposed to go into the files, but Dr. Smith noted a year later that his own was missing from his file.[17]

Dr. Smith's memo was removed from the soldiers' files without an audit trail, since there was apparently no written record of who ordered it. Astonishingly, it is not clear how many files had either the original memo, the substitute altered memo or neither.[18] Dr. Smith assumed that his memo was in all the files

Following the memo alteration, Dr. Smith was transferred to an inappropriate posting in Goose Bay and was subsequently court-martialed for something relatively minor, under a questionable charge that Dr. Smith viewed as a set-up taking advantage of his mental state from frustrations in Croatia and the memo intimidation. Said Smith: "There was no record made of testimony; my request for a polygraph test was denied, my lawyer was supplied by the Judge Advocate General's department; I felt helpless and railroaded."[19] The military judge had spent twenty minutes explaining contradictions in the military police officers' testimony, and then found Smith guilty.[20] Smith subsequently left the navy.

Taken together, the Marsaw and Smith cases sound like the film "From Here to Eternity," in which the stockade sergeant does what he wants with soldiers once they are inside the stockade.

The issue of the exposure and unlawful document removal had first been exposed in late 1998 by Scott Taylor, editor of the military magazine *Esprit de Corps*, and Brian Nolan, in their book *Tested Mettle*. An officer decorated for service in Croatia, Col. Jim Calvin, wrote to the Land Force Command Inspector in April 1998 asking that the toxic substance risk to his men be investigated, because complaints of his men who had fallen ill had produced no action by the military's directorate of medical operations. Colonel Calvin also noted that one of his men had reported the removal from his file of the 1995 warning. For his part, the land forces general having ultimate control responsibility for all army forces, Lt.-Gen. Bill Leach, asserted that he had no knowledge of Calvin's memo until November 1998.[21]

In late 1998 a military officer was assigned to investigate. Not being able to piece things together, he recommended to his superiors in a January 1999 report that a board of inquiry look into the matter. He observed that the evidence suggested that Dr. Smith's letter had indeed been removed from the files. At the time Dr. Smith directed that his letter be put into the files, he noted that a medical colonel in Ottawa had been upset with his action.[22] The colonel would have received Dr. Smith's medical alert the year before.

The investigating officer's final report in early February 1999 would have been preceded by a draft report to someone, as we saw with the famous 1999 internal audit report in the Department of Human Resources and Development. In his final report, the military's investigating officer cautioned against letters such as Dr. Smith's "unless there is documented proof of a health hazard," because it "creates fear and uncertainty." This officer must have known that Dr. Smith knew what the military was unlikely to do for its personnel who later found themselves with medical problems. A military spokesman stated that Dr. Smith's letter had been pulled because it was "not necessarily grounded in scientific or medical fact." While Dr. Smith was operating on the precautionary principle, the military flouted it.

As Scott Taylor, editor of *Esprit de Corps*, put it:

> This letter put the Department on the hook. It made them liable not only
> for additional pension claims but for class-action lawsuits for negligence."[23]

The Department also announced that a team was being sent to Croatia to test the suspect soil that soldiers had used to make sandbags and bunkers. But former Warrant Officer Matt Stopford, suffering from decaying joints and eye problems, stated that the site had been cleaned up in 1995.[24] The Department of National Defence knew of the bauxite hazard at the time, because the department's own documents state that soil tests were lost en route in 1994-1995.[25]

The military further said that a board of inquiry would investigate who ordered the removal of the Smith memos, and when. But as Ottawa access to information researcher Ken Rubin warned,

> Treasury Board allows government departments to create their own rules
> and procedures to investigate what they define as record abuse.[26]

Opposition parliamentarians likened the DND intention of a military internal board of inquiry to the military's Somalia document-shredding aims, and said the RCMP instead should conduct an independent inquiry.

In July 1999 the Chief of the Defence Staff, who was now General Maurice Baril, put Colonel Howard Marsh in charge of the board of inquiry. His mandate was to determine whether soldiers had been exposed to toxic substances in Croatia, but it included the removed memos issue. Yet Col. Marsh had been responsible a year earlier for the investigation into the memo removals. Col. Calvin had given his concerns to Marsh in May 1998 but the investigation had stalled. Col. Marsh saw no problem with the fact that he had assumed responsibility as Land Force Command Inspector for that inquiry, and was now at it again as a board of inquiry president. He said publicly: "I have these board members. They'll say, Colonel, are you aware that you did such and such? And I'll say yes."

Col. Marsh's grasp of the situation was such that he termed the scope of his internal Croatia medical-related inquiry "ten times" larger than the Somalia inquiry because many more troops were involved in Croatia.[27] But the Colonel's 1998 inaction on Col. Calvin's alert and his lack of credibility proved too strong a factor to withstand media criticism and the CDS was forced to replace him as the head of the board of inquiry.

Asked about the fairness of the military investigating itself, General Baril answered in the ministerial style of "the sun is shining."

> Investigating ourselves, this is my job, I don't want to give that job to any-
> body else. I am not giving my job of commanding the troops around the
> world to anyone else. I mean, the Canadian government and the Canadian
> citizens who are shareholders of this big organization have confidence in
> me every day of the week to put men and women's lives on the line.[28]

Inspector Russ Grabb of the RCMP was then borrowed by DND to head an internal military police investigation separate from the board of inquiry. Grabb reported to the Provost Marshall, Brigadier-General Patricia Samson. Aware of this lack of independence, the RCMP made it clear that Inspector Grabb's investigation was a military one, not an RCMP inquiry.

On 5 August Inspector Grabb stated that his staff had been tracking leads and interviewing witnesses in the memo removal since 22 July, when the Opposition raised the issue. They believed that the documents had been shredded, making it a criminal offence.[29]

Borrowing an RCMP officer made things look serious, but the focus on the criminality of shredding was likely designed to divert attention from the real issue: top command's responsibility to have had in place a control system that supported Dr. Smith's concerns rather than suppressed them. Diversion was also helped by the newsworthy suggestion by the Provost Marshall that one of the soldiers claiming Croatia-caused serious health problems was instead poisoned by his men.

The day following the July 1999 newspaper coverage of the health risk, Minister of Defence Arthur Eggleton responded to reporters:

> I can only say to this point in time, it's not very clear that this memo was
> ever put on file. One doctor felt it should have been. Was it ever put on file?
> We don't really know that.[30]

Yet a military spokesman had just finished acknowledging that the memos had been pulled and that a board of inquiry would investigate why. Moreover, a former sergeant had said that he not only saw the memo in his file but also had been told to remove it himself. Worse, the previous Defence Minister, David Collenette, had been briefed in 1995 about Dr. Smith's memo having been inserted in the troops' files.[31]

And since the RCMP officer's shredding investigation for DND had started in July 1999 and was based on Dr. Smith's memos having been in the files, the Minister would surely have known this.

Minister Eggleton also stated that a 1995 DND study gave assurance that there hadn't been toxic exposure. Yet a Department official said that they couldn't find the study but were looking for it,[32] and, as noted above, the samples taken in 1995 went nowhere, so they couldn't have been used for such a study.

Finally, as access to information requests produced more and more evidence, it was shown that Minister Eggleton knew as early as November 1998 that letters had been removed from files. The briefing note for the Minister reads:

> Due to confusion over whether or not the letters should have been included
> in the members' medical files (central staff did not agree that exposure had
> occurred) some letters may have been removed from medical files.[33]

The point is that "central staff" couldn't assure the Minister that harmful exposure had *not* occurred. At the time, the Minister probably read between the lines of this note's obfuscation, because what it probably meant was, "We didn't want the financial contingent liability risk from possible health claims to affect DND's budget, so we pulled Smith's warning letters even though we had already made him water it down." No one was "confused" about the aim.

Either the letters were put in the files and later removed or they weren't, but the evidence is all one way. The minister would or should have known the facts. Applying the Sissela Bok definition of lying – that lying is any intentionally deceptive message that is stated – the defence Minister's July 1999 public statement appears to fit the definition. At best, the Minister appears to have been reckless as to the truth. Top command likely advised the Minister on what to say.

A seemingly-innocuous statement in the middle of a 24 July 1999 article by astute journalists tells us the central issue:

> Discovery of (a 1995 central document) comes as Defence Minister Art Eggleton is trying to downplay the implications of the removal of health warnings from the medical files of peacekeepers who served in Croatia in the mid-1990s.[34]

The key word for Canadians is "implications."

Other Examples

In other areas of senior military competence and motivation:

- A military inquiry determined in January 1997 that a woman captain in the infantry had been singled out and mistreated in a mock execution threat in April 1992 in a Camp Gagetown military exercise because she was an extremely capable person and perceived as a threat to male officers.

   The officer in charge, Captain Michel Rainville, followed this with a similar incident of the same type in May, getting only an oral reprimand in June.[35] This was the same officer who had led a notorious mock raid on the Quebec Citadel in January 1992 (finally being charged in court for this several years later). Notwithstanding the evidence about this person staring them in the face, Rainville's superiors sent him off to Somalia to command the platoon that killed an unarmed Somalia civilian and wounded another in March 1993. He was charged in December 1993 for the Somalia shootings, together with a 1993 weapons charge while back in Canada, but acquitted in his court martial for the Somalia killings.

- When Master Corporal Rick Wheeler was run over and killed by an armoured personnel carrier in a 1992 training exercise, a military investigation at the time attributed it to "negligence of a minor character." His widow, convinced of a cover-up, pursued the case for years. After she succeeded in making the case public in 1996 and placing her concern before a military police advisory group, the military opened a new investigation. In April 1998 Mrs. Wheeler was given a summary of the 2100-page investigation report, which in effect said the training exercise had been uncontrolled. The military did not tell her why it took six years to tell her the truth about what happened. Said Mrs. Wheeler, "I've got closure but I don't feel I've got justice."[36]

- Thirty-four soldiers were placed under investigation in July 1996 for misconduct at a mental hospital that they were guarding in Bosnia in 1993-94. The then land forces commander Lt. Gen. Baril said to the press, "The army has a significant leadership deficiency and I intend to both address it and rectify it."[37] He was saluted all round for his frankness. Had he immediately taken the needed action, the Executive Summary of the Somalia inquiry commissioners report perhaps wouldn't have said what it did about senior officers' conduct.

- Lt. Gen. Armand Roy, Deputy Chief of the Defence Staff at the time he was dismissed in December 1996, had claimed large expenses that he wasn't entitled to between 1992 and 1995. He was ordered to repay the government between $70,000 and $80,000.

- When Corporal Neil McKinnon was killed in a training exercise in March 1995, his death was publicly attributed to his own grenade. After learning that something other than a grenade was involved, his father looked into it and found that in fact he had been accidentally and fatally shot by another soldier while preparing to throw his grenade – something the military never disclosed. In August 1996, fifteen months later, access to information requests about the board of inquiry report promised to his father by the fall of 1995 were still being denied.[38]

- Both the Minister of National Defence David Collenette and the CDS condemned the 1995 spending of $250,000 of taxpayer's money by Major General John McInnis, commander of Land Forces Atlantic, for retirement ceremonies for himself. General McInnis had been the Bosnian commander in 1994. Yet the general was engaged by top command in the same year he retired, for $45,000, to "guide" a leadership and ethics course for senior military officers at the Toronto Command and Staff College.[39] Other expensive contracts have been awarded to officers, even before they retire.

- A November 1996 "amateurish" military mission to Zaire costing $14.5 million, asked for by the Prime Minister, was "ordered into the field without basic military reconnaissance to determine whether it was necessary or practical and without the necessary diplomatic preparation to get its acceptance." It was cancelled within five weeks.[40]

- In January 1997 the Canadian military commander in Haiti was ordered to return to Canada for reported misconduct, having failed to meet "leadership standards."[41]

In July 1997, military police had to rescue a 15-year-old Haitian boy from Canadian Forces peacekeepers after reports that he had been struck repeatedly by soldiers of the Van Doos. Two junior officers were subsequently charged.[42]

- Following testimony she gave before the House of Commons Defence Committee surveying living conditions of military families on Canadian Forces bases in 1998, a non-military former contract worker was sent an intimidating letter by an officer of the Judge Advocate General's office, which she understood as telling her to keep quiet.[43] The Committee's visits to bases stemmed from 1995 revelations of military families using food banks and the then CDS's response that little could be done, and a subsequent survey disclosing that soldiers had lost confidence in their military leaders.[44]

- Soldiers refusing to accept vaccinations, the safety of which was unproved, were disciplined.[45] For example, Sgt. Mike Kipling was court-martialed and when a military judge found him not guilty, the department of National Defence appealed the decision to the federal appeal court.

- Casualty information on soldiers wounded in peacekeeping missions has been wholly inadequate for families and disability claims.[46]

- A 1998 *Maclean's* special report disclosed the extent of sexual assault and harassment in the military as worse than people would imagine.[47] In response, the Chief of the Defence Staff, General Baril, urged women "to come forward because the senior leadership is determined to help them and to stamp out sexism."[48] The assaulted women reported that their assaulters said they would just lie, successfully.

- The navy's missiles failed 70 per cent of the time in three separate exercises in a 14-month period in 1996-97. A resulting navy briefing document stated, "We assess that combat and weapon system knowledge is weak overall" and that crew members' knowledge of their weapons systems was "marginal." When a destroyer fired an armed missile in 1997 at a drone and nearly hit a frigate, the crucial self-destruct control hadn't worked. Minister Eggleton asserted at the time that no danger was involved. The military withheld the facts for over a year and they were obtained only through access to information.[49]

- Officers at the rank of general seek retirement jobs with DND-related corporations, which means that they can put corporations' interests before the public interest while still serving.

- At the military structure level, the military justice system is a misnomer because the Judge Advocate General reports to the CDS, and career fate control over all JAG officers is held by the CDS.

In Ottawa, at 7:30 am 29 September 2000, all flags on government buildings were at half-mast to honour former Prime Minister Pierre Trudeau, who had died the day before. The flag atop National Defence Headquarters still hadn't been lowered. It was lowered later in the morning.

The Pattern

Taken together, rather than news stories read individually or cropping up on TV screens from time to time, the Somalia inquiry disclosures and the scores of other media disclosures on DND responsibilities and performance over several years paint a picture of arrogance, stonewalling and deception by senior DND officials and top command – only a part of which has been summarized here.

When the Prime Minister and an unschooled new Defence Minister in effect dismissed the Somalia inquiry commissioners' report, Canadians did nothing. The state of the military can't be ignored by Canadians as simply "worrisome," "disturbing" or "troubling," allowing us all to turn to other things. The issue is not only the ability and motivation of the most senior military officers. It is whether all ranks, with notable individual exceptions, would support deception aims at the top.

The only reference point for the most senior officers is their own closed society. Because they don't account to the public for their responsibilities for competence and fairness, the most senior officers simply do what they want, in ways that reasonably imply arrogance – including the unwarranted perks they give themselves at taxpayer expense. Hence their insistence on self-investigation, e.g., boards of inquiry and a fettered ombudsman rather than an inspector general. They don't tell us their performance standards.

The give-away is successive chiefs of the Defence Staff talking about "leadership" and not the performance and answering standards they actually have in place and can assert are working. For example, when the 1998 *Maclean's* report on sexual assault and harassment was published, General Baril said:

> We certainly do have a problem, a problem of attitude in integrating women in the Canadian Forces. I'm beyond being patient. Those who quickly cannot change their attitude are in the wrong uniform and in the wrong profession.[50]

Nowhere in Baril's statement about inappropriate attitudes and psychological profiles of people is there a statement of what he was doing to change attitudes and what control processes he had put in place that would prevent assaults and harassment. Provost Marshall Samson, heading the new military National Investigation Service but reporting internally and not even to the CDS but only to his deputy, stated in May 1998, "We're looking at everything." She advised women in the Forces who have been subjected to sexual harassment to "report up the line, and keep reporting it until somebody does something about it." In the newspaper account of her public statement the Provost Marshall made no mention of protection of the person reporting the assault or harassment. [51] In today's world, no one believes that reporting "up the line" in organizations and putting the onus on the complainant will do anything but harm the complainant. (Colonel Samson was later promoted to Brigadier-General).

Statements only about attitudes, people being in the wrong place and where senior officers are looking are empty statements. This should worry Canadians.

At the Minister's level of responsibility, women in the Forces wouldn't find assurance in Minister Eggleton's comment:

> I wish to state unequivocally, that the Canadian Forces is no place for people who abuse, sexually harass and assault their colleagues. [52]

This statement of (obvious) belief by the ultimate accountable directing mind for fairness and justice in the military is not a statement of ministerial executive intention. Nor is it a statement of commitment to action steps that meet a standard. Nor is it a statement of what the Minister had done since taking office to stop the harassment that any new minister would have asked about. As the case of HRDC illustrates, every minister has an important self-informing duty upon taking office. And any Defence minister properly briefed would know that the risk of sexual assault and harassment in the military would be high.

For senior officers, explaining intentions and performance is an unknown obligation because the military is a system of taking field initiative and giving and obeying orders. Within the military, in action, this is necessary. But it in no way means that in peacetime top command needn't answer publicly for its intentions, reasoning and performance standards.

Because they don't have to account, and ministers won't ask them to, senior officers don't meet the standards of competence and fairness in managing the military that Canadians have the right to see met. We saw that management control failure at the top was the central issue in the Somalia and Marsaw cases, and it repeats in the case of the medical files.

At least the spin put out by the senior military, who lack civil service skill at it, is so inept that it's easily recognized for what it is. However, the first stance of the senior military is an indignant "Leave it with us," or simply "We decree." Most letters to the editor and newspaper articles flowing from retired senior officers have a common theme of blind loyalty to top command.

As for ministers of defence installing in top command basic management standards and answering, the ministers might as well not be there. And rather than fix the systemic problems through his power to do so, the Prime Minister stands with the Defence Minister telling the nation that the Somalia commissioners got it wrong. For his part, the Auditor General of Canada reports to Parliament only on certain operating responsibilities of DND, not on management ability, ethics and motivation at the top.

Canadians, if they can't stay in denial, don't seem to know what to do when faced with disillusionment in military top command. Senior citizens remember when the military had honour from having good leaders at the top who had commanded units larger than a company. Younger generations of Canadians either aren't interested or get no cues from their bewildered elders.

The troops have always been told, "Be loyal and you will be looked after." And so they've been loyal – to the point of disbelieving that the senior ranks could break the contract. Now the troops, disillusioned, don't know what to do. And it's clear that ministers don't know what to do with the military. The most important aspects to ministers seem to be defence contracts, and even in that they don't accept the military's recommendations and warnings[53] and don't account to the military or the public for their reasoning.

Installing Accountability Reporting by Top Command

Because the responsibilities of military top command affect people in important ways, the Chief of the Defence Staff, as its directing mind, has the obligation to answer publicly for the discharge of these responsibilities. It doesn't matter that no CDS has ever had to answer, or that none would know how and that no subordinate would either. It's now time they did.

How do we start? We start with the knowledge that successive ministers of the Crown haven't put right the military's operations, and prime ministers haven't had any better grasp of what's needed, and why. So there is no point in looking to them and their predictable advisers. Their job is to approve a publicly challenged set of sensible proposals.

One approach is to assume that top command has been placed in effect in receivership, with the task being to reconstruct its fundamental responsibilities, leadership and management requirements and accountabilities. A task group of three ex-military people, independent of the military as a current or potential contracting or funding client and demonstrably credible with military critics, can be the "official receiver" to recommend key changes, and what top command should answer for and how. This is because the needed public answering identifies and drives the needed performance. (For example, in transportation responsibilities, adequate public assurance reporting for the safety of marine transportation of oil drives the requirement that corporations double-hull their tankers and take other safety measures as well.)

The report of the receivership task group would be public, and would be advanced by an ad hoc parliamentary accountability committee. The committee would comprise the Defence Minister's Parliamentary Secretary and the other parties' defence critics, and would set out the needed reporting standards and staffing specifications for top command. Identifying the military's achievement objectives, fundamental performance standards and rules of conduct isn't a partisan task: we are not talking about defence contracts here.

Senior command can be asked to propose the performance reporting they think reasonable for themselves, to show us what they see as their public answering obligation. The parliamentary committee, not controlled by the government and mandated to get other advice as well, would tell us what they think the public is entitled to receive in military reporting on its intended and actual performance.

Following a round of public challenge, the parliamentary committee would put its conclusions to the House of Commons, stating

- its specifications for the top military posts and how the right leadership can be brought along to replace the current caretakers
- what should be legislated as the military's answering requirements for its intended and actual performance. The committee report would invite the executive government to publicly respond to the proposals
- the rules for nonpartisan parliamentary scrutiny of the military

Since MPs must scrutinize the military's intended and actual performance, they must deal with the difference between the military's peacekeeping and fighting roles. For example, since the major determinants of performance (ability, motivation, organization structure and external constraints) will be different for each of peacekeeping and fighting roles, the CDS's reporting should give the status of these determinants for each main type of military task – and the quality of the management control system that brings them all together. Had this been done for the Airborne Regiment before Somalia, and had the answering been publicly validated, the Regiment would likely not have been sent.

If the accountability committee abdicates the issue of the military's answering for its responsibilities, leaving this to the executive government, and if Parliament simply accepts what the defence ministers don't want as answering, we can expect no improvement in management of the military.

When parliament decides what the CDS should account for, it will clarify top command's primary responsibilities. The CDS's accountability report would be annual and public, formally addressed to the Governor General as Commander in Chief, but would be tabled in the House of Commons. The accounting is thus to the Canadian people. One of the tasks of an Inspector General would be to validate the CDS's report for its fairness and completeness.

The answering has to be specific. For example, "morale" is a conceptual quagmire and too vague a term for accountability reporting to have it identify responsibilities. A CDS could simply assert, "Morale is fine."

The CDS's annual report would state top command's

- ranking of the military's most important responsibilities
- achievement intentions for each major continuing responsibility and assignment and the critical success factors and performance standards for the achievement
- standards for its capital acquisitions (i.e., the quality of the knowledge and skill of Forces personnel to use and properly maintain the sophisticated ships, submarines, planes and equipment purchased (capital acquisitions are about 20% of the military budget)
- actual performance (including compliance with fundamental rules of conduct)
- explanation of significant differences between planned and actual performance (external constraints can be one cause)
- the learning gained by top command and how they applied it

The CDS's performance reporting would also set out the statutory duties of the CDS and his compliance with them, and would state what stands in the way of top command doing its job.

Until an independent Inspector General or similar office is created, an annual report of the military's internal Ombudsman, along the same lines, would be attached to the CDS's report. This would include the Ombudsman's view of external constraints to the effectiveness of his work. The Auditor general would validate the CDS's reporting.

For his part, the Defence Minister would annually report his response to the Desmarais question applied to him: "What would you say are your most important management problems in the Department of National Defence and what are you doing about them?"

Once the public answering requirements became law, the Auditor General could attest to the fairness and completeness of the reporting. As in reliance on internal audit, the Auditor General could rely on the reports of an inspector general, assuming one is appointed. His reports to Parliament would state whether the intent of the legislated accountability has been complied with.

Endnotes

[1] I am indebted to Col. Michel Drapeau for reviewing this chapter, and to Dr. Eric Smith for reviewing the section on medical files.

[2] As a June 2001 report of the Royal Canadian Military Institute stated, in a major critical

assessment of the military, promotion should be based on excellence in the field, not the ability to operate within the bureaucracy at headquarters. (*Ottawa Citizen*, 27 June 2001 p.A1)

3 David Pugliese, *Ottawa Citizen*, 3 September 1996 p.A3

4 A point made by the late General G.C. E. Theriault, Chief of the Defence Staff 1983-1986, speaking to a forum of the Alliance for Public Accountability in Ottawa, November 1996.

5 *Dishonoured Legacy: the Lessons from the Somalia Affair*, Executive Summary, pages ES-1,3,4,7,8,14 and 15 (Minister of Public Works and Government Services Canada. Ottawa, 1997)

6 Annual Report of the Information Commissioner, 1995-1996 (Ottawa: Minister of Public Works and Government Services Canada). p.67

7 *Times Colonist*, 2 June 2001, p.A6

8 Col. (Ret'd) Michel Drapeau, *Maclean's* 5 February 1996 p.22-23

9 Pugliese, op. cit. and 21 August 1996, p.A1

10 *Globe and Mail* 22 January 1997 p.A3 and *Ottawa Citizen*, 23 January 1997 p.A4

11 *Globe and Mail*, 4 April 1996 p.A1

12 *Globe and Mail* editorial, 17 January 1997 p.A20

13 *Globe and Mail* 15 October 1997 p. A4

14 *Ottawa Citizen* 17 October 1997 p.A6

15 *Ottawa Citizen*, 24 May 1998 p.A1

16 *Globe and Mail*, 31 July 1999, p. A4

17 Dr. Eric Smith, "A Dysfunctional Family Called Our Military," *Globe and Mail* 29 July 1999, p.A15 (Dr. Smith had retired from the navy at the time he wrote the article)

18 *Ottawa Citizen*, 14 August 1999, p.A5

19 Interview of Dr. Smith by Peter Worthington, editor emeritus of the *Ottawa Sun* 5 August 1999, p.14

20 Personal communication

21 *Toronto Star*, 28 July 1999, p.A15

22 *Ottawa Citizen*, 22 July 1999, p.A1

23 *Globe and Mail*, 23 July 1999, p.A1

24 Ibid.

25 *National Post*, op. cit.

26 Ken Rubin, "Spinning Military Records," *Ottawa Citizen*, 27 July 1999, p.A15

27 *Globe and Mail*, 30 July 1999., P.A4

28 Interview with members of the *Ottawa Citizen's* editorial board, 13 August 1999, p.A17

29 *Globe and Mail*, 6 August 1999, p. A1

30 *Globe and Mail* 24 July 1999. p. A8

31 The "Advice for the Minister" briefing note was printed in the *Globe and Mail* 27 July 1999, p.A2

32 *Ottawa Citizen*, 23 July 1999, p. A3

33 *Toronto Star*, 28 July 1999, P.A1

34 Daniel LeBlanc and Andrew Mitrovika, *Globe and Mail*, 24 July 1999 p.A1

35 *Globe and Mail* 18 January 1997 p.A4

36 *Ottawa Citizen* 8 April 1998

37 *Ottawa Citizen*, 18 July 1996 p.A1

[38] *Ottawa Citizen* 11 August 1996

[39] *Ottawa Citizen* 14 September 1995 p.A1

[40] *Ottawa Citizen* 18 January 1997 p.A1

[41] *Globe and Mail* 16 January 1997 p.A4

[42] *National Post* 15 July 2000, p.A4

[43] *Globe and Mail* 12 March 1998 p.A5

[44] *Ottawa Citizen* 16 March 1998 p.A3

[45] *Ottawa Citizen* 17 March 1998 p.A7

[46] *Globe and Mail* 1 May 1998 p.A1

[47] *Maclean's*, 25 May 1998

[48] *Globe and Mail* 20 May 1998 p.A6

[49] *Ottawa Citizen* 6 February 1999 p.A1

[50] *Globe and Mail* 20 May 1998 p.A6

[51] *Globe and Mail* 27 May 1998 p.A4

[52] *Ottawa Citizen*, 26 May 1998, p.A12

[53] For example, the Sea King helicopter replacement issue of split contracts versus single, *Times Colonist*, 24 June 2001 p.A5

CHAPTER 11

The Accountability of Judges

Until we install adequate public answering from authorities, harmful things will happen increasingly and unnecessarily, and people trying to stop something or seek redress will increasingly turn to the courts. Yet courts themselves are authorities. In an increasingly litigious society, the "loser pays" practice in Canadian courts for preventing frivolous lawsuits means that corporations and authorities with bottomless pockets for lawsuits can intimidate activists from pursuing important issues in the courts. "Loser pays" also enhances SLAPP strategies ("strategic lawsuits against public participation") in which a challenged authority launches a lawsuit against the activists – or even community residents in a property development protest[1] – to use up the activists' treasuries and energies and distract public attention from the public issues raised by the activists.

Judges are critical to justice in all cases, and we rely on them for fairness. Yet judges are now seemingly able to decide anything they want. They can comply with the law or depart from it without stating the fact, or accounting for their reasons. We must face the fact that we citizens simply don't know the extent to which judges, whom we tend to trust implicitly, serve the law or make their decisions out of personal preference, capriciousness or a felt obligation to someone. Canadians simply do not have the evidence to make that assessment for any set of judges. But faced with the possibility that all is not well with judging, we are likely to go into denial.

The Problems

Judges don't account. Judges determine legal outcomes for people, and for some their fates. But we allow them not to be accountable – to have no answering obligation. This may sound strange, since we can agree that all who affect others in important ways have a public answering obligation. In the Canadian legal system, however, judges are appointed by the executive government. They are not elected. Their tenure is cancelled with difficulty, and only for visible wrongful behaviour; and they haven't been asked to answer for their performance. We make accountability exceptions for members of juries because they are our peers, dragooned and simply doing their best. But in today's world, in common sense, judges cannot be exempted from the obligation to answer for their performance.

We don't hold judges to a standard of performance, and they aren't assessed by any visible credible process. A judge's decision is a decree having the full force of a law enforceable by the Crown unless the decision is overturned by a higher court. Written decisions by judges set out their thinking only to the extent they choose to disclose their motivation. Judges need not report whether they met a set of performance standards, such as compliance with existing law – or their reasoning if they mean in effect to alter it – and how their judgment upholds fairness and natural justice.

In cases involving civil servants' and ministers' duties, for example, we have no assurance that government-appointed judges will try to ascertain whether senior civil servants can be serving someone's interests other than the public interest. More important, and because judges make no performance assertions for themselves, we simply don't know whether a judge's tendency in a particular case is to uphold the law and do justice, or simply to endorse authorities' actions.

Judges are also commissioned by ministers to conduct public inquiries. When the inquiry involves ministers' responsibilities, we don't see judges appointed as commissioners making their first inquiry task the explanation to the public of the responsible ministers' statutory powers and duties in the responsibilities examined. Why is this? Is it deference to ministers because ministers control the appointment decisions that affect judges' careers? Or is it a judicial culture of deference to authority and the existing "system" because judges receive so much deference themselves? We have to face these possibilities.

When a public inquiry into Royal Canadian Mounted Police actions at the 1998 APEC summit meeting in Vancouver pursued the question of influence amounting to direction by the Office of the Prime Minister, the fundamental issue was never addressed. The pepper-sprayed students who had protested at the APEC meeting wanted to know whether the Prime Minister's staff member had conveyed protest-suppression instructions to Vancouver RCMP officials from the Prime Minister. But the Prime Minister's representative didn't have to give instruction. His very presence at preparation meetings with the Vancouver RCMP, a federal police force, would have caused the police authorities to think carefully about what the Prime Minister would want. They would have then honoured those wants. "The limits are understood." People spending their careers in the legal system don't acknowledge the power of tacit instruction.

Nothing compelled the APEC inquiry Commissioner to understand and deal with underlying cause and its effect. But a commissioner could state in his report that the issue of local authorities' acceptance of tacit or implicit instruction (because of its source) could well be the central issue in identifying what happened and why. He could then go on to say, as an accounting, that he couldn't get to the bottom of this issue, given his inquiry mandate.

When we think about it, the collapse of legislative assemblies in protecting fairness in society and the environment means that protection and redress are available only through lawyers and the courts.[2] But since these judges don't answer for their intentions and conduct, we have no assurance that their intentions serve the public interest. With lawyers, we must always ask who their real client is, no matter who they are formally acting for. We simply have no evidence to say that that it is different for judges. The cases of Donald Marshall, David Milgaard, Guy Paul Morin and others are examples of what can happen in total, from the launch of the police investigations to their wrongful time in jail. The judge is the detector and protector of last resort when a charging process is purposefully or recklessly stacked against a defendant, but we have no standards for the judge's ability and motivation.

Our system is a legal system, not a legal justice system. Some of our judges are exemplary, despite there being no system identifying and publicly rewarding and advancing these people. But having exemplary judges doesn't mean that the processes within judges' control designed to ensure justice are in safe hands across the board.

We think we don't believe in tooth fairies, but we adopt blind faith in judges once they are appointed. If we didn't put the force of law behind judges' decisions we would of course have chaos, like a city without traffic lights. But we have no effective precautionary control in place on the appointment of judges and on their intentions and competence. This is like the traffic lights installed whimsically and with no assurance that the lights will work properly.

Executive government doesn't answer for its appointment of judges. We must face the likelihood of provincial and federal executive governments increasingly controlling the courts' functioning through their invisible processes for appointing judges to positions of administrative control – in which they have the power to decide which particular judge is most "appropriate" for a particular case in which the executive government has an outcome interest.

Since the executive government significantly controls, directly or indirectly, the reward system for judges, the precautionary principle tells us that the system must be considered to operate in favour of the executive's wishes unless we can show it to be otherwise. Judges can be appointed to the bench as reward for service to the political party in power, even if it was service in a former capacity years before.

Citizens haven't set the criteria for the Crown's appointments of judges, which are appointments by politicians who have agendas. The criteria used by the executive government aren't laid out publicly, so it's impossible to tell how appointments stem from the executive's unstated agendas. There is no check or veto to prevent self-serving whim by the appointing executive.

The inevitable accolades in the media for the Prime Minister's appointments to the Supreme Court of Canada include sought-out testimonials from former associates about the appointee's fast analytical mind, courtroom prowess, tirelessness and so on. These serve as lulling messages to the public, helping to keep public faith in the system. All these have to do with legal process skills – what the families of those drowned in 1987 in the *Herald of Free Enterprise* called "legal niceties." What isn't assessed publicly before the appointment is how the appointee thinks, what the person's history was in terms of who he or served previously, and who is likely be the appointee's real client once on the bench.

Without forcing the real appointment criteria to be made visible, citizens can't approve them, let alone audit the appointment decision against them. We don't have the elected representative challenge of the appointments of the highest-level judges that the Americans have in their Senate for those nominated by the President for a place on their Supreme Court. This legislator challenge applies to all federally-appointed judges in the U.S. The word "nominee' doesn't apply in the appointment of judges to the Supreme Court of Canada.

Someone visibly harmful to justice won't be appointed to the bench, but there is no control mechanism preventing our executive governments from appointing people whose past associations, inclinations and expected future loyalties (given their promotion aspirations) fit with the underlying aims of authorities. It isn't difficult for the executive government to appoint a committee to screen candidates for competence in law, and this may be done. But a private, unelected screening committee will not delve into the motivations of a candidate and the track record of whose interests they served in the past. Within the set of candidates emerging from a competence screening, the responsible ministers will surely find someone who they think won't be a problem, or who is owed a reward for earlier helpful support. We can't rely on roads to Damascus.

The appointment process is not self-regulating. If a generation of judges is appointed who sufficiently offend the public enough with demonstrable bias, odd thinking or incompetence, the next executive government will appoint more acceptable people – if only for ministers' political safety. But in the meantime, good law can be undercut, questionable law put into the system and injustices done in the courtroom. We don't apply the precautionary principle to the appointment and quality control of judges.

An Ipsos-Reid survey on the Supreme Court of Canada, conducted for the *Globe and Mail* and CTV News, showed strong respect for the Court, but seven in 10 Canadians believe that Supreme Court rulings are influenced by partisan politics. The polling firm inferred that the "broad feeling" of Canadians is that the federal government's appointment of the judges introduces bias toward "lining up" with the federal government.[3]

As a *Globe and Mail* editorial put it, about the appointment of Ian Binnie to the Supreme Court of Canada in January 1998:

> But let's reflect a moment about how he wound up on the bench. A closed, secretive process. No official candidates. No public discussion. Zero public knowledge. Just several weeks of backroom maneuvering followed by an announcement.

> ...Its (Supreme Court's) members are among the most powerful political actors in Canada, and they will still be there long after the elected parliamentarians who appointed them have retired or been tossed out by the voters. Shouldn't we know something about these people before they make it to the bench? Wouldn't a public discussion about the beliefs and values that make a good judge, and an attempt to identify the persons embodying those attitudes, be best held before rather than after the appointment?

> ...The process has to change. There must be a public list of appointees. Parliamentarians must be able to vet the candidates. It should all take place in the open, so that the public can itself scrutinize the quality of the potential appointees, and provide feedback. The old game of innuendo and rumours and who-knows-whom has got to stop.[4]

A start has been made at the provincial level. Alberta in 1997 established a committee to examine appointments of judges and included the issues of term limits for judges and public participation in their appointments.[5]

Government doesn't give public assurance that judges are competent and impartial. This is a crucial factor in court fairness. When executive governments appoint the chief judges who set the case assignments, the chief judges will know which judges have what leanings.

In 1998 the Vancouver-based Defence of Canadian Liberty Committee launched a judicial review suit against the Crown in Federal Court, arguing that the federal government had no jurisdiction to sign, ratify and implement the contentious Multilateral Agreement on Investment. The Committee asked the assigned judge, Mr. Justice Dubé of the Federal Court, to step aside on the grounds of bias because the judge was a friend of Prime

Minister Jean Chrétien (who was named in the suit) and had been a federal minister simultaneously with Mr. Chrétien in 1968-74. (Mr. Dubé was appointed to the Federal Court in 1975). Justice Dubé refused:

> For the past 24 years I have dealt with trials, appeals, motions and judicial reviews in all ten provinces, quite often involving the government. Never have I been asked to recuse myself. I do not intend to do so now....[6]

In the next round of litigation a different judge was assigned by the Associate Chief Judge. Commenting on how they fared with the successor, the Committee said:

> We knew we were in trouble when we saw we had been assigned the judge who has a reputation of being "Mr. Quick Fix".... The judge literally winced painfully at many of the arguments (our lawyer) made. It was obvious the judge did not want that information. The judge kept looking to the lawyer for the government in what seemed like an appeal for help.[7]

The 1992 trial of Guy Paul Morin, following his earlier 1986 acquittal, wrongfully convicted him of murder. During the 1997 commission of inquiry that examined how police, medical experts and Crown attorneys conducted themselves, Morin said:

> The (1992 judge's) distaste for the defence and the efforts we made seemed to be apparent...it was a form of justice that was not really taking place in the courtroom. It seemed (the judge) had already made up his mind[8]

The trial judge did not appear before the Morin Commission of Inquiry. This was because of a 1989 decision of the Supreme Court of Canada on judge's immunity that allows judges to refuse to testify before a public inquiry. This means that unless a judge agrees, he or she can't be asked, in a public inquiry about an injustice, what their performance standards had been, when one of the key issues in the injustice done may have been a trial judge's earlier conduct – such as "warm smiles for the prosecutors and grimaces aimed at the defence lawyer"[9] and a videotape showing the trial judge giving "comradely encouragement" to a police officer facing criminal charges for giving material false evidence instrumental to the wrongful conviction, and who had moreover withheld important information.[10] The Morin Inquiry Commissioner said that his inquiry wasn't a trial and that any misconduct of the 1992 trial judge was a matter for the Judicial Council of Canada, not the Commissioner.[11]

A judge's influence on a jury is itself influenced by the Crown prosecutors, police and other witnesses: all part of what can be termed "tunnel vision"[12] aimed at getting a conviction at all costs – initiated by the police but joined in by other public officials. But the judge's duty is to apply the precautionary principle in assessing the probability of collusion against the defendant and, for that matter, against defence counsel. As Donald Marshall, who spent 11 years wrongfully in prison, understated it when interviewed in July 1997 on David Milgaard's release after 23 years of wrongful imprisonment, "This court system in Canada is not the easiest to fight."[13]

The list of citizens' and lawyers' observations on "minds made up" is legion. The problem is that there is currently no way victims of this can hold a judge to account for bias before the damage is done. People familiar with courtroom processes can detect evidence of bias, whether in a judge's questioning or observations, or body language, but because deference is constantly exacted in the courtroom a participant can't stand up and hold a judge fairly to account.

And bias isn't always easy to attribute. How would we tell if a judge would be inclined not to support the aim of public disclosure of industry-regulator cosiness in a case that involved government's responsibilities? Would it make a difference if the same executive government had made the judge an administrative judge for his area? Is someone awarded a senior court appointment because that person has significantly helped executive government earlier – even a decade earlier – in very important litigation, and might well help again, but this time on the bench?

What is our *evidence* for saying that a judge cannot be "bought"? As citizens, we must obey judicial decisions, but are we required to have blind faith in judges? Where is the contract we signed to that effect? Because executive governments have reward power in the legal system, they can dangle status to overpower a professional person's desire for the stature of a Robinette or a McEachern – especially when the standards of the person's peers are eroding and government knows it.

An administrative judge's power to assign judges to hear cases and to dispense rewards making judges' lives easier is an important possible source of bias leading to unfair trial outcomes. In 1995 Mr. Justice David Marshall of the Ontario Superior Court of Justice, interviewed about his just-published book, *Judicial Conduct and Accountability*, said that judicial independence is threatened by chief judges dispensing assignments, sabbatical leaves, promotions, limousines and education courses. The equality of judges can't help but become a fictional concept when one of their number has greater powers:

> We have gone from a situation of pure, undiluted judicial independence to a very controlled hierarchical judiciary…A manager has to get people to obey him. There has to be a system of rewards and punishments in any managerial situation. As soon as you introduce these, you no longer have judicial independence.[14]

An important task of the judge who is the administrative judge for a region within a province is to assign judges on a rotational basis, usually to courtrooms, although it can be to cases as well.[15] The chief judge for the province may also do assignments, for example to get rid of backlogs, and the senior court clerk is also be involved in the "rota" system. Since the assignment is from an existing pool of judges, someone may be assigned who isn't as competent or objective as a particular case calls for. But it isn't only a matter of competence. Since there are no visible performance standards for judges, including chief judges, and no public and auditable public reporting of judges' performance, we have no assurance that a particular case won't be assigned to a judge who may be biased toward the executive government's interests. The chief judge has the management control responsibility for the selection of judges that produces either fair or unfair decisions. The precautionary principle tells us that we need assurance.

Justice Marshall points out that the executive government can call on the chief judge for suggestions on who should be appointed to the bench, and that this has dangerous implications. He also underscores the point made clearly in recent federal public inquiries: that the executive control the funding of judicial processes, which gives it administrative power over them.[16]

Looking for the ultimate directing mind, we find that the chief judge is appointed by and gets his power and status from an executive government minister, not from his peers. To the extent that judges seek administrative status, the question arises of whose needs will be honoured by chief judges, and to what extent.

If one thinks of the administrative structure of courts as the executive government wants us to think of it – a neutral mechanism that simply provides efficient administration and coordination – then observations from people such as Justice Marshall won't produce audit examination of what is going on, and its implications. But if one views the process of appointing and assigning judges as a process lying within the field of organizational behaviour, the research from the administrative sciences would back Justice Marshall's concerns.

The precautionary principle says that we must assume that the current processes for the appointment of judges and control by administrative judges (chief judges) put justice in the courts at significant risk. This means that the responsible ministers of the Crown, who have effective control over both appointments and administration of the courts, have the obligation to demonstrate to the public, through public answering, whether independence is being assured. Ministers' decrees that all's well simply won't do. And ministers' answering about appointments needs to be independently audited for its fairness and completeness by people such as Justice Marshall. The responsible official in each jurisdiction, the Attorney General, has the obligation to publicly demonstrate why citizens should have faith in the processes as they are now.

Judges can capriciously decide what they will include or exclude as relevant to their decision. Our system gives judges astonishing power to decree and to ignore central issues at stake, or to redefine them into issues that fit the abilities, processes and comfort zones of judges and their profession. They can do this if no one holds them to a standard. For example, is there a high court judge who understands exerted international business power and executive government motivation well enough to identify and understand underlying cause and effect in an issue such as whether the federal executive government should be permitted on its own to commit the country and all its legislatures and municipal councils to a Multilateral Agreement on Investment? Is a judge capable of understanding whether there can be such a thing as irredeemable "bad seeds," in cases of children and teens doing horrific things to others? Can a judge credibly assert to someone in the dock, "You're not a bad person"?

A judge is only confronted with the law if he or she chooses to recognize it. It is true that persons can appeal a judge's decision, but few individuals and non-profit organizations have the resources to do this. An appeal to a higher court examines the reasoning of the lower court judge for errors of law, but we don't know, for example, whether the appeal judges would spot and act on a lower court judge's subtle denigration of expert witnesses, and we don't know the source of assertions of fact made by an appeal judge in a judgment that were not introduced in the trial. These are issues for an appellant's lawyer, but there is another problem. Apart from whether a person can afford to engage an appeal lawyer who would detect bias in the judgment, we can't say that we know for sure who lawyers' real clients are when they come from one of the large firms whose continuing main clients are big corporations and executive government. For most people, then, a judge's decision stands.

An appeal is only a trial of the conduct of a trial. But there should be nothing stopping an appeal court from accepting, as valid challenge of the lower court judge's thinking process, his or her failure to recognize and deal with what the central issue was – such as what management control is and where responsibility for it lay – so long as the claimant's counsel introduced it in any recognizable form.

Yet a judge can be very helpful in giving heads-up informal instruction to a person who strikes the judge as needing help. An example would be a judge subtly conveying, in his or her decision in a preliminary round for a claim, that a plaintiff's own lawyer had put the wrong argument or put something on a wrong basis that in effect killed off the claim. The judge's message could be that the plaintiff should try to find out who his or her lawyer's real client is, and whether there is an actionable claim against the lawyer for incompetence.

In the UK corporate manslaughter trial following the drownings in the *Herald of Free Enterprise*, the corporation may have been charged with the wrong charge, thus predicting failure, but the judge excluded from consideration the company directors' management control responsibility – the central issue in the case. The judge didn't see the case as assessing a corporation's directing minds against performance standards that the public could reasonably expect the company's board to meet.

The conduct of inquiry in science dictates that one has to understand something in order to rule it out as a determinant. As legal processes stand, they allow judges to rule out issues they don't want included, or which they don't understand. Nothing forces a judge to apply the existing common law or to identify commonsense chains of responsibility and accountability. It must be said about the *Herald of Free Enterprise* case that it would have been an exceptional judge who would have grasped the concepts of public accountability and of management control and performance standards as they are generally understood, when the parade of lawyers coming before judges didn't appear to understand or want to understand and apply these concepts themselves. A Denning is an exception.

In a discussion of judges we must include those people acting as judges in military courts martial. If court cases are to re-create reality, the court martial panel for the 1995 military trial of Lieutenant Commander Dean Marsaw didn't force out all the testimony it should have heard and the motivation of the senior officers who charged him, and these were not an issue in the appeal that overturned the panel's verdict.

The February 1996 CBC Fifth Estate TV documentary program on the responsibilities of the federal government's Health Protection Branch for its approval of the drug nifedipine set out to make visible the responsibilities and accountabilities of the federal government as regulator. But it was also to alert viewers to the professional duty and accountability of the Branch's outside medical research advisers. The trial of the CBC three years later for claimed libel in that program didn't deal with these issues. The judge's decision – against the CBC and supported by appeal court judges – helped the government in claiming that its practice for the relationship between the regulator and outside medical research advisers is just fine.[17] A second issue was never exposed in the trial: a medical researcher's professional duty to stay independent and follow through until he or she is satisfied that the "Dear Doctor" advisory letters intended by the Branch for practitioners prescribing a company's drug will faithfully reflect the outside advisory committee's concerns. Without demonstrable follow-through diligence, a researcher's motivation can be rightly questioned. Researchers' responsibilities and accountabilities, regardless whether it was brought out by CBC's counsel, appeared not to have been important to the trial judge or appeal judges.

Relying on case-by-case practice and appeals to develop the law constitute an evolutionary process. This is a true statement, but is it useful? If reasonable performance expectations by citizens, as standards to be met, aren't part of the court process, how do we get them recognized by judges?

Citizens have no way to hold judges to account. We allow ourselves to be blocked from publicly criticizing judges' thinking. We haven't required that transcripts both of closing arguments of trials and the judges' subsequent decisions be made freely available – for example on a comprehensive website, now that computers make this possible. Anyone can ask for a transcript to be typed from the court record, but if a citizen or group who did pay the high cost for a typed transcript was disillusioned by a judge's thinking, they could do nothing with the result. [18] A citizen's letter to the editor or an article for a newspaper or magazine simply wouldn't get published. The social trap we are in is that a citizen's criticism of a judge's thinking is taken as unacceptable disrespect. Yet judges work for us, are paid by us, and affect us in important ways.

The legal profession has accountability for what judges do. The profession doesn't choose or supervise judges, but all judges come from its ranks. There is no reason why the profession should not be required to propose, to the public, criteria for judges' appointments and the standards for their performance and for dealing with aspects of administrative structure that introduce bias. Included in this would be criteria that legislators would apply to attorneys general for their appointment of provincial judges. [19]

Justice depends on judges being aware of what goes on in daily give-and-take in society and government. It also depends on judges demonstrably putting the public interest before strategies to get themselves promoted. The profession collectively has the capability to publicly propose performance standards for judges. Just as we can find out who senior civil servants see as their real client by asking them to propose public answering standards for their political masters, we can do the same for the legal profession. The standards that the legal profession would propose for judges would tell us who the profession's leaders are serving.

Issues for Judges' Accountability Reporting to the Public

The self-regulating value of the public answering obligation was explained earlier. Whoever has important responsibility has a public answering obligation. Judges cannot decree that their office must have unquestioned respect and that they must be fully trusted. Respect and trust must be earned. Nor can judges say that they are unaccountable. Therefore:

- It is reasonable to expect judges collectively to propose the means for achieving greater fairness, making the legal system demonstrably a legal justice system.

    Judges collectively have the experience and commonsense obligation to tell us how the legal processes in Canada can produce a legal justice system. Processes causing wrongful convictions are one obvious example. The needless but predictable legal wrangling that bogged down inquiry commissioners Krever and Richard is another. Converting the military's processes into legal justice processes is yet another. Preventing political-reward appointments to the bench is another responsibility. We can ask the judges to tell us how to convert the legal processes they are familiar with into processes producing continuous justice. When judges collectively tell us how, we will know the extent to which they serve the public interest beyond applying their intellectual technique to individual cases.

Judges needn't simply respond to what lawyers seek in court cases. Judges can propose legislative changes to process without risking their independence. Examples are performance standards for judicial processes, and practice matters such as when class action lawsuits and contingency fees for lawyers are justified.

- It is reasonable to expect judges to propose performance standards for themselves, and give their reasoning for the standards they propose.

Because their decisions are constitutionally to be independent from the executive and legislature, judges can be expected on their own initiative to lay before the public the fundamental rules and basic performance standards for themselves that they think the public can reasonably expect them to meet.

If it is reasonable to expect executive governments and parliaments to formulate performance standards for themselves – and it is – it is also reasonable that the people most critical in the rest of constitutional protection in society do the same, regardless of any umbrage, indignation or outrage by the judiciary at the thought.

What the judges propose can be reviewed by public interest organizations related to the law, such as civil liberties organizations and law review bodies that are free from means of executive government influence. Then the standards can be legislated in the applicable Acts following elected representative review.

- It is reasonable to expect judges to account for their performance.

Given basic performance standards, accountability requires that judges report their own performance against the standards. The reasons for their answering obligation are the same as for other authorities affecting the public in important ways. Exposed failures in judges' performance will have to be assessed by independent others, but the judges' reporting should identify significant external constraints that judges see as operating against their independence or performance. The reporting should be in an accessible public record and made available on an Internet website in each jurisdiction.[20]

- It is reasonable that important accountability reporting be audited.

Since performance reports that are to be relied on should be validated by audit, judges' reporting should be subject to audit of its fairness and completeness. At the outset, however, audit of judges' reporting could be done as an informal review by law-related public interest organizations, and probably would be best done for the accountability reporting by judges whose conduct had aroused concern, such as allegations of racist or sexist comments.

Complaints investigation by the Canadian Judicial Council, comprising the federally-appointed chief justices, doesn't involve citizen representation (unlike Manitoba's Judicial Council, for example). And such investigations are not the same thing as establishing fundamental rules of conduct and basic performance standards and having judges report periodically whether they met them.[21] The effectiveness of complaints investigation processes are ultimately the responsibility of the executive government which has an obligation to report publicly what the investigation performance standards are and whether the investigating bodies met the standards. For example, complaints about judges' conduct get listed by the federal Judicial Council in its annual report, but the names of the judges aren't given.

Nor is the answer only "guidelines," such as the ethical guidelines issued in 1998 by the federal Council. These are about such things as judges

- not speaking out unless the "institution is under attack"
- being wary of appointments to judicial inquiries because of the risk of being caught in political battles
- avoiding racist and sexist comments
- staying off university, church and hospital boards because such bodies are increasingly involved in lawsuits.[22]

The guidelines were criticized by the Canadian Bar Association as not being a code that would allow performance assessment, and there is no discipline element in the guidelines. The Council's only power is to recommend to Parliament that a judge be removed, and that has never happened.[23]

An issue going beyond answering obligations is what citizens should do when their highest court makes a ruling that most of the public find incredible and unacceptable. Examples include the 1994 Supreme Court of Canada ruling that expanded the ability of accused people to use extreme intoxication as a defence, even in sexual assault cases, (as if getting oneself drunk is an act of God). Another was the 1995 Court's ruling striking down Parliament's ban on tobacco advertising, as if the five judges in the 5-4 division had steadfastly resisted understanding the precautionary principle in health despite the annual 40,000 deaths attributable to smoking, and that "free speech" for tobacco corporations, solely to produce cash flow for managers and shareholders from a lethal product, should prevail.

In legislating the tobacco advertising ban as one way of limiting harm to people's health, especially young people, parliamentarians understood that something had to be done. The judge's role is to interpret the law, but citizens must have assurance that judges at least know the legislature's outcome intentions for the laws that the judges strike down, and that judges will therefore give reasoning that citizens can accept as sensible. In terms of the emperor's clothes, citizens must be able to audit Supreme Court judges' decisions against agreed and visible decision standards, and incur no penalty if they call Supreme Court judges irresponsible.[24]

Yet another case was the 5-4 ruling in February 1997 that notes of a rape crisis centre counsellor's interview with a complainant must be made available to an accused at trial, in this particular case two years later (as if a crisis centre is tantamount to an arm of government, with the same duty of keeping everything for later disclosure purposes, rather than the record being there to help counsel traumatized complainants at the time, under commonsense privacy rights). The 1997 decision implied that "missing evidence" could stall prosecutions indefinitely when this is used as a ploy.[25]

Constitutions and the courts provide a sea anchor to protect citizens from themselves and from whim that isn't valid public policy. But the relentless dismantlement of medicare by executive government, pressured by business interests with unlimited money resources, eventually may involve the Supreme Court of Canada in protecting what citizens want. When the public agrees solidly on policy, such as it did in authorizing medicare and its legislated safeguarding through the *Canada Health Act*, the Supreme Court could be asked to decide a claim based on the doctrine of legitimate expectation as it applies to the means of overturning this agreed national public policy. And here we have a problem with Supreme Court Judges signing orders in council as deputies of the Governor General. If an order in council for something, signed by one of the judges, were to be part of an executive government's plan to dismantle an agreed public policy but its legality is challenged, such that it ultimately winds up on the doorstep of the Supreme Court, a conflict arises. The judge who signed the order in council may stand aside, but how would we know whether colleagues on the Court would have signed it, had they been asked, and would they tend to back up the decision of their signatory colleague?

Therefore a reasonable public assertion for the Supreme Court – and other courts – to make about their self-informing is:

> We understand the use of power and money resources and how these operate on executive government – and indeed parliamentarians – to defeat a purpose in public policy that the public as a whole has confirmed and has not rescinded.

Such a public assertion can be audited for its validity.

Endnotes

[1] In England the Department of Transport, wanting to cut through Twyford Down but met with opposition, obtained an injunction that named many property owners as jointly and severally liable for the department's costs and damages, which it asserted to be $3 Million. Pursued for three years, the property owners did what the DOT wanted them to do. They withdrew, rather than forcing the government to seize homes and suffer the public relations consequences. In England, SLAPPs are intended to be effective threats and are not usually carried through to trial. (George Monbiot, *Guardian Weekly*, 31 August 1997, p.25.)

In British Columbia, anti-SLAPP legislation brought in by the NDP government was repealed by the new Liberal government immediately it took office in 2001.

[2] However Judge Barry Stuart of the Yukon court has argued for greater use of Aboriginal sentencing circles for ensuring justice and crime prevention, at least in justice for Aboriginals (*Ottawa Citizen*, 6 December 1997, p.A1)

[3] Kirk Makin, "Canadians Feel Supreme Court Tainted by Partisan Politics," *Globe and Mail*, 3 July 2001, p.A1

[4] *Globe and Mail*, 12 January 1998. p.A18

[5] *Globe and Mail*, 31 January 1998, p.A2A

[6] Network email from of the Defence of Canadian Liberty Committee, January 1999

[7] Canadian Liberty Committee email

[8] Article by Dan Nolan of the *Hamilton Spectator* in the *Ottawa Citizen*, 29 October 1997, p.A8

[9] Kirk Makin, *Globe and Mail*, 29 October 1997, p. A8

[10] Globe and Mail, 25 June 1995. p.A8

[11] Nolan, op. cit.

[12] As put by Reverend James McCloskey of Centurion Ministries in the United States, which works for the wrongfully convicted: "They (the police) get a suspect. Then the pressure is on to close the case. There is a need to satisfy their bosses and the public. They disregard, ignore or suppress any information they come across that might point in a different direction. The human mind has an infinite capacity to justify what it wants to believe." (*Globe and Mail*, 22 July 1997, on the freeing of David Milgaard.

[13] CBC Radio News, 18 July 1997.

[14] Justice Marshall interviewed by Kirk Makin, *Globe and Mail* 27 November 1995, p.A6.

[15] For example, the BC *Provincial Court Act* (1996), applicable to judges appointed by the BC executive government, states:

The chief judge has the power and duty to supervise the judges, justices and court referees and, without limiting those powers and duties, may do one or more of the following:

(a) designate the case or matter, or class of cases or matters, in which a judge, justice or court referee is to act;

(b) designate the court facility where a judge, justice or court referee is to act;

(c) assign a judge, justice or court referee to the duties the chief judge considers advisable;

(d) exercise the other powers and perform other duties prescribed by the Lieutenant Governor in Council. (Section 11 (1))

[16] Marshall interview, op. cit.

[17] Unfortunately the Fifth Estate CBC 1996 intention to serve the public interest wasn't evidenced in CBC's responsibility for a CBC TV Newsmagazine program four years later

that savaged Dr. Nancy Olivieri of the Toronto Hospital for Sick Children in her public stand on disclosure and protection of the integrity of drug clinical trial research.

[18] For example, decisions of cases are available under QuickLaw on the internet, to subscribers. However, retiring BC Chief Justice Allan McEachern has urged that transcripts used in appeals be computerized (*Vancouver Sun*, 18 May 2001, p.B5). This service can be extended and made publicly available, such that both trial judges' and appeal judges' reasoning are available to citizens at no cost. Without this, citizens cannot assess the judicial mind.

[19] For example, the Ontario Attorney General in 1997 rejected the candidates most strongly recommended by Ontario's Judicial Appointments Advisory Committee, created in 1988 by the then Attorney General. (*Globe and Mail*, 12 March 1997 . p.A8)

[20] For someone at his level, Chief Justice McEachern pioneered in putting his judgments on his own website (Neil Hall, "Allan McEachern: A Hard Act to Follow," *Vancouver Sun*, op. cit.

[21] A 1993 report by a Canadian Bar Association Task Force headed by former Supreme Court Judge Bertha Wilson termed the existing complaints investigation system "wholly ineffective" in dealing with racist and sexist behaviour on the bench. (*Ottawa Citizen*, 13 March 1998, p.A5)

[22] Summary of the guidelines by Janice Tibbetts, *Globe and Mail*, 2 December 1998, p.A1.

[23] Ibid.

[24] "Appalling" was the word used by Professor Allan Hutchinson of Osgoode Law School to describe the tobacco judgment giving corporations increased power was (Globe and Mail, 25 September 1995, p.A21) In calling Parliament's 1988 ban on advertising executed by the executive "arbitrary," the editors of the *Globe and Mail* (23 September 1995) seem not to have understood that regulatory power legislatively given to the government is intended to be used arbitrarily by the Crown to protect public health whenever the need arises.

[25] Kirk Makin, *Globe and Mail*, 7-8 February 1997.

CHAPTER 12

The Accountability of Governing Boards

The Board Is the Accountable Directing Mind

If something goes wrong in the safety responsibilities of an organization and people are harmed or killed, the tendency of media and authorities is to go after the on-site employee(s) who failed to take the safety measures. This was the case with *the Herald of Free Enterprise* ("It was the bosun's job to close the bow doors"), the *Exxon Valdez* (the captain), the Westray mine (the on-site mine managers) and many others. But the same tendency can show up in financial affairs, such as the collapse of the venerable Barings Bank, blamed solely on a young trader. It makes a better media story to write about a targeted individual ("the human experience") than the duties of a "corporation." Business observers writing about corporations' performance focus on the chief executive officers of the corporations and their personalities – the John Waynes in the saddle. And when a US congressional committee called the major tobacco companies to testify, it called their chief executive officers, not their boards of directors.

As to which of management and board is the ultimate directing mind, there is no question: business corporation law 70 years ago viewed the board of directors as management,[1] and Lord Denning had made it clearer in the 1950s (see the earlier *Herald of Free Enterprise* case). As the ultimate test, boards also hire and fire the CEO.

In public accountability for safety, the question that hasn't been asked is, "Who, in common sense, has the ultimate responsibility for the effectiveness of the control system that should have prevented X from happening?" Whoever has that responsibility is the person or persons publicly accountable for the harm. Recall that management control causes to happen that which should, and causes not to happen that which shouldn't. There is always an identifiable directing mind responsible for the control system. In a corporation, it is the governing body, the board of directors.

The directing mind of executive government and its entities in the parliamentary system is the ministry, the ministers of the Crown. In the American system, for example, the federal executive directing mind is the President. The work of those trying to indict General Pinochet for crimes in Chile was pioneering in showing that while the head of state may not personally give orders, he or she is none the less responsible for the control system that ensures fairness to citizens – or, in the case of Chile, allows or leads to the torture and killing of people.

In the widespread sexual and other abuses of Aboriginal boys in Canada who had been sent off to reservation schools in the mid-1900s, the major churches operated the schools for the federal executive government. The churches now face massive lawsuits that may cripple their operations. The directing minds of the churches have their own negligence to answer for.[2] But they can rightly argue that, because they operated the schools for the Department of Indian Affairs, the federal government is the directing mind for the aims, responsibilities and control involved. This made it the federal government's responsibility to have obtained the information it should have, on the critical success factors for its policy. Surely fairness to students and their well-being was one of these.

In the deaths from contaminated water in the Ontario town of Walkerton in June 2000, the public focus moved quickly past the water supply operations manager and water commission to the provincial executive government. It was the provincial ministers who chopped the Environment Ministry's protection budget by half in the 1995-1998 period, with predictable results in water testing. It remains to be seen whether the public inquiry launched into the deaths will report who was responsible and answerable to whom, for what, up to and including the responsible ministers, and whether reasonable standards of performance and of preventive answering were met, under the precautionary principle.

Lying between executive governments and business corporation boards in the private sector are the boards of hospitals, regional health districts, universities and colleges and various types of quasi-governmental organizations. But the accountability principle is the same for all: we must identify the ultimate directing minds for the responsibilities we are concerned about and exact adequate public answering from them, before and after the fact. It is not good enough to have the answering come from subordinates or entities whose responsibilities are delegated from the directing minds.

Those ultimately accountable may not be obvious. A health district board is publicly accountable for a range of administrative responsibilities, for hospital accreditation and for practice effectiveness and efficiency. But the executive government who funds it must answer publicly for the care and accessibility standards that it sets for all health districts, and answer publicly for barriers to adequate care, such as minister-ordered staff cuts.

If a university has a teaching and research hospital, the hospital board is responsible for the organization structure needed to maintain the integrity of the hospital's research. But the university sets the research integrity standards that the hospital board is to maintain. This means that the university's governing board is the body who must answer publicly for ensuring that corporate influence doesn't erode the integrity of research. Corporations have more than enough money to entice researchers to do their bidding if institutional donations don't do the trick. Appendix 2 deals with this issue.

Public sector boards may be directing-mind boards setting policy (rare), administrative management boards carrying out government policy (the usual case), or only panels of advisers to officials (which some board members may complain they are). The problem for board members in the public sector such as health district boards is that they may not know what their real power is and may be too deferential to force clarification of it. The public accountability of a board of directors is a function of its power and duty, and all three of these elements must be in balance.[3] But boards such as those of the national Canadian Blood Services and the Ontario Trillium Foundation can be expected to reflect the aims of the executive governments that create them, since their public answering obligations don't suggest independence.

Then there are self-perpetuating organizations like the International Olympic Committee, which has no standards visible to the public for accountability reporting that would provide at least some assurance that the pattern of bribes and conduct uncovered in 1998 wouldn't repeat in the same or other form. The Committee's "Leave it with us" won't do.

The blood, Westray and HRDC examples illustrate the failure of the governing bodies of executive government to control safety and value for money.

Here we will focus on the accountability of the governing boards of the large business corporations. These are unseen people who do not account to the public for their intentions, yet they make or authorize most of the decisions that decide safety and quality of life for people all over the planet. Otherwise insightful writers on the effects of large corporations on society generally use only the word "corporation," and don't deal with the boards of directors as the identifiable directing minds.[4] Yet these writers have the knowledge to draft public answering assertions that we could reasonably expect the boards of the transnational corporations to make.

If auditors report that "the corporation failed to do X", this sends a weaker message to shareholders, public and legislators than saying "the board members failed to cause X to happen." It is one thing for a legal contrivance called a corporation to transact legally as if a person, and take on liability separate from the owners who assume no liability as shareholders. It is quite another to think that something non-human can be held to account. Answering to human beings comes from human beings, not from legal constructs. To talk about "corporate-dominated media," for example, doesn't help until we identify the particular sets of board members causing the dominating, come up with audit samples of the domination and, on the basis of the samples, require the directors to publicly report their intentions and reasoning.

The law has settled the question of who has the ultimate responsibility for what a company does, which means who has control responsibility and the public answering obligation for what the corporation's managers do that affects the public. Regardless of media attention given to chief executive officers, it is the board. Lord Denning's view has been statutory for some time. For example:

Ontario's 1982 *Business Corporations Act* states:

> Subject to any unanimous shareholder agreement, the directors shall manage or supervise the management of the business and affairs of a corporation.[5]

British Columbia's 1998 proposed *Company Act* revision states:

> The directors must, subject to this Act, the regulations and the articles, manage or supervise the management of the affairs and business of the company.[6]

The 1974 federal *Canada Business Corporations Act* states

> Subject to any unanimous shareholder agreement, the directors shall manage the business and affairs of a corporation.[7]

The federal law for government-owned corporations is the same:

> Subject to this Part, the board of directors of a Crown corporation is responsible for the management of the businesses, activities and other affairs of the corporation.[8]

And since the *Canada Business Corporations Act* defines control as the ability to elect the directors, it logically follows that the directors control the company.

Other jurisdictions have similar law.

The Board is Accountable for Adequately Informing Itself

All governing bodies should be able to report in their annual reports that they met due diligence criteria in properly informing themselves for their decisions. The boards need this information to do their control duty – in safety, for example – and to make their decisions on corporate direction and achievement.

As noted in Chapter 2, effective governing bodies:

> understand what constitutes reasonable information for good governance
> and obtain it.[9]

This states two duties, the first being the directors' duty to know what information they need for their decisions, and the second being to obtain the information. To inform themselves adequately, boards must *manage* their information. Since the information doesn't come only from the chief executive officer, they must identify what processes they need for informing themselves, and manage those processes. Board members must know the critical success factors for the organization and obtain the news on each, at the time they should know it. [10]

In the late 1990s, the directors and managers of the infamous mining company Bre-X were reported by the media to have been "deceived" by a field manager.[11] Unchallenged, this word acts to exonerate the officers and board members from their duty to inform themselves adequately for their control duty. We don't know what the Curragh board of directors knew or asked about the Westray mine, before the miners were killed.

In July 2000 the chief executive officer of Canada's largest bank, the Royal Bank of Canada, termed "inappropriate" and "unacceptable" the actions of the Bank's managers of its $30 billion pension investment branch RT Capital, who had manipulated stock prices on the exchange to show high performance for themselves. Under the banner front-page heading, "Bank Chief Apologizes for Scandal," the Toronto *Globe and Mail* burbled, "No bank chairman has ever before issued this kind of public apology for the improper activities of its employees." In his public apology, the CEO said the managers of the Bank's subsidiary Financial Group would "redouble their efforts"[12] but didn't state the management control standards of the Bank's senior management, whom he directed, or the overall company control standards approved by the Bank's board of directors that he chaired.

The Ontario Securities Commission, who reportedly wanted the RT Capital case to "send a message," imposed a $3 million fine, not on the Royal Bank as the accountable entity for control but on the Bank's internal corporation, RT Capital. In pointing out that the fine was less than the Bank's chairman is paid in a year, an alert journalist noted:

> The bank argued... that the fine is meaningful to RT Capital as a smaller
> unit, accounting for about 20 per cent of its net income last year. But for a
> fully-owned entity nestled inside Royal Bank, this hardly seems crippling.[13]

It seems that the Ontario government's Securities Commission keeps its concerns within legal entity boundaries rather than identifying control responsibility up the line to the directing boards.

The practice in large Canadian financial institutions of the CEO also being the board chairman likely persists for personal status reasons. Yet it can be expected to reduce the board members' incentive to inform themselves and to hold the chief executive officer properly to account. Those invited onto such boards by the chairmen-CEOs presumably have no problem with this arrangement.

Effective governance means not only knowing what's going on in the organization and externally what affects it, but also knowing the answers to the "who" questions for proposals coming to the board: who would benefit from what is proposed and who would bear what costs and risks, and why they should. Adequate public answering means reporting what the public has a right to know about boards' control standards, their intentions when these would affect the public in important ways, and their reasoning.

Stakeholders who see inadequate public answering from a board are entitled to question whether the board adequately informs itself or has an intention not in the public interest that it doesn't wish to report. Examples range from corporation-board control of the degree of violence in movies and television, to terminator seeds and boards deciding that the cost to the corporation of increasing the safety of products is more than the cost of probable pay-outs to grieving relations.

No One Holds Boards to Account

Corporate boards are legally asked to account only to a few – these being shareholders, creditors and regulators – and, beyond that, only to certain government agencies who see their duty as regulating *how* corporations operate, not boards' fairness intentions.

The main problem is that when corporations were invented, society failed to install standards for public answering from the owners for what they intended to bring about and why. Through deference to those who owned or managed the corporations, elected representatives over the centuries have given corporate boards increasing power but have failed to require them to account to anyone beyond those who legally own them or who receive corporate reports either through contract or regulation. The accounting to shareholders is simply accounting to a set of financial property owners who comprise a small fraction of the stakeholders significantly affected by what the corporate boards intend and authorize. Corporate boards and officers have never been required to place the public interest first, and to answer for doing so. This is in part because, in North America at least, corporations were launched in the 1700s with charters that served the public interest and people knew who the owners were.[14]

In their classic 1933 work on corporations, Berle and Means show that even by the turn of the century corporate managers and owners had succeeded in eliminating control by the state.

> The evolutionary phase of the modern corporation in recent legal history has been both protracted and confused. Protracted, because it has been accomplished not by any great change either in concept or in statutory enactment, but rather by a long process of grant of management powers piecemeal. The aggregate of these various grants makes up the charter of almost absolute power which the control, commonly through the management, asserts today. Confused, because the various accretions of power appear partly in statutory amendments over more than a century, partly in statutory enactments which purport to recognize or declare the common law; partly in clauses inserted in the charters; partly in powers merely assumed by lawyers and managements, which, becoming traditional, work their way into the system.[15]

By "management," Berle and Means meant the board of directors, elected at the shareholders' meetings. The authors suggest the underlying force and the risk:

> The cynical view of many historians insists that property interests have at all times, visible or invisible, been dominant. Following this grim analysis, one commentator on the rise of corporations (Thorstein Veblen) observed that they had become "the master instruments of civilization." Another (Walther Rathenau) expressed his depression at the fact that the system had at length reached a point definitely committing civilization to the rule of a plutocracy.[16]

and

> The corporate system further commands attention because its development is progressive, as its features become more marked and as new areas come one by one under its sway...This system bids fair to be as all-embracing as was the feudal system in its time.[17]

Seventy years later we have the provision in company law that boards of directors don't serve the public interest. They serve the corporation, whatever that may mean.

For example, the federal *Canada Business Corporations Act* requires that directors "act honestly and in good faith with a view to the best interests of the corporation."[18] Directors use this provision to resist shareholder proposals being placed before annual general meetings. Unless minority shareholders successfully protest something, boards of directors – largely self-perpetuating – are free to define service to shareholders as simply advising the CEO who appoints them, until enough damage is done to make them fire the CEO. They are free to serve their own interests as well. There is no competence requirement. All they have to do is see that the company complies with the law. But external auditors don't even report on that responsibility. Thus there are no standards requiring those directing the corporations to serve the public interest.

The law concerning directors doesn't help us to hold boards to account, and the drafting of that law was purposeful. As we have seen, the law says that directors direct the company, in the sense that citizens understand the directing of an enterprise. The law also requires directors to exercise reasonable diligence – the "duty of care." The only legislated requirement about who the directors are to serve is the provision in companies Acts that directors are to serve the interests of the corporation. Yet the Acts under which the companies incorporate say that the incorporating directors and the corporation are one and the same.

The 1994 Toronto Stock Exchange report on corporate boards of directors is illuminating. It was commissioned because of loss of investor confidence in corporate governance arising from the collapse of large Canadian financial corporations, and inquiries going on in other jurisdictions. The TSE Committee's final report suggests that they ducked the issue of whether corporations are to serve the public interest. The report suggests that they think the public's expression of its interest is an external constraint on the board. After noting that the statutory duty of the directors is to serve the best interests of the corporation, the Committee said:

> The expression of the interests which must be reflected in a board's decisions is often extended from the interests of the corporation to the interests of the shareholders generally on the theory that the ultimate responsibility of the board is to create value for the shareholders and therefore what is in the best interests of the corporation should generally also be in the best interests of the owners…. a definition of board responsibilities to act in the best interests of a broader group than the corporation's shareholders would confuse the board's responsibilities and significantly undermine the accountability of the board of directors.[19]

The message of the TSE Report is that boards serve the public interest only in so far as "public interest" means serving the interests of the corporation and adding to the wealth of the shareholders. And by "interests of the shareholders" the TSE Committee may have meant "the shareholders' impatient wants." The Committee didn't deal with the wants of senior management as opposed to the needs of shareholders at large, and the wants of corporate management and shareholders as opposed to the needs of citizens being affected by what the board instructs management to do.

By "accountability of the board of directors" the report seems to suggest that a board's accountability must be confined to reporting to shareholders, and these reports cover only elements of the company's financial affairs. Yet the public has the right to be protected in safety and respected in fairness by those who have the legal power to kill citizens with unsafe products and to destroy the environment.

Nowhere in the TSE report summary is there a useful statement about the public accountability of corporate boards. Thus the report might lead parliamentarians to pursue setting limits to the legal liability of members of boards of directors, but not to discuss boards' public answering obligations.

In 2001 a joint committee of the TSE, CDNX and the Canadian Institute of Chartered Accountants is expected to issue a report on corporate governance. The adequacy of corporate boards' external answering, surely central to governance responsibilities, appears not to have been something the committee wished to comment on.

The Canadian Democracy and Corporate Accountability Commission, co-chaired by Avie Bennett, Chair of the McClelland and Stewart publishing firm and Ed Broadbent, former national leader of the New Democratic Party, may offer something more useful to Canadians. Their report is planned for release in 2002. In its mid-2001 published Overview of Issues, the Commission defines accountability as "the requirement to explain and accept responsibility for one's actions."[20] But explaining one's responsibilities and accepting the obligation to act is conceptually different from the obligation to *answer* for a responsibility conferred, the federal 1975 Wilson Committee's definition of accountability. And it is the *answering* from governing bodies that is key to having them conduct themselves in the public interest. Responsibility exhortations as the be-all and end-all are obsolete.

We have yet to hold the public debate on the extent to which corporate boards, in serving the financial gain of corporations' owners, are to do that *within* the public interest. This would force debate on what we mean by "the public interest" for boards' actions and answering, and the debate must come.

Even if authorities successfully delay public debate on boards' public answering obligations, do shareholders successfully hold to account for their own interests?

The large corporations created by captains of industry in the 1800s became widely owned because of diminishing capability of family and individual ownership. This shift was achieved through public issue of shares in the equity of these companies. Berle and Means point out that the shift of ownership from owner-manager to perhaps hundreds of thousands of shareholders in the 1930s, coupled with the greater legal control by management, meant separation of ownership from control, that is, owners ceasing to be in control. This in turn meant that boards ceased to be accountable to identifiable governing entities. By contrast, most public sector organizations are ultimately accountable to legislative assemblies, even if indirectly. No one would argue that the boards of large widely-held companies exert effective control over their chief executive officers and senior managers until a crisis occurs. All they do is hire and fire them, even though the boards are at law the directing minds. Thus no one is required to act for the public interest.

In answering, corporations' external accounting has been only to the owners, and only for after-the-fact financial results. Academic argument in the 1960s centered on whether corporate public reporting said anything significant about the corporation that wasn't already known by the market. Today the annual and quarterly financial statements are less informative in an age of fast information exchange. Even with that limitation, the courts, at least in the United Kingdom, seem to be retreating from the idea that potential investors should be able to rely on professionally-audited financial statements. In the United States, one financial writer argues that it has become tacitly agreed that corporate officials can be reckless about whether their published financial statements significantly mislead. The writer doesn't even mention the role of the external auditors.[21]

Notable reviews of corporate governance were undertaken in the 1990s in several countries, but these were confined to internal board practices and corporate reporting in financial matters. [22] The governance issues were only process issues, such as governance committees and audit committees and board awareness of risk.

Who Do Governing Bodies Serve?

The most important issue in directors' public answering is not financial results and auditors' mantras of "relevance," "timeliness" and other aspects of financial reporting convention. It is whether boards are to be required to account publicly for their intentions and reasoning when what they intend would affect the public in important ways. The probable outcomes of their intentions are usually known and, if they are not, the boards have a commonsense duty to know them. What they know, they can report.

It's reasonable to expect corporate boards to serve the public interest. This means being sensible and fair to citizens at large in what boards intend that would affect them. It's therefore reasonable that boards publicly report their intentions. This doesn't contradict the board's legal responsibility to serve the corporation; it simply requires the board to explain their intentions for the corporation's actions, and the reasoning for them.

This is the issue, for example, in regulation of drug companies and maintaining the integrity of clinical research. It is the issue in deciding whether tobacco companies should exist, whether Monsanto's power through patented terminator seeds should be allowed, whether needed forests will be preserved, or whether the safety levels for bulk-carrier ships around the globe should be at a feasible level, or be what the ship owners want.[23] In the case of workplace safety, it's logical that unions take on the role of exacting the needed public answering from corporate boards that makes clear the board's own standards for workplace safety, not just the company's compliance with a regulator's regulations. [24]

As things stand in the case of tobacco, for example, tobacco jobs still exist and shareholders still prosper, anticipating expanding markets for cigarettes in developing countries and China. But horrific numbers of people die, causing huge public health costs before they do. In the case of patented genetically-engineered seeds, plants and other life forms, it is the issue of their unknown effects and their known effects on the livelihoods of farmers across the planet. As Brewster Kneen describes what corporations want:

> Genetic engineering is an expression of ingratitude and disrespect, if not contempt. It is a vehicle, in practice, of an attitude of domination and ownership, as expressed in the assumption that it is possible, reasonable and morally acceptable to claim ownership over life. The claim that it is possible to own life, at least to the extent of being able to claim a patent on a life process or life form, is so outrageous socially and ethically as to be hardly worth debating.[25]

The decisions on who will own what are made by corporate boards and regulators who are not being held publicly to account for their intentions.

Movie and TV violence is argued on grounds of "realism," but its purpose is to tap the fascination of the young for depicted extreme violence without regard to the precautionary principle in terms of violence's possible effects. Corporate accountability for the effects of television lies with the identifiable television broadcasting corporate boards of directors. When corporate executives crank up violence as simply entertainment, it is reasonable to expect that it will cause an effect of some kind on viewers, differentially by age. The evidence we have on the effects of violence on TV suggests that violence should be reduced rather than maintained, and that the need to apply the precautionary principle stares the corporate board members in the face. It could well be the basis of class actions against board members.

The people accountable for the violence depiction are specific, identifiable corporate executives, board members and company owners. They will argue that they are only providing what the public wants in a free-market system. The nature of the effects need to be confirmed by research, but to the extent that common sense suggests showing less violence rather than more, the precautionary principle says that corporations should demonstrate that the effects of depicted violence are not harmful, rather than the proof onus being reversed. The corporation boards can be asked to produce equity statements of who benefits, how, and who bears what risks from different levels of dramatized violence. Those opposing the violence levels can do the same, and each set of statements can be reviewed by the public for its credibility. Such statements would structure the violence issue for public debate, and public challenge would validate the corporate boards' statements for their fairness and completeness.

In addition to accountability for TV violence, public answering can be required for the risk of television recklessly crippling citizens' ability to think things through, thus producing civic incompetence. Neil Postman argues convincingly that most of what we see on TV, made into torrents of images through the technology, becomes simply entertainment, driving out discourse on public issues.[26] Thus citizens can't become "rightly informed," as George Washington put it in 1796. A flood of images doesn't help citizens to inform themselves to do their duty as thinking citizens. Television converts war into entertainment, as it did with the 1991 Gulf war. An exception would be TV documentaries such as those on ship safety and drugs research, where the purpose is to bring the risks to the public's attention.

In matters of safety and health, the aims of corporate boards determine the importance they attach to the precautionary principle. If they can eliminate the precautionary principle as a society imperative, while at the same time raising the level of risk citizens are to accept, they increase their profits. Applying the precautionary principle ourselves, we must expect the large corporations' wealth to be fully applied to "managing" the risk they want citizens to take. This includes buying whatever "expert" research and media opinion it takes to discredit the experts having stature who work in the public interest and who give the warnings.

As to the accountability of large corporations for their collective intentions globally, the proposed Multilateral Agreement on Investment gave us their general intention straight from the horse's mouth (see Appendix 1). In discussing the problems facing the Canadian Democracy and Corporate Accountability Commission, for its public report, Ed Finn likely speaks for activists in arguing that the aim of the large corporations is to "conquer and pillage the world":

> Freed from legislative restraints on their power, answerable only to their major shareholders, equipped with the financial and technological weapons of global conquest, armed with the sweeping rights conferred on them by international trade agreements, their armies of executives, bankers, lawyers and administrators overrun country after country. Servile politicians do their bidding. Media toadies praise their iniquities and ridicule their critics.[27]

In his submission to the Commission, Finn warned: "There is no government in Canada that would dare antagonize its business masters."

Legislatively blocking the action intentions of corporations' directing minds after giving them a free hand through a trade agreement is one thing. But what about asking the corporations to publicly explain what they intend and who, exactly, would gain from what they intend, how, and why they should? And who would lose what, and why they should? As noted earlier in the chapter explaining the public equity statement, this isn't telling boards what to do or not to do. This is the key: it is simply asking them to *explain*. In a democracy, this requirement is unassailable. And if it is unassailable, it can be legislated, even by "servile politicians." The corporations' explanations, made public, would then automatically undergo Lori Wallach's "Dracula Test," which would tell the corporations whether they are apt to be credible with the global citizen suppliers of their needs.

When we think about it, the notion of corporations issuing public equity statements for their intentions is simply a marketing issue in a global competitive market: run something up the flagpole and see who salutes. "Our company's equity statements are better than our competitors." Just as in false advertising, major deception in corporations' equity statements will be found out because their public assertions will be validated by public interest organizations – and unions and the companies' employees themselves, for that matter. Therefore, when corporation lobbyists tell corporation commissions that they like things the way they are, and their supporter politicians agree, they can both be told that legislating equity statement disclosure would be supporting marketing ideals, not an arbitrary imposition by legislatures on corporations' freedom. Requiring answering doesn't tell corporations what to do: it simply requires explanation.

Legislating Boards' Answering Obligations is Feasible

Instead of letting corporate boards shift the onus to citizens to prove that the corporations' intentions are unsafe, we must require corporate boards to account to the public well enough to show whether what they intend is safe. From the answering of the boards, validated by audit, we can establish and deal with the extent to which they put profit before the precautionary principle and feasible safety.

Transnational corporations naturally seek to control their environments. If they can control the votes of national elected representatives in most nations, it helps the corporations overcome citizens' wariness of their products and operations: the government's resulting regulations won't back the views of citizens. An example is corporations fighting product labelling that states the presence of growth hormones or genetically modified organisms.

It is still possible for any sovereign state to require adequate public answering by corporations' directing minds who want to operate in that state. The answering would include the boards' intentions, reasoning and performance standards. No elected representative can credibly argue that this corporate answering shouldn't be given.

The elected representatives in the jurisdictions in which corporations want markets can require from the corporate boards public equity statements for their intentions. For intentions affecting people's safety, workplace conditions and public health, the governments can require boards' assertions about the extent of their compliance with the precautionary principle. Monsanto wasn't told to do this for its terminator seeds. The drug company Apotex wasn't told to do this for its drug deferiprone (see Appendix 2).

Public answering applies to fairness in Southern countries' access to Northern country markets. Southern countries can legitimately ask the identifiable directing minds of the Northern country executive governments and corporations to publicly state the extent of access they intend for the Southern countries, and their reasons. Proposed restrictions on corporate *actions* can be debated: the need for standards for public *answering* by their directing minds is an axiom.

Legislating public answering standards for directors is currently the only way to force explanation of directors' intentions when what they seek would clearly have important impacts on citizens. Having to explain intended outcomes, and for whom, is simply that: explanation. It isn't a directive to do something or refrain from doing something that would run counter to the interests of shareholders.

The boards' explanations before the fact can be in public documents with a title such as "Statement of Directors' Intentions Affecting the Public." The statement would be for boards' intentions that would have safety, justice or environmental effects that should be made visible in the public interest.

Within corporations, the standards for public answering proposed in Chapter 5 apply to corporate management's reporting to the board for its intended and actual performance. For example, an equity statement should accompany each strategic initiative that management proposes to the board. The equity statements for the board provide the basis for the board's disclosure to shareholders (and thus to the public) about its intentions and the effects on shareholders and other stakeholders that would flow from the board's intentions.

As a start in public explanation of the board's intentions, something like the following would do as an amendment to existing companies Acts:

> When the intentions of the board of directors could reasonably be deemed to affect the public in important ways in safety, health, social justice or environmental effect, the directors shall report to the shareholders in a Statement of Directors' Intentions in the corporation's annual report to shareholders or, when promptness is reasonable to expect in the circumstances, through the corporation's website and/or press releases,
>
> a) the board's action intentions for the company and its reasoning and performance standards for those intentions;

b) The extent to which board members have informed themselves about who would benefit from the board's intentions, how they would benefit and why they should, and who would bear what costs and risks from the intentions and why they should, both in the short and longer term;

c) The extent to which board members have used this information in deciding their course of action as the corporation's governing body; and

d) the extent to which the board's intentions uphold the precautionary principle.

Tobacco company intentions are an obvious example. When directors get used to the idea of why this minimum disclosure is needed, we can add to the law – under the axiom that what directors know, they can report – the requirement that the board also publicly report its understanding of who would gain and who would pay under (b) above. The board would also be asked to give its reasoning for its intentions.

In these proposals, reporting to shareholders in effect means reporting publicly. The information in the annual reports to shareholders would be a compendium of the explanations of board intentions and decisions that have already been presented on the corporation's website.

One concept has to be clear: "affect the public in important ways" has the same meaning as "significance" as used by the auditing profession in corporate financial reporting. That is, significant information is that information which, if known, can reasonably be deemed to make a difference to what stakeholders decide to do.

As to the board's self-informing obligation, the challenge for the legal profession is to understand management control well enough to be useful in the question of the adequacy of boards' self-informing, when boards are sued for not controlling diligently.

Had intentions statements been legislated and enforced at the time:

- The board of the Canadian Red Cross Society would have publicly stated its performance standards for its blood and blood products safety as soon as risk appeared in the medical scientific and regulatory community in Europe and the United States.
- The directors of the parent company of the Westray coal mine would have publicly stated their mine safety standards for the mine, so that regulators, legislators and a Nova Scotia public familiar with mine deaths could have assessed them for reasonableness and compared them with opinions of mine experts.
- The directors of the major companies producing tobacco and genetically engineered organisms would have publicly stated the risk they intended the public to take, so this could be compared with the views of the independent scientific and

regulatory communities on who and what would be affected and how by the companies' marketing intentions. (The directors of tobacco companies today should be required to state their marketing intentions for Southern countries and China, as smoking risk awareness of North Americans builds in force.)

- The directors of Exxon would have publicly stated, on the advice of the company's officers responsible for marine operations, that they intended to authorize passage of supertankers down the pacific coast without coastal pilots and no timely assessments of captains' competence.
- The directors of North Sea ferry companies, on the advice of naval architects, would have publicly stated the stability of their "roll-on, roll-off" ships in an emergency at sea.
- The management of Morton Thiokol and NASA would have publicly stated their safety assurance for the *Challenger* for a lift-off at 50 degrees Fahrenheit.

These statements can be publicly audited for their fairness and completeness by related public interest organizations and regulators.

There is nothing stopping boards from installing in their corporations' by-laws reasonable standards for management accountability reporting to the board and for the board's external accountability reporting. And there is nothing stopping corporate shareholders or members of other organizations from telling the boards what they think of the adequacy of the boards' current by-laws. Legislated requirements for by-laws content are overlooked mechanisms for self-regulation and answering.

In summary, we mustn't carry on with the public thinking that boards of directors ensure good management and largely protect the public, with statutes saying that the board serves only the best interests of the "corporation," with board members being continually re-elected because of proxies but knowing the chief executive officer in charge, and with the CEO accounting only to the board.

The role of corporate boards and the duties of their members has to be re-thought outside the mindset of traditional financial management and property stewardship.

Public answering is needed from boards not so much to make corporations compete better as to make them compete within rules that have them serve the public interest and answer to the public adequately. The latter would include explaining to shareholders the relationship of the CEO's salary and bonuses to the value of the company beyond what the CEO has done simply to relieve pressure on current earnings per share – actions that may have the effect of clouding future prospects.

The public accountability of the board as the directing mind is two-fold: it is to answer to the public for the reasoning for its decisions that affect the public in important ways, and to answer for holding management to account. The boards' accountability reporting includes asserting how well the board informs itself for what key responsibilities. The board's formal answering should state whether the board sees itself as the directing mind, and whether it sees itself accountable only to the shareholders or to a broader group of stakeholders – the citizens affected by its decisions.

All agree that the corporate form of getting things done is efficient. But the meaning of efficiency is dependent on fairness aims. Just as elected representatives must control the fairness aims for government policy, citizens must tell boards the fairness and disclosure standards they are to meet. Given the consistency of observations over the past 60 years, from Berle and Means to David Korten and other current observers, the corrective lever to be installed by citizens through their elected representatives is the requirement for public answering from boards that meets a reasonable standard of answering. The answering must inform citizens for their civic duty with respect to corporations. No one would argue that the *obligation* to account for fairness is new. What is new is holding to account effectively: exacting full and fair answering from those accountable.

Since boards of directors constitute corporations' directing minds, public interest organizations can commission various groups of smart students (the young will understand accountability) to come up with rating criteria for public answering from boards. They could grade the adequacy of boards' answering for key responsibilities affecting the public – an F for "fail" – and, through their public reports, invite the boards to give better answering. For the transnational corporations, the grading can be coordinated worldwide on the Internet, and means found to give the ratings to citizens lacking computers. Suddenly, tangible public stigma can attach to identifiable persons directing corporations' actions who don't account well before and after the fact. Citizens purchases of those corporations' goods and services could be affected as a result. Some of the government-allowed harmful effects of autonomous corporations could thus be capped, or even reduced, in the 21st century.

Endnotes

[1] See Adolf A. Berle, Jr., and Gardiner C. Means, *The Modern Corporation and Private Property*, New York, Macmillan, 1933

[2] The legal profession's "vicarious liability" is being used as the basis for a case against a former Catholic archbishop of Newfoundland for knowing but doing nothing about sexual assaults by a priest from 1960-1981 (CBC Radio 5 July 2000). This significantly moves the control responsibility up the line to the top, and will likely be used for other cases against other churches.

[3] The importance of the balance of power, duty and accountability for governing bodies was pointed out by Barrie Webb, QC, and Robert Taylor at the 1994 annual conference of the

national foundation CCAF-FCVI.

[4] For example, "Board of directors" is not a separate entry in the indexes in the following sample of books about corporations: Richard Barnet and John Cavanagh, *Global Dreams*, Touchstone, New York, 1994; David Korten, *When Corporations Rule the World*, Berrett-Koehler Publishers, San Francisco, 1995; Ralph Estes, *Tyranny of the Bottom Line*, Berrett-Koehler Publishers, San Francisco 1995

[5] Ontario *Business Corporations Act* 1982, Section 115.

[6] British Columbia's 1998 Discussion Draft for the *Company Act*, Section 159

[7] *Canada Business Corporations Act*, 1994, Section 102

[8] *Financial Administration Act* 1988, Part X, Section 109

[9] CCAF-FCVI op. cit.

[10] Cornelius Burk and Henry McCandless, "Fulfilling the Need to Know," *Business Quarterly*, University of Western Ontario, London, Spring 1997

[11] CBC Radio News, 4 May 1998.

[12] John E. Cleghorn, giving a public apology for a "situation" as Chairman and CEO not of the Royal Bank as a whole, but of its Financial Group. *Globe and Mail*, 14 July 2000, p.B5.

[13] Janet McFarland, writing in the *Globe and Mail*, 21 July 2000. p.A1

[14] Estes, op. cit.

[15] Berle and Means, op. cit., p.127

[16] Ibid, p.2

[17] Ibid, p.9

[18] *Canada Business Corporations Act*, Section 122(1).

[19] *Where Were the Directors?": Guidelines for Improved Corporate Governance in Canada*, Report of the Toronto Stock Exchange Committee on Corporate Governance in Canada, (Toronto, TSE, December 1994, Paras. 4.11 and 4.16)

[20] Canadian Democracy and Corporate Accountability Commission, "An Overview of Issues," Toronto, 2001, p.iii

[21] Reed Abelson, "Justice – Corporate Style" *New York Times Service*, quoted in *The Globe and Mail*, 8 August, 1996, B6

[22] For example, Cadbury (UK - 1992), King (South Africa - 1994), Dey (Toronto Stock Exchange - 1994), and Percy (International Capital markets Group - 1995).

[23] For example, the 1992 Australian parliamentary inquiry report "Ships of Shame" (as if a hull can have shame) and the 1993 BBC Panorama TV documentary on ocean bulk carriers were not really about sub-standard ships. They were about sub-standard owners. The cited rate of 30-40 crew members per year drowned continued off Canada's east coast in 1993-4, with the *Gold Bond Conveyor* (38 drowned) and the *Marika 7* (36 drowned). The Reverend David Craig, a former Australian seafarer who ran the Halifax Missions to Seamen in the early 1990s, was transferred in 1994 to the Mission's London headquarters for publicly taking the shipping companies to task for what he knew of their operations. In fact he was talking about boards. It is significant that nearly half the Halifax Mission's funding came from shipping companies and the Halifax Port Authorities. The London-based International Marine Organization (IMO) failed to deal with public accountability and the responsibilities of shipping company boards of directors in its 1994 International Safety Management Code. In any case, a code is simply exhortation.

[24] See Ed Finn, op. cit., on workplace deaths and injuries. And as an editorial in the London

Independent pointed out, commenting on everything from Creutzfeldt-Jakob Disease to ferry groundings, "We no longer choose to take risks; we have them thrust upon us." (The *Independent*, 28 March 1996, quoted in the *Ottawa Citizen* 23 April 1996, p.A11)

[25] Brewster Kneen, *Farmageddon*, New Society Publishers, Gabriola Island, British Columbia, 1999, p.29

[26] Neil Postman, *Amusing Ourselves to Death: Public Discourse in an Age of Show Business* (New York: Penguin, 1985)

[27] Canadian Centre for Policy Alternatives *Monitor*, Ottawa, May 2001, p.4

CHAPTER 13

The Accountability of Professionals, Academics and Journalists

Professionals

Guilds were set up centuries ago to ensure crafts and services and a standard of quality, with special status granted in return. The professions that emerged from the guilds were distinguished by an intellectual technique, acquired by special training unavailable to the laity, and which was to be applied for the benefit of society. In return, professionals got rights such as monopolies and public status.

Because professions affect the public in important ways, they are answerable to the public. Yet the public and our regulatory bodies keep faith in the idea of professions regulating themselves and are patient when professional failures occur. The professions say, "Leave it with us. We'll take care of it." Then they talk about the need to tighten up standards and to have their members reminded of their professional obligations. If no changes are noticeable, more rules and regulations may result, but not public answering for the discharge of their responsibilities.

When a profession applies its technique primarily to gain money from a market, it yields its claim to be a profession. At a conference in 1991, Justice Willard Estey, who headed the inquiry into the collapse of two western chartered banks, told the auditing profession in Canada:

> "You rejoice under a licensed monopoly. You are not in a business; you are in a profession. Unhappily, some of you have stopped thinking in those terms."[1]

In these few words Justice Estey had explained to us why auditors refer to their professional work as "products;" why they now describe a corporation's accountability reporting to shareholders as "communication" rather than answering for responsibilities; and why in mid-2000 the *Wall Street Journal* described the parties in the split-up of a big professional firm as members of the "accounting and consulting industries"[2] One of the other large accounting and auditing firms took a full-page advertisement in a national newspaper to tell readers that it was helping pharmaceutical companies to get their drugs onto the market in under ten years.[3]

Supreme Court of Canada Justice Frank Iacobucci repeated Justice Estey's comment at a 1998 conference on the future of the legal profession. He noted the emergent emphasis in law firms on billable hours for profit maximization as an end in itself, and that:

> There is a clear tendency to be a hired gun in promotion of a client's cause
> rather than an active and constructive participant in the course of justice.[4]

To the extent that professionals seek to be professional entrepreneurs first and to serve the public interest when it is accommodated within their own self-interest, they can be termed skilled technicians and be asked to pay their own training and other costs in gaining the incomes and social status they seek.

Professionals think that if they have good skills to offer they apply these skills, the public must necessarily benefit. Attention to improving the "how" of the technique causes the technique to be honed and expanded, but the public doesn't know how much professionals fit societal problems to their existing techniques. An example is the legal wrangling in public inquiries introduced at full fees that blocks unearthing the truth. The issue of whether the public interest is being served is important, because universities funded from the public purse give professionals their skills, and legislators give them their status.

Professionals tend to think about their work in one of two broad ways. They can think that if they do work that meets high standards of intellectual technique and service to the public interest, and manage their affairs properly, they will get the status and money they want. The other view says that one need acquire only the professional skill and ethical standards that earns the money and status that the professional would like to have. We can think of professional leaders of both types, but thirty years ago there still seemed to be a few leaders of the first type. Now all professionals are trained to think "saleable products." In the professions, stature used to be all-important. Now it is defined as status – the ability to generate revenue for the firm. The point is that citizens don't know the extent to which professional firms go with the flow, and therefore their monopoly status is problematic.

But from their practice experience, all professionals should be able to tell us what we can fairly expect in public answering from the organizations they work with in their professional areas. For example, individual doctors obviously hold beliefs about drug companies and their marketing pressures. How do doctors act on those beliefs? Are general practitioners unswayed by the drug company representatives, the researchers unswayed by drug companies' funding, and their professional associations unswayed by the revenue from ads in their glossy journals that are not put there to convince anyone about anything technically? Do doctors publicly question the adequacy of "Dear Doctor" letters from the federal Health Protection Branch on drug assessments? Does the medical profession counsel the public and government's regulatory agencies on how to hold drug companies fairly to account?

Do the architecture and legal professions do the same for property developers? Does the accounting profession do the same for transnational corporations determining the fates of countries?

The issue is what performance accounting is reasonable to expect from professional bodies. Self-regulation by the self-accredited must be accompanied by public answering for the discharge of their responsibilities. Yet we have never asked the professions to publicly answer for the discharge of important responsibilities that are reasonably theirs.

Consider external auditing. It is not the shareholders of corporations that engage auditors' professional skills; it is management and the board of directors. In a speech to the Ontario Institute of Chartered Accountants in 1999, the Chairman of the Ontario Securities Commission warned the auditors that the Commission would take "renewed interest in disciplining" in the trend toward "aggressive accounting" that constitutes "interpretations of accounting standards beyond all reasonable limits." [5] The President of the Institute responded, "We have to push back on that," meaning that he conceded cause for concern. But this isn't an assertion that the Institute, which governs practice, will stop such practice. Later the same year the Commission Chairman, speaking to another group, was quoted as saying:

> Corporate directors need to beef up supervision of their auditors to ensure
> financial statements aren't pumped up to meet market expectations.[6]

This is a remarkable statement, considering that the external and presumably independent auditors have the statutory duty to express their professional opinion on the fairness and completeness of corporations' public financial reporting approved by the directors.

The auditor's duty is to be expert in serving the financial reporting relationship between the corporate directing minds and investors. But auditors offer only the techniques and skills that management and the business sector are willing to pay for. Hence auditors don't report a corporation's compliance with the law. While the external auditor's client is the shareholders, the auditors would never question the use of proxies in perpetuating the power, mindsets and continuing terms of existing board members – or propose that companies Acts require directors to report their intentions and reasoning before the fact when what they intend affects the public in important ways.

The accounting profession's apparent crusade to apply its generally accepted accounting principles (GAAP) to every type of undertaking on the planet is a case in point. Unschooled elected representatives and civil servants worldwide haven't the time and knowledge – or interest – to question the accounting profession when the spokesmen of the profession say to them, quietly and insistently, "GAAP is what you need. It is the Answer for government's financial reporting." The profession hasn't reported its understanding of what parliamentarians need to make their fairness and value for money decisions, and why GAAP is the answer to their needs.

GAAP is a set of financial reporting conventions, not principles, and wasn't designed for decision-making for governments, even when made over for the public sector. It was designed for merchandising and manufacturing businesses, to match financial expenditure against accomplishment to arrive at an accountant's measure of profit or loss. Its purpose was to prevent self-serving whim in businesses' reporting of their financial performance. GAAP then became used for other types of businesses and then, for all businesses, to measure earnings per share for short-term corporate performance assessment in the stock market. Since short-term corporate performance appearances were needed to keep up share prices in the market, pressure for "flexibility" in the use of the accounting conventions grew.

But in government, the GAAP issue isn't "creative accounting." Legislators, whose business is making equity trade-off decisions in society and deciding what to fund and not fund, need to know the fairness implications for citizens, but also the short and long term cash implications of their decisions. They aren't in the business of generating profit. Their bottom line is the effectiveness of programs and projects: did they make the intended difference? Governments and legislatures need equity statements or their equivalent to make fairness trade-offs in intentions, and the financial information they need is the information that helps them choose from among alternatives. The financial statements they need most are validated schedules of key information that help them choose between options. GAAP doesn't provide this.

Elected representatives don't use financial statement edifices created by accountants who wish to apply a one-best-way business-profits reporting method to the use of public money. To the extent that generally accepted accounting conventions are needed for the public sector – and they are – they are best developed by starting with a clean piece of paper and the identified major trade-offs in each decision situation and devising the reporting most useful for decision-making and public answering for decision reasoning. The usefulness of private-sector concepts such as depreciation of historical cost for decision-making in governments and public sector agencies hasn't been challenged.

As to auditing, the profession is at a crossroads. With financial auditing practice at its maturity for earning fees, the profession can expand its expert validation role – its intellectual technique – to the broader range of public answering we need from directing minds of corporations and other institutions, for their intentions and performance. The range is vast: safety, social justice, health, environmental protection and many other responsibilities. Or the profession can shift out of its public attestation role and simply work for management, as consultants.

Auditors are in the business of public accountability, but as a profession they don't ask themselves, "How can we advise citizens on holding organizations' directing minds to account for their decision-making affecting the public and the environment in important ways?" We are long past the question, "What do we need in our professional handbook to guide us on disclosure of potential liability from purchasing polluted property?"

If the profession chooses to restrict its attestation work to financial accountability relationships, it is still accountable for telling stakeholders how the financial reporting helps them answer the all-important "who benefits, who pays?" questions. Otherwise after-the-fact financial attestation is not only too late for financial decision-making; it's not relevant to answering for the key fairness decisions being made in society.

The medical profession is publicly accountable for *preventing* illness and getting research funding distributed fairly, not just installing artificial organs and treating disease. The profession should be able to assert, for example, that the incidence of unnecessary surgery is everywhere held below agreed tolerance levels. It should be able to assert that doctors don't prescribe drugs without knowing the true level of assurance behind regulatory agencies' "Dear Doctor" letters about drugs' safety, and without knowing with reasonable assurance the effects, individually and in combination, of the drugs they prescribe. The profession should be able to assert that doctors don't prescribe drugs that are expensive and paid for by the public purse but which have only marginal beneficial effects and uncertain risks.

As to accountability at the doctor-patient level, an example will serve. A 63-year-old stroke patient is in the extended care side of an extended care/rehabilitation hospital, suffering debilitating central pain affecting her limbs that developed several months after the stroke. She therefore needs several different doctors' help. Although she has been in the hospital for over four months, and is predictably angry and resentful and equally hard on the staff and her own family, the family see no evidence of a hospital progress program for her.

The family thought that the doctors who logically related to her condition would get together as managers of a patient, produce a coordinated program beyond trial and error in drug combinations, and present it to the patient and her family. The family doesn't know what the doctors are doing among themselves. The patient can't hold to account because no one person is in charge of her or the hospital. The family tend to liken it to a refugee camp. As a hospital RN put the treatment issue in the first Patient Review Meeting, a month after her admittance (not having been examined by any doctor), "It would be nice if a doctor would step forward."

The hospital-designated visiting GP, having 15 other patients at the hospital and running a maternity practice, says, after the fourth month, "A lot has been going on." To the patient, this meant only that a rehabilitation doctor and a psychiatric doctor had each visited her bedside – no sophisticated tests had been done. The family feels that hard questioning of doctors, unused to accounting to anyone as opposed to hearing only supplications, would likely be met with umbrage.

Teachers are accountable for knowing what constitutes effective education for students' life skills, efficacy and citizenship, and can account publicly for what they are doing to produce it – including what they are doing to prevent negative effects of government-prescribed curricula, or of television.

Lawyers can answer for justice, because they own the legal system. They are answerable for the system being a legal justice system, not just a legal system. And their profession can reasonably be expected to assert whether the system meets a standard that has been agreed with the public.

Ill-intentioned directing minds can't defeat the public interest alone: they need the help of lawyers. But lawyers can collectively make validated public assertions that will tell us whether they put their client's wants before the needs of the public interest. When their client's wants are in conflict with the precautionary principle, lawyers fight against the principle. How would tobacco industry lawyers refute the assertion that they are simply legal mercenaries? In a court case, how would big-firm lawyers refute the proposition that they are engaged to help keep clouded the relationships between regulator, outside research advisers to drug companies who serve on the regulator's committees, and the drug companies? Working against the precautionary principle doesn't bother lawyers whose sole goal is to win – and who congenitally put property rights before environmental and health protection.

As one letter to the editor put it, in response to Justice Iacobucci's 1998 observations on the profession cited earlier:

> ...the *de facto* purpose of a trial, or legal action, is not, as it should be, to determine truth and secure justice but to select a winner by any acceptable means, with legal trickery at a premium. The "winner" is usually the one with the most prestigious/expensive lawyers.[7]

Moreover, when big-firm lawyers go to court on behalf of organizations or individuals trying to take on large corporations or institutions, citizens have no means of telling who the real client of the law firm is – whether the firm plans to "take a dive" for greater reward down the road from those with the greatest power. It's alarming to hear lawyers say, "Never mind; we'll win on appeal" – especially when the same team of lawyers acts at each appeal level, after losing. Even in government we simply can't tell whether the civil-servant lawyers in justice departments serve the public interest or simply what they anticipate as the wants of their political masters in crushing challenge.

Who else other than lawyers design SLAPPs (Strategic Lawsuits Against Public Participation) to ensure uneven playing fields? As noted earlier, SLAPPs are suits without substantial merit that are brought by private interests to stop citizens from exercising their political rights or to punish them for having done so. And why should citizens salute a profession that produces judges who decide that people are blameless in their killing of others because they take drugs or alcohol to an extent they ought to know will impair their thinking?[8] When the loved ones of those drowned in the *Herald of Free Enterprise*, killed in the Westray mine, or dead or dying from lethal blood transfusions try to get redress, they see themselves getting only legal niceties from a legal system, not redress from a justice system.

As to the "few bad apples" cliché constantly trotted out to suggest that there is nothing basically wrong with a profession, one lawyer quipped, "It's the ninety-five per cent of the profession that's giving the rest of us a bad name."

Economists collectively, or at least those who call democracy a "political market,"[9] should formally assert the extent to which they understand social justice and behavioural cause and effect and how it should affect economists' thinking and their professional recommendations. Within their intellectual technique, it is reasonable to expect economists collectively to assert, for example, whether continued use of the measure Gross Domestic Product (GDP) as the measure of a government's success makes sense (where GDP is the value of all final goods and services brought about in a defined jurisdiction). The GDP score is increased for Southern countries by trade policies economically harmful to their citizens. GDP is also increased by body shop work repairing cars smashed on unsafe highways. Dysfunctions raise the GDP. It is therefore reasonable to have the economics profession formally assert whether more useful measures of achievement have been possible and could have been put in place before now, and whether most economists know this.

The same holds for the Tobin tax proposal on the transactions of currency speculators that don't benefit the public and cause problems for economies. Where is the equity statement from the profession that gives the profession's fair assessment of this proposal, as to who would benefit, how, and why they should, and who would bear what costs from legislating the proposal, and why they should? The profession probably doesn't want to touch it, but has a public duty to explain the implications to citizens.

Architects should be asked to assert whether they put their own acquired tastes in the design of public buildings before citizens' preferences in streetscapes for the places where the citizens have to live. Architects' jargon for conveying their own aspirations doesn't let us understand what they are trying to achieve for the public good. Only critics of architecture such as the Prince of Wales would appear to have the clout to bring about such public answering.

Applying the precautionary principle, we must not allow "leave it with us" responses by each profession. Each profession creates "due process" committees to come up with recommended professional practice. And once their deliberations are finished, they deem themselves to have produced the right result simply because "due process" was used.

There is another kind of problem with professions, apart from the issue of their duty in the public interest. The scholar and former priest, Ivan Illich, writing in the 1970s, argues that in an elitist-oriented society people can form themselves into "self-accredited elites" called professions, who impute needs to people that only the elites can treat. As Illich sees it, professions disable people by making them think they have more treatment requirements than they really have. "They turn the modern state into a holding corporation of enterprises which facilitates the operation of their self-certified incompetencies...."[10]

Londoners in World War II saw their relations being smashed and killed in the Blitz. They didn't mentally collapse. Obviously, trauma counselling is often a great help, but we now seem to have trauma counsellors instantly on site in every situation that is at all stressful for anyone. Extending the Illich argument would predict that trauma counsellors will seek to become a self-accredited profession, which then actively expands the range and variety of stresses calling for trauma counselling. Illich sees people being disabled by thinking that they can't cope on their own with stress incidents in life which they observe. He predicts the coming of a "post-professional ethos," in which citizens figure out for themselves what they don't need from professionals.

Professions' Answering to the Public

Protecting the public is a responsibility common to all professions, but it mustn't be the professions that rule on the extent of their own responsibilities and accountabilities. It must be citizens. Because they affect the public in important ways, professions can't be accountable only for the quality of their techniques and not for their intentions. Self-regulation needs first to be oriented to the professions' public answering for their responsibilities, not to internal discipline committees, lobbying for monopolies and avoidance of external regulation. If professions account to the public, we can expect this to produce a self-regulating effect because the obligation to answer influences how well people discharge their responsibilities.

Professions can draft standards for their public answering for their responsibilities as professions, set them out for adequate public challenge, and govern themselves accordingly. The professions would say to the public, "This is what we think we are publicly accountable for. Is it what you had in mind?" If the professions won't do this, in a time of increasing need for public answering by all authorities, citizens and organizations interested in the effects of professions' practices will have to write the answering standards for each profession.

Citizens can do this through small-scale "constituent assemblies" of stakeholders affected by each profession. The first item on the agenda of each group can be the statement by the particular profession, supported by evidence, of the extent to which Justice Estey's observations accurately portray their profession. The main agenda item would be what can reasonably be stated as the profession's responsibilities and reasonably expected as the profession's public answering.

Each profession in its reporting can be expected to state what they seek to bring about in the public interest and what they think they have achieved. We must require the professional bodies formally to tell the public *whose* needs they are honouring, in what priority, and how, and whose they are not.

Therefore it is reasonable that each profession publicly state:
- who, exactly, it is serving and how, and why the service is needed
- its specific *achievement* objectives in the public interest, in terms of results – end states or conditions – that it seeks to bring about
- its own performance standards for the achievement (not just descriptions of activities or standards for how technique is applied)
- its own specific performance standards for:
  - ensuring the honesty of its members
  - dealing with complaints
  - accounting to complainants for what happened, and why
- the extent to which its achievement objectives have been met
- what it has learned about serving the public interest and how it has applied the learning.

There will be much squirming over first drafts, but we must ask professionals to publicly make these assertions. The public answering obligations of the professions need to be included in their qualifying curricula and certification exams.

As well, each profession can produce useful information for the public. The pioneering work of B.C. Chief Justice Allan McEachern in providing citizens with computer access to his court judgments was noted earlier.[11] Expanding that service, provincial law societies can set out, in Citizen Information websites, useful "heads-up" information, such as:

- expiry times for suing local, provincial and federal government for different types of important responsibilities
- pitfalls to know about in suing the Crown
- the workings of class action suits and the restrictions on their use

Academics

The issue in the public accountability of academics is to have them tell us what they think they are fairly and publicly accountable for achieving in the public interest, given that they influence the thinking of the young and their salaries and pensions are paid 80% or more from the public purse.

Cited in a 1990 Carnegie Foundation study, Derek Bok, former president of Harvard University, sums up the issue of academics' responsibility:

> Armed with the security of tenure and the time to study the world with care, professors would appear to have a unique opportunity to act as society's scouts to signal impending problems long before they are visible to others. Yet rarely have members of the academy succeeded in discovering the emerging issues and bringing them vividly to the attention of the public.[12]

One reason is that they are not encouraged to scout – to investigate beyond interesting twists earning them journal publications. Activists then have to do the scouting for society, but have no tenure. A second reason is that academics related to the workings of governments and large organizations and funded by them are expected not to fundamentally challenge existing power arrangements. They are expected to help keep responsibilities blurred and accountability "complex." Academics who don't go with the flow may not get funded. One indicator is authorities' ready acceptance of academics' attention to codes of ethics for business and government. These are only exhortations, unless the conduct is audited and the code includes standards for public answering that are enforced. Codes of ethics are not rules for public answering that mustn't be broken.

In the sciences, especially medicine and agriculture, academics know the large corporations' profit aim of getting citizens to take ever higher risk and to keep the public's attention off the precautionary principle. But because funding of research has been largely transferred from government to the corporations, and government funding organizations have been politicized to the point where their funding rules require a corporate funding "partner" in each case, research academics are expected to honour corporations' wants if they want to be funded. The safety wall between the scientists and shark-infested waters has been largely removed. This means that we can expect more and more scientists to rationalize to themselves that the convergence of their research results with corporations' and executive government's wishes is a coincidence.

We have probably never had a period in society where the power of corporations, up front or behind the scenes, together with deception by supposedly democratic governments, has been greater. As a consequence, in the areas of political science and public administration, academics don't go to the bone. Economic policy and trade academics swarmed to support the proposed Multilateral Agreement on Investment.

One test for government-related academics is whether they write about public accountability to help citizen competence in holding authorities fairly to account. The writing simply isn't there. Yet the question why we don't have adequate public answering from authorities, and what it takes to get it, has been facing scholars ever since the university faculties most closely linked to the work of authorities were formed.

A valid priority in academic research is to identify the cost of the *lack* of public answering to a reasonable standard. It will be a large amount, even without non-quantifiable costs. It will include the cost to society of failure to publicly account for the application of the precautionary principle in safety and social justice, for example in contaminated blood, unsafe mines and wrongful convictions; the cost of fighting and lobbying as a result of lowered trust in institutions stemming from inadequate answering; the cost of audit needed to dig out the performance information from authorities who should have been providing it in the first place; and the public purse cost of people in authority repeating their effort with greater armament when their decisions haven't been accepted because of inadequate public answering before the fact.

At the universities and colleges, where the professional intellectual techniques are taught, there must be a shift in mindset. Given the main purpose of universities – training people to think critically – the public accountability of professionals must be made a solid issue rather than being ignored or made simply an appearances tack-on to technique.

Can professors serving the professions at public cost validly assert that they teach what public accountability means for each of their disciplines, how it works, and what should be examined in current cause and effect? If university students taking auditing courses, for example, find that their textbooks don't explain accountability and how auditing is to serve accountability relationships (which has been the very purpose of auditing for over a hundred years) [13], and that their professors don't teach accountability relationships, students have the right to ask their professors why they teach only auditing technique.

Students in economics can ask their professors to tell them how the GDP is currently used, by whom, to influence, in what ways, what key decisions of which decision-makers affecting what segments of society. Students should also ask their professors to tell them who, on the planet, is discarding the GDP as a basis for policy decisions, and why. If a professor cannot lay this out, the students can agree on a reasonable time by which the professor will find out and report back.

Students in other disciplines can ask equivalent questions about their own professions' public accountability. The best-rated and worst-rated faculty responses can be posted on Internet student networks. If professors of political science, public administration and business don't think that their curricula should include the public answering obligation by authorities related to their disciplines, their students can ask them to explain why not.

Academics' Answering to the Public

Academics can reasonably be expected to publicly state performance standards for themselves that would confirm whether the Derek Bok observation applies to them. This obligation in no way restricts their work. It is a reasonable explanation requirement, because their salaries and pensions come largely from the public purse.

Academics in the social sciences can be asked to tell us why whistleblowers aren't supported by citizens at large. Government-related academics can tell us what it takes to achieve a level of public trust in executive government and politicians that makes society work properly. When academics comment on election outcomes, they talk about political parties' credibility, but don't explain cause-effect relationships between politicians' public answering and their credibility. These are areas of research that lie outside the lamplight of the drunkard's search, but citizens need the research done and assessed for its implications.

With some exceptions, members of the academy don't explore the implications for citizens of basic propositions such as J.D. Thompson's – that organizations seek to control their environments and buffer them if they can't[14] – and how this should decide what the directing minds of organizations should report to the public. Funded research and consulting contracts whose scope doesn't threaten power arrangements are hard to resist. A test of the worth to society of the work of academics related to governments and corporations is what their work usefully says to citizens about the effects in society of good and poor public answering by authorities.

Journalists

We rely on journalists to tell us what's going on. Thus they affect the public in important ways. They have a direct effect on the climate of opinion shaping fairness decisions in society. They also have intellectual technique in their facts reporting. In indicating pattern and suggesting deception, the better journalists use a seemingly innocuous manner to ensure that the story gets printed, but the information is usually there if the reader detects it in the article. Journalists' coverage of the Canadian military and HRDC are examples.

But journalists stop short of explaining for citizens the deception techniques by the authorities they quote or write about. Since journalists are employees taking direction from media management, or having to accept management's terms if, as freelancers, they want their work published, we will confine the term "media" to mean managers and owners of media corporations, such as newspapers and radio and TV broadcasters. The accountability problem is determining who makes what decisions about what we are to read, as between visible journalists and their invisible bosses. This includes who puts the headings on journalists' articles and reports, since the headings can distort. This isn't a minor matter.

Viewed as professionals in the public exposure of what goes on, journalists can fairly be expected to publicly assert what we can expect all professional bodies to assert: what they specifically intend to achieve for society and what their performance standards are. They should also find a way to tell us what or who stands in their way of producing fair and complete reporting, whether it's media management or anyone. Codes of ethics and monitoring boards for journalists aren't the same thing as public answering for responsibilities. Journalists have been criticized, blamed and threatened, but not asked to state publicly and clearly their own standards for their fairness and usefulness. It's also fair to require the directing minds of media corporations to account publicly for constraints they place on journalists' scope.

In Canada, journalists were strongly criticized by former federal government minister John Crosbie at the February 1995 conference of the Canadian Association of Journalists, in St. John's: "You're out to titillate and entertain, rather than inform...you want to destroy things." So too in the United Kingdom, where in 1995 Sir Edward Heath ranked the British press as "among the worst in the world in terms of its responsibility."

Crosbie's criticism brings out one of the most disappointing and dysfunctional practices of journalists: the attempt to convert every issue into conflict, controversy or combat, presumably to sell more newspapers. If something isn't a conflict between people, journalists seem to want to make it one. Contriving conflict clouds the issue of who has what important responsibilities and performance standards and whether they are meeting them. Simply finding a person with opposed views to someone else won't produce this information.

Journalists like to be the first to report horror stories, but the important thing in harm or waste attributable to authorities is what the responsibility and accountability issues are. Simply reporting harm without pointing citizens to the questions they should ask may make a news story, but it isn't being as helpful as journalists could be in the right role as nonpartisan observers and investigators. Pointing readers in the right direction isn't telling them what to think.

When the reporting has to be prolonged, such as in the late 1990s coverage of the military, HRDC and the legal system, journalists get serious about pattern, short of proposing underlying causes. Examples of rigorous sustained coverage are the reporting of David Pugliese of the *Ottawa Citizen* on the military, and the reporting of Kirk Makin of the *Globe and Mail* and Paul McKay of the *Citizen* on the legal profession.

However, once inquiries shut down or are shut down (as in the Somalia case) journalists' attention goes elsewhere and we don't know who or what dissuades journalists from follow-up. Journalists follow responsibility stories only to the point where events shift to a behind-the-scenes state, such as the RCMP investigating something as a result of harm being exposed, or a highly-controversial Bill passing through a legislature. We don't see follow-up. Someone doing a review of newspaper clippings would find all the initial events and people's reactions to them, but no later coverage tracking what came of it. It's like auditors or management consultants reporting on performance but not following up to see what happened to their recommendations.

Journalists' ready acceptance of euphemism is another problem. The classic example is "ethnic cleansing" used universally in print, radio and television rather than "mass murder." Journalists are accountable for explaining the reasons why they aid and abet purposeful distortion of meaning in language.

When governmental or military euphemism is accepted and used by the media, it becomes dangerous. Those writing on the language adopted by the media during the 1991 Gulf war have pointed out the practices.[15] But what will prevent critics from having to write yet another round of books when it all happens again? Orwell had already described it over 50 years earlier: planes bombing defenceless villages in a countryside was called "pacification". As Orwell warned, state control over citizens will be complete when the language is perfect.

Edward Herman cites a typical example:

> [President] Reagan's election was the culmination of the corporate campaign of the 1970s "to get the government off our backs," which, translated from doublespeak, means, among other things, that the government should reduce or eliminate attempts to protect the public from price-gouging, misrepresentation, and threats to worker, consumer, and environmental safety.[16]

A different issue is how the media themselves are used by, and succumb to, those in power. Herman and Noam Chomsky, in their famous *Manufacturing Consent*, explain it as the "propaganda model."[17] But surely what Orwell taught in the 1940s about inexact or evasive language permitting defence of the indefensible has been a mainstay in the curriculum of every school of journalism in the western world.

There are limits on what journalists can do. As James Winter points out:

> Far from being independent-minded professionals, most journalists are employees who do the job the boss wants in return for a pay cheque. They have virtually no professional protection akin to that of a medical doctor, a nurse, teacher or lawyer; none of the academic freedom afforded to professors. Like the rest of us, they have spouses and kids and mortgages and they want to keep their jobs. Some are well-intentioned and daring, some are excellent journalists, but most are not. Even the outstanding among them are severely limited by economic and organizational constraints.[18]

Winter further notes that what journalists write may be rejected or else edited and headlined the way management and the editors hired by management want to see it emerge.[19]

An example of headings making a difference was the *Ottawa Citizen*'s front-page headline for the coverage of Supreme Court of Canada Justice Iacobucci's 1998 speech quoted earlier: "Judge Scolds 'Greedy' Lawyers." The page 2 heading continuing the story was "Greedy." The editors' headline made a Supreme Court judge say that all lawyers are greedy. In fact Justice Iacobucci had said that lawyers' striving for billable hours gave the public the impression that lawyers are self-interested and greedy. A more recent example is the heading *Globe and Mail* editors, presumably seeking to be cute, gave to an August 2000 article on control of fresh water by Maude Barlow, Chair of the Council of Canadians – "The Fight for Liquid Assets."[20] The heading suggested an article to be found in the Business section of the *Globe*, with water being a market commodity. Barlow's message was that the scarcity of fresh water on the planet dictates that water be declared a human right and not turned over to corporations as a commodity.

Headings condition readers' thinking before they get to what the journalist says. Thus it is a major responsibility issue when the wording of headlines editors exonerate authorities from their responsibility or reinforce invalid decrees, such as "Defence Minister Dismisses Somalia Inquiry Report," or when journalists portray what government announces as fact by failing to insert the all-important "The Minister *claims* that..." Another is a newspaper headline saying, about Canadian energy exports to the U.S., "Protect Canada, Minister Urges,"[21] as if ministers can only urge, and when the entity they would "urge" is themselves.

Newspaper management can reasonably be asked to state their performance standards and performance for faithfulness of headlining to the journalists' intended message. This issue includes what veto rights journalists have over headlining which can nullify an important article or even give an opposite message. If the editor rejects a journalist's proposed headline and has to do one to meet a deadline, while the journalist is off on another story without a cell phone, faithfulness rules must be in place. When a newspaper opinions page editor writes, "Our writing coach selects the best headlines for monthly praise,"[22] it gives us a clue to whether journalists have any control over the headlines written by others for news stories that distort or even nullify the journalist's intended message. The vehement view of editors the world over, that their whim has primacy, doesn't help journalists convey to citizens the true picture of what's going on.

Related to "territory," newspapers tend not to pick up on important radio news stories that ought to have good newspaper journalist coverage as well as radio coverage. CBC Radio reporters, for example, have been doing increasingly important work in investigative reporting. Examples are federal Health Protection Branch responsibilities for drug safety, suppression of scientists' views in issues such as bovine growth hormones and genetically engineered foods, and radio journalists' investigative reporting of police forces. But the issues they cover aren't picked up and given support by the newspapers. If we hear an important issue being examined on the radio and look for it in the newspaper in the next two days, we will often see nothing. The public doesn't know whether the print journalists' invisible superiors are making the coverage decisions, and who makes the decisions isn't publicly explained by newspaper management. The same is true for letters to the editor.

Journalists don't appear to have sorted out whether they are energy units working for corporate owners and accepting this role, or whether they are professionals with an obligation to decide their role in the public interest, find a way to carry it out and account for their effort. They collectively have to find a way to deal with management interference with their lines of inquiry.

Journalists can report the adequacy of authorities' explanations of their intentions and actions by asking those they interview to answer simple questions amounting to accountability questions. Journalists should be able to do a good job of this if they take the time to understand accountability and holding to account, and why it is a society imperative. Questions by activist organizations are often simply ignored by the accountable; questions about public answering that are put by interviewing journalists can't be ignored.

Journalists can help citizens focus their attention on the responsible and accountable directing minds by interviewing the chairpersons of the governing bodies of organizations, not the CEOs who are subordinate to the boards of directors. The journalist can ask, "Who would you say has the ultimate responsibility for X, and what in your view would be adequate answering to the public for the responsibilities?"

Investigative journalists can identify deception, spin and unsupported decree and expose it. At the same time, they can encourage public answering by decision-makers in authority by repeatedly asking them basic questions about their public answering obligations. Journalists can expose arrogance, dishonesty and deceit in government and corporation public statements, saying to us, like auditors serving accountability relationships, "This is what we've found: is it what you had in mind?" To the extent that those in authority claim to be adequately answering to the public, the journalists' role is to check their assertions against what the journalists have found out to be going on.

The famous Watergate investigative reporting in the United States was a case of journalists doing this audit. Obviously, there would never have been public answering by the Executive that would have allowed journalists to comment on the fairness and completeness of the answering. Like auditors, journalists can say to the public, "One would think that authorities X and Y would have been answering for A, B and C. Since they haven't, we will tell you what we have found out about it, to help you demand the accounting."

If authorities are required to produce equity statements or their equivalent for what they propose, journalists can condense them for citizens in half a page of their newspaper. Or, if authorities such as ministers of the Crown refuse to produce public statements of equity trade-offs for what they propose, journalists can take to them the equity statements developed by public interest organizations, and ask for the minister's response to each major element of the activists' statements. Journalists have a better chance of wresting answering from ministers than activist organizations do, because ministers can't live without journalists if they want to get their views out.

The trap journalists have to avoid is being chosen and co-opted by authorities. For example, a minister can give a particular journalist special attention and interview time, and the journalist succumbs to the attention. Truly challenging executive power takes courage, but when it isn't challenged we get journalists' acceptance, for example, that a feasible test for hepatitis C was not available to Canadian government authorities before 1986.

Journalists' Answering to the Public

As noted, the first consideration in journalists' public accountability is to have journalists tell us what they are trying to accomplish and why, and tell us their performance standards and the extent to which they think they've lived up to them. Answering publicly doesn't limit journalists' freedom, but it does let us know what they see as their duty to the public interest. Journalists' answering should tell us the distinction they make between journalism, entertainment and provocation, and how they help citizens do their civic duty.

Organizations such as the Canadian Association of Journalists can state:

- journalists' intended achievement (in terms of what they seek to bring about, not just a vague statement of effort activity),
- journalists' basic performance standards (including standards evidencing fairness and rejection of co-opting effort by authorities), and
- the public answering that journalists think is reasonable to give citizens about their intentions and performance (which includes media management action hindering their service to the public, described clearly enough for the public to act on).

The public answering obligation applies as well to the professors directing the schools of journalism, who can discuss in their courses journalists' responsibility to expose spin in public answering that claims to be accountability reporting.

Journalists can start their public answering by collectively accounting for their performance against Orwell's criteria stated by George Woodcock in the CBC documentary cited earlier. For example, journalists can be invited to make the following performance assertions:

- We write plainly and vigorously, without euphemisms that anaesthetize people's brains such that they fail to ask the questions they should
- We expose language that appears intended to narrow the range of the public's thinking

And, taking on a new responsibility in aid of public answering, journalists can assert:

- For the issues we identify, we try to make clear who is or isn't answering to whom, for what responsibilities, and who seems to be saying what in the answering

Without being partisan, journalists can also point out what they see as obvious missing answering. Thus the journalist's work parallels that of an external auditor but is "online" rather than after the fact, and has more freedom than auditors' mandates allow.

Journalists should be able to meet these basic standards and decide their own scope for their reporting. If corporate management distorts or suppresses what they want the public to know, journalists must either collectively expose this through their organizations and identify what the public can do to help prevent it, or remain doing only what they are told to do and garner less respect as a result. The public can back them up if the limits placed on their scope are made visible, just as investors back professional auditors who report imposed limits on their audit scope.

Endnotes

[1] Editorial, *CA Magazine,* July 1991

2 "Arthur Andersen, Andersen Consulting Split," reprinted in the *Globe and Mail* 8 August 2000 p.B1

3 PricewaterhouseCoopers ad in the *Globe and Mail* 15 April 1999 p.B9

4 *Ottawa Citizen* 30 March 1998 p.A1

5 David Brown, quoted in the *Globe and Mail* 9 June 1999 p.B3

6 *Globe and Mail* 15 September 1999 p.B5

7 A.D. McKay, letter to the editor, *Ottawa Citizen*, 12 April 1998 p.A15

8 "Court Quashes Conviction Against Ontario Drugged Teen," *Globe and Mail*, August, 1994, p.A5

9 Professor Bill Watson of McGill University, debating with Professor Mel Watkins of the University of Toronto on the merits or harm of the "Chicago School" of economics, CBC Radio Morningside, 13 October, 1995.

10 Ivan Illich, *Disabling Professions* (London: Marion Boyars Publishers, 1977) p.16.

11 *Vancouver Sun*, 18 May 2001, op. cit.

12 Ernest Boyer, *Scholarship Reconsidered: Priorities of the Professoriate*, Carnegie Foundation, 1990, p.76

13 An example is W. Morley Lemmon, Alvin A. Arens and James K. Loebbecke, *Auditing: an Integrated Approach*, Scarborough, Prentice Hall, 5th edition, 1993.

14 Thompson, op. cit.

15 For example, see Edward S. Herman, *Beyond Hypocrisy: Decoding the News in an Age of Propaganda* (Montreal: Black Rose Books, 1992)

16 Herman, p.85

17 Edward S. Herman and Noam Chomsky, *Manufacturing Consent: the Political Economy of the Mass Media* (New York, Pantheon, 1988).

18 James Winter, *Democracy's Oxygen*, (Montreal, Black Rose Books, 1997) 139-40

19 Winter, Chapter 5

20 Maude Barlow, *Globe and Mail* 16 August 2000 p.A11

21 *Globe and Mail*, 19 May 2001, p.A7

22 Letter by editorial page editor of the *Ottawa Citizen* 18 September 1995 to the Ottawa Centretown Citizens' Community Association, in response to the Association's inquiry about quality control over the paper's headlining of reporters' articles.

PART III

Holding to Account

CHAPTER 14

Holding to Account

The Concept

Holding to account means getting adequate answering for important responsibilities. It doesn't mean supplicating, hoping, fighting, or blaming. Exacting the answering means that we prevent the answering obligation from being ignored, shifted to others, thwarted through deception or impeded through delay. Having the answering meet a standard means that the answering given by those with the responsibilities is honest and complete. Under the precautionary principle, we don't trust blindly: we validate important answering. Thus adequate answering is answering audited for its fairness and completeness.

The answering obligation tells no one what to do; it's simply a fairness obligation to explain intentions and, later, what came of them, Therefore, this obligation can't be refused by authorities in a democracy, and if it is refused in a dictatorship it tells citizens that whim is the only criterion of the authorities.

Holding fairly to account means that those in the legitimate role of holding to account act fairly on the reporting given, and don't evade their own responsibilities. It means that political candidates or opposition parties in legislatures don't seize on reports of lack of success to criticize those with the responsibilities, just for partisan or self-serving purposes. It further means not holding authorities to account for intentions and actions they can't control. But it does mean having them answer for how they are dealing with external constraints.

The main reason for holding authorities to account is to better predict their conduct and to cut down the time, energy and emotion citizens spend in fighting with authorities, whether it's to block something or gain access to information. Instead of guessing or ferreting out what authorities intend and why they intend it, we simply ask them to tell us, but we audit what they say. All authorities have the obligation to answer. It's just that we haven't asked them to answer. If we had, Access to Information commissioners would have been public accountability commissioners for the areas of responsibility not covered by professional audit.

In terms of driving and restraining forces, exacting adequate public answering from authorities slows their driving forces coming at us on uneven playing fields. An example was the executive government of Ontario using its obedient legislature members to push through several upheaving changes at once in the late 1990s. The ministers knew that citizens couldn't cope with a legislative blitzkrieg transferring local control to the ministers in municipalities, hospitals and education. The related budget slashes and privatization led to Walkerton, among other outcomes. Public answering and its validation slows authorities' driving forces because it forces out authorities' intentions and reasoning for public challenge. Executive governments can't claim as adequate answering, "We were elected to do this" because pre-election platforms meet no standard of public answering for the clarity or specificity of intentions and the reasoning behind them.

Reducing authorities' driving forces is better than trying to increase restraining forces, because authorities have greater forces to deploy. If they know that their intentions will be publicly exposed through their answering, because what they say will be publicly validated, authorities may think twice about what they intend.

In the late 1960s when "lateral thinking" became a new expression, Edward De Bono offered a little exercise for people to test themselves. But it was both an exercise and a revealing fable. It went something like this:

> Wicked landlord of house of elderly frail man and his demure beautiful daughter forces the daughter into a difficult choice: she to marry wicked man or no home for father. But he gives her a sporting chance. While standing on a gravel pathway of stones, he invites her to reach into a pouch he's holding and draw a stone. He says that he has put into the pouch a white one and a black one. Draw black and they stay in the house. Draw white and she goes with him. The bag contains two white stones.

What to do?

> Daughter draws the stone but, without showing which colour it is, "accidentally" drops it on the path where it's immediately lost among the rest. After apologizing for her clumsiness, she points out it that doesn't matter because the stone still in the bag must be the opposite colour of the one she drew.

Wicked man allows her and her father to keep the house.

A plausible reason why the furious man wouldn't ignore his deceit and simply evict, using the force he had, is that he couldn't stand the disgrace he would suffer in the eyes of the beautiful daughter. Public loss of face is a very powerful deterrent – except perhaps for the totally arrogant.

Holding to account is like using the other person's body in jujitsu. If directing minds must publicly state their intentions and justify them, but their real intentions would lead to harm or unfairness, public validation of what they would likely say would expose it as a lie. That would incur public loss of face, self-imposed, unless they are unabashed and immune to the stigma of being exposed as liars.

But we may simply have to fight, to counter arrogance in authorities who won't account. Seattle in 1999 was an example of broad-scale restraining forces by both WTO-affected Southern countries and activists from all participating countries. They were protesting against global big-business agendas for which there is no public accounting. A more laser-like fighting approach was used in Clayoquot Sound where, to get the logging companies' attention and force them to talk, activists put nails in target trees, leaving the trees growing but too risky for sawmill saws. Regulations and codes of conduct for forestry operations, however comprehensive, deal with actions of people. They don't produce public accountings of intentions and reasoning for public challenge, or of performance.

Gandhi's passive resistance teaching was a very big nail. The English should have accounted to the people of India for their intentions a hundred years earlier, but if it had been asked for it would have been met with arrogance. There is a nail equivalent for all authorities who refuse to account for their intentions.

When the answering also includes authorities' intended performance standards and how they intend to report their results, citizens shouldn't have to spend hours after work to come up with standards for the authority. We should be assessing what the authorities assert as their performance standards and validating their reporting of their achievement.

Adequate public answering for intentions will make clearer to us the risks authorities want us to take. We need it, for example, from those who proposed the 1997 Multilateral Agreement on Investment, with its relentless spirit evident in the protested executive governments' meetings since. Because we know the risks with tobacco, what we need from the corporations intent on selling cigarettes predicted to kill tens of millions people this century is their reasoning for what they're doing, not just the response, "Promoting smoking and selling cigarettes is legal." Their answering better equips us to act. If we know what authorities intend and why, we can commend it, alter it or stop it. Waking up and taking action after the fact is too late – as in blood contamination, Westray, Walkerton and intentions such as the dismantlement of medicare.

Getting Rid of Supplication

Supplication is often straightforward, out of deference to authority, such as in a community group's letter to an authority saying, "We would be grateful if you would consider..." The irony is that the letter is being written to people whose salaries are paid by the taxes of those doing the supplicating. Or an organization's spokesperson may say, "We urge government to ..." or, "I hope they take into account..." Or an Opposition Member of Parliament may say, "I hope the government will stand firm on...." If we suspect we have cancer, hope is a relevant word. But as citizens with the duty to help bring about fairness, "hope" and "urge" should be no more part of our vocabulary than it is for professional auditors.

We can tell forms of supplication by the absence of stated legitimate *expectation* for someone to meet a performance and answering standard. For example, an expectation letter to an accountable authority can say: "We think it reasonable that you do what you can to bring about A, B and C. It is also reasonable that we know your action intentions and reasoning by date X, so we can decide what action we need to take." The test is whether those having the concerns are saying – and meaning – "This won't do," or simply hoping.

We have thus far used a standard type of language. For example, in mid-2000 the Council of Canadians sent to its members across Canada a form protest letter for its members to sign and send to the federal Trade Minister, Pierre Pettigrew. The letter asked the Minister to "withdraw Canada from the current World Trade Organization's services negotiation until our Medicare and public education are given full protection." In view of what we have been seeing at the federal level, and the Council's knowledge, the letter was justified. But following three paragraphs setting out the major concerns, the letter concluded:

> I join with thousands of other citizens – and the Council of Canadians – in urging you to use your position to preserve our social programs.
>
> I await your reply.

The purpose of such a form letter is to have the Minister's staff tally it to gauge the strength of public opinion on an issue and let the Minister know. But to "urge" is only to supplicate.

If the aim is to send a serious shot across the bow of the responsible minister about ministers' intentions affecting all Canadians and future generations of Canadians, the closing part of the letter could say:

> I think you know that most Canadians want our Medicare and public education protected, and that Canadians don't believe that a sovereign country

is powerless to protect its core policies. You have not told us your government's intentions at the WTO, and your reasons. Would you therefore please tell us what you action you will take at the WTO that would assure protection of our Medicare and public education system? Canadians have not given you power of attorney in this matter.

The language of reasonable expectation is neither deferential nor insulting. It simply asks for explanation. No minister can refuse to respond to a fair question put by a citizen unless the refusal can be carried off successfully in the legislature and in the media. The minister's staff will realize that citizens signing an expectation-based letter understand very well what they are asking. The minister wouldn't want to have newspapers print the number of refused responses, because the form letter would then be printed right across Canada. If a minister doesn't respond or responds inadequately, the citizens who wrote can write again – and again, if necessary.

We don't have to hammer authorities as the alternative to supplicating. Invitations to account can be put as questions, such as,

> "For safety in (blood, water, the workplace or other situations), do you agree with the experts that the following responsibilities are critical success factors? If you do, is it reasonable that you report publicly on your performance for these responsibilities?"

Many people talk about the state of poverty or injustice in countries of the South and even the industrialized North – whether in articles in international magazines, letters to the editors and op-eds or in Internet exchanges. The pattern is one set of people describing and others writing letters responding with their feelings about the issue. Basically all say, "This is terrible," or, in outrage, "We protest," or "We call for…" Or, in the case of the early 1999 Kosevo bombing by NATO, a church leader concerned about stopping the bombing says, "A way must be found…" without suggesting who has the obligation to answer publicly for finding the way and implementing it, and by when.

Describers may identify responsible governments and call for "political will," but written concern or outrage that doesn't include steps for exacting the needed answering amounts only to supplication. Protest can be kept up so long as the energy is there, but protest alone doesn't address how the beliefs of the outraged convert to levers that actually alter the conduct of the responsible and accountable authorities.

Until articles and letters to editors specifically propose who must do what and when to have a good chance of making a difference, and until the writers identify the specific accountable directing minds and how they are to be made to answer publicly, protest language will remain in the streets. Public protest can create a climate of opinion influencing authorities, but without also holding to account we will likely get only appearances in response. The agenda is then carried on behind closed doors. To make a difference in authorities' conduct, the climate of opinion has to be strong enough not only to stop something but also to force powerful people thereafter to explain their intentions publicly before the fact, and have their stated intentions publicly validated and challenged.

Forging Public Answering Standards

Since we don't have public answering standards, it will take too long for them to simply evolve, like the common law. Too much needless harm will occur in the meantime. Therefore we have to use legislation to make adequate answering the law. Compliance with the law will be a major issue, but auditors and the courts still function. Ensuring compliance is a lesser problem than coping with the lack of answering standards.

How do we forge the public answering standards? We can start by asking citizens' organizations and the major public interest organizations to get together to draft, for their areas of concern, reasonable public answering standards for the authorities relevant to their work. In virtually every area of citizen concern there are public interest organizations or groups working on the issues. Other countries have their equivalent organizations that can be tapped for insight. Then we ask our elected representatives to convert the drafts into Bills to legislate the obligation to answer, and the basic answering standards. Basic standards for accountability legislation were offered in Chapter 5.

Pilot projects would be an effective way to see how writing and installing standards can be done, working from consensus on common principles of public accountability. The drafting groups would have to be demonstrably non-partisan and resemble constituent assemblies. They would work in consultation with representatives from the authorities and elected representatives in each of the responsibility areas where public answering standards are needed. Where a set of responsibilities extends from local government through province or state to the federal government, such as in health, elected representatives from each jurisdiction of government would participate.

As well, current and retired staff of legislative audit offices and the civil service could volunteer their time to help identify responsibilities and advise on reasonable public answering standards. Community colleges' outreach programs could logically house the accountability pilot projects – or some of the large public interest organizations could. Government and the large philanthropic foundations should see such groups as helping the public interest and thus be willing to help fund the groups' out-of-pocket costs. All it takes in each area of accountability concern is for one public interest organization to call a coalition together to draft the standards.

The sequence is roughly as follows:

- identify and rank authorities' responsibilities (just as auditors general have to do for their audit scope decisions in government auditing)
- rank situations, processes and responsibilities in which the lack of public answering creates a significant risk to safety, social justice or the environment
- decide the basic standards for public answering reasonable to expect, including, for intentions, the equity statement or its equivalent
- identify plausible causes of probable refusal to answer
- ask decision-makers to declare their intentions for adequate public answering for their responsibilities

Public interest organizations can allot part of their work specifically to accountability and talk to other groups about principles and standards for public answering. Each can organize public meetings as citizens' forums in their areas of concern and use these meetings to seek consensus on the public answering that goes with the responsibilities. Use of the equity statement approach can be tested in such meetings, and approaches that produce effective results can be shared on the Internet.

Websites for the pilot projects could track and show the progress of the projects and the barriers in the way of legislator acceptance at each level of government. The drafting groups would also put their work into print form for citizens who want to follow the progress but who aren't on the Internet. Community networking could then help circulate the pilot work and mobilize support for putting the answering standards into legislation in several jurisdictions.

Seniors' organizations can work effectively on virtually any aspect of public accountability because seniors remember what duty and standards mean and why they are important. Their numbers include people who have worked for years in virtually every area of public responsibility. Seniors have the power[1] and collectively those who are able-bodied have the brains and time. Increasingly, they will have modems to communicate on the Internet.

In addition to protecting marginalized fellow seniors, those seniors who are able can use their collective power to help install public accountability of governments and corporations to a standard. It is not far-fetched to say that working to install public accountability can produce renewed sense of purpose. The young, now having fewer options unless they are techno-wizards, may fairly argue that able-bodied seniors should try to help turn around what the seniors' generation in authority allowed to happen. But the young will grasp the idea of public accountability and be their own force for it, especially through the Internet.

Getting Equity Statements to the Public

We saw in Chapter 5 the purpose of the equity statement. It is a public statement by accountable authorities that basically says,

> We realize that what we intend would affect the public in important ways. This is a statement of what we intend, and why, giving our view of the fairness trade-offs involved. We are prepared to clarify for you the intentions and reasoning we give in the statement.

Any intention of an authority that can be called a proposal – whether the authority's own intention or someone else's that the authority is asked to approve – can be explained for the public by means of an equity statement. A first cut at it can be done on the back of an envelope.

The catch is that public answering shares power. That means that only forward-looking governing bodies who believe in citizens being better informed would likely volunteer public equity statements for their intentions. If, for example, a journalist were to ask the federal Health and Trade Ministers whether the government would produce an equity statement for not supporting clear labelling of genetically engineered foods, the types of responses would be predictable: "Several well-established forms of government information will give you our position on that," or, "Equity statements aren't generally accepted practice for governments," or, "Healthy debate on genetically engineered foods is already going on in Parliament."

What wouldn't be said is that while the Europeans intend to make labelling the law, the Canadian federal executive government sides with the United States on virtually every trade matter concerning corporations. This includes food, because the American government sees food only as a trade issue. Not so France, for example. The Canadian federal ministers know that a validated equity statement for the blocking of compulsory labelling would be impoverished and arouse public questioning of the government's motivation.

And if a journalist were to ask tobacco corporation representatives if they would be willing to put out an equity statement for the promotion and sale of cigarettes, knowing the deaths and public health care expense, they would say that so long as it's legal to sell cigarettes there's no issue of public answering. They are just carrying on business as they are expected to do in a society that promotes business, and they stand ready to pay any ultimately successful legal claims that happen to survive a decade of lawsuit challenge – like the unpaid court-awarded claims against Exxon for the *Exxon Valdez*.

If authorities, when asked, refuse to explain their intentions to a reasonable standard of answering in equity statements or their equivalent, we shift strategy in holding to account. An appropriate public interest organization concerned about the authority's intentions can lead the drafting of the equity statement that the authority should have provided.

We then publicly ask the authority to respond with what they think is a more accurate picture of their intentions and the fairness trade-offs.

Just as health-related public interest organizations can draft an equity statement for the restriction of something, such as tobacco companies' sales, they can draft them for what they argue for. In the genetically-engineered foods labelling issue, for example, public interest organizations can draft a public equity statement for the labelling proposal.[2] It must be as objective as possible to give the government no "hooks" to use as straw men. These organizations can then formally ask the government to publicly give its opinion about the fairness and completeness of their equity statement, which would be available on an Internet web page. They can show on their website the government's response, verbatim.

Whoever refuses to come up with a reasonable equity statement for the public yields credibility to those who do.

To the extent that public interest organizations do such statements for important proposals and submit them to public challenge, whether for authorities' proposals or their own, the practice of drafting equity statements for the public's attention will catch on. For example, in the earlier-cited newspaper op-ed article by Council of Canadians Chairperson Maude Barlow, on control of the world's scarce fresh water,[3] she states:

> "The answer (to the threat of corporate control of water) is to demand that governments accept their responsibilities and establish full water-protection regimes."

Since the responsible governments haven't declared such regimes, and our own government has given us no evidence that it wishes to lead such an initiative, the Council could get together with other organizations concerned about water supply on the planet and write an intention for governments to adopt as their reasonable control. The coalition could draft its proposal as an equity statement, have it challenged by knowledgeable people and present it to the next Stockholm Water Symposium. Following the Symposium's critique, the coalition would present its equity statement to the responsible executive governments and parliaments and ask them to tell their citizens whether they agree with the statement – and if not, why not. Because Canada has disproportionately so much of the world's fresh water supply, it would be the first government formally presented with the equity statement and the obligation to respond to Canadians.

The catch here is the North American Free Trade Agreement. Mel Clark, a former trade negotiator for the Canadian government, warns in an article for the Canadian Centre for Policy Alternatives:

> "Contrary to the reassurances of federal politicians, Canada's water resources are not protected under the terms of the North American Free Trade Agree-

ment (NAFTA). They were protected under the General Agreement on Tariffs and Trade (GATT), which gave Canada complete control over its water, but in signing NAFTA the federal government in effect yielded control of the country's water to the United States.

> "…Americans are given the same rights as Canadians to our water. NAFTA cancels our right to tax water exports to the U.S., overrides the constitutional right of the provinces to control the water within their boundaries, and accords U.S. corporations the right to sue the federal government if it – or a province – fails to respect the terms of NAFTA. Nowhere in NAFTA is there any wording that gives Ottawa or the provinces the right to limit or embargo water exports to the U.S.… The only way to prevent this loss of our water is by terminating NAFTA (and the FTA) and returning to trade with the Americans under the GATT. The suggestion by the Council of Canadians and other critics that the terms of NAFTA and the FTA could simply be renegotiated to restore the protection of our water simply won't work…" [4]

It is possible to apply the structure of the equity statement to a proposal that Canada unilaterally cancel the offending provisions of the NAFTA, but Americans wouldn't be impressed by Canadians saying, after signing the Agreement, "Wait a minute; we were stupid. We want to change it." Holding the Canadian federal government to account means citizens asking the Prime Minister to confirm publicly, to Canadians, the legal status of Canada's rights over its water. But it also means asking the Prime Minister to show us what a diligent public equity statement for accepting the NAFTA with respect to protection of water, Medicare, education, labour and environmental protection core policy in Canada, would have shown, at the time the then executive government handed over Canada's sovereign rights. In the case of water, the Prime Minister can obviously be asked to state what the executive government intends to do, if anything, to ensure Canadian control over Canadian water. Were the executive government to try to duck this answering by saying, "That was a previous government," its obligation to account to us is still there – for what the current executive intended for the NAFTA once it took office, and what it now plans to do.

To resolve the water issue for Canada, there must be one or more proposals put forward by someone. Every major proposal is subject to public equity statement explanation so that citizens can grasp what is happening and who intends what, and why.

If public interest organizations repeatedly produce credible public equity statements for authorities' apparent intentions, citizens will come to understand their usefulness for assessing fairness trade-offs. We can then expect authorities to be forced to follow suit, issuing what they think the equity statements should be. This progression is no different from the norm in corporate financial reporting practice over the past century: if one major corporation improves its financial accountability reporting, others soon follow. The difference is that equity statements are more useful to citizens, being before-the-fact reports. We can then expect citizens to be better informed in commending, altering or halting what authorities propose.

But citizen response is key. Following an equity statement round, citizens will be better informed, but they have to act. Otherwise the authorities simply carry on with their intentions. We therefore have to tell our respective elected representatives what we expect of them.

Exacting Answering for Performance Standards and Results

Having authorities tell us their performance standards clarifies what they intend to achieve, for whom. It tells us the specific responsibilities they accept, whose needs they are honouring and to what extent, and what they agree to be accountable for. Asking people to tell us their own performance standards is central to holding to account.

A very simple household example will illustrate:

> In the mid-1980s I bought a small second-hand 1930s upholstered chair that needed the legs refinished. I asked the store owner if he could have his refinishing shop do it. When his shop delivered it, I found that part of the upholstery hadn't been tacked back on the chair and there was a large white chalk-like smudge on the back. I called the owner, whom I knew, described generally the look of the chair and said, "All I ask is that you drop in next time you're making a delivery in the neighbourhood, stand in my living room, look at the chair and tell me whether it meets your own standard." He said simply, "I don't need to. I'll pick it up tomorrow morning. I'm sorry this happened. I'm surprised."

In the cases cited earlier of contaminated blood, ferry drownings, the Westray mine, the court martial and the conduct of senior military officers and the federal job-creation grants, we find that the authorities' performance standards for ensuring safety and fairness weren't visible to the public. This meant that the standards could be inadequate or non-existent – and they were.

After authorities act, we must require them to tell us the outcomes of their actions, as they see them, and how they applied the learning reasonably to be gained from what they did or authorized others to do. Again we validate the reporting to ensure that it isn't self-serving. The answering after the fact tells us what needs to be encouraged, altered or stopped in authorities' future performance, and what confidence to place in authorities for the future. Exacting and validating answering before and after the fact tells us whether to change the people constituting the authorities, but more important is installing the performance and answering rules that all authorities must comply with.

Changing Our Relationship With Elected Representatives

Citizens may find it daunting to call up their elected representatives, sit down with them and hand them expectations, however reasonable, especially if the elected representative is a minister of the Crown. But those who grasp the implications of the missing public answering for safety, health, social justice, education, environmental protection and other major responsibilities of authorities and who feel that we must now have adequate public answering, can at least do something that doesn't take much effort.

Citizens can individually write to their elected representatives at each level of government and ask them a few simple questions along the following lines:

1. Do you believe that authorities such as ministers, municipal councillors and governing bodies of corporations, institutions and other organizations should account to the public for the discharge of their statutory and commonsense responsibilities, both for what they intend and why, and the results and learning from their decisions?

2. Do you believe that the reporting by these people should meet standards for fair and complete public answering that citizens can reasonably expect to see met, so that citizens are adequately informed to assess the authority's performance?

3. Would you please tell me whether the current law in your (council's or legislature's) jurisdiction requires public answering by major types of authorities for their performance, and sets standards for explaining authorities' intentions before the fact that citizens can reasonably expect to see met?

4. To the extent that a solid review were to show that legislation for your jurisdiction does not require fair and complete public answering by authorities, are you prepared to put forward a (council motion or legislative Bill) that would install in the law reasonable basic answering standards, with provision for validation of the answering?

5. If you would not launch this initiative yourself, would you please tell me why? And, if you would not, would you vote for a set of standards proposed by another legislator, regardless of political party, that would constitute public answering standards that citizens have the right to see met?

This would be a fair letter. Today it is an elected representative's duty to know what adequate public answering means and why it is important. If the elected representative does understand, he or she can tell the constituent what that understanding is. The letter should close with the request that the elected representative respond with specific answers to each of the questions asked. Chapter 5 proposed six basic answering standards to be legislated. But more effective than simply attaching these to a letter would be each citizen's own view of what the basic standards should be.

What happens if no one responds, or responds with fog? Since most elected representatives haven't thought very much about working to improve public answering, they may not want to respond to the request letter. Yet they will realize that the request is a fair one. So each person writing a letter may have to telephone or drop a note to their elected representative, reminding them to answer. The point is that citizens have the right to answers from their elected representatives to fair questions, and shouldn't allow deference to inhibit their insistence for adequate answers.

Citizens are concerned about many issues. They can be local property development proposals, school or hospital closings, grotesque escalation of provincial gaming revenues,[5] workplace safety, dismantlement of universal Medicare and public schooling, proportional representation in voting, lethal tobacco effects, and national sovereign power sell-outs. For each perceived intention, citizens can ask their elected representatives to produce equity statements or their equivalent for what the authorities intend, however roughly drafted. The motto is, "What you know, you can report."

Predictable Objections to the Answering Obligation

Opposition in principle. Because they don't want to share power, people in authority will decree that the existing political processes and regulations applied to them suffice, and that these processes generally sort things out. Academics will call basic answering standards "too simplistic," asserting that you do indeed have to be a carpenter to tell if a door jamb is crooked. Darwin scholar Richard Dawkins pointed out that the likely reason that academics and scientists didn't accept Darwin's theory at the time was that it was too simple.[6] Yet the tenured scouts for society resist even agreeing on the meaning of accountability. For their part, large activist organizations may say that holding to account is naive because authorities will simply lie if made to explain their intentions and reasoning and their performance standards and results. But if answering before the fact had been adequate, we likely wouldn't have had the blood, water and coal mine deaths and the wrecked lives for others that followed.

There is a difference between, on the one hand, the Sierra Club, Greenpeace, Suzuki Foundation, Council of Canadians, Centre for Public Policy Analysis or a Public Citizen and, on the other, a group of inner city parents trying to stop a school closure. It is the power of the large public interest organizations to convince citizens of what they ought to conclude about government and corporate directing minds who refuse to answer when that obligation is axiomatic. If made to answer in an age when commitment to "account-ability" appears in every second statement by authorities, arrogant and deceitful authorities would shoot themselves in the foot.

Straight dodges. The fairness argument – that the answering requirement is simply the unassailable obligation to explain, and doesn't tell people what to do in their jobs – won't be debated head-on. Instead, those in authority who don't want to answer to the public will simply use the decree approach.

Politicians will say that because holding to account isn't the way government and society work, it's out of step with reality. Moreover, it isn't the Canadian way, which is to trust those in authority. It's a recipe for disrespect and anarchy rather than compliance with authority and "due process." Anyone who wants standards for public answering is seeking to de-stabilize governments and the business community – worse, a Robespierre. Yet accountability is perhaps the simplest regulator in the public interest.

Politicians will say that authorities having to draft equity statements for their intentions for public challenge would simply be mini-referendums flooding the country. Yet equity statements are succinct briefing documents for legislators and citizens that show fairness trade-offs.

Politicians, sensing the self-regulating effect on themselves of required public answering, will say that it will make life dull and unimaginative, meaning that answering before the fact and allowing challenge would rob them of trumpeting a fait accompli that hasn't been put to citizens for assessment – like the NAFTA.

Politicians will say that in any case the need for adequate public answering is a political matter properly left to the political debate processes of legislative assemblies. Yet, as we have seen, government majorities in legislatures combined with opposition ineptness can kill off the answering obligation. The response to this is to ask them if they disagree with George Washington's observation on citizens having "a right understanding of matters."

Elected representatives as executive governments, and corporate boards as directing minds will chorus that accountability means openness and transparency, which they are already committed to producing for their organizations. Regardless how "open" and "transparent" these organizations claim to be, those terms don't mean answering for responsibilities.

Senior civil servants will say that public answering from them isn't necessary because they are dedicated individuals working constantly in the public interest and why wouldn't everyone accept that? The evidence says that we simply don't know their motivation, and that no one can be given blind trust.

Members of governing bodies will say that good people won't want to become board members if they must publicly account for their intentions and control performance, to the extent proposed in these chapters. The real issue is that people who don't want to account should not be allowed to be board members. And if someone claims that we need to raise elected representatives' salaries to attract good candidates (when perceived impotence and frustration in the legislature may be the key barriers), their public answering obligation had better be a condition of getting the pay and pension.

As well, people in authority will say that answering to standards will take up so much time that they won't be able to do their jobs properly – conveniently ignoring that they have to be well-informed to do their jobs properly, and what they know they can report. In fact, the better they report the greater the public trust they will have.

But one concern of ministers and civil servants is totally valid. If they account in good faith, their answering mustn't be used simply for political partisanship purposes, to blame. In the HRDC case the ministers' answering was deceptive, bringing hostility from the Opposition. But if answering given in good faith is used unfairly, there won't be further answering.

Answering costs too much. The human and financial costs of dealing with sub-standard conduct leading to harm are largely costs from the *lack* of public answering before the fact.

The cost of reporting fairness reasoning, performance standards, compliance and results will certainly be argued by those not wanting to answer to a standard. The fallacy is that the cost is already there: it's not a significant marginal cost. The cost that we readily accept is the cost of people we place in authority obtaining the information they need to do their jobs properly. Recall the CCAF-FCVI's fourth characteristic for effective governance, that governing bodies will "understand what constitutes reasonable information for good governance and obtain it." If accountable authorities – governing bodies and executive governments – are informing themselves to a reasonable standard, what they need to report to us is something they should already know for their jobs.

One of the reasons people in authority don't want to account is that they may not be as well informed for their duties as they should be. The obligation of governing body members to manage the information they need to be well informed and to be able to account publicly and adequately is largely missing in today's organizations. It not just that governing bodies are encouraged to leave key decision-making and control to the chief executive officer. It is also because money that should be spent on information has been spent on information technology rather than on creating and maintaining the processes that inform. [7]

Responding to access-to-information requests will also be cited as an answering burden. But giving out information only when coerced by law, and only to those who know specifically what to ask for, isn't public answering. Most access-to-information requests stem from inadequate answering in the first place, which led to low trust in the accountable institutions, which in turn led to the access claims to know what's going on. Good answering would reduce costs of access and the policing of compliance with access to information laws.

Moreover, organizations' costs of complying with access requests increase with the time and effort staff spend trying to defeat the intent of the access laws. An example for Canadians was access to information attempts regarding the conduct of the military after the Somalia killings. Defence personnel had deliberately and significantly altered information legitimately asked for by a journalist.

Then there is the issue of the combined total cost of external examiners of various kinds as the checking regime: auditors and inspectors general, information and privacy commissioners, ombudsmen, coroners, inquiry commissioners and other examiners in the public sector. These people stand outside the accountability relationship between the accountable and those legitimately holding to account. Adequate answering by authorities for their intentions and performance would likely cut the cost of these examinations by half. The work the federal Information Commissioner was forced to do in the Somalia inquiry is a case in point.

And if government departments and agencies accounted properly, auditors general, likely for the same or less cost as their direct performance audits, could cover a greater range of government responsibilities through attestation auditing. The problem is that governments don't report their performance against agreed standards, and the legislatures haven't been making them because legislators have thus far been free to leave accountability reporting to auditors general. So auditors general, having no power to force adequate answering from governments, try to fill in by doing the public reporting that governments should be giving.

To be sure, audit costs are necessary to validate important accountability reporting by authorities. This is a desirable expenditure. It's no different from the annual external audit of the financial reporting of corporations. We require it under the precautionary principle, regardless whether the company has a long track record of good reporting. Validation costs will drop to a minimum as norms of answering quality get installed, directing minds start to report more usefully, and public stigma attaches to authorities who refuse to answer to a standard.

The cost of developing standards for public answering through well-focused task groups as suggested here is minimal when compared to the money governments throw away with impunity. If the standards-drafting job is given to bureaucrats and academics, they will be funded either for quick and dirty appearances work or for unending study. Nor have they experience in writing answering standards for authorities that achieve what *citizens* need. For their part, accountants would tend to fit public answering standards into their own conventions of "relevance" and "timeliness" and the like, which don't address *what* should be reported to citizens. Regular reporting would likely be modelled on the conventions for corporate financial reporting.

Public answering standards must be developed by citizens, using a clean sheet of paper and drafting the standards through coalitions. We have no body of expertise – we have to develop it – but developing the capability is quite feasible.

"We Have Met the Enemy, And He Is Us"

If the lack of public answering for responsibilities before and after the fact can be causally linked to harm, the only people who can force authorities to answer adequately are citizens – us. Chapter 2 suggested reasons why we haven't installed adequate public answering. They include the erosion of standards in society, lack of understanding of the purpose of answering, undue deference to authorities (which includes blind faith) and citizen apathy (which means increasing tolerance of deception).

The public cases of lethally-contaminated blood, Somalia and Westray haven't done the trick in creating public answering obligations for authorities. Walkerton's contaminated water can be the Canadian turning point in holding to account. In Walkerton it wasn't public crucifixion of a water system manager, like the captain of the *Exxon Valdez*: the focus moved quickly past those running the water supply to the executive government of Ontario. And it wasn't lawyers looking for deep pockets. But it remains to be seen how much citizens will take, before saying "enough is enough" and actually holding to account. Other countries will have their own turning-point series of harmful events. It's a truism that no major change in organizations occurs until some powerful person or group is hurting badly enough. The question is the hurt threshold of citizens as a whole.

The aim of holding to account is to make visible the real intentions and performance standards of directing minds, so we can predict them better and know what action to take as citizens. We may have to take no action, but the precautionary principle says that we should have the evidence to support that decision. Here we have looked at only a few examples of harm associated with failure to answer. Other examples need to be examined for their accountability lessons. These range from wrongful convictions that point to public answering standards needed for police, prosecution and judges, to dangerous government secret service activities affecting all citizens, to inadequate environmental protection laws that lack answering requirements.

To lessen the chances of us remaining the enemy, action for installing adequate public answering can start at any of three levels:

Minimum individual action. People who don't wish to be activists can still help bring about greater fairness. Given a statement by a coalition of public interest organizations of why standards for adequate public answering by authorities are important, they can simply sign their agreement to a question put to them: "Should basic standards of public answering be installed in the law and met by all decision-makers in authority?"

Stronger individual action. Accountability isn't just for safety and health. People in their daily lives being served by businesses and governments may think a particular service is sub-standard yet within the control of a particular service unit. They should find and ask the manager to state the organization's own performance standards and whether the manager thinks they are living up to them. An indifferent or self-satisfied response is an indicator that the real client isn't the citizen. The idea is not to leave the premises before getting an answer to the questions or the name and address of the person who should answer. Then ask that person what his or her own performance standard is for the service.

Those who want adequate answering the norm for governments, corporations and other institutions can write to their elected representatives and election candidates and ask them their intentions for it. The questions set out earlier in this chapter can be used for this. It means following up to get the elected representative's answer, and giving a copy of it to an appropriate public interest organization if the response doesn't show commitment to answering standards. In addition, citizens can cite both their expectations letter to their elected representative and the response they got in a letter to the editor. Some of these letters will be printed.

Action by a group. We have local concerns and broader concerns. A local example would be a proposal for a casino, or Toronto shipping its garbage to abandoned mine shafts in northern Ontario. Any community group can ask the responsible elected representatives to produce an equity statement for the proposal for public challenge, so that community groups can see whether important trade-offs are being considered by those giving the approvals. To repeat, if no statement is forthcoming, community groups can draft their own equity statement and ask the elected representatives whether it fairly presents the trade-offs. Given that the community's equity statement is reasonable and points to either yes or no, the elected representatives' subsequent votes on the issue have to be justified. This approach holds for issues at all levels of government, and for intentions of corporations that affect the public in important ways.

It is reasonable to demand of elected representatives that they produce equity statements for public challenge of their intentions before they vote. For example, if city school trustees seem to act as agents of the provincial executive government rather than public servants acting on parents' behalf in school-closing intentions of the government, they can legitimately be asked not to vote until they have produced a challenged equity statement for their closure intentions. The same holds for the provincial executive government's directives to school boards of "Close five schools or no funds," when the demographics show that the schools will be needed within five years. The challenged reasoning for the intentions laid out in such a statement will show up whether demographics, costs and benefits that stare the decision-makers in the face support the intentions. It will show, if it is the case, school board failure to properly challenge the government and mere ideology and control zeal as the force behind the executive government's intention.

If the school board and government refuse to produce equity statements or their equivalent for their intentions, parents' groups can produce them themselves and publicly demand that the authorities tell the public what's wrong with the parents' statements of who gains and who loses, and how.

If the authorities still refuse to answer adequately for their intentions before voting, parents could try the approach of legal action under the doctrine of legitimate expectation. In other words, since the government's duty to provide adequate schooling is established major policy, the authorities' refusal to answer adequately means that the process intent of appropriate hearings and consultation legitimately expected for overturning agreed policy hasn't been carried out. While this is a shift from holding to account to action through the courts, the issue in the claim is based in accountability.

Last-Resort Strategy in Holding to Account: Citizen Audit

When the actions or inaction of an authority cause us major concern, common sense will tell us who has what responsibilities. Those responsibilities will suggest the public answering that the authority should be giving for its intentions, performance standards and results. For every important responsibility there is accountability. Since the actual public answering by an authority is there for all to see, we can decide whether it's adequate to tell us what's going on, and we can validate it. If the authority's answering doesn't tell us what's going on, the precautionary principle tells us to try to see for ourselves what the authority is doing or not doing, and why. We will often find that the usual professional or regulator audits being done are not addressing what we are concerned about. The available evidence will tell us what the authority's apparent performance is for its responsibilities and what its current answering is. This will suggest the public answering we need from the authority.

We can call this approach citizen audit. It is a systematic way of publicly identifying the responsibilities of an authority's directing minds, their apparent performance and the adequacy of their public reporting, so as to force better public answering from them. Citizen audit is based on the proposition that citizens can learn and assess enough about an authority's performance and answering to support a public invitation to its directing minds to produce adequate answering. It can be used for any body called an authority, whether it's an agency of government, a corporate board or an institution or organization of any kind. Citizen audit would be more systematic and in-depth than journalists' inquiries because journalists have only limited time to cover any one issue and they don't use an audit structure. But the work of journalists is critical to citizen audit information-gathering.

Citizen audit uses the standard concept of audit, which is the assessment of reporting or observed performance against a standard or criterion and the reporting of the assessment to someone.

Professional audit produces an opinion at a professional level of rigour – for example, whether financial statements are fair and complete. The idea is that people can rely on the validity of the audit opinion and act on it. For their audits, professional auditors have access to information not available to the public. Citizen audit is not at the level of rigour of professional audit. It assesses observed performance and answering based mainly on information available to the public. It is more like the preliminary review stage in a professional audit that identifies risk areas that should be examined in the audit. It is also similar to a parliamentary committee's work assessing a ministry's performance. It requires only common sense and fairness, but it must close the accountability escape hatches.

The purpose of citizen audit is to produce enough evidence about an authority's responsibilities to show what its governing body should be reporting fully and fairly to the public about those responsibilities. If critics say that audit can only be done by professional auditors, it is saying that citizens are not entitled to a right understanding of matters. The purpose is not to authoritatively "find" against an authority that is the subject of the audit, as professional performance audit or a court would. There is no intent of malice in a citizen audit, but there is no deference or euphemism either.

If an authority doesn't think the citizen audit's assessment has got it right, it will usually be because the authority hasn't adequately accounted for its responsibilities. What the authority does report is of course there for all to see. But failure to answer forces citizens to draw inferences from the evidence available. Citizen audit simply suggests a picture that has to be confirmed. If the available evidence used for citizen audit is incomplete, the authorities need only account – validly – to set the picture straight. With no answering from authorities, and no audit, we will never get the real picture of what they are deciding in their offices and boardrooms. It is obviously insupportable for authorities to claim that the only allowable audit on the planet is narrow-scope professional audit. Sensible citizens can do citizen audits, just as sensible citizens can serve on juries. If citizen audits appear damning, rigorous audit evidence may show a worse picture.

Citizen audit reports can show our ultimate regulating bodies – the legislatures – what any authority's public answering should be. And if the governing political party in the legislature likes things the way they are, citizen audit can then focus on them and their ministers.

The main steps of citizen audit are:
1. When concern about a responsibility area arises, we determine who is reasonably responsible for what, in the public interest
2. We see what the public answering is from the responsible authorities, to assess how much we have to find out about the authorities performance
3. We keep a running inventory of press clippings, statements on radio and TV and articles in magazines and journals on the responsibilities. When we put these together, we will likely see pattern emerging that may not be discernible from single news items taken one at a time
4. We connect with people who can supply valid letters, minutes, transcripts and documents shedding light on who is doing what or failing to do what
5. From the information we have, and from inside information made available that would withstand challenge, we set out publicly:
   • who we think has what reasonable responsibilities
   • the apparent performance of those with the responsibilities
   • who should answer publicly, and for what
   • how the answering should be validated.

Appendix 2 is an example of a citizen audit report by the Alliance for Public Accountability, condensed from the full audit report which was more rigorous than most such audits would be. It deals with the responsibilities and public accountabilities of two prominent institutions, the University of Toronto and its research hospital, the Hospital for Sick Children, in the Apotex affair. This is the well-known case (but only one of many such cases) of a drug company intimidating a research doctor of stature who produced research evidence on one of the company's drugs that the company didn't want disclosed.

The Appendix shows the basic approach in citizen audit. With practice, the audit should normally be reportable in about 20 pages or less, with a back-up briefing binder to support the report. The logical groups to do citizen audits are issue-based public interest organizations and activist groups, large labour organizations or groups specifically formed to bring about adequate public answering for particular responsibilities. Once an organization has done a citizen audit or two, it can help "train the trainers."

Public interest organizations can use citizen audits to demand from authorities the public answering that, when validated, helps to disclose authorities' intentions. For their part, unions can do the same for authorities' assertions of their performance standards and their actual performance for workplace safety, health care and equity. In other words, when there is no answering by authorities, unions and others can become direct auditors of performance, using the citizen audit approach. They would report their audits to the public. They have an advantage in that their access to information will likely be greater than an ad hoc citizen group formed to try to cope with a concern.

To sum up, we must now apply the precautionary principle to all major responsibilities of authorities. Getting adequate answering from authorities before the fact is necessary if we want to prevent harm. And if authorities won't answer, we must relentlessly and publicly lay out their responsibilities, apparent performance and answering inadequacies through means such as citizen audits, until they are hurting so much that they decide to account to a standard, or are made to by legislators feeling the heat.

Whistleblowing as Last-Resort Public Reporting

The issue. Whistleblowers as employees of conscience hold to account as citizen audits do, only the risk of being alone is enormous. In sounding an alarm, the whistleblower says, "This is what's going on; I invite the right people to confirm it." Whistleblowing happens when employees acting in the public interest think reasonable performance standards aren't being met, won't be met, and harm (or more harm) will come of it. Whistleblowing means reporting misconduct, violation of laws, rules or regulations, gross mismanagement, gross waste of funds, abuse of authority, or acts that are a substantial and specific danger to public health and safety.[8] All of these relate to duties that are subject to the answering obligation. But included in wrongful acts or omissions must be failure to uphold the precautionary principle in matters of public health and safety.

Whistleblowers give the answering that the authorities should have given but refused to give, or wouldn't give honestly. The conditions giving rise to whistleblowing are many, but a common denominator is inadequate answering requirements, which in turn stem from citizens not demanding them.

Whistleblowers report publicly in the only way they see open to them to prevent harm from happening, recurring or expanding. But they know they will be punished for their actions by their organizations and be rewarded by no one, and they know that the general public won't protect them even when they have acted clearly in the public's interest. A recent article gives a riveting summary of what the whistleblower faces:

They dare to do what most of us fear – to speak out in the face of swift and life-altering retribution. For most people, going public is a last resort. Their motivation is rarely self-aggrandizement or personal gain, but the public good.

In return, they often lose their jobs, their savings and sometimes their families. They can become the targets of death threats. They can be shunned by co-workers, or have their reputations vilified. They can sink into depression, even contemplate suicide. They are labelled as disgruntled or obsessive, often in an effort to undermine their credibility and make them more vulnerable to attack. And, when the media's attention is eventually consumed by other matters, they often are left to endure all of this alone.[9]

Since whistleblowers perform basically the same public service as auditors and other external examiners – giving citizens a heads-up – the reasons why the public leaves whistleblowers to their fates need to be explained. Citizens must see how their failure to protect whistleblowers is a signal to authorities to carry on with arrogance and misconduct. The lack of citizen support may reflect cultural psychological baggage attached to the words "informant" and "complainant," even when the lives or health at stake can be that of the loved ones of those who wouldn't stand up in defence of whistleblowers. Or perhaps it's a broader Kitty Genovese syndrome.[10] There is more to it than that, but it will take research to explain it. Yet academics seem to avoid this obvious area of research. Perhaps it is because no authority would fund it – a citizenry on the side of whistleblowers would be a palpable hindrance to people in authority, and might get to the state of encouraging whistle-blowing for authorities flouting the precautionary principle.

Citizens must decide whether they will accept the results of their failure to help whistle blowers, with the results only getting worse as standards of decency and fairness fall, precisely because citizens failed to protect in law those who take high risk to try to protect the public.

Perhaps the leading government in whistleblower protection is the United States federal government. Congress passed its *Whistleblower Protection Act* in 1989 to protect citizens who report misconduct. The American legislation implies that their federal legislators are serious about protecting whistleblowers. But it is not clear whether legislative intent means actual support for whistleblowers in their organizations. In a 1992 report on the *Whistleblower Protection Act*, the United States General Accounting Office observed:

> Fear of reprisal for reporting misconduct continues to be a concern for many federal employees. Further, many employees did not know whether their agencies would support whistleblowers and most had minimal knowledge about their right to protection from reprisal.[11]

An American judge in a 1993 whistleblower suit against the General Electric Company observed, "This is not the first time where this court has noted antagonism of the Justice Department to a whistle-blower."[12] There is no evidence that the Canadian federal government departments would act differently.

The Canadian federal Liberal Party had included whistleblower protection legislation as a campaign promise in the 1993 election:

> Public servants who "blow the whistle" on illegal or unethical behaviour should be protected. A Liberal government will introduce whistleblowing legislation in the first session of a new Parliament[13]

But this was not in the Speech From the Throne for the ensuing Parliament. Both provincial and federal governments have inserted protection clauses here and there in their policies and regulations, but to date there has been no substantial action by the federal government.

It took a Canadian Senator, Noël Kinsella, to introduce a private member's Bill for whistleblower protection in the Senate in December 1999. As at August 2001 the Bill was at third reading stage. The Bill illustrates the problem in getting effective legislation.

It provides for one of the federal Public Service Commissioners to be designated the Public Interest Commissioner, who would receive allegations by civil servants and act. The Commissioner would be appointed by ministers, not by Parliament, and would not be someone from outside the government's influence ambit, screened by an all-party parliamentary committee. This aside, immediately the term "allegation" in the Bill becomes important because of the psychological baggage attaching to the word. It can mean not only the simple act of alleging something, in the sense of asserting something , but also "an assertion unsupported and by implication regarded as unsupportable." (Webster's dictionary).

In the Bill, the scope of complaints to the Commissioner by an employee is confined to wrongful acts or omissions (defined much as the American law describes them) by "another person working for the Public Service or in the Public Service workplace." This does not suggest that a set of senior officials or a contractor for government would necessarily be a "person" coming under the provisions of the Bill. For example, a set of senior officials overruling scientists' warnings given under the precautionary principle would likely be called "due process in management" rather than a "person" under the legislation.

The commissioner need not prepare a report if he or she thinks the employee "ought to first exhaust review procedures otherwise available," or if the commissioner thinks an appropriate procedure lies in another Act.

"Exhaust review procedures otherwise available" typifies a cancer in Canadian law. If a person in an organization feels unjustly treated, he or she is expected to go back up the line to get redress. This means appealing to the various officials at different levels who themselves had the management control responsibility to prevent what happened. In Canadian law, the deck is always stacked against someone who complains against power. This is one reason why the federal executive government refused to appoint an independent inspector general for the military, a central recommendation of the Somalia Inquiry Commission. An organizational ombudsman of some kind cannot bring independent pressure to bear both to protect the whistleblower and fix the problem.

The Kinsella Bill has the Commissioner laying his or her report on the responsible minister's doorstep, with no Commissioner power to exact adequate response by the responsible top civil servants and minister (with the help of the Auditor General if necessary). The Bill tells ministers, on receipt of the Commissioner's report, to "consider the matter and respond to the Commissioner," stating what action they will take – or that they intend no action. It doesn't call for public accountings by the responsible officials of what they actually did, following the Commissioner's report to them, and what public assurance they give about preventing wrongful acts or omissions in the future. The needed response would be the ministers' and senior civil servants' explanation of the extent to which they discharged their commonsense duties in the issue – not just a lulling statement.

As to reprisals against employees (termed disciplinary action), the Bill lists the prohibitions and provides a fine of up to $10,000, although not making clear that this must be paid personally and not automatically reimbursed out of the public purse. The Bill doesn't require the minister to have a management control system specifically to prevent harassment or other actions, which the Auditor General could then assess for Parliament.

Thus the assigned Public Service Commissioner may achieve nothing more than bring something to the attention of the minister. The Commissioner's own reporting, through the Public Service Commission's annual report to Parliament, would not be accountability reporting. The Bill asks only that the Commissioner report on his or her activity, not achievement.

The Bill appears to do the minimum, perhaps to increase its chances of being passed in both Senate and House of Commons.

Whistleblowers do have obligations if they are to avoid the "15 minutes of fame" charge so often laid against them. The first to try to test the hypothesis that if he or she knew the reasoning of those at the higher levels, the whistle needn't be blown. But there are obvious limits to what subordinates can be expected to know, or to find out.

Intelligent senior management will account credibly to questioning by subordinates whose technical and professional knowledge leads them to raise an alert. Senior management's answering may explain the actions taken (or the lack) satisfactorily, in which case the organization is saved needless public embarrassment. But, as in the case of the *Challenger* space shuttle, subordinates, in concluding on the extent of a problem, will usually have better technical evidence to support a concern than will their superiors. (The *Challenger* wasn't a whistleblower case as such, because the engineers alarmed at the intention to launch didn't have the time before lift-off to speak out to save the crew's lives.)

In accounting to their subordinates for their actions or inaction, superiors may resolve issues that could otherwise result in whistleblowing. But if the rationale for a decision wouldn't stand the light of day inside the organization, it won't likely be credible outside, once known. If senior management isn't trusted because it arrogantly refuses to account properly to subordinates, it will simply bring on whistleblowing. The problem is expecting senior management to answer fairly to subordinates when the performance at issue is the responsibility of the superiors and the superiors believe that they don't have to account to subordinates.

This is where unions come in, since they have the clout to require senior officials to account to employees for their standards in matters of fairness and safety. The union's actions will tell its members whether or not the union officials are simply an extension of the human resources department of the organization.

We create the trauma for employees of conscience because we haven't required validated public answering from authorities. This would show the extent to which reasonable performance standards are being met for safety (as in the blood, Westray and *Herald of Free Enterprise* cases) or value for money (as in the HRDC example) which would tip us off to risk. Writing and exhorting on ethics and drafting codes of all kinds won't suffice. The choice is to accept the wages of citizen indifference to whistleblowers or to install effective whistleblower protection. Good legislation, diligently administered by people who answer for that diligence, is by far the less costly answer – whether we are talking about saving lives, protecting justice and the public purse, or simply common decency to people who go beyond the call of duty in the public interest.

Endnotes

1 Canadians are well aware of the clout of seniors in such issues as pensions. In the United States, for example, the Republicans' "Contract for America" for 1995 was slated to cut $15 billion of federal nutritional programs for schoolchildren but not $500 million for seniors' food programs. On the Democrat side, all programs for seniors escaped cuts while almost every other spending program was sliced.("Senior Power Rides Again," *Newsweek*, 20 February 1995, p.31)

2 An Ipsos-Reid/Globe and Mail/CTV poll showed that 63% of Canadians would be less likely to buy a food product that is genetically-modified or contains genetically modified ingredi-

ents. "It's clear that Canadians want to be able to choose," said the polling firm's spokesman. (*Globe and Mail*, 30 August 2001, p.A1)

[3] Maude Barlow, op. cit.

[4] Mel Clark, "Control of Canada's Water Yielded to the U.S. by NAFTA," Canadian Centre for Policy Alternatives *Monitor*, Ottawa, July 2000

[5] By 2001, Canadian provincial gaming revenues were $5.5 billions in total – equal to alcohol and tobacco combined and three times more than this revenue eight years earlier. (CBC Radio 30 August 2001)

[6] Eleanor Wachtel interview with Richard Dawkins, CBC radio 27 July 1997

[7] Burk and McCandless, op. cit.

[8] Since the U.S. has moved to protect whistleblowers with legislation, and Canada has no effective legislation, we use here the definition of whistleblowing of the United States General Accounting Office, as set out in its November 1993 report to the U.S. House of Representatives on its survey of whistleblowers' views of the federal agency designed to protect them, the Office of Special Counsel.

[9] Andrew Mitrovika, "Blow the Whistle on Government Secrecy," *Globe and Mail*, 24 May 2001, p.A15

[10] Kitty Genovese was the New York woman who was repeatedly attacked and stabbed to death under the windows of an apartment building. No one responded to her screams and called the police.

[11] GAO, Washington, Fact Sheet 249141, July 1992

[12] Amal Kumar Naj, "Whistle-Blower in GE Case Gets Record Award," New York, *Wall Street Journal*, 8 December 1992.

[13] "The Liberal Approach to the Public Service", 9 September 1993, quoted in "Lifting the Silence," *Dialogue With Parliament 1994*, Ottawa, 1994, The Professional Institute of the Public Service of Canada, p.8

CHAPTER 15

Summary

- Apply the precautionary principle
- Identify the directing minds, exact their intentions and reasoning and validate what they say
- Know their performance standards and their performance
- Don't supplicate – state reasonable expectations instead
- Be fair in holding to account, and do something sensible with accountings given in good faith
- But be relentless: "No public answering, no decision taken."

Gaining Control

This book cites only a few instances of harm, injustice and risk that we needlessly tolerate if we don't ask for preventive answering from authorities. The less answering we ask for, the more authorities can become arrogant. Those in power who argue against standards for public answering are counting on our deference and apathy. We need only to look at the evidence to decide whether authorities should account to a standard. If they should, each of us has a civic duty to do something, however limited, to help produce that public answering.

Have we the evidence to say that legal systems are legal justice systems, or that transnational corporations' directing minds won't cause harm on the planet? Do we assume that executive government decisions to under-staff our health care institutions and poorly resource home care will somehow force efficiency? Do we assume as never-ending the work of the tens of thousands of people in Canada who staff food banks, shelters and other support centres because we haven't held our elected representatives to account? And what is the responsibility of citizens to detect and block the advance of a politician showing signs of working against fairness in society? Why are these people removed only after the harm is done? Is it too much to expect authorities to answer well enough to allow citizens ultimate decision-making control?

We have two options: we can choose to blindly trust what authorities do that affects us, set no standards for their performance and answering and know we will be deceived whenever they choose to deceive us. Or we can choose to have our authorities answer to us, meeting the standards we set for them. We can't use our democratic processes to fix something durably without public answering.

If we want to keep Medicare, for example, we now not only have to tell our politicians what to do, but also make them answer to us for doing it. As it is, they keep telling us what can't be done in fairness and value for money because they aren't motivated to make it work properly as a government-run system. Our provincial ministers are too busy fighting the federal government for control of health and the tax money for it; the federal ministers want to keep up appearances of overall control of standards already lost; neither level of government is subject to useful rules for their public answering; and the civil servants involved portray more "technology" as the answer to decision-making in the public interest. What begins as the need to question motivation must lead also to questioning officials' competence – something we have never had to do in the past.

It is a matter of deciding priorities in fairness, and citizens have to do the deciding. We can't just vote for a political party and then simply hope. If we choose to control our authorities, we must hold them fairly but relentlessly to account. Control won't work without the public answering obligation, and important answering must be validated.

Those reasonably well off seem to be in balance among themselves, in a type of homeostasis. The large corporations seem happy enough, increasingly controlling our governments. National elected representatives pretend to be in control, citing a ritual activity that has already lost them their power over the executive government. Activists describe, re-describe and fight authorities with effort that periodically interrupts but doesn't stop the continuing power shift to those with the money. The political "right" is content to define itself as people who avoid dealing with social problems that have to be dealt with, and the "left," seeming not to know how to achieve power arrangements to bring about what it wants as outcomes for people, contents itself with fighting or going with the flow. No one proposes to all citizens how we do our civic duty by facing the truth of what's going on, deciding what needs to be protected, and figuring out a way to control authorities.

Holding to account does change the relationship between citizens and authorities. By holding to account and doing something sensible with the answering, we can control authorities instead of being controlled by them. If we think we're being abused by those we placed or accepted in authority, it is because we gave someone a free hand.

Holding effectively to account is a good indicator of civic competence. It *is* possible to increase fairness on the planet. We *can* stop the slide toward every person for himself and all submitting to corporate marketing plans. But only if we cease being our own enemy and decide to know what authorities intend to do and why, before they act, and respond to it. We can know this if we exact public answering from them and put the force of law behind their obligation to answer fully and fairly.

With no strong keel politically, our civic incompetence has allowed Canada to resemble the Eaton's retail operation, to be picked up piecemeal or whole by the United States whose transnational corporation panzer divisions use trade agreement armour made in Canada. Some people may say what they are thinking: "But we really don't have to learn how to fix our country ourselves. All we have to do is join the United States. They'll do it for us." If that is the thinking, an even better idea is to sell Canada at auction to the highest bidder – lock, stock and barrel. A transnational consortium would get all our resources (think of water sales alone) and we would each get a cash payment.

We can alter future probabilities by vigorously applying the precautionary principle not only to safety, health and the environment, but to politics generally. This means that we must cancel public trust in institutions and make their directing minds earn it back through fair and complete answering for their intentions, performance standards and results. Instead of operating on blind faith and accepting the onus of proving whether authorities' intentions are suspect, we must fairly and relentlessly order authorities to account, so that we know whether their intentions are serving the public interest. If the large public interest organizations won't take on this task, concerned citizens must themselves form groups to publicly show the answering that should be given by authorities, and for what. The demand for answering for responsibilities can't be rejected, regardless whether statutory provisions for the answering exist.

As Ursula Franklin pointed out in a mid-1990s networking conference in Ottawa, the concern is not that our senior officials are well-intentioned but poorly informed; the worry is that they are well-informed and ill-intentioned. But to help protect authorities from themselves, we must require our elected representatives to legislate what we need as the simple obligation to account and the basic standards for the public answering. That way, people in authority can be made to answer to us properly. And if they lie, they can be sued.

We can start by putting authorities who don't answer into credibility receivership. We then use the processes described earlier: we form issue-based citizen committees and "audit" brigades to assess the present quality of answering by authorities. We then ask the authorities to meet basic answering standards and propose, in the drafting groups de-scribed earlier, what needs to be legislated for their answering. When a few authorities start to give reasonable answering, we will see how easily people who seek positions of authority take to the answering obligation. We don't supplicate. We simply state reason-able expectations for people's responsibilities and for their answering obligations. If some directing minds still hold out and won't answer, we work to remove them from office.

In proposing the needed answering from authorities, we can be guided in the drafting by the work of authoritative observers of how the institutions of our society are operating regionally, nationally and internationally – many of whom this book has cited. We can translate what their insight tells us into accountability assertions that we ask the authori-ties' directing minds to make. It can be done simply and systematically in each country, with international collaboration meetings based on common issues. We need to create a set of non-governmental organizations for public answering.

The total annual time of citizens in all countries taken up with lobbying elected rep-resentatives, sleuthing, going to meeting after meeting and government "public consulta-tions," writing briefs and articles, issuing pamphlets, holding vigils, rallying with placards – and all the other fighting activities in the public interest – would be an astonishing sum were it estimated. Worse, the fighting has to be repeated for every new and worrying apparent intention of authorities – even for the same intention, if it is withdrawn after its discovery and presented again in a different guise. Because of deception by authorities, there is already an army out there that could make the answering obligation work for us to reduce the deception and give us the information to make fair decisions in the public interest.

Just as citizens, and indeed shareholders, had lost public control of corporations by 1900, and Parliament had lost control of the public purse by the mid-1970s, citizens have given control to their elected representatives without giving them fundamental rules for their performance and answering. This was on the unwarranted assumption that elections constituted adequate accountability.

Those in power in the governing political parties created procedural rules for the legislative assemblies that keep power in the hands of the few and with no public answer-ing for the extent to which the assembly processes serve the public interest.

Our legislators pretend these things haven't happened. As an example, consider the important issue of spending authorization. In the Canadian federal Parliament, the Esti-mates – the documents placed before Parliament stating the executive's requests for de-partmental funding from the public purse – are automatically deemed passed after a certain date, regardless of debate on the achievement intentions. Rank and file elected representa-tives accept their impotence, even when they are new to Parliament.

While legislators were losing power to the executive governments, the executive was handing over its powers to the private sector – to corporations. It doesn't matter whether this stemmed from ideological beliefs, buck-passing desire to have someone else like the "market" resolve the issues that elected representatives should resolve, expectation of future positions with corporations, or as simple reciprocity for campaign contributions.

Today we need more than exhortations about "caring societies" and "safety nets." No political party has public answering as a central plank in its platform, let alone the assertion that they would install answering to a standard, were they in power. But, thus far at least, elected representatives still hold legislative power, regardless whose bidding they may do, and they can be held publicly to account for doing something about public answering obligations.

The encouraging thing about citizens holding to account is that those in power don't know how to block the requirement that they must publicly account. This is because they have never had experience with it. They have strategies for dealing with virtually all activists' arguments, but they have never had to publicly state, and have publicly validated, their reasoning for their intentions or their performance standards. This makes holding authorities to account an adventure, not a chore.

The central issue, returning to the work of Day and Klein cited in the Introduction, is that as soon as we say the word "democracy," simple logic leads to the answering obligation by authorities as a critical part of the democratic process. The fact that those in power don't want public accountability for themselves and have thus far quietly prevented the answering obligation from being debated by citizens is beside the point.

Provisions in international declarations of human rights have recently, and justly, been given much attention. We can safely say that authorities' failure to account qualifies as injustice. If that is the case, and because public answering is a politically neutral obligation, the obligation to answer can be added to the appropriate Articles in such declarations, along the following lines:

> When the intentions of civil or military authorities would significantly affect the moral and legal entitlement rights of people, those who would be affected have the right to full, fair and public explanation by the authorities for their intentions and reasoning, including independent validation of the answering, before those authorities act.

"Have the right to" doesn't mean that citizens will *get* the answers, since human rights declarations are not orders to executive governments. But what authorities know, they can report.

Including public answering in human rights helps in three ways. First, validated public answering formally tells citizens whether decision-makers in authority apply the precautionary principle, not only for safety and the environment but also for social justice. Secondly, it tells citizens before the fact what those in authority intend that affects them in important ways. This means that citizens then have the chance to judge the fairness of the intentions and how burdens would be shared so as to predict possible outcomes and to act to alter future probabilities. Thirdly, it tells citizens what happened as a result of the decisions taken, which affects trust in authorities for the future.

This will sound naive for dictatorships, but those regimes don't pay attention to human rights declarations in any case. While funding organizations like the World Bank have a challenge trying to prevent the funding for projects in dictatorships from being siphoned off, the demand that authorities publicly answer for their responsibilities is unassailable and the result is fully visible, unlike the funds trail. No public answering to a minimum standard, no funding.

As to deception in answering, it will be found out and publicly exposed. Unabashed lying by authorities that is claimed to be adequate answering can be held out like a large neon sign. This exposure can be expected to erode authorities' credibility with the public. When citizens suspect an authority in all its reporting, tangible public support can be expected to quietly evaporate.

The obligation to answer is axiomatic in any culture that teaches fairness. To the extent that nationhood is defined by innovation in the use of power, bringing about adequate public answering would be an innovative and productive use of power. Collapsing to "survival of the fittest" isn't. Good answering makes our lives easier because it helps reduce citizen time and emotional energy spent in forcing out information and in countering powerful self-serving lobbying. If people in authority refuse to answer for the discharge of their responsibilities, their motivation must be questioned.

But, to hold to account, we and our elected representatives and all those staffing our institutions need to have the same understanding of what accountability means. For example, "transparency" is not answering. It simply means, "We won't stand in your way if you already know where to look." Within organizations, reciprocal accountability between superiors and subordinates mustn't be twisted into a "new management technique" offered by consultants. And in the public sector, civil servants mustn't be allowed to twist "accountability" into "a new policy technique." Good public answering should cause opportunistic civil servants to self-destruct.

Yet the nagging question still remains: do citizens *want* the information that good public answering would give them? Many might not and simply say, "I'm concerned, but I've got too much on my plate in mortgages and educating my kids. And I don't understand accountability." Or, "I'll be frank. In today's world, it's everyone for themselves; accountability is not something I'm interested in." Or, "I admit it; I don't want to know what's really going on.. I prefer putting my faith in people in authority." Citizens who don't want to know that the emperor has no clothes can at least support those willing to work for greater fairness. When powerful forces produce needless inequity, people should at least *decide* what their effort is to be as citizens, even if it is to do nothing.

The standards and rules for public answering must be set by citizens. But politicians and civil servants should first be told to propose the standards and rules, so that we can see what each of these groups thinks is fair answering. That is important. Citizens' groups can then assess the proposed standards, raising them as necessary to meet citizens' reasonable expectations, and tell elected representatives in each jurisdiction:

> Adequate public answering can be achieved, to a demonstrable, reasonable standard. Please tell us what you intend to do yourself to install basic answering standards in the law in your jurisdiction, and how you ensure that you adequately inform yourself on major issues before you vote on the issues.

Those used to supplicating to authorities rather than stating reasonable expectations of them may find this action too aggressive. But the scores of examples of harm and unfairness that could have been prevented through answering before the fact should show us why the fair expectations approach is needed.

Citizens' groups must develop a ground swell of demand for adequate public answering, and here the Internet will help profoundly. We saw the great value of the Internet for alerting citizens and groups internationally to the MAI and for helping to make the implications of authorities' intentions clearer. The Internet provides the means for citizens to exchange perceptions and strategies. Those on the net will gravitate to those with the best ideas.[1] Secondly, if the question is put to an issue-oriented network, "For issue X, who should account to whom, for what responsibilities and intentions, and what should they be asked to report?" it will produce nifty suggestions.

Thirdly, we can use the Internet to learn from others effective methods of holding to account. This includes performance standards and alternatives to what is proposed, perhaps even backed by simulations and models if people are willing to offer them. Citizens' organizations can transfer the information to those who don't have access to the Internet. Fourthly, as those in authority increasingly "go on the net" and answer to people, they themselves will understand better the legitimacy of public answering and be more likely to improve their own accounting to those they affect by their intentions.

Keeping Citizen Control: Educating for the Longer Run

To achieve and maintain adequate public answering we must start teaching the young what it means, why we need it, and how to ensure adequate public answering for important responsibilities. Understanding the purpose of answering and what constitutes fair standards for the answering come first.

But one of the first teaching priorities in accountability should be community outreach programs specifically to help elected representatives, public interest organizations and other activists understand and apply public accountability principles. Community colleges are ideally suited to this, through seminars and workshops. Outreach programs can help those seeking to hold fairly to account learn how to go about it at a practical level, for the safety and social issues they're concerned about.

If government-funded community colleges don't want to touch public accountability as an evening course (despite the fact that it is politically neutral), activist organizations can get together and teach themselves how to hold to account effectively. Seminars on holding to account make sense because opportunistic commercial organizations are already offering instruction on how to defeat public opposition to something. Concurrently with seminars, citizens can use Internet networking among communities to share ideas and practice in holding fairly to account.

Courses in our schools, colleges and universities can be built from pilot programs. Academics can start research in cause and effect for the current inadequacy of public answering in all sectors: why people shy from the answering obligation and shy from holding to account, and why citizens don't support whistleblowers. Students in the social and physical sciences as well as those in the business schools need to work with the idea that people must publicly answer for their responsibilities. For example, Dr. Ernest Pavlock, of the graduate business school of Virginia Tech in the United States, pioneered with his seminar course on accountability in the late 1990s. Although it was a business course, students consistently presented thoughtful papers on a variety of self-chosen public issues going well beyond financial accountability issues.

It's reasonable to expect that all who get academic degrees largely at public expense, and who earn their livelihoods because of that public investment in them, should have a good idea of what is meant by answering for responsibilities and why it's important. Students should grasp what adequate public answering means in various settings. Those in political and policy-related programs and professional schools should leave with a sound understanding of public accountability and be able to distinguish between adequate and deceptive public answering. When students go into professional schools, they should know that professions have public answering obligations for their service to the public. If, after their degrees, they choose to serve themselves only and not the public interest, they will at least have been exposed to the choice.

The challenge will come in academic courses in public administration. Rather than simply teaching students how to be successful in the civil service, they should teach the duty of appointed officials to help citizens exert fair control in the public interest. Political science students can study causes and effects of good and poor public answering. Students in the behavioral sciences can take on the issue of reciprocal accountability as it affects trust within organizations, and challenge existing ways of thinking in the public administration and political science disciplines. The professions must be asked by our elected representatives to include their own public answering obligations in their professional courses and pronouncements. Education programs in accountability will fail if they are simply submerged into existing curricula headings and ways of thinking.

For at least the next decade, university librarians should hold to account the academic faculties and professional schools for supplying the missing literature on public answering related to their discipline areas. Because accountability is common to all areas of human interaction, community librarians can help people in the community identify resources in holding to account and develop directories of related networks.

The schools are the best bet for the long run. In our schools, we can teach students to think about the concepts and implications of responsibility and public accountability, and to consider what constitutes fair expectations in answering, in various types of situations. For example, we can teach students what deception is and the effect of euphemism, in the sense that George Orwell explained it, of anaesthetizing the brain to prevent questioning of what should be questioned.

The idea of education programs in public accountability should withstand parental opposition, since the religions and cultures of parents don't block being decent to others – which is presumably the common core of the great religions. The problem will be education ministers not taking kindly to teaching young citizens how to hold to account.

Through understanding of the concepts of responsibility, accountability and standards, students can be introduced to the idea of legislated responsibilities and accountabilities. They can practice holding fairly to account and answering to each other in social relationship simulations. These and actual situations are increasingly being incorporated into classroom teaching because of increasing aggression and violence in the schools – some of it lethal. Students should then be better fitted to later teach their own children about responsibility and accountability. They might even help their own parents hold more firmly to standards.

A Final Comment

In holding to account we citizens don't scream at those in authority to stop what they are doing and do something else. We simply tell the directing minds to explain publicly, before they act, their reasons for their intentions and their most important performance standards, including those for upholding the precautionary principle. We then respond fairly and ask them to later report what they think they have achieved and how they have applied their learning.

To achieve fairness in society we need institutions. But to have them work properly we have to have valid trust in both the fairness and competence of their directing minds. Installing public answering to a standard will help produce that trust, but the installation process must be kept up at a reasonable pace. Comfort zones can't be allowed to block the progress. Full and fair answering will show us the good performers.

If we can say that we have developed a way to fix one of the main shortcomings in democracy, we can share our learning with others on the planet.

Endnotes

[1] I am indebted to networking authority Garth Graham for pointing this out.

Appendices

Applying Equity Statement Disclosure to the Intent of International Agreements

The Idea of the Equity Statement

(Note: the Chapter 5 explanation of equity statements is summarized here to make this appendix more helpful as a stand-alone guide.)

The equity statement (EqS) applies the precautionary principle we apply in safety, health and the environment to the intentions of authorities in other issues of social justice. The purpose of the statement is to make clear, for all and before the fact, what authorities intend that would affect the public in important ways and why they intend it.

The statement explains, in summary form:

• who would benefit from what is intended and how, both in the short and longer term, and why they should benefit,

• who would bear what costs and risks, both in the short and longer term, and why they should, and

• if the intention were to go forward, who would answer publicly, and for what.

The equity statement lays out authorities' intentions in a reasonably simple way for public review and challenge before decisions are taken. Citizens are then better informed to commend, alter or halt the intentions. The statement is like a projected balance sheet, showing fairness trade-offs – who would have what outcomes from authorities' intentions. Authorities intending action that would significantly affect the public, or who plan to authorize someone else's intentions (such as corporations), can fairly be asked to present equity statements for what they intend, for public challenge for their fairness and completeness. Applying the precautionary principle means that we make authorities tell us what they intend and why. We then validate what they say: we don't have blind faith.

Equity statements are in the conditional, for example, "the intention would..." We must not say "the intention will," because "will" concedes that the intention is fait accompli and that the debate is simply about how the decision is to be carried out.

If the authorities refuse to explain their intentions to a reasonable standard of explanation, public interest organizations can draft equity statements from their own knowledge of the intentions, present them to the responsible lead authority and publicly ask the directing minds of the authority to state publicly what they think is a more accurate statement of their own intentions and the likely outcomes. In either sequence, successive rounds of public challenge clarify the intentions at issue and the likely outcomes, for whom.

The onus is not on citizens to conclusively prove that a set of directing minds has a particular intention not in the public interest. That isn't practicable. But if we have plausible indicators of an authority's intention, the application of the precautionary principle says that the onus is on the directing minds to publicly make clear what their intentions and reasoning are.

Applying the Equity Statement to the Intentions of the OECD's Multilateral Agreement on Investment

The following equity statement framework, applied to the 1997-1998 intentions of the Organization for Economic Cooperation and Development (OECD) for the Multilateral Agreement on Investment (MAI), illustrates how such statements can be used to lay out for elected representatives, public interest organizations and citizens at large the implications of authorities' intentions and of particular core provisions in intentions.

The example is not a statement ready to place before authorities or the public for challenge; it is presented as a work in progress and only to show how an equity disclosure statement can be structured in a useful standard way. Financial balance sheets, for example, are structured in a standard way to make them easier to follow. An equity statement for the MAI set out for public challenge would be developed by those knowledgeable about the implications of the proposed MAI written agreement.

Suppose that each of the OECD countries had installed a national law following World War II that said:

> No international trade agreement shall be signed by an executive govern-
> ment until an equity statement for the proposed agreement, jointly pro-

duced by the intended signatory governments, has been laid before the citizens of each country and the opportunity given them to publicly challenge the fairness and completeness of the statements of what is proposed.

We may then not have had the Seattle and other street demonstrations in other countries before and after Seattle. They clearly showed a dysfunctional level of citizen distrust of authorities such as WTO, APEC, FTAA, IMF and World Bank and all the other organizations and institutions who do not account to citizens and are seen as keeping and enhancing the power of business – what Charles Dickens called the "vested interests."

Jim Stanford of the Canadian Centre for Policy Alternatives reports an example of worldwide economical and cultural 'harmonization' through dispute-settlement mechanisms. A dispute panel of the WTO recently ruled that the Japanese must convert to driving on the right side of the road to accommodate the North American and European auto producers, who argued that Japan's practice raised an unfair barrier to imports of their cars and trucks. Canada's Trade Minister, Pierre Pettigrew, pronounced it "a victory for free trade," and added, "They can now stop driving on the wrong side of the road."[1] Using this traffic law case, US beef growers intend to launch a trade challenge to Japan's sushi industry. Said a beef association lobbyist,

> Japanese consumers are indoctrinated to eat raw fish from the time they are toddlers. No wonder they won't buy our meat. That's completely unacceptable.

The American aim was summed up by a US official assigned to the WTO:

> Basically it won't stop until foreigners finally start to think like Americans, and – most of all – shop like Americans.[2]

Were it not real, this example could be a comedian's satirical skit.

Background: the apparent aim of the MAI. The OECD and its member executive governments proposed the MAI as a set of rules to "liberate" international investment for the benefit of all. The October 1997 statement to the OECD by the international coalition of non-governmental organizations saw it differently:

> The intention of the MAI is not to regulate investments but to regulate governments.

The executive governments forming the governing body of the OECD have never explained to citizens the implications of the MAI as they see them – what the proposed agreement would lead to and not lead to, if legislated in the signatory countries.

The Canadian federal government gave the following MAI purpose on its 1997 website of the Department of Foreign Affairs and International Trade:

> The central purpose of this agreement is to provide a broad multilateral framework of agreed principles and commitments governing the treatment of foreign investment so that all countries can participate on an equal footing in the international marketplace for investment. An investment agreement negotiated among the OECD countries would set a high standard of investment protection and establish the basis for a wider agreement embracing many more countries.

What is not included in the Canadian government's statement is whether "international marketplace for investment" is meant to replace countries' sovereign power. Behind this text, drafted by civil servants and opaque to citizens, is the central issue: primacy of corporations' aims.

While the stated intention is unrestricted movement of capital in and out of countries, the reasonably inferred outcome intention for the MAI is that transnational corporations would have unfettered access to actual and potential consumers and business opportunities in all countries signing the agreement, and be able to override a country's laws and policies not convergent with corporations' profit aims. "Liberalizing investment" is an intentionally deceptive term unless the large corporations have hitherto been limited in their operations – which hasn't been the case. They haven't been hurting.

The MAI implies that countries who are not initial signatories would have economic pressure put on them to submit to the MAI. This is why the MAI has been termed by activists as a "charter of rights and freedoms for corporations," paving the way for corporate rule over everything that the large corporations don't already control.

The MAI does not forthrightly state, as a preamble, "Nothing insurmountable is to be placed in the way of corporations' market and cash flow aims in target countries." Nor have the drafters of the MAI and the executive governments responsible for it given public assurance of what the MAI does *not* intend to bring about, and why the MAI couldn't be used by corporations in ways that bring about harmful results. The OECD drafts, exposed by public interest organizations, have been coy.

The precautionary principle tells us that the MAI should first be regarded as putting the force of law across the planet behind the profit aims of the transnational corporations. Signatory countries would be bound by it. A seemingly innocuous set of provisions, once accepted, leads to continual acceptance of stronger successive provisions, year by year, until the ultimate aim is attained. Berle and Means had pointed out in 1933 that this was the way corporations had eliminated one by one the limitations of statutory provisions that had been imposed on them in the public interest in the early days of the development of the corporation. Corporations largely had their own way by 1900.[3]

Our politicians in general don't seem to have grasped what Berle and Means were telling us. But there may be some politicians who do, very well. Rather than being well-intentioned but simply ill-informed, they can be, as Ursula Franklin worried, well-informed and ill-intentioned. When the Norwegians in 1945 shot their wartime Nazi-collaborating premier, Vidkun Quisling, his name went down in history. The question is whether modern-day use of the term can be apt for people in a position to sell out fairness in society.

Much of the public's concern over the MAI stems from the OECD and its member-country governing body having no visible intention to make the planned agreement public, for challenge. The 1997 OECD draft, exposed by activists, was marked "Confidential." As Peter Newman put it in a *Maclean's* article in May 1998,

> Considering that 29 countries, including Canada, have been negotiating the new trade accord since May, 1995, the proceedings have been kept amazingly secret. There has yet to be a full-scale parliamentary debate on the issue; it is as if the future of this country had surreptitiously been relegated to senior civil servants, apparently with a mandate to sign the country away. They have done virtually all the negotiations to date, and no one with any degree of public accountability has had much of a look-in. This is not only wrong, it is stupid.
>
> Nobody understands the likely impact of the MAI...Unless it doesn't mean what it says, and is a statement of philosophy instead of intention, its provisions will rob national governments of the ability to impose sovereignty inside their own territory, Once that is gone, what is the point of pretending you're still a country?...If Wal-Mart decided to build near a village square, and the locals won a referendum halting the superstore's construction, Wal-mart could then sue under the MAI, and win.[4]

Adequate public explanation is important because such an agreement would sail through any OECD member country's legislature having a government-party majority obedient to the executive government. Through the force of law, the agreement would effectively nullify national and local government core policies in those countries more quickly and comprehensively than the countries' own law-making processes could. In Canada, the example of the Free Trade Agreement (FTA) signed with the United States in 1987 despite a majority of Canadians opposing it, and compensation for the pre-1986 hepatitis C victims of contaminated blood denied by the unanimous vote of the governing Liberal party in House of Commons in 1998, shows the parliamentary voting compliance on anything the executive wants.

Once the MAI was exposed, the outcry started, because the MAI was shown to be an expansion of corporate powers even beyond those awarded by the FTA. There were no public answering provisions attaching to the corporations for what they intend, and none for the dispute resolution tribunals provided for in the MAI.

But not until October 1997, eight months after the first public leak of the 1997 MAI draft, did Canada's federal Minister of Trade, Sergio Marchi, direct that a House of Commons committee hold public hearings. And the timetable given the sub-committee was unrealistic: 50 witnesses from selected groups heard over the single month of November, with deliberations to be concluded in time to get the formal report in English and French to the Minister before the Christmas recess of the House. The Minister portrayed this as "thorough and constructive dialogue with Canadians on the MAI,"[5] but failed to say what standard of public consultation he had met.

The December 1997 report on the MAI by the House committee[6] dealt with concerns about implementation, not the outcome implications of the MAI.

In the Canadian parliamentary system, with the governing party forming the majority membership of House of Commons committees, the committees don't take the initiative to examine on their own an issue that the ministers don't want them to examine – as we saw with lethally-contaminated blood. A minister refers an issue to them for "parliamentary input." Because of the government membership majority, the committee reports are usually predictable. But in the Trade Sub-Committee's report on the MAI it was also because of where most Members stood ideologically on the MAI. The second recommendation, of 17 made by the Sub-Committee, is illuminating:

> The Government should continue and increase its efforts to inform Canadians of the merits of negotiating a MAI, while addressing the concerns brought forward by this Committee's public hearings.[7]

In other words, the Members of Parliament wanted a "tell and sell." Recommendation 4 may look promising at first glance:

> The Government should consider undertaking a full impact analysis which will note the reason why Canada should take part in the MAI. Where relevant, this will include a discussion of foreseeable, economic, environmental, social and cultural effects of the agreement and the obligations imposed by the final terms of the agreement.

The recommendation is not that an impact analysis such as an equity statement must be done; only that doing an analysis "be considered" by the executive government, with the executive being free to decide whether a concern is "relevant."

The minority report of the New Democratic Party Members of Parliament on the Sub-Committee stated in part:

> ...There is no urgency to protect further the rights of those who are already very powerful... What is urgently needed is new forms of global governance that can hold global corporations accountable to the common good in the way that national governments were once able to discipline earlier forms

of corporate activity in the interests of society. For instance, we urgently need an enforceable rules-based global economic regime that requires all countries and corporations to adhere to the core labour standards of freedom of association, free collective bargaining, prohibition of forced labour, elimination of child labour exploitation and non-discrimination in the workplace. Those who are content to complete or perfect the enshrining and enforcement of investor rights, while leaving the enforcement of corporate responsibilities and the rights of workers, the environment, and societies for another day, perhaps even another generation, have much to answer for by way of moral reasoning.[8]

By May of 1998 the OECD was forced to shelve the April MAI draft because of the problems the executive governments of most member countries were having with its terms – principally France. France's pull-out from the Agreement effectively killed off the first round, and was critical because the other executive governments, through their legislature majorities, may have been able to ram the MAI through. But activist campaigns against the MAI put that in doubt, because they had mushroomed in punch. In Canada, these were causing concern to the federal legislators otherwise obedient to the executive government.

The precautionary principle says that the shelved MAI provisions must be presumed simply to have been put on hold until the right time or occasion arrives to bring them forward again in a different form. In fact a number of alternative vehicles for pursuing the MAI aims were already proposed by January 1999, such as the World Trade Organization. And the basic aims were running concurrently, through bodies such as the Asia-Pacific Economic Cooperation forum (APEC) and formal economic alliances with Europe, and more recently the Free Trade Association of the Americas.

But the answering obligation doesn't lie with the transnational corporations, whose aims are clear, unabashed and wholly understandable. The public answering obligation lies with the executive governments who collectively still have the legal power to decide what corporations may or may not do.

Spin was important.[9] For example, the Canadian federal executive government claimed that a draft agreement by definition isn't something that exists as an intention, and therefore can't be challenged. Or International Trade Minister Sergio Marchi asserting, "I have undertaken a thorough and constructive dialogue with Canadians on the MAI."

Intentions disclosure through the equity statement. This appendix illustrates a reasonably simple way of structuring the "who" questions for the MAI, and the answers. As noted, the example is offered at an inexpert level of knowledge of the MAI and is incomplete. It is meant simply as an illustration of how interested citizens could be helped by having the major MAI intentions laid out in an understandable way that is also comprehensive. Those who know what each provision implies in technically-written international agreements can produce a more complete and accurate set of equity statements for the several most important MAI provisions. Doing that would also make clear what the OECD's provisions purposefully don't say, which also needs public explanation of the reasons.

To the extent that public interest organizations find the equity statement structure useful, they can draft and consolidate such statements for every significant MAI provision into a statement for the MAI as a whole, and then present the set to elected representatives and the public.

This approach can then be applied to future intended agreements coming down the tracks.

The available evidence about the MAI and the responsible executive governments' lack of public answering makes the precautionary principle essential for such proposed agreements. This means that the apparent MAI benefits, costs and risks proposed by critics as needing equity statement disclosure should be taken as reasonably valid unless a validated equity statement from the executive governments shows that the concerns are unfounded.

Equity statements can point to the need for citizen audit (see Appendix 2), but each citizen audit will usually identify what public equity statements we need from what authorities, for what apparent intentions.

Equity Statement Structure for the MAI Intentions

Note: An equity statement for a proposal written by the proponents will state the intentions that the proponents wish portrayed. Similarly, if the challengers were to write the equity statement, their statement of the authorities' intentions will be what they infer those intentions to be. Thus the reasoning set out in equity statements will be those of the people making the arguments, whether for or against, and whether fair or unsound. But forcing proponents to publicly lay out their reasoning can cause them to self-destruct – something captured by Lori Wallach of Public Citizen's Global Trade Watch in her "Dracula Test" for MAI intentions. Since the MAI proponents have not issued a public statement making their intentions and reasoning clear, the MAI intentions section below is written as what the author infers their intentions to be.

Whenever there is a perceived intention by an authority, an equity statement can be drafted for it. Equity statements can be drafted for the perceived intentions of the WTO and other globalizing organizations which would affect the public in important ways. They can also be drafted for tribunals' decisions, as a means of publicly auditing the reasoning of the panelists.

Sections of the Statement

Following the format for the equity statement outlined in Chapter 5, sections of an equity statement for the MAI would be:

1. The inferred MAI intention
2. Who would benefit from the MAI, how, immediately and in the future?
3. Why should the beneficiaries benefit?
4. Who would bear what costs and risks, immediately and in the future?
5. Why should those bearing the costs and risks do so?
6. Who would be accountable to whom, and for what, if the MAI went ahead?

1. The inferred MAI intention.

Citizens have no evidence that the MAI expects foreign corporations to honour the core policies of a signatory country and to plan their corporations' affairs, in and affecting that country, in conformity with the policies set within that country in its public interest. From all the evidence, the outcome they seek through each country's adoption of the agreement can be reasonably inferred as follows:

> Through the force of law, once the executive government of a country signs the MAI, the market aims of foreign corporations will take precedence over a country's policies produced by that country, even though the policies were produced through the country's due process operating in the public interest of its citizens.

Canadian Medicare is an example of such a policy.

The strategic means for achieving this corporate aim are also reasonably inferred: "In general, the MAI's substantive provisions are broad, vague and unspecific."[10] The MAI drafts were not written to be understood by lay persons, which means that most elected representatives who tried to understand it would likely give up and simply vote the way their party told them to vote.

The MAI gives corporate aspirations primacy by giving foreign investors a general right of entry in all economic sectors of a signatory country. It limits the extent to which governments can regulate business to achieve core economic, social or environmental objectives – especially important for developing countries, such as in domestic ownership of farm land. And it opens up the business operations of nations' cultural sectors to unrestricted foreign competition.[11]

The MAI uses the earlier NAFTA's provisions for prohibiting "expropriation," in effect saying that a government doing something that thwarts a corporation's profit planned to flow from an investment in that country – whether or not the corporate action is in the public interest of the country – is "expropriation."

Measures against unjust expropriation are understandable, in the generally understood sense of a jurisdiction confiscating property. But it is hard to believe that citizens with "a right understanding of matters" would accept a legislated MAI that would not only place planned corporate profits for a particular group of investors before a country's regulations in the public interest, but also require the state to compensate the corporation (if it were thwarted by the state) for whatever sum the corporation could successfully decree. Not all limits on corporations currently give rise to compensation[12] For example, a federal food and drug agency can order a product off the shelves.

The MAI would further prohibit a country, to a greater extent than the NAFTA does, from imposing performance requirements on corporations. It doesn't matter whether these are logical (for example, to exact concessions to promote economic development objectives or local investment needs) or to address particular economic, social or environmental problems. Examples of prohibitions would be domestic content or purchasing requirements, balancing of imports and exports, local sales restrictions, or mandatory exporting requirements.[13]

The MAI drafts suggest that if the profit plans for a foreign corporation's assets are blocked or significantly reduced by the statutes and subordinate legislation of a signatory country, such as its environmental protection regulations, the corporation simply alleges that the state has breached its obligations under the Agreement, "causing loss or damage" to the corporation's investment that would then be interpreted as an "expropriation" – even if the "lost profit" was simply planned profit as calculated by the corporation's marketing group.

The corporation could then sue that country in a court of its choosing, arguing that the legislated trade agreement provisions applicable to that state prevail. These are already installed in law in Canada under the FTA and NAFTA, and would be installed in other countries through the MAI, in expanding the NAFTA provisions.

The corporation would have the power to by-pass the courts and administrative tribunals of the signatory state and submit the dispute to resolution through binding arbitration under the MAI. This would be under MAI-recognized international rules or conventions for arbitration by tribunals. The panel would render a binding decision, one not appealable. The claims filings under the NAFTA, for example, are not public and thus far the public doesn't know how many claims have been filed, for what.

Thus adequate public explanation by the OECD governing-body executive governments for the MAI outcome intentions and their reasoning is important.

It is clear that the Canadian executive government, before signing the FTA and NAFTA, did not explain to Canadians how clauses prohibiting "expropriation" could nullify legislation to protect Canadian core policy for health, social and environmental protection aims. Nor did the federal government explain the implications for Canada of the wording it agreed to. Because Canadians were not given this accounting before the fact, we know neither the motivation nor the ability of the NAFTA negotiators instructed by the executive government. The precautionary principle says that we trust only when we have the evidence to do so.

A spokesman for the Canadian Department of Foreign Affairs stated in September 2000, after Mexico accepted a NAFTA tribunal decision against it in its suit against Metalclad Corp:

> We would like to revisit Chapter 11…. In our view, it's not being used in
> the way it was designed to be used[14]

(Chapter 11 gives foreign corporations the right to sue governments if they think their assets have been unfairly treated.).

This suggests that public exposure of the NAFTA terms and implications before the fact would have caused Canadian citizens to listen better to the critics, focus more attention on the implications of the provisions being written, and ask for public explanation by the government. Instead, a decade later, the Canadian government is forced into supplicating after the fact with a "We didn't realize…" The Canadian civil servants working on the NAFTA knew the design intention. The statement, "We would like to revisit" means, "Don't count on it."

This means that we have no basis for trusting the motivation and ability of our executive governments that have been pushing the MAI, and have no basis for trusting our federal government for MAI clones in the future.

A foreign corporation's claim can be based on estimated profits lost if blocked from fully exploiting sales of its products in a target country. The basis of a claim under the MAI would be that the halting of a corporation's marketing plan was equivalent to "expropriation" prohibited under the MAI.

A foreign corporation can go to an MAI arbitration panel – as Ethyl Corp. started to do before the Canadian government threw in the towel on the corporation's MMT gasoline additive in the late 1990s – with a claim that would overturn a country's steps to protect its environment. Astonishingly, the claim could be based simply on the corporation's unaudited *estimate* of profits not to be attained in the future because of the government's stance. Any country's restrictions that could be interpreted by a foreign company's accountants as loss of potential profit, at whatever the company set as the dollar figure, would presumably serve to claim under the MAI. The corporation could expect a reasonable probability of success, in view of the aim of the MAI, and its wording as understood in the community of business and the dispute panelists.

The lack of provisions for public answering for the MAI's invisible arbitration panel process hasn't been dealt with. We lack the evidence to place blind faith in tribunals of people coming from and making decisions in a business-oriented arena.

(Note that an equity statement for the intention to ban MMT would have been an appropriate way to publicly examine "who gains and who loses" from banning MMT for health and environmental reasons. This is a separate issue from using equity statements to make the implications of the MAI visible. And since the tobacco companies used the NAFTA challenge threat in 1994 to kill off the Canadian federal government's planned legislation prohibiting tobacco advertising on cigarette packages, the merits of the existence of tobacco companies and/or their sales rights in target countries could also be examined through the equity statement approach.)

2. Who would benefit from the MAI, how, immediately and in the future?

Connected to the corporations and their subsidiaries and parent companies, financial beneficiaries include the investor owners, directors, managers and employees of the corporations and their affiliates, suppliers of goods and services to the corporation, others involved in the corporations' financial success such as professionals, other people working in the chain from production to development branch management for the target country, and the dependents of all these people. Corporate managers and board members would gain job satisfaction and recognition.

Immediate beneficiaries in the target country include all those serving in the foreign corporation chain through to retailers, and their dependents, and suppliers of goods and services to the corporation's operations in target countries. The immediate benefits would be cash or equivalent wealth from salaries and bonuses or other form of business profit in the chain from supply to sales points.

Thriving corporate operations in a country contribute to the economy of the country which includes the creation of payrolls not otherwise created.

But corporate income tax revenue for a target country as a benefit is nowhere near what it used to be, relative to personal income tax flowing into the public purse. And transnationals pay little tax. The shareholders of the transnationals are increasingly foreign. R&D is not apt to be conducted in target countries by MAI investors whose aim is only sales in those countries. As to labour, a foreign corporation may create a payroll but will seek the lowest labour costs, which may not be more than minimum wage levels in the target country, or could even be less. Then it could simply shift the payroll to another country that offers its workforce for less.

At the national level, the MAI would force complacent countries to "get with it" in international competitive trade effort – the argument the Canadian government told Canadians about the NAFTA. (but see the "who pays" section)

Dollar amounts can be estimated, such as estimated annual incomes for the estimated numbers of people in a state in the employ or gaining from the business of the foreign corporations' in the state – less what these same people would be apt to have in income without the MAI. The "who" receiving economic benefits can be estimated in numbers and dollar effect.

Tax revenues for the corporation's headquarters country may or may not be significant.

The longer-term benefits from corporations' sustained and increasing cash flowing from a market target state would include sustained and increasing salaries, bonuses and dividends and related-business profits to the direct beneficiaries and, as well, capital gains and interest and other forms of financial benefit to those investing in the corporations. [Again numbers could be estimated]

Perhaps most important, longer-term predictability of profit would be assured from the effective 20-year lock-in time for the MAI. While the NAFTA has only a six-month written notice requirement for a country's withdrawal, the MAI's five-year membership commitment is backed by a further 15 years of lock-in for commitments existing at the time notice is given.

3. Why should the beneficiaries benefit?

Proponents would argue that anyone has the right to benefit from corporations' activities that are legal, and the MAI provisions would have the force of law in the target countries. If an enterprise is legal, like the sale of tobacco, other considerations should not take precedence.

4. Who would bear what costs and risks, immediately and in the future?

Citizens of the signatory countries would immediately start to lose control over what they want their country to keep in employment policy, health, education, agriculture, values and social justice, and what they want to protect in the environment. As reasonably understood, the MAI provisions would have the law honour the wants of foreign corporations' directing minds over the needs that a country's citizens had decided for themselves.

In health, for example, we decide what we need done by government through Acts of our legislatures and the regulations under the Acts. Any change, such as greater home care operated by government, would be subordinated to corporate investment intentions so long as any part is already being done by businesses. As soon as a government with a government-delivered system of health care privatized any part, the MAI would make competition for that service open to foreign corporations whose lobbying and influence resources and claims of better efficiency would likely beat out domestic corporations; whose values in such matters as privacy of records and levels of service would be suspect; whose R&D wouldn't be local; whose efficiency wouldn't be controlled by Canadian governments; and whose profits would flow to other countries and be lost to local re-investment – including large sums paid from the country's public purse when health services are contracted out.

As to the MAI making target countries' complacent businesses stand on their own two feet, this may apply to the Bombardiers of the world (who still get subsidies or loan guarantees), but it would leave workers and farmers to the wolves as investment capital moves vagariously from country to country to maximize owners' cash flow, and corporations decide who will grow what and how, or work at what, where, for the corporations' benefit. Imaginative successful entrepreneurs in a country should earn success internationally, even within other countries' regulations, if what they offer is sought strongly enough by others. But if the most powerful and richest companies win out through influencing politicians to deny smaller competitors an even playing field, we have no evidence that it wouldn't carry on under an MAI.

The NAFTA/MAI premise – that people in all countries and cultures, not just in the business communities, are to embrace all-out competition as the only culture in the public interest – is the opposite of needed cooperation across the globe in social justice, and the opposite of the teachings of the great religions. Lethal sales of arms is to be seen as simply good business practice. Government-supported media and publishing, protecting and building existing cultures, is to be viewed as only the business of entertainment. It is therefore not to be protected in ownership, yet all foreign ownership has "cultural baggage" attached to it.[15] Or protected from overwhelming transnational resources applied to conditioning target country consumers or their government officials, who may think the winning side to be on is that of the corporations. Entertainment is conceptually the opposite of standards. The cost of a country legally being unable to "discriminate" (as the MAI puts it) to buttress its cultures is a cost and a loss of quality in life that most citizens understand.

In the labour force, signatory countries' loss of the right to impose their core labour policies on corporations – such as job-creation obligations in return for public purse grants, local hiring, or other performance requirements – would thwart the country's economic development plans tangibly benefiting the country's regions. Fairness would be lost if the MAI ruled out, as its drafters apparently intend, core labour standards such as those of the International Labour Organization of the United Nations and OECD's Guidelines for Multinational Enterprises[16]

The ability of governments to ensure environmental protection would be crippled unless adequate protection standards were supported in the MAI. But as critics point out, the MAI comprises state obligations benefiting corporations yet is devoid of corporate obligations.

The magnitude of transnational corporations' resources, deployed in predictable directions, heightens the risks and costs to countries because the corporations' resources make possible:

(i)   pervasive advertising to influence citizens' beliefs and attitudes such that they ignore what is actually happening,

(ii)   the co-opting of senior politicians and civil servants having duties in regulatory oversight and legislation drafting, and

(iii) the hiring of the target state's professionals to help bring about the outcomes the corporations want.

A signatory government can legally impose domestic limits on a foreign corporation's freedom but, as in the MMT case, the MAI would say that the government then pays in compensation the anticipated profits that the corporation successfully says it would lose in its claim under the MAI arbitration processes.

As to corporations seeking arbitration panels, there is no governmental mechanism to screen the fairness of investor claims. More important, the MAI sets no standards for MAI dispute panelists in adjudicating cases. What a government would get is the arbitration process of one of three trade-oriented bodies. "The fact that money and prestige are at stake for dispute bodies builds in an incentive for panels to come out with rulings favourable towards investors."[17]

Although the state nominates one of two panelists and shares the nomination of a third presiding panelist, the panelists – usually lawyers – are unaccountable to the public. It's important to remember that the nominee of the state works for the executive government of the state, not the people of the state. If the executive government is known to place business interests first, for example through de-regulation, privatization and tax policies, the state's public interest may not be represented at the tribunal.

Moreover, those knowledgeable or expert enough to deal with the matters involved comprise a pool or community of professionals having, to a significant extent, common ideas and associations. And they can be expected to want to get along with each other. With no visible standards and no accounting to the public, citizens simply don't know whose needs are being honoured in the arbitration decision-making and whose are not.

Equally important is the risk of a government ideologically tied to corporate priorities being half-hearted about contesting a claim. The executive government could even counter a corporation with argument purposefully constructed to destroy its own case – in effect taking a dive. One of the biggest threats to justice in litigation systems is citizens not knowing whether a firm acting for them has someone more powerful as their real client.

The roll-back provisions of the MAI, aimed at eventually eliminating laws and policies counter to the MAI aims, would be an opportunity cost in the signatory country for those laws and policies that currently produce a net benefit to the country.

The "lock-in" provision in the MAI would carry effects demonstrated to be harmful for 20 years – 15 years beyond the five years of committed compliance before a country could give notice to withdraw from the MAI. (The concern about MAI clones and lock-ins, combined with distrust of the federal executive government, is one reason why anti-NAFTA critics in Canada seek to have the government withdraw from the NAFTA.)

Citizens of developing countries can expect equivalent risks and certain costs, given the demonstrated power of business to set policy such as "structural adjustment" requirements enforced through the main financial aid institutions such as the International Monetary Fund.

Perhaps even worse for the longer run is predictable decay of active democracy as citizens lose interest in political debate because of the increasing extent to which corporations control outcomes. A "what's the use" attitude could be expected to set in, not only for citizens at large but also for those dedicated civil servants working as protection regulators in the public interest.

5. Why should those bearing the costs and risks do so?

Again, in the absence of answering by MAI proponents, the reasons must be inferred. Those owning property (which includes shares in corporations) have been traditionally free to deploy it in whatever way they and no one has created law that says they shouldn't continue to do so. The Scottish clearances were an early classic example, and the name Berle and Means gave to their 1933 watershed book, *The Modern Corporation and Private Property*, was purposeful. As a legacy of English law, lawyers tend to view people's property rights as sacred, and to place them before any definition of the public interest.

By the year 2000 property rights have come to include unrestricted deployment and re-deployment of capital, regardless of the effects. The directing minds for the MAI collectively portray as net beneficial to society the unfettered global access for corporations' operations, free movement of capital and resources and the absence of public answering obligations for transnational corporations for their intentions and effects. But to honour these aims as property rights requires the final removal of control by countries over the aims and conduct of corporations.

Large corporations haven't shown that they are hurting under the present structure of country sovereignty, and that the public at large is therefore hurting because of it. The questions, "Why do the large corporations really need an MAI?" and "What is their justification?" haven't been answered by the executive governments intending to authorize such agreements. More important, the OECD governments haven't laid out the costs of the proposed MAI to the citizens of each country who would be affected by it.

6. Who would be accountable to whom, and for what, if the MAI went ahead?

The MAI contemplates no answering by corporations to anyone for the powers and rights that would be granted to them under the Agreement.

But had there been an accountability section in the MAI faithful to the reasonably-inferred MAI intent, it would have been worded something along these lines:

> SECTION XIII - PUBLIC ACCOUNTABILITY
>
> Given the benefit to society of investors' rights and states' obligations as provided in the Agreement, there is no need for any investor or signatory executive government to publicly explain investor intentions and reasoning, investor performance standards, and subsequent outcomes related to investors' use of the powers given them under the Agreement.

In other words, it is the apparent intention of the MAI drafters that investor corporations do not account to the states they affect for corporate responsibilities that are reasonably theirs in the public interest. It may be for that reason that the drafters have not asked the states to account to the corporations for compliance with the MAI terms. The MAI directing minds would likely not want executive governments to rigorously explain to citizens the costs.

Comment

Based on the evidence we have about the MAI, fairness outcomes seem to be the following:

(1) Because of the secrecy, the opaqueness of the agreement and the lack of provisions

for public answering, the overall hallmark of the MAI's directing minds has been plain, ungoverned arrogance, bordering on contempt for citizens – the belief that it is the right of property owners (shareholders), directors and business managers to have the law automatically put their wants before the equity needs across society that citizens have decided and re-worked through due process over centuries.

It is not just a case of a few business owners seeking to do something questionable and wanting legal permission. That would be at the level of a local property developer's aspiration to increase his family's wealth at community cost. The worrisome thing, when all the buzzwords such as "liberalization of investment" are stripped away and explanations forced, is that what is sought by a very small number of people on the planet is the operation of what is reasonably termed plain greed, regulated only by market forces that are themselves to remain unregulated. The universal role of governments – to intervene to ensure fairness in society – still applies, but the large corporations constituting the investors under the MAI would effectively overrule a government's intervention effort, were the MAI to become law in the country.

(2) The federal elected representatives in Canada, with the exception of some, have thus far appeared to be serving the directing minds for the MAI more than the citizens of Canada. The argument for this worry is that these MPs have not given evidence that they truly understand the implications of the MAI. But the real issue is not the political ideology of those elected representatives who think corporations' self-serving aims are axiomatically beneficial to society. It is that citizens simply don't know whether the federal executive government had intended to run the MAI through Parliament as an unaccounted-for reversal of its formally stated pre-election position against the NAFTA, and would they try again for future MAI clones, willingly assisted by their senior civil servants?

As proposed in Chapter 14, citizens' coalitions must publicly set out fundamental answering rules as instructions for governments, and the validation needed for the answering. These rules would require executive governments to state the global equity problems they are working on (real problems, not straw men) and to publicly account for their stage-by-stage intentions and progress in proposing solutions. The governments would identify, for what they recommend, who would gain and who would lose, how, and why they should, and who would answer publicly, for what.

Then, if ministers and their civil servants bring us something which, when deciphered, doesn't wash, and our elected representatives say, "We have read what is proposed but we can't understand the drafters' equity statements for the main provisions," we say to the responsible minister, "Go away and do it again. That's what you're paid for."

For the future, the needed rule of thumb is: No public answering before the fact, validated for its fairness and completeness, no international agreements signed.

Endnotes

[1] Canadian Centre for Policy Alternatives *Monitor*, November 2000

[2] Ibid.

[3] Berle and Means, *The Modern Corporation and Private Property*, op. cit.

[4] *Maclean's*, 2 May, 1998. p.51

[5] Letter from International Trade Minister Sergio Marchi to Ottawa MAI-Not! activist Terry Cottam, 11 May 1998

[6] International Trade, Trade Disputes and Investment Sub-Committee of the House of Commons' Standing Committee on Foreign Affairs and International Trade

[7] "Canada and the Multilateral Agreement on Investment," Third Report of the Standing Committee on Foreign Affairs and International Trade, House of Commons, Ottawa, December 1997, p.3

[8] Ibid.

[9] The government's non-disclosure about the MAI had its origins in the Free Trade Agreement signed in the late 1980s. The *Toronto Star* in September 1985 published excerpts from confidential government documents for a government public relations program "calling for Prime Minister Mulroney to focus exclusively on the possible benefits of free trade, to avoid mention of job losses, to discredit Liberal and New Democrat MPs who raise concerns about the free trade negotiations and to isolate groups opposed to the trade talks. 'It is likely the higher the profile the issue attains, the lower the degree of public approval will be.... The strategy should be less on educating the general public than on getting across the message that the trade initiative is a good idea...Benign neglect from a majority of Canadians may be the realistic outcome of a well-executed communications program.' ...The Prime Minister would tell Canadians that Canadian national interests, values or social programs, such as medicare, will never be sacrificed." (article by Bob Hepburn, Metro Edition, 20 September 1998, p.1)

[10] "MAI Provisions and Proposals: an Analysis of the April 1998 Text," Public Citizen, Washington, D.C., July 1998, pp. 4-7

[11] Public Citizen, p.24

[12] Public Citizen, p.14

[13] Public Citizen, p.18-20

[14] *Globe and Mail*, 2 September 2000, p.B3

[15] Gray Report (Report of Canadian federal minister Herb Gray on foreign ownership in the early 1970s)

[16] MAI Alert #1, Canadian Labour Congress, Ottawa, January 1998

[17] Ibid, p.22

An Example of a Citizen Audit: the Audit of Responsibilities, Performance and Accountabilities in the Apotex Influence Issue at The University of Toronto's Hospital for Sick Children, 1996-1999

This appendix comprises extracts from the February 2000 citizen audit report of the Ottawa-based Alliance for Public Accountability (APA). Citizen audits as proposed in Chapter 14 would be less detailed than this example, and shorter. The APA citizen audit was the first of its kind, and because it dealt with central research issues in the research community it had to be as rigorous as the available evidence allowed. The structure and content of citizens' audit reports would be tailored to what citizens doing their own audits need. The language of the APA audit is in the past tense because the actions described took place from 1996 through 1999. (More went on after that.) But citizen audits can be "on line" – which is even better – dealing with current responsibilities and answering obligations so as to head off something harmful.

(Note: A 500-page examination of the Apotex affair was published in October 2001 by the Committee of Inquiry of the Canadian Association of University Teachers, Ottawa.)

I. Introduction to Citizen Audit

(Note: as with the equity statement example in Appendix 1, citizen audit as described in Chapter 14 is summarized here to make this appendix more helpful as a stand-alone guide)

Citizen audit is a structured examination by citizens' organizations of authorities' particular responsibilities and answering. It is based on evidence available to the citizens, and produces a public report. It can be done whenever authorities are not answering for their responsibilities, yet those responsibilities affect the public in important ways. Citizen audit is based on two propositions.

The first proposition is that you don't have to be a carpenter to tell if a door jamb is crooked. Citizens don't have to be professional auditors to fairly assess whether authorities are serving the public interest and answering adequately. The authorities are not only governments; they are governing bodies of all kinds.

The second proposition is that we must now apply to our public and private sector institutions the precautionary principle we apply to safety and environmental protection. The precautionary principle of demonstrating reasonable assurance of safety before proceeding with an intention must now be applied to fairness precautions for authorities' decision-making in all our institutions. For our own safety we must reject the notion that the onus is on citizens to conclusively prove that the intended action of authorities would lead to harm. The onus is the opposite. Authorities must demonstrate to us that what they intend is not harmful. They must publicly explain their intentions and reasoning, and their performance standards. Citizen audit can be invoked when they won't publicly account.

Citizen audit applies basic aspects of performance audit to authorities, but aims at the answering obligation. It uses available information to report:
- who is responsible for what, including performance and answering expectations for the authorities that citizens have a right to see met,
- what the apparent performance and answering is; and
- who should answer publicly, and how, for what responsibilities.

If those in authority reject the citizen audit observations, they can lay out what they think is better evidence, along with their reasoning for their performance. In other words, they publicly account. They are invited to explain their intentions and performance standards, their performance and the learning they gained and how they applied it, and to accept validation of their answering.

The purpose of citizen audit is not to attack people or produce journalistic conflict. It is to present enough evidence to invite accountable authorities to account to a reasonable standard of public answering. This will help place public trust in governing bodies and other authorities on a better footing. Citizen audit is a relatively simple means of assessing authorities' performance and answering: "Does the performance and answering of those who direct the authority support public confidence in them?" Doing the audit shows citizens a means of overcoming undue deference to people in authority and how to prompt adequate public answering from them.

Given this basic approach, public interest organizations can audit important responsibility areas in any area of concern to them when the available evidence suggests that people in authority are not discharging their responsibilities properly and/or are not answering for them fully, fairly and publicly.

This is the case with the directing minds of the Hospital for Sick Children and of the University of Toronto, and with the responsible authorities related to these institutions, in a late 1990s series of events. These authorities failed to protect a drugs researcher of stature from legal threats by a large drug company, Apotex, when she wished to publish research results unfavourable to the company.

The Toronto case is one of several major cases, which makes it important to illustrate what concerned citizens and professionals can do in inviting authorities to publicly account. In fact, the incidence of drug company funding-threat pressure and responsible authorities' failure to protect the independence of researchers led medical journal editors in mid-2001 to collectively take a stand on behalf of researchers:

> Editors at the world's most prominent medical journals, alarmed that drug companies are exercising too much control over research results, have agreed to adopt a uniform policy that reserves the right to refuse to publish drug-company sponsored studies unless the researchers involved are guaranteed scientific independence.[1]

II. Introduction to the APA Citizen Audit Report

Purpose of the Report

The report intends to show, from the available evidence:
- who had what important responsibilities and accountabilities during the Apotex affair, and
- whether those with the responsibilities appear to have met reasonable performance standards and whether they answered publicly for their responsibilities.

Using public documents, newspaper and scientific journal articles, and letters and other documents supplied by the research doctors, APA compared the apparent performance of accountable people with performance and answering standards reasonable in their circumstances. The APA report is based on common sense in governance and management obligations. It is not a report trying to change the rules of hockey in the third period and apply them back to the first period.

The report is intended to be useful to all groups and organizations concerned with protecting scientific research integrity. This includes a range of organizations such as the Canadian Association of University Teachers, the Canadian Health Coalition, Doctors for Research Integrity and other research-related professional bodies and journalists in Canada and elsewhere.

The report also aims to overcome the understandable limits to media coverage. However diligent their reporting, print journalists report events as they occur; they don't intend their work to be a comprehensive report of pattern, and of who had what responsibilities and whether they discharged them. And some reporters will report with the bias prescribed by their corporate bosses.

Who Had What Responsibilities and Accountabilities?

The responsibilities and accountabilities included in this report are those of the following:
Hospital for Sick Children Board of Trustees
Hospital executive management (CEO)
Hospital medical/scientific senior officials
Hospital researchers
Senior officials of the University of Toronto related to the Hospital's management
The federal Health Protection Branch (the drugs licencing authority)
The Medical Research Council of Canada (a policy-making body)
Apotex Inc. (the corporation seeking to market deferiprone)
The audit did not examine the oversight roles of the Ontario Ministers of Health and of Education.

The responsibilities of each of the above authorities are reviewed through the following periods:
- The launch of the Toronto deferiprone (L1) trials,
- The conduct of the trials and disclosure issues up to the time Apotex cancelled the trials in Toronto,
- The aftermath of the trials cancellation
- The publication of the Naimark report in December 1999
- The Hospital Board's firing of Dr. Olivieri and University President's January 1999 reinstatement arrangement.

(Note: events subsequent to January 1999 were dealt with as an epilogue in the APA's 15 February 2000 report)

Principles and Concepts Used in the Report

The precautionary principle. This principle, as applied to people in authority, means that one does not proceed with important intentions without reasonable assurance that it is safe to do so. And if the safety of proceeding is in doubt, authorities err on the side of caution. The preventable explosion of the US *Challenger* space shuttle and Canada's disgraces of lethally-contaminated blood and the Westray mine are examples of people in authority being allowed to disregard the precautionary principle. In health, the precautionary principle is at the heart of the federal *Food and Drugs Act*, the supreme law in Canada governing, among other things, responsibilities in safety of drug research. The *Act* imposes the intent of the precautionary principle on all those coming under the *Act*'s jurisdiction.

The principle of directing-mind responsibility. This principle, supported in law, says that every organization has a body that can be deemed the responsible "directing mind and will" of the organization (as the law puts it). In a corporation the directing mind is the board of directors. In the case of the Hospital for Sick Children, this is the Board of Trustees, and for the University, the Governing Council. It is reasonable to expect governing boards to set the values for the organizations, direct management and answer for what they and their subordinate managers do or fail to do.

Boards are not simply panels of advisors. Even in owner-managed corporations boards have responsibilities. They have the obligation to answer publicly for their commonsense duties as well as their statutory duties. The by-laws of the Hospital for Sick Children state that the Board "...shall be responsible for the governance of the Hospital, and shall have ultimate authority with respect to the Hospital, its operations and its officers." The by-laws also state that the Hospital's administrative head, the Chief Executive Officer, is "subject to the direction of the Board in all things.")

The principle of self-informing. This commonsense principle, as summarized by the respected governance research foundation CCAF-FCVI says:

> Effective governing bodies understand what constitutes reasonable information for good governance and obtain it.

The CCAF-FCVI also states that effective governing bodies:

> Once informed, are prepared to act to ensure that the organization's objectives are met and that performance is satisfactory.

In other words, it is not good enough for members of a governing board to passively receive information and react as if only a responding panel of advisers. Board members must identify and obtain adequate and timely information to discharge their governance and supervision duties with due diligence. They have a commonsense duty to question, validate and supplement the information they get and act in the public interest.

The principle of management control. Management control means effectively engaging those abilities, motivations, processes and structures that cause to happen that which should happen and cause not to happen that which shouldn't. Control applies to safety precautions, fairness, and corporate achievement and deals with people's abilities and motivations, organization structure and coping with external constraints.

The Hospital's Board of Trustees has the management control responsibility for the Hospital. As the owner of the system of control within the Hospital, the Board has the obligation to approve the control systems for the Hospital's main functions of treatment, research and teaching.

As part of their self-informing duty, Board members have the obligation to ensure that they know currently how the critical success factors for each main function are working. A Board cannot divorce itself from "management." It must be able to report publicly whether its control systems are working satisfactorily in the public interest. In the case of research, the Board must effectively govern the critical success factors for research achievement and for protection of research integrity.

The same holds for the University's Governing Council at its level.

The concepts of responsibility and accountability. Responsibility is the obligation to act. Accountability is the obligation to answer for the discharge of responsibilities. These are related but separate obligations. Both must be met, because the obligation to answer can be expected to exert a self-regulating effect on people's performance. Failure to require adequate answering amounts to jettisoning the precautionary principle and running on blind faith in authorities. Holding to account, that is, exacting adequate answering, doesn't direct people's decision-making. It simply asks them to explain.

The concept of public accountability. As a matter of fairness, those whose responsibilities affect the public in important ways must answer publicly and adequately for their responsibilities. This includes explaining what they intend to bring about as achievement, their performance standards, their actual results and the learning they gained and how they applied it.

The following is a condensed version of the Alliance for Public Accountability's February 2000 citizen audit report.

Main Message of the APA Report

In APA's view, from the evidence available, senior officials of the Hospital for Sick Children and of the University of Toronto are not meeting the performance and answering standards for the protection of medical research integrity that citizens have a right to see met. At immediate risk is public safety. A researcher of international stature who did her ethical duty to protect patients was and is still being savaged as a result. This suggests that research integrity at the University of Toronto is in peril. The most senior officials of the Hospital and University have the duty to account to the public fully and fairly for their respective responsibilities, but they have given no such public answering.

(Note: In October 2001 the new President of the University, Robert Birgeneau, wrote an astonishing "decree" piece in the *Toronto Star*. He asserted that "Whenever there has been threat to academic freedom, the University has vigorously defended the rights of its faculty in their research." This is simply not true. He then claimed that the "Dr. Nancy Olivieri/Apotex dispute" was something that happened outside the University's scrutiny and control, implying that if an issue involves corporation sponsorship of University researchers, the University's "reach" doesn't extend to ensuring the "academic freedom"... "invoked by faculty members in their relationships with parties other than the University.

Birgeneau went on to say that the cases of Dr. Olivieri, and more recently Dr. David Healy, didn't fall within his definition of academic freedom. Birgeneau's article twisted the issue. What he avoided conceding was that the Apotex issue was a major case of a researcher's *duty* to report research results under the precautionary principle, regardless of what Birgeneau views as "academic freedom," and that the University didn't do its duty. The new President was silent on the University's management control for ensuring even the "academic freedom" that he didn't define.)

Summary Citizen Audit Observations

1. At no time since the Apotex drug company affair commenced in early 1996 has the Board of Trustees of the Hospital or top management and Governing Council of the University explained publicly their responsibilities and performance in dealing with the aims of corporations – and indeed governments – that threaten the integrity of scientific research carried out by researchers of conscience working in the public interest.

   These authorities – and the Medical Research Council and federal Health Protection Branch – have their reasons, but no excuses for not dealing with the influence of corporations. They all know that corporations' aims to control their environments are totally predictable and unabashed.

2. There is no visible evidence that either Hospital or University officials supported Dr. Nancy Olivieri in her clear ethical duty as a clinical-trials researcher.

3. There is no visible evidence that Hospital or University officials placed the precautionary principle first in their decision-making in the Apotex affair.

4. Neither the Hospital Board nor University top management had a system of control ensuring that the influence attempt by Apotex Inc. to prevent Dr. Olivieri from disclosing her findings would be quashed and that researchers of conscience would be protected from corporations exerting financial and other influence to produce favourable test results for their products.

5. The public statements of the Hospital Board and management officials about their duties can best be described as alternating spin and decree.

6. Apotex Inc. proposed a $20 million donation to the University of Toronto for a biotechnology research centre, which would trigger government matching grants and other donations to a total of $92 million for the centre. Although the Apotex donation was ostensibly withdrawn in late 1999, the project is proceeding. This raises the question of the University's motivation in failing to ensure fairness for Dr. Olivieri.

7. The Koren hate-mail issue is not simply a matter of Dr. Koren's personal relationships with other researchers. Dr. Koren's activities and publications with respect to Apotex's drug deferiprone have helped the company. This raises doubts about the University's objectivity in dealing with Dr. Koren in its disciplinary decision resulting from his confessed harassment letters. The decision is being taken behind closed doors without the process of a hearing, let alone a public hearing which could bring out the facts.

8. There is no evidence available to Canadians giving assurance that research institutions in Canada are not becoming simply pools of "product-testers" serving corporations seeking to purchase the research results they want.

Summary Recommendation

Groups and organizations striving to protect the integrity of health-related scientific research must work together with researchers of conscience to draft public expectations for research institutions' performance and public answering. The expectations should be written in the form of fundamental rules and should be presented to elected representatives as proposed amendments to protective legislation upholding the precautionary principle.

General Observations

Medical research is a main engine of the Hospital for Sick Children, an acclaimed research and teaching hospital of the University of Toronto. Yet neither the Hospital's Board of Trustees, as the Hospital's governing body, nor the University, as the employer of medical researchers, has a visible policy or effective control system to deal with known threats to the quality of medical research and disclosure of research results. A major threat to modern research is sponsoring or "partnered" corporations exerting influence to produce research results favourable to their product marketing. This includes the truncation of adequate testing and other means of controlling unfavourable research news about their products.

The Hospital Board of Trustees and University officials knew, or had the duty to know the risk implications of the federal government's policy of deregulation. Deregulation increasingly turns government health protection responsibility over to corporations, with no attaching answering obligations. The federal government expects research institutions increasingly to get their funding from corporations rather than from the public purse. Yet the Board and University had no control system for supporting researchers upholding the precautionary principle and putting research disclosure in the public interest before corporations' cash flow aims. The Hospital Board in December 1998 stated that it looked to the federal Medical Research Council to develop research hospital policy on corporate influence. Yet this Council, which certainly knows the issue, avoided dealing with corporate influence in its 1998 guidelines and has yet to provide guidance on institutional conflict of interest.

No one in governance authority in the Hospital or University accounted to the public for asking themselves the following questions, and acting diligently:

> What is our institutional ethical position in dealing with governments and corporations whose aims conflict with publication in the public interest?

> What support do we give researchers to protect research integrity and research disclosure in the public interest?

> Does Canadian law permit a corporation do what Apotex threatens to do?

Senior medical officials of the Hospital and University had no visible ethical position guiding their response when Dr. Nancy Olivieri requested their protection from Apotex's unethical legal threat.

No one spending even a week examining what happened at the Hospital for Sick Children and University of Toronto throughout the Apotex affair could help being struck by the authorities' lack of visible action in the public interest compared to the sustained courage of Dr. Olivieri and the colleagues supporting her. The doctors were unaccustomed to having to confront executive authority on matters of effective governance and control.

And they were unaccustomed to being intimidated and threatened. They discovered a continuous stance from the Hospital CEO and Board that said in effect, "A public pronouncement by us is sufficient to maintain the Hospital's credibility." These officials appear to have sought to protect their governance and administrative public image rather than understand and come to grips with their duty in the public interest.

Throughout the four-year period since Dr. Olivieri first made known her concern about harmful effects of Apotex's deferiprone, none of the Board of Trustees and senior administrative and medical management of the Hospital or University officials has evidenced, through public answering, that they were acting in the public interest with respect to the issues of corporate influence and the need to support researchers working in the public interest.

Board of Trustee members are people of status and are undoubtedly well-intentioned in patient care. But they have not dispelled the perception that, because they constitute the governing body of an institution that has high international stature, they feel entitled to think that they and their CEO:

- could not have been lax in their self-informing or significantly wrong in their perception of the Apotex affair and its implications, or wrongly motivated in their decisions about how to deal with the issue;
- had the right to substitute Board decrees for adequate public answering for the Board's and CEO's performance;
- did not need to apologize for their inaction and later actions with respect to Dr. Olivieri and her colleagues, despite the fact that:
  - Hospital Board and management added to the stress on Dr. Olivieri and her colleagues rather than removing it, and that
  - the redress conditions for Dr. Olivieri included in University President Prichard's 25 January 1999 agreement made their performance failure clear; and
- are adequately addressing the issue of government policy and corporate aims that erode research integrity.

The Board apparently hasn't grasped the point made by a University of Toronto medical faculty member in a 1998 letter to the *Toronto Star*:

> (Board Chairman) Pitblado should not confuse the Hospital's reputation with that of his administration.[2]

The governance point is not that public-spirited members of a Board of Trustees simply bungled issues new to them; it is that they had a duty to know what the issues were and take a strong, visible ethical stand in the public interest. Corporate influence practices were well known to the senior members of the Board in business, including Chairman

James Pitblado and his successor Alexander Aird. The conduct of the Hospital Board of Trustees, senior Hospital administrative and medical research officials and University of Toronto officials, and their lack of public answering, has heightened concern in medical research internationally.

A growing problem for Canadians, and indeed citizens of all countries, is that in important safety and health issues, those with appointed status are increasingly being allowed to overrule and/or suppress the concerns and views of those with stature earned through their expertise. What is set out in this report may seem surprising, but Canadians must face the fact that such conduct happens regularly in public and private sector institutions following action in the public interest taken by employees of conscience.

The University of Toronto, as the Hospital's "mother ship," stood for nothing visible until the January 1999 meeting of its President with American and British research leaders. None of the authorities has made clear their duty to support researchers working in the public interest.

And none of the supervisory agencies involved appear to have acted visibly and usefully. This includes the Health Protection Branch of Health Canada as the drugs licencing regulator, the Medical Research Council as Canada's major policy-making body, or the Ontario government as the funder and supervisor of Ontario hospitals and universities.

The available evidence suggests that the Hospital Board of Trustees resisted and still resists its obligation to publicly explain its understanding of the basic issues and its responsibilities. The Board has never asserted what it has learned and applied. The Board says in effect to the public, "Leave things with us. We will get things back to normal."

No senior group in the community related to the Hospital and the University, nor any government official or minister, has yet come forward to durably alter the beliefs, attitudes, intentions and conduct of the Hospital Board of Trustees and senior management and to install adequate public answering by them.

In the absence of adequate public answering, the conduct of the Board and senior Hospital officials is fairly seen as lacking in governance and research management prudence, unclear in motivation and burdened with hubris. Taken together, the public statements of the authorities involved, from mid-1998 through 31 December 1999, would suggest inability to comprehend responsibilities and public answering obligations. But in today's world of litigation, the horseshoe nail and the kingdom suggests that Board failure to support Dr. Olivieri, were this to lead to licencing of deferiprone not in the public interest, might lead to individual and class actions in the event of attributable harm. The Hospital Directors might then be involved as well as the federal regulators.

If those whose responsibilities and accountabilities are reviewed in this report feel indignant at being cited, they can easily respond. They can explain fully and fairly to the public their responsibilities, intentions, performance and learning, and submit their answering to public challenge. In fact the purpose of this report is to help produce that answering.

III. What Happened at the Hospital

The deferiprone (L1) research. In April 1993, Dr. Nancy Olivieri and Dr. Gideon Koren, both of University of Toronto's Faculty of Medicine and appointed to the Hospital for Sick Children for carrying out research, signed a contract with Apotex Inc to undertake clinical trials of Apotex's drug L1, deferiprone. The drug was to replace a reliable but burdensome form of treatment. Patients with thalassemia incur iron build-up in their blood from the necessary transfusions. At the time of the Apotex contract, Dr. Olivieri was in her fifth year of her long-term study of the drug funded by the Medical Research Council of Canada (MRC).

Following discussions between Dr. Olivieri and the U.S. Food and Drug Administration (FDA) in August 1993 about further development of the drug, the FDA specified four criteria for a licencing application: continuation of the long-term trial, a randomized three-year trial comparing diferiprone with the standard therapy deferoximine, a 200-patient trial of 12 months per single patient to evaluate L1 bone marrow toxicity, and a drug company to be involved in the synthesis of the drug.

In early 1994, Apotex's Vice-President Dr. Michael Spino, a pharmacist without experience in thalassemia or related trials methodology, asked Dr. Olivieri and Dr. Gary Brittenham of Case Western University in the U.S. to organize and supervise a multicentre toxicity trial to be done in the U.S. and Italy. Dr. Olivieri continued the Toronto long-term efficacy study, and launched a randomized comparative study, co-funded by Apotex and the Medical Research Council under an MRC industry grant, with Dr. Olivieri being principal investigator of both these studies. While toxicity was extensively tested in the Toronto trials, the U.S. Food and Drug Administration had mandated doctors Olivieri and Brittenden to conduct a 200-patient one-year trial. With Dr. Brittenden, she also chaired the steering committee for the multicentre toxicity trial, and wrote and supervised the protocols for these trials in Italy and the United States – until Apotex abruptly dismissed Dr. Olivieri from the steering committee chair and cancelled the Toronto trials. Apotex Vice-President Spino placed Dr. Koren on the steering committee.

Warning signs. By September 1995, Drs. Olivieri and Brittenham noticed declining effectiveness of deferiprone in many patients and, in another patient subset, hepatic iron concentrations rising – meaning danger. From September 1995 to May 1996, Drs. Olivieri and Brittenham repeatedly detailed their concerns to Apotex's Michael Spino and gave him a modified completed protocol for deferiprone patients who could benefit from the modification. Despite having no other medical consultant involved in the Toronto trials apart from Drs. Olivieri and Brittenham, Vice-President Spino "did not agree" with their interpretation of the data and rejected implementation of their modified protocol.

Frustrated by Apotex's stance, Dr. Olivieri in February 1996 discussed her concerns with the Chair of the Hospital's Research Ethics Board, Dr. Stanley Zlotkin, who asked Dr. Olivieri to produce a revised patient consent form for the REB's review. This meant full disclosure to the adult patients in the trial and to the parents of the child patients, and to the REB, the independent review committee required to oversee such a trial.

Apotex's inaction on the Olivieri and Brittenham concerns prompted Dr. Zlotkin to tell Dr. Olivieri in early April 1996 to inform the Health Protection Branch of her actions. Dr. Zlotkin told Vice-President Spino in May 1996 that full disclosure is required when unexpected study findings are identified.

Apotex's action. Following transmittal of revised consent forms to the REB and Apotex on 21 May 1996, Apotex's Michael Spino that same week wrote to Dr. Olivieri terminating the Toronto trial and dismissing her from the international trial. He stated:

> All information whether written or not, obtained or generated during the term of the LA-01 agreement... shall be and remain secret and confidential.... Please be aware that Apotex will take all possible steps to ensure that these obligations of confidentiality are met and will vigorously pursue all legal remedies in the event there is any breach of these obligations.

Spino's action was contrary to the recommendations of the Hospital's Research Ethics Board and of Dr. Olivieri. Dr. Koren, not an expert in the area of thalassemia and iron and not an active participant in the actual work of the trial, was held out by Vice-President Spino as authoritatively disagreeing with Drs. Olivieri and Brittenham.

Vice-President Spino convened his own panel in July 1996 to challenge the Olivieri-Brittenham conclusions, but this was unsuccessful. The Apotex panel produced uncertain results from its review of the trial data because it was not given the data Dr. Olivieri had supplied. It was given Apotex's summary of the data. The panel's methodology and criteria were challenged by Drs. Olivieri and Brittenham. The researchers on the Apotex panel giving opinions on the trial could not be considered financially independent of Apotex.

Thus the conclusion that deferiprone was producing a new series of risks for thalassemia patients, being ineffective in the majority of patients with iron overload and appearing to lose effectiveness over time, was not overturned. But in scientific meetings worldwide, Apotex continued to attach the name of the Hospital for Sick Children to Dr. Koren's and its own interpretation of the deferiprone trials: namely that it is effective and safe in the majority of thalassemia patients.

The disclosure issue. In a June 1996 Apotex letter to Dr. Brittenham, Vice-President Spino stated:

> Based on the position that Nancy (Olivieri) took – that the drug was working only in a minority of patients and was losing its effect in some patients, we felt it was no longer appropriate to conduct trials with her as the Principal Investigator. Since we do not concur with her assessment of the drug's effectiveness, we could not allow such information to be transmitted to patients, thus misinforming them. In addition we could not justify Nancy as the Principal Investigator in studies of a drug she does not believe works.

This action is similar to a corporation's management seeking to change the shareholders' external auditors because it doesn't like the audit firm's opinion on the fairness of management's financial statements. As to the position of the Hospital for Sick Children, Hospital officials issued a statement attributing Apotex's termination of its trial to "protocol violations" by Dr. Olivieri, yet these were not significant.

But scientific consensus on the deferiprone trial results was not the issue. Regardless of researcher disagreement about data meaning, the universal duty of researchers and their institutions under the precautionary principle is to take action to ensure patient safety and prompt, responsible risk communication in the face of uncertainty.

The 1995 consultancy contract Dr. Olivieri signed with Apotex had a clause, as did the earlier Apotex contract she had signed with Dr. Koren, requiring Apotex's permission before disclosing trial results data even to the Hospital's Research Ethics Board and the federal drugs regulator. The earlier grant for diferiprone research funded by the Medical Research Council alone had no such restriction. Because the Research Ethics Board had told Dr. Olivieri to go ahead and inform patients of perceived risk, Dr. Olivieri wrote to the Hospital administration in May 1996 about Apotex's legal threat.

In December 1996 Drs. Olivieri and Brittenham became aware of a 1994 study showing toxicity effects in animals treated with a compound closely related to deferiprone. This prompted them to do an immediate liver biopsy review of the 21 patients that had been part of Drs. Olivieri's and Brittenham's 1995 trial. Tests carried out by Toronto Hospital hepatopathologist Dr. Ross Cameron indicated progressive hepatic fibrosis in a substantial number of the deferiprone-treated patients.

Dr. Olivieri presented her cumulative findings to a meeting of the American Society of Hematology in December 1996, notwithstanding Apotex's continued legal threats and Vice-President Spino's personal attempt to have the Chair of the conference session prevent her presentation. One month later, for a 1997 thalassemia conference at Malta at which Dr. Olivieri was invited to present her data, Dr. Koren, in an extraordinary act, sent to the conference convenors an abstract he co-authored with Apotex in support of deferiprone. Dr. Koren was a co-investigator but did not actively participate in the deferiprone research. He none the less used the data of investigators Olivieri and Brittenham without notifying or consulting either of them.

Drs. Olivieri and Brittenham again notified Apotex of their concerns 4 February 1997. Drs Olivieri and Cameron had convened a meeting the same day of all patients and parents of patients at risk to offer those still taking deferiprone the option of discontinuing. Dr. Olivieri also informed the patients in the other short-term trial.

Hospital officials' and Board's response. As Apotex's threats continued and the August 1998 *New England Journal of Medicine* publication date loomed for the article on deferiprone that Dr. Olivieri had submitted, the Hospital's administrative and medical research officials' conduct became more hostile toward Dr. Olivieri and colleagues supporting her. The result was a letter, signed by more than 120 physicians, scientists and allied health professionals summarizing the issues, delivered to Dr. Manuel Buchwald, the Hospital's Chief of Research, in August 1998. The letter called for an external independent and competent inquiry into the L1 events, including the issue of corporate influence affecting the Hospital and the lack of Hospital support for Dr. Olivieri.

In August the *New England Journal of Medicine* published Dr. Olivieri's peer-reviewed deferiprone findings, making the issue public. By the end of August 1998 the Apotex affair was producing significant newspaper coverage, and soon feature articles in *Maclean's* and *Elm St.* magazines.

The researchers' call for an independent review into the issues arising from the trials was at first rejected by the Hospital's CEO, Michael Strofolino, and the Board. The CEO apparently threatened to resign if an independent inquiry were to be launched. But by September 1998 public pressure had forced the Board of Trustees to act. To produce an external review, the Board chose the approach of a consulting assignment, but refused to include the Apotex influence issue in the assignment. The Hospital Board asked a consultant, Dr. Arnold Naimark, to review the "facts and circumstances" of the Toronto deferiprone trials and report back to the Board. Once the Board had accepted his report, it would become public. The research doctors, the University of Toronto Faculty Association and the Canadian Association of University Teachers saw Dr. Naimark's association with industry as putting him in a conflict of interest and viewed him as not independent in terms of conclusions and recommendations. Dr. Naimark had been President of the University of Manitoba at the time of substantial Apotex funding to the University, and modern-day university presidents are highly involved in funding effort.

Because the researchers did not trust the use Dr. Naimark would make of the information they held, the researchers refused to provide it – information fundamental to the credibility of Dr. Naimark's report. Further pressure from the researchers and external pressure on the Board resulted in the Board appointing two other persons to the Naimark review. But this was only 10 working days before the report was scheduled to be released to the public. Moreover, the Board's process and criteria for these added appointments resulted in one highly credible candidate refusing to join the panel. Those chosen were not acceptable to the researchers.

In his lengthy report to the Board, released to the public 9 December 1998,[3] Dr. Naimark noted the lack of procedure-level internal checks in the Hospital in research contract review – something the Hospital's internal auditors could have dealt with. Dr. Naimark's report suggested that Dr. Olivieri had failed in her professional duty to inform the Research Ethics Board about potential harmful effects of deferiprone from hepatic-fibrosis biopsies done during the clinical trial. Yet Dr. Olivieri had already taken the necessary precautionary steps with her patients.

After two attempts by Hospital medical officials to dismiss Dr. Olivieri during the Apotex affair, the Hospital's Executive on 6 January 1999 dismissed Dr. Olivieri from her administrative position in clinical research. This effectively blocked her from directing clinical research at the Hospital. The University of Toronto Faculty Association immediately added this event to an existing grievance with the University on behalf of Dr. Olivieri. At the same time, the Canadian Association of University Teachers began to organize its own examination of the Apotex affair and of its implications for research integrity.

In late January 1999, two international leaders in research, Dr. David Nathan, President of Harvard's Dana Farber Cancer Institute, and Sir David Weatherall, Regius Professor of Medicine at Oxford, exacted a two-day meeting with University of Toronto President John Prichard. Dr. Olivieri and senior Hospital Board and University officials attended. By the end of the meeting, President Prichard had drawn up a 16-point agreement apparently reinstating Dr. Olivieri's research position, but in the Toronto Hospital as well. Among other things, the agreement compensated Dr. Olivieri for her legal expenses. It was signed by Dr. Olivieri and Hospital CEO Michael Strofolino, but not by the Chairman of the Hospital Board, James Pitblado.

There is no evidence that the Hospital executive and Board thereafter changed their thinking or attitudes toward Dr. Olivieri about the research integrity concerns identified by the researchers and outside eminent supporters of the researchers. The related events of 1999 included the investigation and discipline action flowing from Dr. Koren's mail harassment and Dr. Olivieri's continued attempt to have the Commission of European Communities' drugs licencing agency withhold the marketing licence for deferiprone.

IV. Responsibilities, Performance and Answering

1. The Hospital Board of Trustees

The Board's responsibilities. To discharge their governance duty, the members of the Board of Trustees have the obligation to obtain a sound understanding of:

- each of the main functions of the Hospital – treatment, research and teaching – and the critical success factors for discharging each of these responsibilities in the public interest,

and, in the case of research,

- how the Hospital is to serve the public interest in drugs trials, which includes understanding and heading off threats to research integrity such as corporations' influence strategies and federal regulator lack of diligence.

These commonsense responsibilities go beyond Board members' concerns for finances and resources and how best to obtain funds.

The Board's responsibility includes setting the values for Hospital staff, which means stating clearly how the Board applies the precautionary principle to safeguard the public interest in Hospital-approved drugs research. This would be done through:

- Hospital policy that installs the Board's values,
- a Hospital-wide control system that detects and deals with risks to research integrity and includes fundamental rules, and
- the Board, as the Hospital's directing mind, "walking the talk."

It is therefore reasonable to expect that the Board of Trustees would have in place a Board-approved control system ensuring that:

- Hospital researchers and their superiors are competent and motivated in the public interest and know their ethical duty to put the interests of patients first
- in their conduct, all officials of the Hospital with research-related responsibilities uphold the precautionary principle for health safety
- research agreements with corporations that fund research involving HSC staff and resources are written under the precautionary principle – in particular that HSC research staff will comply with the precautionary intent of law related to their work and will strive to publish the research results they produce.

During the Apotex clinical trials, the Board had the responsibility to know whether the critical success factors for the Hospital's performance and credibility in research were managed properly. The Board cannot be passive and simply react to those issues and problems the CEO thinks the Board should be told about. "Management by exception" is no longer sufficient in an era of too many instances of board failure to properly discharge their directing-mind duty.[4]

The Board can be expected to have ranked the types of information it needed for its assurance on critical success factors and to have ensured that it obtained the information. This would include the Board:

- knowing whether and how company influence was being applied to the Hospital's clinical trials, and knowing whether Apotex's legal threat against Dr. Olivieri to prevent her communicating her research conclusions was valid in law;
- acting on the information to protect research integrity when there is suspicion of harm, including nullifying Apotex's legal threats to Dr. Olivieri
- accounting to the public for its intentions and actions.

Yet Apotex's threats to Dr. Olivieri dragged on, making the affair a public issue by August 1998. At that point, however belatedly, the Board had the responsibility to learn what had been going on and why it happened, understand what research integrity means and why it is important, and fix the problem durably in the public interest – at least for the Hospital's research.

For its own credibility, the Board had the commonsense duty to commission an independent, competent and credible examination of the responsibilities, performance and answering of all those significantly involved in the Apotex affair – which included the Board.

(Note: The APA's citizen audit report set out a separate statement of apparent performance for each responsibility set out in the report's responsibilities sections. Here it is summarized. "No available evidence" means that there appears to be no public evidence, nor evidence available to the APA arising in exchanges between Dr. Olivieri and her supporting colleagues and the Hospital and University officials)

The Board's performance. There is no available evidence that the Board discharged the above responsibilities.

The Board's public answering. It is unlikely that the Board of Trustees has ever included in the Hospital for Sick Children's annual reports to the public the issue of protecting research objectivity from corporate influence, and commented on the Board's policy and its performance standards for the Hospital to deal with this risk. The Board's 1997-98 and 1998-99 public Annual Reports on the Hospital are silent on the Apotex affair.

The available evidence indicates that at no time the Board stated:

- its understanding of what the fundamental issues are in the Apotex affair or that it intended to get to the bottom of what was going on and identify underlying causes[5]

- its standards for support of researchers acting in the public interest
- its answer to the basic question applicable to all research institutions, posed by Dr. John Polanyi of the University of Toronto in a letter to the *Globe and Mail*, which is whether research conclusions are simply to be purchased[6]

The board did not make clear who was running the Hospital, and at no time publicly explained why it had either instructed or allowed its CEO to take a decree/confrontation stance with researchers of stature on what the researchers were trying to get across to the Board.

Nor did the Board explain how the Hospital got into the conflict of interest issue of HSC anticipating the benefit of a $20 million Apotex Foundation grant toward a new university health sciences facility, or the fact that the Hospital kept laboratory space in its building for Apotex Vice-President Spino[7] for deferiprone-related activity.

The Board made no public statement on anything until, responding to external pressure, the Board overruled the CEO's refusal to carry out the independent competent review asked for by the research doctors, and declared in September 1998 that there would be a review by Dr. Naimark.

The Board fostered the public impression of a rigorous independent inquiry by asserting that its consultant was independent and that the report would be public. But it did not answer the objections from researchers and other knowledgeable observers that Dr. Naimark did not qualify as being independent or sufficiently competent if working alone.

The Board deceptively stated, in a large advertisement in the *Toronto Star* one week before the release of the Naimark report:

> Dr. Naimark and his distinguished panelists are currently conducting an independent review of the Apotex L1 clinical trial issue. They have examined thousands of documents and conducted scores of interviews. We all look forward to receiving the facts.[8]

Officials would have known that the two persons added mid-November 1998 would not have had time to do interviews and examine documents, and by the time of this advertisement on 2 December the report would have been completed and likely in the Board's hands (or, if not, a draft in the typing stage).

The Board has not publicly reported on Hospital compliance with the President's Agreement of 25 January 1999. Nor has it reported what it learned from all events up to and including the U of T President's Agreement, and how the Board has applied its learning. The most Chairman Pitblado said as a public statement on release of the December 1998 Naimark report was that the Board was "prepared to learn" from what happened. This is not a statement of intended achievement in the public interest.

The Board has made no clear public statement on the importance it attaches to the integrity of research and what it plans to do to protect it, as a leading research hospital. The only related statement was by Vice-Chair Mary Mogford (significantly not by the Chairman-elect, Vice-Chair Alexander Aird, a management consultant) which was that such policy would be left to the federal Medical Research Council to develop. [9]

2. Management

The by-laws of the Hospital state that the Chief Executive Officer shall "report to the Board any matter about which it should have knowledge." (S.5.04)

The CEO's responsibilities. It was the CEO's responsibility to:
- ensure that new members of the Board were briefed on the research function of the Hospital, which included the nature and extent of the known risk of corporate influence and how this influence is exerted by corporations, directly or indirectly. This includes corporate influence on funding intermediaries such as Medical research Council and the federal regulator, not just influence attempts on researchers;
- propose for Board approval, from consultation with the Hospital's research officials, the needed control system for maintaining Hospital research integrity under the precautionary principle, which would include having institution officials stand between corporations and researchers whose job is to do research, and having fundamental rules;[10] and
- regularly report to the Board whether the control system for this critical success factor for research was working.

So long as Hospital staff were doing clinical trials, it was the CEO's responsibility to know of important challenges to research integrity by sponsoring corporations, to take action to neutralize any corporate intent for the Hospital which was not in the public interest, and to call on the Board for support as necessary. But the CEO's responsibility also included ensuring that Board members could not claim "plausible denial" (i.e. "we didn't know") and thus duck their directing responsibility for known risks.

More specifically, in view of the well-known major examples of corporate suppression of unfavorable research results, it was the CEO's responsibility to maintain a management control system that ensured that
- all Hospital-related research agreements with corporations involving Hospital staff and resources are:
  - written to include precautionary-principle standards such as provisions pro-

tecting researcher disclosure, and
- screened by Hospital legal counsel for provisions contrary to law, and that
• both management and staff performance are faithful to Hospital policy.

Regardless of the existing quality of management control, from the time the CEO learned of Apotex's apparent intentions, he had the responsibility to ask the right questions and understand and report to the Board the issues and the validity of the Apotex legal threat against Dr. Olivieri. It was also his duty to know whether Apotex's action contravened the intent of the *Food and Drugs Act*.

In a pivotal letter to the editor of *Maclean's*, following that magazine's 16 November 1998 story on the Apotex affair, Queen's University former Dean of Law, Emeritus Professor Dan Soberman made clear the Hospital CEO's and Board's self-informing responsibility:

> One important point was not mentioned in your very interesting and informative story on Dr. Nancy Olivieri. The article refers to a confidentiality clause in Dr. Olivieri's contract with Apotex restricting her right to disclose. But there is no mention of the overriding question of public policy: under common law, any contractual clause is void to the extent it offends public policy. Accordingly, to the extent that such a clause prohibits disclosure of information about a medicine that might reasonably be believed by a researcher to cause harm to the health of a person taking that medicine, the clause is void. Period.[11]

Equally important, Canadian law as pointed out by Professor Soberman converges with what Dr. David Nathan of Harvard stated in a December 1999 "60 Minutes" television interview as the long-standing duty of all researchers such as Dr. Olivieri, regardless whether they sign a contract with a secrecy clause.

Until the Apotex threat had been nullified, the CEO had the responsibility to:
• obtain from the Research Ethics Board its views and reasoning in the Apotex trials issue brought to it by Dr. Olivieri,
• act under the precautionary principle in responding to the research disclosure concerns of researchers rather than take the view that researchers pointing out fundamental issues are simply malcontents telling management how to do its job. The CEO had the responsibility of supporting HSC researchers of stature in their right to voice their research conclusions until, under the precautionary principle, there was reasonable assurance that the precautionary action they took could be safely relaxed.
• ensure no harassment of researchers, defined in Hospital harassment policy as:

> unwarranted, pressing, or persistent behaviour on the part of one employee

towards another that is, or reasonably ought to have been known to be, unwelcome to the victim, and includes verbal threats, unwarranted voice mails, emails and letters.

The CEO's performance. Because much of the CEO's involvement dealt with the Board and senior research officials, there is no available evidence whether the CEO had discharged the foregoing responsibilities. But there is no available evidence that he did.

Following publication of Dr. Naimark's report in December 1998, it was presumably the CEO who told Dr. Hugh O'Brodovich, Paediatrician-in-Chief, to fire Dr. Olivieri from her HSC trials position 6 January 1999, without evident credible cause. The evidence suggests that the decision was based on the views of the Hospital's clinical division chiefs, which including Dr. Koren, and that these views were not documented.

The CEO's answering. There is no available information on what CEO Strofolino reported to the Board on:

- Hospital control for ensuring that the precautionary principle governs Hospital research and dissemination of results.
- the risk of corporate influence eroding the integrity of research and what the CEO was doing about it in the research responsibility areas of the Hospital
- The CEO's own understanding of the public interest issues in the Apotex affair, the action he took in the public interest and the reasoning, and
- the intentions, reasoning and performance of his administrative and medical research officials having advisory and management duties.

Only after the Naimark report was published 9 December 1998 did the CEO concede, through the statement of his press officer, Cindy DeGiusti,

> The Hospital could have done a better job of providing her (Dr. Olivieri)with (legal and moral) support, so we're obviously sorry that took place, (but) over and over again the management of the Hospital backed her right to publish the material. They talked to people at Apotex and told them to back off. Unfortunately...we failed to let her know how much discussion was taking place.[12]

However, there has been no evidence presented by "management of the Hospital" that they took any such action, let alone that they determined whether Apotex's threat against Dr. Olivieri was legally valid. Given the facts of the Apotex affair, dissembling is the most charitable adjective that can be applied to the statement the Hospital's press officer was presumably told to make. The press officer's statement offers no glimmer of an accounting for executive performance against a reasonable performance standard. And had the CEO and Board been genuinely sorry for anything in the Apotex affair, a formal public apology was called for.

CEO Strofolino was reported in the press to have said himself on 10 December that the Hospital could have done a better job of supporting Dr. Olivieri: "She felt she wasn't getting sufficient support, and for that we're sorry. We could have been more visible."[13] The words, "could have been" do not imply a Hospital performance standard for fairness, and the words "she felt" are reasonably seen as patronizing, suggesting that Dr. Olivieri, a distinguished researcher with respect for and belief in evidence, had only a feeling or impression with nothing to back it up. Since the CEO had not by December 1999 apologized direct to Dr. Olivieri for anything and his responses were the same as his press official, a reader of his quoted remarks is entitled to conclude that they were designed by the CEO (and Board) simply as a "socially desirable response."

3. Senior Medical Research Officials' Responsibilities, Performance and Answering

Research officials' responsibilities. It is the responsibility of senior medical research staff to identify formally, for researchers, executive and Board of Trustees, what comprehensive research policy should mean in the Hospital. This includes:

- what the precautionary principle is to mean in Hospital research practice, especially for research funded by corporations, and
- the research standards and disclosure protection the Hospital needs to apply to protect the public interest in safety.

It is also their responsibility, jointly with the University, to advise the Hospital executive on how the standards should be applied in support of researchers. This means support for caution when researchers have significant concerns about the safety of trial drugs – especially when they have a track record of competence and principles. It also means having the courage to defend researchers when Hospital leadership hasn't made clear that it has discussed known threats to research integrity and hasn't taken a visible stand.

Senior research officials are responsible for having in place control systems ensuring that the Hospital's fundamental rules with respect to research contracts are adequate, known to all research staff and complied with. They are also responsible for ensuring that guidance from the Research Ethics Board upholds the precautionary principle and is useful and timely. These officials had the responsibility to:

- safeguard HSC research integrity and researchers' disclosure of worrisome risks and trials results
- ensure that they had a monitoring system to tell them of significant incidents of

drug company influence in clinical trials running counter to research practice in the public interest and, when instances are suspected, to deal with it to the limit of their powers
- formally call on the Hospital executive for help in removing barriers standing in the way of researchers acting in the public interest

They had the control obligation to:
- confirm the professional and scientific duties of the researcher and Apotex's duties in the public interest
- tell Apotex the limits to corporate influence on researchers and, depending on Apotex's reply
- make a recommendation to the Hospital CEO for action by the Hospital as a corporation, to the extent that the senior medical research officials could not themselves deal effectively with Apotex

and had the obligation to:
- brief the CEO and Board on:
    - what research integrity and disclosure means, how it is key to the Hospital's research accomplishments in the public interest, and why, under the precautionary principle, corporations must not be able to prevent disclosure of important trials conclusions,
    - the role of the Hospital's Research Ethics Board in the Apotex trials issue,
- brief the CEO and Board on what was happening in the United States in the area of corporate influence and intimidation, since by mid-1997 several "heads up" articles had appeared in US journals such as the *Wall St. Journal* and coverage by *Science* of the Knoll corporation affair in mid-1996,
- act under the precautionary principle themselves in responding to the research integrity concerns of researchers, rather than take the view that researchers pointing out fundamental issues to the Hospital executive are malcontents.

Research officials' performance. There is no evidence that the senior research officials had discharged these responsibilities.

Dr. Peter Durie, a senior researcher and colleague of Dr. Olivieri, stated that the Hospital had no mechanism to ensure its researchers received legal advice before they made their arrangements, and that the Hospital lacked a proper system for overseeing such contracts.[14]

When Apotex's intention to prevent circulation of Dr. Olivieri's concerns became known to the research officials, the officials claimed that the issue was simply a scientific controversy, best settled within the scientific community.[15] This was not the issue.

The available evidence indicates that, in the period from the time the deferiprone trials were halted in February 1996 through January 1999, the Hospital's senior medical research officials:

- permitted Apotex's Vice-President Spino to be part of the Hospital's Research Institute into 1998.[16] This included having Dr. Spino's name on the letterhead of the Hospital's Division of Pharmacology headed by Dr. Koren, and providing him Hospital laboratory space at least through 1998, and joint supervision of two post-doctoral researchers on L1;

- initially distanced themselves from the Apotex issue, with Dr. Buchwald saying, as if he were outside the Hospital looking in:

  The Hospital was in a somewhat difficult position at the time, I understand, because they believed they were in a scientific dispute and they were asked to take sides in a scientific dispute[17];

- gave Dr. Olivieri no support in her request for legal help,

- cancelled, through Dr. O'Brodovich, a 1997 arrangement with Dr. David Nathan of Harvard to do a peer review of the Hospital's haemotology and oncology division after Dr. Nathan stated his concerns about the Apotex affair;

- provided no indication to the Hospital's research doctors whether senior officials had intervened with Apotex on Dr. Olivieri's behalf,

- authorized, or issued themselves, an internal memo, subsequently emailed to scientists across Canada, that ignored the precautionary principle and claimed that Dr. Olivieri was wrong on the basis that "both Apotex and other (unspecified) scientists involved in the deferiprone trials disagreed with Olivieri's interpretation of the data,"[18]

- allowed and/or contributed to other defamatory conduct. As Dr. Durie put it:

  Some of my superiors were sending e-mail messages to scientists across Canada with incorrect, untruthful, defamatory statements....Plus nurses were being asked to come up with letters being critical of Dr. Olivieri, and letters were being sent to former trainees asking them to comment on her competence.[19]

- falsely interpreted a 15 April 1998 letter from Dr. Olivieri requesting more staff as a resignation threat and promptly "accepted," knowing full well that resigning was the last thing Dr. Olivieri intended.[20]

Research officials' answering. There is no evidence that senior medical research officials reported to their superiors and peers on the responsibilities and actions cited above, or for their views on the Board's Naimark assignment criteria and what should be examined as a second stage. Officials did not acknowledge the Hospital Research Institute connection with Apotex.

4. Researchers

Researchers' responsibilities. The role of researchers is to carry out research that meets competence and integrity standards reasonable for the problem being researched, and the particular circumstances. Because objectivity is paramount to research being useful, researchers can expect their administrative heads to protect them from the influence of the profit aims of drug companies who pay for the research. Currently, the protective role falls to Hospital boards, Universities, the Medical Research Council and the federal drugs regulator.

Assessment of the responsibilities, performance and accountabilities of the researchers in HSC must take into account the lack of researcher protection from what Dr. Ursula Franklin, Professor Emeritus of the University of Toronto, calls "shark-infested waters."

In complying with the known fundamental rules of the Hospital, researchers are entitled to rely on the Hospital to ensure that precautions for preventing sponsoring corporations from compromising the precautionary principle are in place and made clear to all staff.

Researchers are furthermore entitled to precautionary advice from senior officials on relationships with corporations and how to deal with them.

If the researcher suspects a significant problem, he or she is to:

- notify the patients concerned, the sponsoring organization and the Research Ethics Board
- decide whether to continue trial treatment under strengthened monitoring, modify the protocol, or stop the treatment.
- determine how best to proceed, which mean seeking the views of the relevant research ethics board, and
- comply with the administrative rules of the hospital.

Dr. Olivieri's duty was clear. As Harvard's Dr. David Nathan put it on North American television:

> If she believes that a drug is either ineffectual or toxic, even if she's wrong, in the end, it's her absolute duty to do what she did.[21]

When asked if the Apotex non-disclosure agreement she signed in 1995 legally prevented Dr. Olivieri from doing what she did, Dr. Nathan said:

> I don't care if she signed the Gettysburg address. That's a fundamental responsibility of a principal investigator.[22]

Researchers' performance. In the case of Apotex's trials, Dr. Olivieri dealt with a corporation that put into the research contract a clause that Apotex ought to have known contravened medical research ethics. Dr. Olivieri had no previous experience in dealing with corporations in research. Given that the Hospital holds itself out as a leading research institution, its senior medical management could be expected to know both ethics conventions and corporations' tendencies. Dr. Koren, as the Hospital Research Institute's Associate Director, apparently found no problems in the 1993 Apotex contract he signed with Dr. Olivieri. Because of his extensive experience with Apotex, she was entitled to rely on his acceptance of the contract. Moreover, the Hospital had no visible required process for researchers to submit contracts to a Hospital screening unit.

On the other hand, as Dr. Olivieri herself stated, she had been naive about the 1995 contract, even though that contract had added to the 1993 contract wording a lulling provision that any Apotex-caused delays in publication would not be unreasonable.

The net result in onus is that it would have been helpful if Dr. Olivieri had laid before the Hospital's medical administrators Apotex's proposed disclosure restriction provisions in the 1995 contract. But Dr. Koren had contributed to Dr. Olivieri being lulled about research contract clauses through their 1993 contract. Hospital management had the obligation to protect researchers from corporations and from their own ignorance about what corporations tend to do and cannot do.

During the period of the trials, the evidence shows that Dr. Olivieri discharged her responsibilities of due care, including

- alerting the federal Health Protection Branch and the US Food and Drug Administration and complying with the Research ethics Board's instructions.
- presenting her findings at scientific conferences in late 1996 and 1997
- submitting an article on the drug's problems to *the New England Journal of Medicine* published in August 1998

As to her colleagues, over 120 concerned researchers and others sent an August 1998 letter to the administration, calling for the Hospital to convene an outside independent inquiry into Apotex's influence attempt and Hospital officials' failure to support Dr. Olivieri. Once the issues became public that month, researchers gave interviews to journalists, CBC and other media to explain the issues as they saw them.

Dr. Olivieri and her colleagues refused to participate in the Naimark work because:

- they viewed Dr. Naimark as not independent, and not sufficiently competent without other acceptable panelists
- they believed that the Naimark review was an internal procedures study of limited scope, for the Board's own PR use, and not an independent competent external

inquiry, free from conflict of interest, that would examine fundamental issues including those the researchers had pointed out and make recommendations;

- the persons they proposed to supplement Dr. Naimark were either unacceptable
  to the Board or refused to serve because they would be given no real power in the
  panel's scope, questioning or conclusions; and
- they did not trust that important information they could give Dr. Naimark would
  be used fairly in the public interest, as opposed to being buried within the review's
  scope and having spin put on it to serve the Board and CEO.

Researchers' answering. There are no apparent norms for researchers answering for their
responsibilities in drugs trials, except perhaps to a Hospital administrative unit reviewing
intended arrangements. Nor are there formal performance reporting processes for researchers
in HSC and no norms for researchers to answer publicly for their work in an accountability sense. However, research doctors of conscience presumably stand ready to account for
their performance standards and their actual performance.

5. The University of Toronto

University responsibilities. Related to the Apotex affair, the University's management and
Governing Council had the responsibility to establish and maintain policies and monitoring to protect academic freedom in publishing, prevent unethical and other forms of misconduct by its members, and to act to the limit of its power to protect the integrity of
research generally.

The University had the management control responsibility to see that University policy
protecting research integrity was applied to the work of its research and teaching hospitals.
This means that the Dean of the Faculty of Medicine and related University officials can
be expected to have:

- adequately informed themselves about the influence practices of corporations and
  what types of influence attempts have no legal merit;
- installed faculty control systems to identify and nullify any corporation's attempt
  to influence University faculty members in any way running counter to the public
  interest; and
- supported the conclusions of a professor having demonstrated international research stature until such time as the extent of the risk from the trial drug became
  clear.

The University had the same responsibility as Hospital senior research officials to
know the emerging literature on corporate-influence horror stories, such as the celebrated

case of Knoll Pharma Inc. threatening a University of California research professor, Dr. Betty Dong[23] and to learn from them and act.

While the Hospital had the immediate obligation to protect the public interest in its research, the University's Faculty had the duty to have a control system that told the Dean not only whether the Faculty professors appointed to the Hospital for research were carrying out research competently under the precautionary principle, but also whether they were being subjected to influences not in the public interest.

As soon as Dr. Olivieri drew the matter to the attention of the Dean of the Faculty of Medicine, Dr. Arnold Aberman, he had the obligation to find out whether the Hospital administration was dealing with the situation satisfactorily and to act vigorously to safeguard the integrity of work by University faculty.

It was the Hospital's role to be the first to tell the corporation to withdraw its Olivieri intimidation, but if the Hospital failed to act the Dean had the responsibility to draw on the full power of the University, its law faulty and its business community supporters to cause Apotex to withdraw. This meant more than the Dean's reported meeting in a coffee shop with an Apotex official.[24] In any case the Dean, reporting to the President of the University, had the responsibility to assess the issue as important, report the researcher's and Apotex's actions to the President, and be able to tell the Hospital's Board of Trustees the stand being taken by the University, i.e., the President and Governing Council.

Given the precedents of corporate influence, the Dean also had the responsibility to work with the other medical research deans in Canada to ensure that the Medical Research Council and the federal Health Protection Branch publicly stated their understanding of the corporate-funding-influence issue and dealt with the risk to research integrity and researchers' vulnerability. The HPB had known the influence issue for decades, and the MRC likewise.

As well, the University's President had the obligation to sort out at the University governing body level and explain publicly the University's intentions with respect to Apotex's proposed donation of $20 million toward a new health sciences complex, named the Centre for Cellular and Biomolecular Research.

University performance. The available evidence indicates that University officials did not take a leadership and control responsibility and did not discharge the responsibilities set out above.

Alerted to the problem by Dr. Olivieri, Dean Aberman's initial personal response to Dr. Olivieri in May 1996 was that the University would not become involved in the Apotex affair because he regarded the deferiprone trials issue as simply an academic dispute.[25]

Beyond Dean Aberman's October 1998 statement to a *Varsity* reporter that he had attempted to mediate,[26] and an assertion to the same effect by Dr. Naimark in his report, there is no available evidence of Dean Aberman seeking to establish whether Apotex's threat to Dr. Olivieri was valid, nor of the extent of the Dean's intervention with Apotex at a senior corporate level.

At the University Governing Council level, the University would have had the clout to head off Apotex speedily if University officials had faced the issue and visibly put the precautionary principle for research ahead of funding concerns.

In the fall of 1998, Dr. Nathan of Harvard called Dean Aberman to tell him that the Apotex issue was of enormous importance to the reputation of the University. Dr. Nathan was reported in the *Globe and Mail* to have felt that Dean Aberman trivialized the importance of the issue.[27]

University President John Prichard stated to the *Globe and Mail* that, after the Apotex affair had become public in mid-August 1998, he had thoroughly reviewed the affair and concluded the Dean and senior faculty members had acted appropriately.[28] In a telephone call to Sir David Weatherall, in which Sir David had expressed his concerns, the President said that the case was being handled properly.[29] It is not clear whether the President's call was to understand Dr. Weatherall's concerns or simply to tell him and other international research leaders that the University administration was happy with its handling of the Apotex affair.

It is not clear whether University officials knew that the Hospital CEO and Board were going to fire Dr. Olivieri on 6 January 1999 and, if they did, what stand they took.

Based on the evidence to 25 January 1999, it is doubtful whether Dr. Olivieri would have had the reinstatement agreement had not Drs. Nathan and Weatherall come to Toronto with the express purpose of making University officials involved come to their senses. The international reputations of the University President and Faculty of Medicine officials were clearly at stake. There is no available evidence whether President Prichard requested Board Chairman Pitblado to sign the agreement (the Chairman did not) to demonstrate Board of Trustees' commitment to carrying out the President's agreement.

There is no available evidence of actions by President Prichard to see to it that the letter and spirit of his 25 January agreement reinstating Dr. Olivieri was upheld by the Hospital Board, CEO and medical research officials.

University answering. It is reasonable to expect that the University would be answering to the provincial Minister of Health, the federal regulator, or publicly, for having a control system that protects the integrity of faculty research from corporate influence operating against the public interest. Audits of universities have thus far not included the adequacy of universities' policies and answering for the protection research integrity, yet the conflict between researchers' integrity aims and university corporate funding aims is growing, not diminishing.

At the time it should have been given, the University officials chose not to issue a clarifying public statement on the conflict-of-interest implications of the proposed $20 million building donation from Apotex, for a Centre for Cellular and Biomolecular Research. When the $20 million donation surfaced in the media in the fall of 1998,[30] the public thought that the conflict of interest issue would end the proposal. But media articles in the fall of 1999 portrayed the project as still very much on the rails. The Apotex donation triggers roughly matching grants from each of the federal and provincial governments, totalling about $50 million, with private donations funding the balance of the estimated $92 million total for the Centre. [31] Not only would the Apotex name be prominent; the research done could be expected to ensure Apotex commercial opportunities.

As to the Naimark assignment, University of Toronto President Prichard stated in November 1998, "It will be a very thorough review...."[32] and that "The University from the outset has called for a full review and public disclosure of all the facts surrounding this matter." This is misleading, because the President's 25 January 1999 agreement instructing the Hospital about Dr. Olivieri suggested more than simply "calling for an inquiry" It suggested that whatever standard of inquiry the University demanded for the Apotex issue would have to be met by the Hospital. Regardless, the University had overall responsibility for the soundness and credibility of any review.

In simply quoting from the Hospital Board of Trustees' instructions to Dr. Naimark, "the facts surrounding this matter," President Prichard doesn't tell the public whether the University had asked for review and disclosure of the central issues – the issues of who had what responsibilities and accountabilities and whether the obligations were met.

The University of Toronto's Governing Council has issued no evident statements on the discharge of its responsibility for dealing with the protection of research integrity.

6. The Federal Health Protection Branch (HPB)

HPB responsibilities. The regulatory responsibilities of the federal government's Health Protection Branch (HPB) are stated here by Dr. Michèle Brill-Edwards, MD, formerly the Branch's senior physician for prescription drugs regulation in Canada. As she put it:

> If HPB were doing its job to uphold the *Food and Drugs Act* the Apotex case could not occur. The Act and regulations control the conduct of human research in Canada for new drugs. (All clinical trials in Canada involving humans taking new prescription drugs are governed under the *Food and Drugs Act*. Throughout the trial, minute-to-minute control of the trial lies with the federal Health Protection Branch and the Minister of Health.)

Specifically, when new adverse drug reactions arise in the course of research, there are explicit regulations requiring the researcher to inform the manufacturer and the manufacturer to fully inform the HPB of all relevant information, including adverse interpretations by the researcher. HPB then takes control in the public interest to safeguard the research subjects. HPB has the power (and the duty) to alter and/or stop the trial if it deems necessary. The manufacturer is then expected to notify other jurisdictions of the HPB intervention.[33]

Flowing from the federal Health Minister's duties to protect the public under the *Food and Drugs Act*, the Health Protection Branch has the responsibility to know what drugs are slated for what clinical trials and when, and how the trials are progressing. Although citizens can fairly conclude that having the Branch rely solely on drug companies to report the success of their products is unacceptable, that is in fact the practice of the Branch. Astonishing as it may be, the Branch conducts no field audits and requires no progress reports and collects no independent data for safety monitoring during the conduct of a trial.

Research contracts with researchers are not reviewed by the Branch. Conflict of interest statements are not required by the Branch. By contrast, the United States Food and Drug Administration policy requires declaration of all funding and benefits from the sponsor of the research to the investigator.

When informed of problems by a manufacturer or researcher, Branch officials must use the their regulatory power to protect the public. The Branch has more power than a hospital research ethics board: it is the only authority in Canada with the legal power and the duty to order a manufacturer to stop a trial or alter it. The changes can be made instantaneously, if need be, to protect the lives and well-being of trial subjects. For example, the manufacturer must identify, for speedy communication, a company staff member whose name and contact numbers, valid at all times, are known to all the trial investigators and the Branch. This is to ensure rapid reporting to the company of serious adverse events and deaths. The drug company is to report promptly to the Branch, because the events may signal danger for other patients in the same study wherever the trial is being conducted.

But there is no mechanism to deal with deliberate non-communication of a drug's failing efficacy or adverse events occurring in a trial. Moreover, Canadian regulations are silent on the right or duty of a researcher to communicate serious events directly to the Branch.

Any new information that suggests the drug may endanger users is to be reviewed by Branch staff who determine what changes must be implemented rapidly for the protection of subjects in the trial. Nothing stops the regulator from calling for whatever information it deems necessary to assess risk. HPB staff are precluded from having or receiving any benefits from drug sponsors.

HPB performance. The Branch took no discernible stand in the Medical Research Council's policy decision on obligatory corporation "partnership" in research funding involving MRC funds.

Dr. Olivieri reported her concerns about deferiprone's loss of efficacy and Apotex's cancellation of the clinical trial to the Health Protection Branch in 1996, as directed by the Research Ethics Board. Branch officials chose not to deal with the hazard, taking the stance that the issue was solely an efficacy issue. Yet the Branch's duty is to immediately identify and deal with emerging hazards in such trials. Clearly, the failure of efficacy (i.e. loss of beneficial effect) in halting the progression of a fatal disease is a hazard. The Branch had the authority and safety concern to compel action by the manufacturer to protect the patients. At minimum, this should have included both active investigation by HPB and instruction to continue monitoring the patients for evidence of further damage even if the drug was stopped. If the Branch deems it necessary, it has clear and ample legal authority to cause the manufacturer to alter the trial.

Branch officials told Dr. Olivieri that they could not assure her that any action would be taken by the Branch to notify patients elsewhere who were treated by the drug. Yet other jurisdictions rely on the integrity of the Branch to fully and accurately assess safety concerns in Canadian trials, compelling the company to communicate them.

When researchers have safety concerns, such as in the case of deferiprone's failure of efficacy and, later, worsening of liver and heart fibrosis, agencies of other jurisdictions expect that the Health Protection Branch will investigate. The Branch creates a danger if it allows the manufacturer to stop a trial "voluntarily" (i.e. for reasons other than safety), based on a manufacturer's allegation that the research is faulty from "protocol violations," and does not investigate. The risk is not only for trial patients; other jurisdictions will then assume that the Canadian regulator has in fact investigated and agrees with the manufacturer's assertions.

Thus the federal Health Protection Branch not only failed to help Dr. Olivieri in protecting Canadian subjects in the deferiprone trials; its failure to investigate assists Apotex to portray to the rest of the world that Dr. Olivieri's research conclusions need not be addressed. If that aim is successful, no other agency will likely evaluate the important safety concerns arising from the Canadian deferiprone trial results. A major issue in point is European Union approval or disapproval of deferiprone. This carries great weight because of the potential huge Eurasian market Apotex seeks, which the EU decision would influence.

Were the Health Protection Branch to ignore the extensive documentation supplied by Dr. Olivieri and accept Apotex's allegations about the Olivieri work without investigation, this would constitute federal regulator behaviour amounting to fraud against citizens. The Health Minister has the statutory duty to protect the public and cannot be reckless as to the truth of Olivieri's work and of Apotex's allegations. If the Branch accepts Apotex's portrayal of valid Canadian clinical trial evidence as invalid, it can lead to unsupported Canadian market approval in Canada. It could also allow Apotex to successfully promote the other trials in other jurisdictions as the only "pivotal" trials that any regulator should consider.

Health Protection Branch answering. There is no accountability structure or law requiring the Branch to report publicly on the discharge of its diligence in drugs licencing, let alone for its involvement in each clinical trial for the purpose of licencing. On the contrary, all Branch drug decisions and supporting evidence are confidential. Even under the federal Access to Information Act, access is essentially limited to what the manufacturer is willing to disclose.

7. The Medical Research Council (MRC)

MRC responsibilities. As a federally-funded agency reporting to Health Canada for its funding, MRC has responsibility for policy guidance for the research it funds. As soon as the risk inherent in corporations sponsoring research surfaced in the international health arena, MRC had a duty to act. As the agency developing and carrying out Canadian research funding policy, MRC had the duty to know the significant instances of corporate influence attempts and to recognize the implications for protection of research integrity in Canada and take the necessary action to ensure the protection. The Council should, but apparently no longer does, stand between researchers and "shark-infested waters."

In formulating its funding policy requiring part of the funding to come from a "partner" corporation, MRC had the obligation to know the extent of the risk. This included risk to the integrity of both research scope and trial results, and risk to adequate disclosure of research conclusions. It is not rocket science to know that corporate influence to produce favourable published trial results in drugs would lead to what Dr. John Polanyi called "purchased" research conclusions.

MRC may have been working as early as 1993 on the August 1998 Tri-Council policy on Ethical Conduct for Research About Humans (jointly with the Natural Sciences and Engineering Research Council and the Social Sciences and Humanities Research Council). MRC therefore had the lead-agency obligation to deal with the corporate sponsorship risk in those research guidelines, regardless whether the other Councils acknowledged risk.

The fact that the MRC works within the federal executive government's policy and the responsible minister's aims does not relieve the MRC's governing body from putting on the public record its views on cause and effect in corporate threats to research integrity.

Because of MRC's duty to serve the public interest, it had a commonsense duty to take an interest in Apotex's contract provisions that the corporation expected Drs. Olivieri and Koren to sign in 1993. This would mean spotting the disclosure restriction clauses and telling Apotex that they were contrary to the public interest the MRC was expected to serve.

Given that Apotex abruptly terminated the trial in February 1996, MRC, as public purse co-funder, had the obligation, in terms of value for money at the least, to hold Apotex to account for its reasoning.

MRC Performance. The purpose of having the federal government fund MRC from the public purse is to ensure that funding is available to researchers in Canada to do independent important research. Yet MRC required Dr. Olivieri to have a corporate co-funder for the deferiprone clinical trial. MRC, without evident attention to the precautionary principle in the protection of research independence, had launched a "partnership" policy. This may serve ministers' aims of corporate funds replacing public purse spending on research, but it threatens researchers' independence and increases rather than reduces risk of corporate influence in drugs trials outcomes, thus producing higher, not lower risk to Canadians' safety.

It is not evident that MRC properly evaluated the likely effect of this policy before setting it. It is not evident that MRC has since evaluated the results of its policy, despite the fact that Canada is among the lowest of industrialized countries in public research spending per capita.

The fundamental policy change by MRC's governing body requiring corporation funding set the stage not only for Apotex's actions suppressing research results when they indicate harm, but also for the Hospital's and University's actions in denying backing to Dr. Olivieri.

As Dr. Drummond Rennie, Deputy Editor of the *Journal of the American Medical Association,* put it, in the "60 Minutes" TV investigative program cited earlier,

> Universities are discovering that this is a great way to make money: money flowing in from drug companies to do trials…. Where are all those studies where the new drug was no better, or even quite a bit worse? Where are they?

MRC hasn't answered Dr. Rennie's question.

MRC took no visible interest in what Apotex was attempting to do in its contract with Dr. Olivieri. Apotex's threats of legal action against Dr. Olivieri could not have gone unnoticed by MRC officials. There is no available evidence that MRC expressed concern at Apotex's conduct, let alone took action with Apotex.

Nor is there evidence why MRC officials excluded the risk of corporate influence attempts from the new 1998 Tri-Council policy on Ethical Conduct for Research About Humans. Having decided the policy of requiring corporate "partners" in MRC funding, MRC did not advise research institutions and researchers on to how to deal with perceived corporate influence attempts. Nor did its officials advise research institutions on conflict of interest at the level of institutional governance.

Both researchers and research institution administrators were entitled to look to this set of standards, promulgated by the major research funding arms of government, to give them guidance on dealing with their institutions' conflicts of interest in corporate-sponsored research such as Apotex's. But the policy, dealing largely with the research plan, patients' rights, consent form practice and ethics involving patients, is silent on corporate influence.

MRC answering. MRC appears to answer to no one for its duty to ensure the protection of research integrity in work that it funds. In the case of deferiprone, this means that, if asked, MRC would have been in a position to publicly report whether it was satisfied that the corporation's contract terms with the Principal Investigators served the public interest."

Under the precautionary principle, MRC had the obligation to explain to Parliament and to the research community why its intended corporate "partnership" policy does not put research integrity at further risk. Even as late as August 1998, MRC had not issued a public statement explaining why it omitted policy guidance on corporate influence from the Tri-Council policy and why it confined the policy scope and guidance to within-institution ethical issues and relationships with research subjects.

Given MRC's knowledge of the Apotex affair and earlier experience in Canada and other jurisdictions in research involving corporate sponsorship, the public had the right to expect the Council to have answered publicly for its responsibility to deal with the corporations issue.

Apotex Inc.

Apotex's responsibilities. As a corporation, Apotex had the responsibility of knowing the generally accepted research integrity conventions of the research community. Vice-President Spino had the responsibility to know the precautionary intent of the governing *Food* *and Drugs Act* and follow it for clinical trials of Apotex products. The company had the responsibility to employ trained and competent personnel to oversee clinical trials and to advise top management. A corporation claiming a place in the drugs development arena cannot plead ignorance of research disclosure norms in the public interest, or of the law on public interest.

More specifically, in the Toronto trials of deferiprone, Apotex had the responsibility not to block dissemination of researchers' conclusions upholding the precautionary principle. Vice-President Spino had the duty to know that he was required to inform the Health Protection Branch of researchers' adverse findings, regardless whether earlier trial results published by Dr. Olivieri looked promising. Whether the company didn't like what Dr. Olivieri was seeing in the later Toronto trials is beside the point.

Moreover, Apotex's legal staff and Vice-President Spino had the responsibility to know what the common law would invalidate in Apotex's contract terms with Dr. Olivieri – the issue pointed out by Professor Soberman of Queen's University. They may well have known.

Apotex's performance. Since it can be presumed that Apotex officials knew that the restrictive provisions they drafted for Dr. Olivieri to sign were against anyone's view of the public interest, their conduct cannot be said to have met a reasonable and commonsense ethical standard, quite apart from what the law said.

On receiving Dr. Olivieri's concerns about deferiprone, Vice-President Spino appears to have ignored the Hospital Research Ethics Board's instruction to Dr. Olivieri in his decision to threaten Dr. Olivieri with legal action, and ignored her international stature in calling her expressed concern about deferiprone "misinformation."

Having engaged on contract a panel of doctors to challenge Dr. Olivieri's conclusions, he did not give the panel the data that Dr. Olivieri had given to him and instead gave the panel an Apotex synthesis of the data.

Apotex unilaterally, apparently without consulting the federal Health Protection Branch, cancelled the Toronto deferiprone trials. This was against the advice not only of Dr. Olivieri but also of Apotex's own panel. The HPB, had it been alerted to Vice-President Spino's intention to cancel the trials, might have required that the trials continue, under conditions set by the Branch.

Apotex's answering. At present there is no law or business convention requiring corporations to demonstrate in their external reporting whether and to what extent they place cash flow to themselves before the public interest in safety. Generally accepted reporting standards for Canadian corporations' annual reporting to shareholders exist for the benefit of financial investors, and apply only to the disclosure of significant information affecting the fairness and completeness of corporations' financial statements.

In the case of a pharmaceutical corporation, for example, the company's reporting would not include audited assertions by management of the extent to which it is complying with the *Food and Drugs Act* , let alone whether it is following generally accepted research ethics practice for the research it commissions.

Apotex's answering to the federal Health Protection Branch is limited to what the Branch requires from the corporation under the federal regulations. The political policy intentions of ministers determine how senior officials of the Department of Health interpret regulations pertaining to disclosure.

— — —

The February 2000 APA citizen audit set out other information that was not central to the illustration of a citizen audit report, and is therefore not included here. For example, the APA report included recommendations for:

- setting responsibilities and performance and answering standards for all research-related organizations
- setting within-organization performance and answering standards
- making the law and its intent clear to all.

Public interest organizations or citizens' groups carrying out citizen audits should include in their reports recommendations to those with the power to set answering standards and hold to account.

Endnotes

[1] "A Stand for Scientific Independence," Susan Okie, *Washington Post*, 5 August 2001. p.A1

[2] *Toronto Star* 5 December 1998 letter by Dr. Paul Ranalli of the University of Toronto.

[3] "Clinical Trials of L1 (Deferiprone) at the Hospital for Sick Children in Toronto: a Review of Facts and Circumstances" (Naimark Report), December 1998. p.5

[4] Areas of concern about boards of directors range from directors' responsibilities in the 1992 Westray mine explosion to the conduct of financial corporation directors prompting the 1994 Toronto Stock Exchange study, "Where Were the Directors?" to boards' responsibilities for environmental protection.

[5] In August 1998 Dr. Brenda Gallie told the *Globe and Mail* that the Hospital administration had "made it very clear that there would be no effort to investigate the many questions left hanging by the Apotex drug trial issue." In the same interview, Dr. Helen Chan warned that "Other centres will question whether there was any complicity to hide the truth." (28 August 1998, p.A3)

[6] *Globe and Mail*, 7 September 1998 p.A10

[7] *Globe and Mail* 22 August 1998 p.A27

[8] *Toronto Star*, 2 December 1998

[9] CBC Radio1 interview with Mary Mogford, Vice-Chair, 10 December 1998

[10] IBM Canada, for example, has rules for its employees that are considered fundamental to the corporation and are the fewest possible in number that are not to be broken or waived without the permission of those who set the rules.

[11] Letter to *Maclean's*, 23 November 1998.

[12] *Toronto Sun*, 15 December 1998

[13] *National Post* 11 December 1998

[14] *Globe and Mail* 13 August 1998 p.A4

[15] Dr. Miriam Shuchman, *Toronto Star* 2 November 1998 and *McLean's* 16 November 1998

[16] Dr. Nancy Olivieri letter to the editor of *Nature Magazine*, January 1999

[17] Dr. Buchwald, *Globe and Mail* 13 August 1998 p.A9. The article states that Dr. Buchwald was speaking on behalf of the Hospital's administration

[18] *Maclean's* 16 November 1998 p.69

[19] *The Medical Post* 17 November 1998 p.5

[20] Michael Valpy, *Elm St.*, Nov.-Dec. 1998, p.36

[21] TV investigative program "60 Minutes" aired in December 1999

[22] Ibid

[23] *Science*, 18 July 1996 and "60 Minutes" December 1999

[24] Naimark Report p.33

[25] Dr. Miriam Shuchman, *Toronto Star* 2 November 1998

[26] *Varsity*, 5 October, 1998.

[27] Michael Valpy, *Globe and Mail* 2 November 1998, p.A9

[28] Ibid

[29] Ibid

[30] The *Varsity* student newspaper featured the $20 million in an article 13 October, two months after the Apotex influence affair became public.

[31] Toronto Star, 4 September 1999 and University of Toronto Magazine Autumn 1999

[32] *Varsity*, 30 November 1998

[33] Dr. Michèle Brill-Edwards, personal communication 30 November 1998

Reasonable Expectations for Elected Representatives' and Civil Servants' Duties and Answering Obligations

I. Elected Representatives

The following duties and answering obligations are proposed as reasonable for elected representatives at large in local government, provincial/state or federal government. Citizens have the right to see them met. (Ministers of the Crown require a more rigorous set, proposed in II.)

Duties. Citizens can and should reasonably expect their legislators to:
- inform themselves for their decision-making, in all their major responsibility areas, to a standard of self-informing that citizens can reasonably expect them to meet
- for each major proposal by or supported by executive government, cause an equity statement or its equivalent to be drafted by the proponents, well before decisions are taken, and to be placed in an accessible public record such as a known website
- understand, for their jurisdictions, and make clear for constituents, who has responsibility for what, and the performance standards that those with important responsibilities can be reasonably expected to meet
- establish nonpartisan interparliamentary committees to write reasonable standards for legislators for upholding the precautionary principle in all their decision-

making – not only in public safety and health and in environmental issues, but also in issues of fairness and equity for citizens

- know what public accountability means and why adequate public answering is needed, and install in legislation the basic standards for all authorities' public answering for their responsibilities in their jurisdictions, both before and after the fact
- know how to make executive governments answer fully and fairly for their responsibilities, which includes the executive's direction of civil servants in the public interest, and regulation of corporations and other agencies

Answering obligations. Because they form the ultimate governing body in their jurisdiction, elected representatives can reasonably be asked to first tell their constituents what they see as their own powers, duties and accountabilities. This can be done in their first "householder" pamphlet and/or on their website.

Answering about authorities' intentions: From their self-informing, elected representatives can be expected to report accurately to their constituents the intentions of those authorities over whom they have jurisdiction, and their own assessment of those intentions. They should be able to report:

- their understanding of the fairness trade-offs in current government programs, based on their own assessment of who is getting what benefits and who is bearing what costs and risks
- the extent to which they have informed themselves about proposals for which they have decision-making or review responsibility
- what they have done that demonstrates that they are dealing with – not ducking – issues which are theirs to deal with. Examples would include causing public statements to be drafted for the main fairness trade-offs implicit in important proposals and put out for challenge by legitimate stakeholders, and reporting to their constituents their own reasoning on the issue, and causing audits of responsibilities about which there are performance questions
- in an age of "globalization" and increasing public alarm about large corporations' powers, their view of the rights given large corporations in society, and their reasoning for the extent of their acceptance of profit aims of corporations' directing minds taking precedence over established public policy (such as Medicare)
- the extent to which fairness issues are being portrayed as technology issues – something that deftly submerges fairness concerns and paves the way for increased government and corporate control, leading to a compliant society
- what they have done to convey to their constituents and fellow councillors, politi-

cal party caucus members and responsible ministers, their positions on important proposals and their reasoning

Answering about effectiveness of legislators' control: Elected representatives should be able to report to their constituents, with respect to their governance duties:

- the extent to which, if they are members of the governing political party, they obtain adequate explanation of the executive's (ministers') intentions before the fact, and the extent to which the prime minister or premier controls their challenge and voting in the legislature
- the extent to which, if they are members of the political opposition, they have achieved adequate government answering, and what barriers stand in the way
- what they see as fundamental rules for both legislative assemblies and government operations that are not to be broken, to prevent both elected representatives and civil servants from saying "The rules weren't clear"
- the standard of compliance with the law and its spirit that the legislators expect the executive government and departments and agencies to meet
- what they understand as adequate management control and the critical success factors for the responsibilities of the departments, branches and agencies of government to which they relate as legislators – for example, reward systems that uphold the precautionary principle in regulatory departments and control ensuring fairness in contracts awarded in public works
- their understanding of the relationship between fairness and efficiency. For example, government departments can be inefficient in pursuing fair aims and efficient in pursuing unfair aims. Social assistance units of government can be rated as efficient but not be reaching all those entitled to the assistance. Local governments can be efficient in laying asphalt and concrete for cars and paving over inner city grass, but not working to reduce the use of cars in cities and save trees
- their view of the adequacy of ministers' performance standards for departments – for example, whether activity intentions are being portrayed as achievement objectives
- the extent to which ministers of the Crown and their officials are discharging their decision-making and control duties under the precautionary principle – for example, the extent to which, in workplace safety and health protection, the alerts of government inspectors and scientists are acted upon
- the extent to which they have monitored the executive government's action on recommendations of inquiry commissioners or coroners, and have given their opinion publicly on the adequacy of the action

- their view of the efficiency standards that civil servants propose for themselves and the adequacy of civil servants' reporting on their own performance and learning
- their perception of the extent to which senior civil servants are serving the wants of ministers and large corporations as opposed to the needs of the public, and the evidence supporting their perception
- for their scrutiny role, their understanding of the basic determinants of performance by civil servants in their jurisdiction, such as:

    Ability – the ability of people to meet reasonable performance expectations of them, which includes the quality of their training

    Motivation – the values and rewards systems that surround the civil servants

    Organization structure – regularized patterns of interaction in organizations

    External constraints – the external influences affecting civil servants' performance that are beyond their control and how they cope with them, including "ministerial override"

    and how, in their view, the executive government is dealing with each of these determinants, in the public interest
- their understanding of how the legislature ensures that learning reasonably to be gained from government programs and operations has been gained and applied
- their expectations for the executive government's accountability reporting to the legislature, both before and after the fact, for fairness, efficiency and compliance with the law
- their view of the adequacy of the executive's answering in the legislature and what action they have taken, whether as a government or opposition elected representative, to ensure adequate answering. For local government councillors, who comprise the municipal executive, this means reporting what they have done to achieve adequate answering from staff and adequate reporting from themselves to the community

About audit: Elected representatives should report
- what they see as needed validation of the executive government's accountability reporting, and what they have done to ensure such audit reports

The work of the committees of the legislative assemblies should normally supply most of the information elected representatives need to make most of the above assertions to their constituents. But government majorities can block inquiry by committees into government responsibilities, and block effective holding to account by the committees. Opposition members will then have to explain this blocking to their constituents and to the public at large, making it an election issue if necessary.

Other answering matters. It is reasonable that all elected representatives report to their constituents, and ministers to the legislature, on the discharge of their responsibilities, meeting standards of answering set by citizens. Where citizens have the right of recall, it should be invoked only when the elected representatives have been asked to answer for their responsibilities and when the answering, validated, shows recall to be warranted. Otherwise recall can give unfair power to mobilized partisan whim at the constituent level.

At the legislative assembly level, there is no reason why each legislature and the Senate of Canada can't start doing what assemblies have never done: issue an annual report to citizens, stating the assembly's achievement objectives and its performance standards and whether it met them. The reports would be signed by the assembly Speakers.

II. Ministers of the Crown

Although ministers act as representatives of their constituents and as leaders in their legislatures, their responsibilities as their jurisdiction's executive are dominant. Because of their position of power as the executive, and the statutory powers and duties given them individually, ministers can be expected to inform themselves to a much higher degree that other elected representatives. The Westray mine example illustrated this. In addition, as ministers of the Crown they must comply with the law as well as proposing what should be the law.

For each type of responsibility – executive, legislative and constituent representative– ministers have public answering obligations. That being the case, citizens have legitimate expectations for ministers' public answering.

Standards for ministers' public answering. Given the evidence, citizens are entitled to be worried about the fairness and completeness of ministers' answering to the legislatures and direct to the public. Moreover, ministers may not feel obliged to answer – even acknowledge – fair questions sent to them by organizations knowledgeable about the minister's duties and answering obligations.

Ministers can publicly state why the following expectations are unreasonable, if they think they are:

1. Ministers collectively will tell the legislature, in a Statement of Executive Accountabilities, what they think are reasonable standards for their disclosure of their intentions and reasoning in policy and compliance, and for their performance and results.

The logical person to issue the Statement is the prime minister or premier. The Speech from the Throne for each new parliament is the logical occasion to make the statement. The Governor General or Lieutenant Governor would say, "In public answering for their responsibilities, my ministers will meet the following standards…"

It is up to the Queen's representatives giving the Speech From the Throne whether they will read out appearances statements about accountability given them by ministers of the type, "My government is committed to openness and transparency." This is clearly not a commitment to *answer* for the discharge of responsibilities.

2. For each of their key statutory responsibilities, ministers individually will tell the legislature (and therefore the public) in a Statement of Minister's Responsibilities and Accountabilities tabled in the legislature at the outset of their taking office and annually thereafter, what they understand as their statutory powers and duties and public answering obligations.

Legislators and citizens need this information as a starting point for any semblance of control over government, whether it's for workplace safety, health protection, fairness in the military, protection of the country's core social policies or protection of the environment. Referring people to particular Acts isn't helpful; what citizens need to know, within a month after a new minister takes office for a portfolio, is how each minister interprets his or her statutory powers, duties and answering obligations.

3. For important proposals that they initiate or intend to authorize, ministers will produce equity statements or their equivalent for public challenge.

Examples would be ministers' intentions in legislative Bills or proposed policy or agreements, or proposed elimination of government regulations – whether for workplace safety, food safety, drugs licencing or environmental protection.

4. In annual reporting to their legislatures on policy or program decisions made, ministers will:

- state their performance standards for the key functions of their departments and agencies
- state whether they and their departmental officials are complying with the intent of the law applicable to their responsibilities
  (It is not up to citizens or legislators to make access to information requests and do other detective work to find this out)
- state the extent to which they have informed themselves for their decisions
- state the extent to which they have applied the precautionary principle in their decision-making
- state what they have achieved (not just their activities) and how they have applied the learning they ought to have gained

In fairness issues, such as welfare and unemployment, ministers' self-informing should approximate the learning they would gain if they had agreed to the request: "Will the Minister come and live in our circumstances for two weeks, to see what our life is like?"

Given the 1990s actions of the federal government, the federal Minister of Health, for example, has the fairness obligation to lay before the public:

- the evidence supporting the government's claim that the federal Health Protection Branch's laboratory functions were not shut down or significantly reduced during the 1995-2000 period
- the evidence that the federal money expended for Health Protection Branch functions was not halved or significantly reduced over the 1995-2000 period

The stated performance standards would include, in addition to those for upholding the precautionary principle and other regulatory duties, compliance with the law, fairness in value for money and efficiency.

Some will say that a minister's public answering obligations are adequately dealt with by the concept of "ministerial responsibility" and by having to stand for re-election periodically. The evidence refutes this.

5. Ministers will ensure that the rules of procedure for their legislatures are changed to require fair and complete answering in the assembly for fair questions put to them by opposition members.

The Speaker would rule on the fairness of the questions and of the answering given in the legislature.

On taking office, each minister should be required to meet – initially and then annually – with the standing committees of the legislature related to the minister's department to explain to the committee's members the minister's view of

- his or her powers, duties and accountabilities
- the most important policy and departmental management problems facing the minister and how he or she is dealing with them.

The committee members would then ask the auditor general, who would be invited to these meetings, to comment on the adequacy of the minister's answering for his or her responsibilities. Since auditing serves an accountability relationship, expressing an opinion on the adequacy of ministers' answering is a reasonable task for auditors general.

III. Senior Civil Servants

Duties

Whereas elected representatives are responsible for fairness decisions, civil servants are responsible for carrying out executive decisions efficiently and economically. But civil servants don't carry out decisions contrary to law or those that they know will lead to harm and/or injustice or otherwise jeopardize the public interest. Blind obedience and loyalty to ministers' definitions of the public interest can mean serving ministers' wants at the expense of citizens' needs. Regardless of norms to date, senior civil servants can be reasonably expected to account for the advice they give to the executive, because their advice is to be non-partisan and in the public interest.

Citizens in any jurisdiction of government can therefore reasonably expect senior civil servants to:

- Give the executive government and legislators politically-neutral information useful to each for making fairness trade-offs in decision-making in the public interest
- For each policy proposal by the executive (or proposals by others needing government authority and /or funding to do something that affects the public in important ways), produce for the executive an equity statement or its equivalent as a means for making clear the intended outcomes and fairness trade-offs. Draft the statement to withstand public scrutiny of its fairness and completeness[1]
- For the intended policy achievement, determine the critical success factors for it and propose to the executive performance standards and public accountability reporting reasonable for those with significant responsibilities under the policy. Those others will include corporations mandated to carry out the elements of the policy (e.g., food and drugs safety)
- Propose to their ministers what they think constitutes reasonable public accountability reporting standards for ministers for fair and complete reporting on the discharge of their responsibilities
- Propose, for executive approval, the fundamental rules for public servants and rank their importance.
- Confirm with the executive the efficiency/service standards for themselves, that they think are reasonable in their circumstances, for supporting the fairness objectives of programs and meeting the reasonable needs of users of government services. These will be a basis for being held fairly to account. (Standards that are too low will lose credibility for civil servants.) Developing the standards includes consulting users of services on what they regard as their priorities and, later, on whether the services met their needs. Be able to assert to the executive, legislature and public that the standards are achievement standards and are not simply activity intentions or intentions for doing what technology makes it easy to do.
- Manage the achievement of the fairness intent of programs or projects, to the extent civil servants can control this achievement, and meet reasonable standards for efficiency and compliance with fundamental rules.

- If a fundamental rule ought to be broken to achieve better service in the public interest, justify it to those who set the rule. This means legislators, if it is the spirit of the law or regulations, and the executive if the rule is an executive direction.
- Meet the agreed performance standards:
  - know the department's own capability in terms of ability, motivation, organization structure and external constraints
  - apply available benchmarks and other good practices comparisons
  - make the reward system match the planned achievement, to the extent possible within their sphere of control
  - train staff for their responsibilities, including ability to identify risk to citizens and feasible means of government limiting the risk
  - structure for task achievement, not status attainment
  - remove barriers standing in the way of people doing a better job
- Determine the actual accomplishment of programs and projects and people's performance for each significant responsibility
- Determine the performance against the agreed performance standards and, as accurately as possible, attribute the underlying causes of variance from the achievement plan and determine the learning that ought to be gained and applied.

Answering obligations

Citizens can reasonably expect senior civil servants in every jurisdiction to:

- Set out, in a public record (given their knowledge of the issues) what they think are reasonable standards for public answering by their ministers or other forms of executive for: what the executive proposes that would affect the public in important ways, what was achieved, and significant unintended effects
- Report, through the executive, to legislators and publics served:
  - the program and project accomplishment, as they see it
  - significant variances from planned achievement and performance, and their attribution
  - how external constraints are being dealt with
  - the learning gained from what was done and how it was applied
- Make annual performance reports to the executive and legislature on civil servants' compliance with the law, especially in safety or health regulatory tasks (including their application of the precautionary principle)
- Explain any re-negotiations sought and obtained in fundamental rules to enable more efficient and innovative performance.

Endnotes

[1] For its own political aims, the executive government may withhold the equity statement from public scrutiny. It is up to elected representatives to exact such statements, but it is imperative that civil servants be able to say in a public record that they produced such statements as their politically neutral responsibility in serving public accountability.

Index

ISBN 155212957-8

9 781552 129579